LIFE IN KINGS

ANCIENT ISRAEL AND ITS LITERATURE

Thomas C. Römer, General Editor

Editorial Board:
Mark G. Brett
Marc Brettler
Corrine L. Carvalho
Tom Dozeman
Cynthia Edenburg
Konrad Schmid

Number 30

LIFE IN KINGS
Reshaping the Royal Story in the Hebrew Bible

A. Graeme Auld

SBL PRESS

Atlanta

Copyright © 2017 by Society of Biblical Literature

All rights reserved. No part of this work may be reproduced or transmitted in any form or by any means, electronic or mechanical, including photocopying and recording, or by means of any information storage or retrieval system, except as may be expressly permitted by the 1976 Copyright Act or in writing from the publisher. Requests for permission should be addressed in writing to the Rights and Permissions Office, SBL Press, 825 Houston Mill Road, Atlanta, GA 30329 USA.

Library of Congress Cataloging-in-Publication Data

Names: Auld, A. Graeme, author.
Title: Life in Kings : reshaping the royal story in the Hebrew Bible / by A. Graeme Auld.
Description: Atlanta : SBL Press, [2017] | Series: Ancient Israel and its literature ; number 30 | Includes bibliographical references and index.
Identifiers: LCCN 2016056517 (print) | LCCN 2016056912 (ebook) | ISBN 9781628371710 (pbk. : alk. paper) | ISBN 9780884142126 (hardcover : alk. paper) | ISBN 9780884142119 (ebook)
Subjects: LCSH: Bible. Kings—Criticism, interpretation, etc.
Classification: LCC BS1335.52 .A95 2017 (print) | LCC BS1335.52 (ebook) | DDC 222/.506—dc23
LC record available at https://lccn.loc.gov/2016056517

Printed on acid-free paper.

Contents

Abbreviations vii

1. The Story So Far 1
2. Life 29
3. More Words 39
4. God-King Communication in Jerusalem 59
5. Cultic Matters: The Synoptic Tradition 69
6. Toward the Synoptic Narrative 89
7. Samuel Revisited 103
8. Prophets and Kings in Israel 117
9. Rewriting Judah's Kings 141
10. Isaiah and Hezekiah 163
11. Reading Written Kings 191
12. Shared Text Sampled 205

Bibliography 279
Hebrew Bible Index 289
Author Index 320

Abbreviations

AASF	Annales Academiae Scientiarum Fennicae
AB	Anchor Bible
AIL	Ancient Israel and Its Literature
Anab.	Arrian, *Anabasis Alexandri*
ANEM	Ancient Near East Monographs
ATD	Das Alte Testament Deutsch
ATANT	Abhandlungen zur Theologie des Alten und Neuen Testaments
BETL	Bibliotheca Ephemeridum Theologicarum Lovaniensium
BibInt	Biblical Interpretation Series
BKAT	Biblischer Kommentar, Altes Testament
BZAW	Beihefte zur Zeitschrift für die alttestamentliche Wissenschaft
CBQ	*Catholic Biblical Quarterly*
CEV	Contemporary English Version
CSIC	Consejo Superior de Investigaciones Científicas
DCH	*Dictionary of Classical Hebrew*. Edited by David J. A. Clines. 9 vols. Sheffield: Sheffield Phoenix, 1993–2014.
DJD	Discoveries in the Judaean Desert
DtrH	Deuteronomistic History/ian
DtrN	nomistic Deuteronomistic source
ErIsr	*Eretz-Israel*
ET	English translation
FAT	Forschungen zum Alten Testament
FRLANT	Forschungen zur Religion des Alten und Neuen Testaments
HB	Hebrew Bible
HSM	Harvard Semitic Monographs
HSS	Harvard Semitic Studies
ICC	International Critical Commentary

JBL	*Journal of Biblical Literature*
JDT	*Jahrbuch für deutsche Theologie*
JSJ	*Journal for the Study of Judaism*
JSJSup	Journal for the Study of Judaism Supplements
JSOT	*Journal for the Study of the Old Testament*
JSOTSup	Journal for the Study of the Old Testament Supplement Series
LCL	Loeb Classical Library
LHBOTS	Library of Hebrew Bible/Old Testament Studies
MSS	manuscripts
NEB	New English Bible
NRSV	New Revised Standard Version
OTL	Old Testament Library
OTS	Old Testament Studies
RB	*Revue biblique*
RSV	Revised Standard Version
SBT	Studies in Biblical Theology
SBLStBL	Society of Biblical Literature Studies in Biblical Literature
SOTSMS	Society for Old Testament Studies Monograph Series
SSLL	Studies in Semitic Languages and Linguistics
SSN	Studia Semitica Neerlandica
STDJ	Studies on the Texts of the Desert of Judah
TECC	Textos y Estudios "Cardenal Cisneros"
ThW	Theologische Wissenschaft
TZ	*Theologische Zeitschrift*
VT	*Vetus Testamentum*
VTSup	Vetus Testamentum Supplements
ZAW	*Zeitschrift für die alttestamentliche Wissenschaft*

1
The Story So Far

This book is about writing and rewriting the biblical book of Kings—it is a book about words and their use and their reuse, about meanings and changes in meaning. Observing changes helps the telling of history. And history is doubly implicated in the process: a story about reuse and rewritings is waiting to be told, and the words themselves are also telling about times past. However, our principal concern is with the words themselves.

1.1. The Fathers Who Framed the Debate

1.1.1. Wilhelm M. L. de Wette

The decades around 1800 were an exciting time for scholarship in many academic fields. Old orthodoxies in medical and physical science as in humanities and theology were being challenged by fresh arguments. Long-established worldviews were being confronted by new evidence and reevaluated in fresh scrutiny of the long-familiar. Jena was an important center of the ferment. In biblical studies the radical contributions of Wilhelm Martin Leberecht de Wette remain monuments of the period.[1] Two of his early scholarly moves have had lasting influence.

Many authorities since ancient times had associated the book of Deuteronomy with the book of the law found in the Jerusalem temple during renovations launched by King Josiah (2 Kgs 22), but without doubting that Deuteronomy was Mosaic in origin. However, in his doctoral dis-

---

1. The following paragraphs on de Wette draw on two important studies: Rudolf Smend, *Wilhelm Martin Leberecht de Wettes Arbeit am Alten und am Neuen Testament* (Basel: Helbing & Lichtenhahn, 1958); and John W. Rogerson, *W. M. L. de Wette, Founder of Modern Biblical Criticism: An Intellectual Biography*, JSOTSup 126 (Sheffield: Sheffield Academic, 1992).

sertation de Wette argued that the legislation in Deuteronomy was not simply more developed than the laws of the previous pentateuchal books but stemmed from a much later period than Moses. The shift in teaching about the proper place for sacrifice—from a plurality of altars to a single altar—was crucial.

Even conservative scholars of the period admitted that Chronicles was a relatively late biblical book. But they held that it could still possess historical worth because its author had worked with written sources contemporary with or at least close to the events they reported. Johann Gottfried Eichhorn, who had left Jena (for Göttingen) before de Wette began his studies there, had explained the agreements between Samuel–Kings and Chronicles on the basis of shared ancient sources: a life of David, a life of Solomon, and many others. Because the Chronicler had copied these rather faithfully and not concealed his own additions, he should be reckoned a trustworthy, not a tendentious, historian.

De Wette's devastating critique of the Chronicler precisely as *historian* arose out of his case against the Mosaic authorship of pentateuchal legislation and was a necessary corollary of it.[2] A century and a half later, Rudolf Smend, also in his mid-twenties, would explain the matter as follows.[3] Before de Wette's analysis, the contradiction between the religious world of the books of Samuel and Kings, on the one side, and Chronicles, on the other, had not been systematically faced. Since all were persuaded of the genuineness of the Mosaic legislation, no one could suspect the thoroughly Mosaic stability of the cult in Chronicles; and the divergent presentation by the authors of Samuel–Kings was simply held to result from their lack of interest in religion and cult. De Wette's trenchant critique was aimed at the claim that Chronicles was historical. Against Eichhorn's assumption of an early life of David,[4] he argued: (1) There is no historical trace of such a biography. (2) What Samuel and Chronicles share about David is paltry and incomplete. (3) The shared elements are very varied and lack organic cohesion. (4) Organic cohesion is best illustrated in the reportage of the books of Samuel. (5) Eichhorn's explanation of the differences as resulting from divergent revisions of the common source placed empty hypothesis

---

2. W. M. L. de Wette, *Beiträge zur Einleitung in das Alte Testament*, 2 vols. (Halle: Schimmelpfennig, 1806–1807).

3. Smend, *De Wettes Arbeit*, 40–45.

4. Johann Gottfried Eichhorn, *Einleitung in das Alte Testament*, 3rd ed. (Leipzig: Weidmann, 1803).

on empty hypothesis. (6) His hypothesis would have no historical worth even if it were true, for we do not know to which period the supposed life of David belongs.

Today there is widespread agreement over de Wette's (negative) conclusion about the Chronicler as historian,[5] and much of his case against Eichhorn remains valid. Yet the young de Wette did have a tendency to exaggerate evidence, and the fact that his case has had overall success has obscured the weakness of some of his arguments. A baby has disappeared with the bathwater. His alternative to Eichhorn's common source(s) had to be that the Chronicler rewrote the earlier Samuel–Kings; and this perspective on the origins of Chronicles, though it took many decades to be fully accepted, has been largely unchallenged ever since. Yet, once we detach arguments 2 and 3 from the constraints of the original historical polemic, it is easier to see that at least these two of his six arguments deserve reassessment. In this present study I claim that consistent attention to an alternative perspective will—at the very least—help test the adequacy of a longstanding scholarly consensus.

1.1.2. Julius Wellhausen

Julius Wellhausen put his seal of approval on de Wette's early work some seventy years later in one of his own early and very influential studies. The textual work undergirding what we now know as his *Prolegomena* was first published in sections in the *Jahrbücher für Deutsche Theologie* of 1876, 1877, and 1878; and in 1889 these were combined along with a supplement in a single volume as *Die Composition des Hexateuchs und der historischen Bücher des Alten Testaments*.[6] In 1878 he published what he had intended as the first volume of a two-volume history of Israel.[7] In 1883 a revised edition was retitled *Prolegomena …*, since he no longer intended to prepare the second volume.[8] In *Die Composition des Hexateuchs*, he mentions the

---

5. The issues are usefully explored in M. Patrick Graham, Kenneth G. Hoglund, and Steven L. McKenzie, eds., *The Chronicler as Historian*, JSOTSup 238 (Sheffield: Sheffield Academic, 1997).

6. Julius Wellhausen, "Die Composition des Hexateuchs," *JDT* 21 (1876): 392–450, 531–602; *JDT* 22 (1877): 407–79; Wellhausen, *Die Composition des Hexateuchs und der historischen Bücher des Alten Testaments* (Berlin: Reimer, 1889).

7. Julius Wellhausen, *Geschichte Israels*, 2 vols. (Berlin: Reimer, 1878).

8. As early as 1 June 1877, Wellhausen had told Abraham Kuenen he hoped to

Chronicler only very briefly here and there, and this already suggests that he did not deem that work to be of significant use in analyzing the earlier historical books.

The main argument of Wellhausen's *Prolegomena to the History of Israel* is laid out in two corresponding and mutually supportive sections. The first relates the history of worship: this explores the developing cultic legislation in the Pentateuch, from its earlier "Jehovistic" strata, through Deuteronomy from the late monarchic period, to the postexilic Priestly Code.[9] The second concerns what he calls the history of tradition.[10] Here he reviews the large-scale biblical narratives about the past in three steps: he starts at the end of the historical development with Chronicles, "which properly speaking forms but a single book along with Ezra and Nehemiah";[11] moves next to Judges, Samuel, and Kings; and concludes with the narrative of the Hexateuch. His principal conclusion with relevance to this study is stated in the following sentences:

> In the Chronicles the pattern according to which the history of ancient Israel is represented is the Pentateuch, *i.e.* the Priestly Code. In the source of Chronicles, in the older historical books, the revision does not proceed upon the basis of the Priestly Code, which indeed is completely unknown to them, but on the basis of Deuteronomy. Thus in the question of the order of sequence of the two great bodies of laws, the history of the tradition leads us to the same conclusion as the history of the cultus.[12]

While preserving many elements from earlier times, the books from Judges through Kings had undergone a consistent revision in the exilic period. "If ... we are fully justified in calling the revision Deuteronomistic, this means no more than that it came into existence under the influence of Deuteronomy, which pervaded the whole century of the exile."[13] Wellhau-

---

combine a history of the tradition with the already completed history of worship under the title "Prolegomena zur Geschichte Israels und Judas" (*Briefe*, ed. Rudolf Smend [Tübingen: Mohr Siebeck, 2013], 39 n. 41).

9. Julius Wellhausen, *Prolegomena to the History of Israel*, Reprints and Translations (Atlanta: Scholars Press, 1994), 17–167.

10. Ibid., 169–362.

11. Ibid., 171.

12. Ibid., 294.

13. Wellhausen, *Die Composition des Hexateuchs*, 280.

sen identified both Judg 17–21 and 2 Sam 21–24 as inserts into Deuteronomistically edited Judges and Samuel.[14] While he distinguished clearly between the historical worth of Judg 17–18 and the worthlessness of Judg 19–21, he made no similar pronouncement on the several elements of 2 Sam 21–24.

For both Wellhausen and de Wette, the main point about the Chronicler was that his total conception was unhistorical, whatever accurate detail might or might not be included. Wellhausen was scornful of de Wette's critics: "many a theological Sisyphus has toiled to roll the stone again wholly or half-way up the hill"![15] Against F. C. Movers, who had returned to Eichhorn's (pre–de Wette) view that the Chronicler had access to sources older than the books of Samuel–Kings, Wellhausen insisted that appeal to such sources (even if they had existed) was beside the main point: "the historical character of the work is not hereby altered in the smallest degree, it is merely shared by the so-called 'sources.'"[16] On the Chronicler's sources he writes: "It would seem … very natural to identify the work alluded to in Chronicles with our present canonical book [of Samuel–Kings]."[17] However, "the conclusion is forced upon us that the Book of Kings cited by the Chronicler is a late compilation far removed from actual tradition, and in relation to the canonical Book of Kings it can only be explained as an apocryphal amplification."[18]

His main case may be unimpeachable, but some details of his supporting argument go too far:

> It is indeed possible that occasionally a grain of good corn may occur among the chaff, but to be conscientious one must neglect this possibility of exceptions, and give due honour to the probability of the rule. For it is only too easy to deceive oneself in thinking that one has come upon some sound particular in a tainted whole. To what is said in 2 Sam. v. 9, "So David dwelt in the stronghold (Jebus), and he called it the city of

---

14. Ibid., 232–38, 263–64.
15. Wellhausen, *Prolegomena*, 222–27.
16. Wellhausen, *Prolegomena*, 223. On Movers, see Kai Peltonen, "Function, Explanation and Literary Phenomena: Aspects of Source Criticism as Theory and Method in the History of Chronicles Research," in *The Chronicler as Author: Studies in Text and Texture*, ed. M. Patrick Graham and Steven L. McKenzie, JSOTSup 263 (Sheffield: Sheffield Academic, 1999), 28–31.
17. Ibid., 226.
18. Ibid., 226–27.

David, and he built round about from the rampart and inward," there is added in 1 Chron. xi. 8, the statement that "Joab restored the rest of the city (Jerusalem)." This looks innocent enough, and is generally accepted as a fact. But the word חיה for בנה shows the comparatively modern date of the statement.... In many cases it is usual to regard such additions as having their origin in a better text of Samuel and Kings which lay before the Chronicler; and this certainly is the most likely way in which good additions could have got in.[19]

We shall return to the synoptic texts on the taking of Jerusalem in the next chapter (see 2.1). Suffice it to note that Wellhausen does not consider the literal sense of חיה ("let live") either here or in his earlier discussion of the text of Samuel.[20]

1.1.3. Martin Noth

Martin Noth's lasting and most famous contribution was to focus more closely on the Deuteronomistic achievement, many aspects of which had already been identified. The first volume of his classic *Überlieferungsgeschichtliche Studien* (1943) shows in several respects the influence of Wellhausen's *Prolegomena*. The title chosen, "Studies in the History of the Tradition," immediately recalls the heading of the second main part of the *Prolegomena*; and, like that forerunner, Noth's studies are organized in three sections with somewhat similar subject matter. They deal in turn with the Deuteronomistic work, the Chronistic work, and the Priestly writing and the redaction of the Pentateuch.

The main novelty in these tradition-historical studies was Noth's presentation of the Deuteronomist, together with its implications for his approach to the Pentateuch. The first major section was published in English translation as *The Deuteronomistic History*.[21] *The Chronicler's History* followed some years later, and this translation included the appendix on the implications for the Pentateuch of Noth's Deuteron-

---

19. Ibid., 224.

20. Julius Wellhausen, *Der Text der Bücher Samuelis* (Göttingen: Vandenhoeck & Ruprecht, 1871), 164. In his discussion of the synoptic chapters, he pays close and sympathetic attention to the evidence in Chronicles.

21. Martin Noth, *The Deuteronomistic History*, JSOTSup 15 (Sheffield: JSOT Press, 1981).

omistic hypothesis.²² E. W. Nicholson prepared a short introduction for the 1981 translation, and Hugh Williamson wrote a rather fuller one for the 1987 volume.²³ Unfortunately, however, Noth's own foreword of September 1943 was neither translated as it stood nor incorporated or even mentioned in either of these fresh introductions. Less important is its second paragraph, where Noth mentions overlapping studies by Gustav Hölscher and Fr. Ahlemann published after the completion of his own manuscript. More significant is the statement with which he concludes the first paragraph:

> The investigation submitted²⁴ singles out the earliest monument in human history known to us of true history writing, the only such monument in the ancient Orient, in order to appreciate it in its particularity—and attaches the investigation of a later offshoot from this work.²⁵

In one sense, Noth's Deuteronomist was simply Wellhausen's exilic reviser of the books of Judges, Samuel, and Kings. He revised once-separate traditions about the judges, the beginnings of monarchy, and the kingdoms of Israel and Judah—and also about the settlement under Joshua and the core of Deuteronomy itself. But where Noth went beyond Wellhausen was in his claim that the Deuteronomist, by contributing substantial linking narratives and interpretive speeches uttered by major characters, and by coordinating a consistent chronological framework, had brought—and had been the first to bring—this wealth of diverse materials into a *single* narrative. His Deuteronomist, therefore, deserved to be called a true historian. He recognized that a few passages in the Tetrateuch (such as Exod 23:20-33) had also been augmented by the Deuteronomist, but insisted that they had never been part of the single overarching redaction observable in Deuteronomy–Kings.²⁶ In the appendix to these studies, Noth

---

22. Martin Noth, *The Chronicler's History*, trans. H. G. M. Williamson, JSOTSup 50 (Sheffield: Sheffield Academic, 1987).

23. Noth, *Deuteronomistic History*, vii–x; Noth, *Chronicler's History*, 11–26, respectively.

24. To the Königsberg Learned Society (Königsberger Gelehrte Gesellschaft).

25. Noth certainly makes a similar point, though not quite so strongly (*Überlieferungsgeschichtliche Studien: Die sammelnden und bearbeitenden Geschichtswerke im Alten Testament* [Halle: Niemeyer, 1943], 2 n. 2). The English translation (*Deuteronomistic History*, 100 n. 3) does not quite catch his claim.

26. Noth, *Deuteronomistic History*, 104 n. 2.

began to explore the implications for the Pentateuch (or "Hexateuch") of his demonstration that Deuteronomy had been (re)written as the beginning of Deuteronomy–Kings.

The relationship between Noth's historian and his sources is nicely illustrated in the discussion of chronology: "We do not propose to inquire into the sources which Dtr. used for the chronological material, but would note simply that he intended to supply and in fact did supply an unbroken chronology for the period of the Israelite and Judaean monarchies using specific and, as we can show, on the whole reliable sources."[27]

On the surprising note in 1 Sam 13:1 about the (only two-year) length of Saul's reign, he comments:

> Admittedly, it is generally thought that this data has been subject to damage at a late stage, or that the whole verse was added by a much later hand. The verse is missing in LXX^B and several other Septuagint manuscripts, but this means little, given the liberties which the Septuagint takes with the Hebrew text, especially in the "Books of Kingdoms."[28] It would in fact be very surprising if Dtr. with his interest in chronological questions did not give a date for the reign of Saul. 1 Sam. 13:1 was certainly inserted by Dtr. at the appropriate place after 1 Sam. 12 in the style of his formulaic introductions to the reigns of kings elsewhere.[29]

The Deuteronomist was also responsible for contributing the regnal information about Saul's son and about David.[30] Noth's view that the evaluations and the chronological information at the head of the report of each king's reign were Deuteronomistic has been hugely influential.

In the first and third sections of the *Überlieferungsgeschichtliche Studien*, Noth refers to Wellhausen, but not in the second, on the work of the Chronicler.[31] Like Wellhausen, however, Noth held that the Chronistic work had

---

27. Ibid., 18.
28. What Noth wrote was "Books of Kings" ("Königsbüchern"; see *Überlieferungsgschichtliche Studien*, 24).
29. Noth, *Deuteronomistic History*, 23. Wellhausen (*Composition des Hexateuchs*, 246) had also held that 1 Sam 13:1 belonged to the chronological redaction.
30. Noth, *Deuteronomistic History*, 125, 127.
31. In the English translation, references to Wellhausen appear only in passing in Williamson's introduction (*Chronicler's History*, 12) and several times in the appendix on "The 'Priestly Writing' and the Redaction of the Pentateuch" (107–47), while de Wette is mentioned only once, in Williamson's introduction (12).

included Ezra-Nehemiah. He sets the date of the work between 300 and 200 BCE, based on arguments relating to Ezra-Nehemiah. The history of the Davidic monarchy related in the book of Chronicles has 2 Samuel–2 Kings as its main source—not the text of the original Deuteronomistic History (DtrH), but instead the familiar separate books that included post-Deuteronomistic additions such as 2 Sam 21–24. Though Noth dates the Chronicler to the early Hellenistic period like Wellhausen, he is more open than the latter to recognize quality in some of his sources: he may have used an older source (or extract from it) on military matters. "The very existence of the work of Dtr. is sufficient to show that the annals themselves or at least some extracts of this sort were not all destroyed in 587 BC."[32]

> For the period after Solomon, as is well known, he extracted from [2 Samuel–2 Kings] only those portions which dealt with the kings of Judah and ... more or less ignored the history of the state of Israel. Only occasionally, when it was a question of something significant for Judaean history, did he include some material from sections dealing with the Israelite kings, sometimes in a brief summary, as at 2 Chron. 22.7–9, and sometimes in full, as at 2 Chron. 18.2–34."[33]

That the Chronicler's source for the David story included 2 Sam 21–24 (and hence was post-Deuteronomistic), that 1 Kgs 22 // 2 Chr 18 was a story dealing fundamentally with a king of Israel,[34] and that 2 Chr 22:7–9 is a summary of 2 Kgs 9–10 rather than one of its sources are all straightforward judgments to make if one *knows* that the Chronistic work was composed long after the Deuteronomistic one. However, I have argued elsewhere that the exploits of David's heroes against Philistine giants and the census insisted on by David were already available together to the author of the Samuel coda (2 Sam 21–24) just as we find them in 1 Chr 20:4–8 and 1 Chr 21.[35] I will argue in the course of this study that 1 Kgs 22 // 2 Chr 18 was an integral part of the story of Jerusalem's kings. As

---

32. Ibid., 60–61.
33. Ibid., 90.
34. In these first two judgments, Noth was anticipated by Wellhausen. We noted above his view that 2 Sam 21–24 was an appendix to Samuel ("ein Anhang am Schluss"); then in *Composition des Hexateuchs*, 287–88, he had assigned 1 Kgs 20; 22; 2 Kgs 3; 6:24–7:20; 9–10 to a northern source distinct from 1 Kgs 17–19; 21.
35. A. Graeme Auld, *I and II Samuel: A Commentary*, OTL (Louisville: Westminster John Knox, 2011), 10–11.

for 2 Chr 22:9–11, it may instead have been the acorn from which one of the mighty oaks of 2 Kgs 9–10 grew, just as the note in 1 Kgs 12:15 // 2 Chr 10:15 about Ahijah may have prompted the composition of the wider Ahijah complex within 1 Kgs 11–14.[36]

Noth's thesis about a Deuteronomistic History has proved remarkably successful despite being much revised. Rudolf Smend proposed a second (also exilic-period) Deuteronomist (DtrN) on the basis of some portions of Joshua and the beginning of Judges, and Frank Moore Cross argued that a first Deuteronomistic edition before the collapse of Jerusalem was more supportive of monarchy (Dtr[1]), while an exilic reedition was more critical (Dtr[2]).[37] Each of these leaders was followed and their proposals further modified by a series of students. Timo Veijola and Walter Dietrich elaborated Smend's lead into studies of Judges, Samuel, and Kings; and Richard Nelson followed Cross and argued for a dual redaction of the whole history.[38] Against that trend, both Hans-Dettlef Hoffmann and Robert Polzin argued that a single Deuteronomist had been responsible for all or almost all of the material in Deuteronomy–Kings (with fewer exceptions, if any, than Noth had allowed).[39]

Noth's proposal has remained classic even even where important elements of it have been departed from.[40] Very many scholars—often appar-

---

36. Similar points can be made about Michal and about the Jabesh story, both also mentioned in Noth, *Chronicler's History*, 90.

37. Rudolf Smend, "Das Gesetz und die Völker," in *Probleme biblischer Theologie: Gerhard von Rad zum 70. Geburtstag*, ed. Hans Walter Wolff (Munich: Kaiser, 1971), 494–509; Frank Moore Cross, *Canaanite Myth and Hebrew Epic: Essays in the History of the Religion of Israel* (Cambridge: Harvard University Press, 1973), 274–89.

38. Timo Veijola, *Das Königtum in der Beurteilung des deuteronomistischen Historiographie*, AASF 198 (Helsinki: Academia Scientiarum Fennica, 1977); Walter Dietrich, *Prophetie und Geschichte: Eine redaktionsgeschichtliche Untersuchung zum deuteronomistischen Geschichtswerk*, FRLANT 108 (Göttingen: Vandenhoeck & Ruprecht, 1972); Richard Nelson, *The Double Redaction of the Deuteronomistic History*, JSOTSup 18 (Sheffield: JSOT Press, 1981).

39. Hans-Detlef Hoffmann, *Reform und Reformen: Untersuchungen zu einem Grundthema der deuteronomistischen Geschichtsschreibung*, ATANT 66 (Zurich: Theologischer Verlag, 1980). See Robert Polzin's series Literary Study of the Deuteronomic History: *Moses and the Deuteronomist* (New York: Seabury, 1980); *Samuel and the Deuteronomist* (San Francisco: Harper & Row, 1989); *David and the Deuteronomist* (Bloomington: Indiana University Press, 1993).

40. It has been substantially assessed and represented by Walter Dietrich in "Die Vorderen Propheten," in *Die Entstehung des Alten Testaments*, by Walter Dietrich,

ently impervious to larger and smaller changes that have been argued in subsequent discussion—simply use "DtrH" as shorthand for the books of Joshua, Judges, Samuel, and Kings, the books of the Former Prophets in the Hebrew Bible. This surely indicates both Noth's success and his failure (he himself insisted on Deuteronomy as the start of DtrH).

1.2. Some Recent Discussion

In 1983, I hazarded the suggestion that it would be easier to think together the development of the Deuteronomistic and Chronistic works if the story of David in his court (2 Sam 9–20 + 1 Kgs 1–2) and the Elijah/Elisha narratives (in much of 1 Kgs 17–2 Kgs 10) were considered "*supplements* to the Deuteronomist's work, not *sources* for it," observing that "the Chronicler is deafeningly silent over each corpus."[41] The paper was something of a counterfactual essay before these became more popular.[42] John Van Seters argued quite independently in the same year that the court history was a supplement to David's story.[43] Shortly afterward, Steven McKenzie proposed that the Chronicler had worked not from the books of Samuel–Kings as they stand, but from a text close to Cross's Dtr[1]: "although C[hronicles] is not a completely reliable criterion for isolating Dtr 2 material, at least where C has a parallel to a K[ings] passage, one must be extremely cautious about attributing the latter to Dtr 2."[44] In his second book, McKenzie went on to argue that much of the Elijah-Elisha material was a later addition to Deuteronomistic Kings.[45]

Both of McKenzie's moves—relating the first draft of Chronicles to a penultimate draft of the Deuteronomists' work and recognizing the major prophetic collection at the heart of Kings as an addition to the

---

Hans-Peter Mathys, Thomas Römer, and Rudolf Smend, ThW 1 (Stuttgart: Kohlhammer, 2014), 167–282.

41. A. Graeme Auld, "Prophets through the Looking Glass: Between Writings and Moses," *JSOT* 27 (1983): 16.

42. The background to its preparation is sketched in A. Graeme Auld, *Samuel at the Threshold: Selected Works of Graeme Auld*, SOTSMS (Ashgate: Aldershot, 2004), 4.

43. John Van Seters, *In Search of History: Historiography in the Ancient World and the Origins of Biblical History* (New Haven: Yale University Press, 1983), 277–91.

44. Steven McKenzie, *The Chronicler's Use of the Deuteronomistic History*, HSM 33 (Chico, CA: Scholars Press, 1985), 206.

45. Steven McKenzie, *The Trouble with Kings: The Composition of the Book of Kings in the Deuteronomistic History*, VTSup 42 (Leiden: Brill, 1991).

book—seemed to provide very substantial support to my 1983 proposal. Acknowledging the stimulus that his two monographs had supplied, I advanced the more radical argument[46] that the books of Samuel-Kings should no longer be privileged as the main source of Chronicles, but that Samuel-Kings and Chronicles should both be recognized as independent appropriations of and developments from a common source, a narrative focused on the house of David and the house of Yahweh in Jerusalem—a narrative I subsequently named the Book of Two Houses (BTH).[47] בית יהוה ("the house of Yahweh")[48] and בית המלך ("the house of the king")[49] are two of the most constant elements of the synoptic tradition and very often found as a pair.

Noth had supposed that the Chronicler took over from Kings "only those portions which dealt with the kings of Judah and ... more or less ignored the history of the state of Israel. Only occasionally, when it was a question of something significant for Judaean history, did he include some material from sections dealing with the Israelite kings."[50] I proposed instead that, for the period after Solomon, Chronicles used a precursor of our book of Kings—a history of the kings of Judah with occasional mention of Israel, to which the connected history of the kings of Israel had not yet been added. I also asked, "Are there still questions about the writing of the books of Kings whose best answer is 'The Deuteronomists'?"[51] Also in 1994, Ernst Würthwein argued that the primary direction of influence

---

46. See A. Graeme Auld, *Kings without Privilege* (Edinburgh: T&T Clark, 1994).

47. So named first in "Prophets Shared—but Recycled," in *The Future of the Deuteronomistic History*, ed. Thomas Römer, BETL 147 (Leuven: Peeters, 2000), 19–28 (reprinted in my *Samuel at the Threshold*, 127–34).

48. 1 Kgs 6:37 // 2 Chr 3:1; 1 Kgs 7:45 // 2 Chr 4:16; 1 Kgs 7:51 // 2 Chr 5:1; 1 Kgs 8:11 // 2 Chr 5:11–14[!]; 1 Kgs 8:64 // 2 Chr 7:7; 1 Kgs 9:1 // 2 Chr 7:11; 1 Kgs 9:10 // 2 Chr 8:1; 1 Kgs 10:5, 12 // 2 Chr 9:4, 11; 1 Kgs 14:26, 28 // 2 Chr 12:9, 11; 1 Kgs 15:18 // 2 Chr 16:2; 2 Kgs 11:13, 15, 18, 19 // 2 Chr 23:12, 14, 17, 18; 2 Kgs 12:10 // 2 Chr 24:8; 2 Kgs 12:8–14 // 2 Chr 24:9–16; 2 Kgs 14:14 // 2 Chr 25:24; 2 Kgs 15:35 // 2 Chr 27:3; 2 Kgs 16:8 (, 18) // 2 Chr 28:21 (, 24); 2 Kgs 21:4, 5 // 2 Chr 33:4, 5; 2 Kgs 22:3, 5 (2x), 8, 9; 2 Kgs 23:2 (2x) // 2 Chr 34:8, 10 (2x), 15, 17, 30 (2x).

49. 1 Kgs 9:1 // 2 Chr 7:11; 10:12 // 2 Chr 9:11; 14:26–27 // 2 Chr 12:9–10; 15:18 // 2 Chr 16:2; 2 Kgs 11:16, 19 // 2 Chr 23:15, 20; 2 Kgs 14:14 // 2 Chr 25:24; 2 Kgs 15:5 // 2 Chr 26:21; 2 Kgs 16:8 // 2 Chr 28:21.

50. Noth, *Chronicler's History*, 90.

51. Auld, *Kings without Privilege*, 150.

ran from Kings to Deuteronomy rather than the other way round.[52] The title of his contribution can be translated as "Reflections on the So-Called Deuteronomistic History: A Sketch." (The *so-called* in the title of his sketch would be adopted in Thomas Römer's masterly 2005 introduction to matters Deuteronomistic.[53])

The following year, a wholly different approach was advanced by Isaac Kalimi. Against both medieval Jewish scholars and contemporary specialists, he insisted that the books of Chronicles were not דרש or commentary on Samuel–Kings: Samuel–Kings could not have had authoritative or canonical status, or the Chronicler would not have been able to be so free in his modification of their text. Instead, he was a historian who chose from older sources what seemed to suit him and brought this into his chosen order and literary form.[54] That the several literary devices employed in Chronicles are found throughout the text persuades Kalimi of the substantial unity of the work.[55]

McKenzie brought the above-mentioned monographs of Auld and Kalimi into dialogue in his discussion of "The Chronicler as Redactor." After considering "Who Redacted?," he turned to "What Chr. Redacted: Auld's Theory of a Shared Source," and finally "How Chr. Redacted: Kalimi's Analysis of Redactional Techniques in Chronicles."[56] I was given the opportunity to answer most of McKenzie's questions and criticisms in an essay in the same volume,[57] but one of them (about Ahijah's oracle in 1 Kgs 12:15 // 2 Chr 10:15) had to wait many more years.[58] My millennial study

---

52. Ernst Würthwein, "Erwägungen zum sog. deuteronomistischen Geschichtswerk: Eine Skizze," in *Studien zum deuteronomistischen Geschichtswerk*, BZAW 227 (Berlin: de Gruyter, 1994), 1–11.

53. Thomas Römer, *The So-Called Deuteronomistic History: A Sociological, Historical and Literary Introduction* (London: T&T Clark, 2005).

54. Isaac Kalimi, *Zur Geschichtsschreibung des Chronisten*, BZAW 226 (Berlin: de Gruyter, 1995), 7.

55. The first section of his monograph is available in English as Isaac Kalimi, "Was the Chronicler a Historian?" in Graham, Hoglund, and McKenzie, *Chronicler as Historian*, 73–89.

56. Steven McKenzie, "The Chronicler as Redactor," in Graham and McKenzie, *Chronicler as Author*, 70–90.

57. A. Graeme Auld, "What Was the Main Source of the Books of Chronicles?," in Graham and McKenzie, *Chronicler as Author*, 91–99.

58. Until my "Isaiah and the Oldest 'Biblical' Prophetic Narrative," in *Prophets and Prophecy in Stories: Papers Read at the Fifth Meeting of the Edinburgh Prophecy*

then probed the consensus view as a counterfactual: "What If the Chronicler Did Use the Deuteronomistic History?"[59]

Two articles published in 2001 usefully probed significant differences between Deuteronomy and the so-called Deuteronomistic History, with particular reference to the role of the king. Gary Knoppers put the issue like this:

> If much of the law of the king (Deut. 17:14–20), or of the constitution for office holders (16:18–18:22) of which the law of the king is a part, stems from Deuteronomistic hands, as some scholars contend, how likely is it that the Deuteronomists who edited Kings wrote such texts? However one dates the material in Deut. 16:18–18:22—before, contemporaneous with, or after the work of the primary Deuteronomistic editor(s) of Kings—the disparities between the two works remain.[60]

Bernard Levinson charted "discontinuities in the royal ideology of Deuteronomy and DtrH": over the king as final court of appeal, as responsible for the cultus, as divinely adopted, as leader in war, and (associating Jer 34 with the spirit of DtrH) as responsible for economic relief.[61] This was his solution: "So radical was [Deuteronomy's blueprint] in its own time that, shortly after its promulgation, it was effectively abrogated, as the Deuteronomistic Historian, while purporting to implement the norms of Deuteronomy, restored to the king precisely those powers denied him by Deuteronomy."[62]

My *Kings without Privilege* received different sorts of support, sometimes indirect, from several of my doctoral candidates. James Linville envisaged the book of Kings as a significant work of the postexilic period.[63] Lydie Kucová explored mutual influences on the development of

---

Network, Utrecht, October 2013, ed. Bob Becking and Hans Barstad, OTS 65 (Leiden: Brill, 2015), 47.

59. A. Graeme Auld, "What If the Chronicler Did Use the Deuteronomistic History?," in *Virtual History and the Bible*, ed. J. Cheryl Exum, BibInt 8 (Leiden: Brill, 2000), 137–50.

60. Gary N. Knoppers, "Rethinking the Relationship between Deuteronomy and the Deuteronomistic History: The Case of Kings," *CBQ* 63 (2001): 414.

61. Bernard M. Levinson, "The Reconceptualization of Kingship in Deuteronomy and the Deuteronomistic History's Transformation of Torah," *VT* 51 (2001): 529.

62. Ibid., 533–34.

63. James R. Linville, *Israel in the Book of Kings: The Past as a Project of Social Identity*, JSOTSup 272 (Sheffield: Sheffield Academic, 1998).

the Joash and Josiah traditions.[64] Craig Ho wrote perceptively about the transition from Saul to David in the tradition behind Samuel and Chronicles.[65] Robert Rezetko's work on the synoptic reports of the transfer of the divine ark to Jerusalem was not only important in itself;[66] it also launched him on a substantial critique of the mainstream view of the history of Biblical Hebrew.

Some early encouragement came from Kurt Noll and David Carr.[67] But the most substantial support has come from Raymond Person Jr. His early study of *The Kings-Isaiah and Kings-Jeremiah Recensions* offered a good blend of text-critical and redactional study.[68] Then his interest in "two different scribal groups with their differing theological traditions" as responsible for Chronicles and (what he prefers to call) "the Deuteronomic History," already indicated in an earlier study, was more fully sketched in an article in honor of my work.[69] Against those who held that the Deuteronom(ist)ic History was substantially complete by the end of the exilic period, he deployed some of the conclusions of his *Recensions* study. He had demonstrated there that editing in Deuteronomic style remained alive and well much longer; and the later stages were contemporary with the separate rethinking of the shared project that produced Chronicles. He

---

64. Lydie Kucová, "Common Source Theory and Composition of the Story of the Divided Monarchy in Kings with Special Emphasis on the Account of Josiah's Reform" (PhD thesis, Edinburgh University, 2005).

65. Craig (Yuet Shun) Ho, "The Troubles of David and His House: Textual and Literary Studies of the Synoptic Stories of Saul and David in Samuel–Kings and Chronicles" (PhD thesis, Edinburgh University, 1994); Ho, "Conjectures and Refutations: Is 1 Samuel XXXI 1–13 Really the Source of 1 Chronicles X 1–12?" *VT* 45 (1995): 82–106.

66. Robert Rezetko, *Source and Revision in the Narratives of David's Transfer of the Ark: Text, Language and Story in 2 Samuel 6 and 1 Chronicles 13, 15–16*, LHBOTS 470 (London: T&T Clark, 2007).

67. Kurt L. Noll, "Deuteronomistic History or Deuteronomic Debate? (A Thought Experiment)," *JSOT* 31 (2007): 311–45; David Carr, *The Formation of the Hebrew Bible: A New Reconstruction* (New York: Oxford University Press, 2011), 73–77.

68. Raymond F. Person Jr., *The Kings-Isaiah and Kings-Jeremiah Recensions*, BZAW 252 (Berlin: de Gruyter, 1997).

69. Raymond F. Person Jr., *The Deuteronomic School: History, Social Setting, and Literature*, SBLStBL 2 (Atlanta: Society of Biblical Literature, 2002), 143; Person, "The Deuteronomic History and the Books of Chronicles: Contemporary Competing Historiographies," in *Reflection and Refraction: Studies in Biblical Historiography in Honour of A. Graeme Auld*, ed. Robert Rezetko, Timothy H. Lim, and W. Brian Aucker, VTSup 113 (Leiden: Brill, 2007), 315–36.

offered his full approval to the challenge launched by Robert Rezetko and Ian Young against the consensual (but circular) argument about Standard Biblical Hebrew (SBH) and Late Biblical Hebrew (LBH): the literary language of the monarchy (SBH) continued to be used by the early returnees to Persian Yehud; "those who remained in Babylon much longer developed a Hebrew with more Aramaic influences (LBH)."[70]

A wide-ranging monograph followed, *The Deuteronomic History and the Book of Chronicles*, its approach indicated in its subtitle, *Scribal Works in an Oral World*.[71] In dialogue with a wide array of scholars, Person argued that Samuel–Kings as we know them and Chronicles were divergent appropriations of a shared source that already had substantial Deuteronomic characteristics. On the one side, his critique of many of the critics of my project is very perceptive;[72] and on the other, he has set my proposals in a fresh intellectual environment. While I had conceived the separate development of Samuel–Kings and Chronicles as (simply?) the efforts of scholar-scribes at their desks, Person insists on setting the work of these scribes in the wider intellectual context of a predominantly oral world. He judges that attentiveness to orality is important in two different ways. Oral performances are at least tolerant of—and may even encourage—the practice of synonymous variation: the use of an alternative word or phrase within what is accepted as being the same text.[73] Then, in face of a hypothetical, older, written Solomon story that, like the Chronicler's, mentioned the daughter of Pharaoh only once (Solomon moving her to her own house in 2 Chr 8:11),[74] Person supposes that its readers would not have been puzzled. They knew many more stories than were written down; they were already familiar with Solomon's Egyptian wife, and

---

70. Person, "Deuteronomic History and the Books of Chronicles," 335.

71. Raymond F. Person Jr., *The Deuteronomic History and the Book of Chronicles: Scribal Works in an Oral World*, AIL 6 (Atlanta: Society of Biblical Literature, 2010).

72. He endorses seeing the death of Saul (1 Sam 31 // 1 Chr 10) as the start of the shared source (ibid., 91).

73. "Given this reconstruction of the process of the interaction of texts and the broader oral tradition in ancient Israel, Auld's thesis of a smaller common source behind Samuel–Kings//Chronicles has some validity. However, Auld's attempt to reconstruct this one source must be corrected with the idea that this common source existed in multiple forms from the beginning of its history, none of which would have been understood as so authoritative as to dismiss the authority of others" (ibid., 129).

74. He has a careful critique (ibid., 111) of Zipora Talshir's criticism of *Kings without Privilege* on this point.

not necessarily as we find her in (different versions of) Kings. What they looked out for was how the Chronicler was retelling this fragment of the familiar story. Other such fragments are Saul's daughter Michal scorning David from a window in Jerusalem and Ahijah's oracle about Rehoboam's impending loss of most of Israel.

I have sympathy with this approach but am not wholly persuaded of its relevance in every such case. We have no information—indeed, we can have no information—independent of Samuel–Kings and Chronicles about what more the writers or readers of these texts may have known about Michal or the Egyptian princess. As far as Michal is concerned, I have sketched a possible development back from her scorning the new king to her love for the new hero who had killed Goliath, each step belonging to a new broad layer of the development of the book of Samuel.[75] The analysis repeated later in this volume of the story of David and Bathsheba deduces that all but one of its characters and many of its themes already featured in the shorter synoptic history of David. But what about Bathsheba herself? Was she widely known in lore about David and his women? Or was she created by the author of 2 Sam 11–12? How could we know?

Two further challenges from Person require a response. One concerns the proper use of the term *Deuteronom(ist)ic*. Rightly (I think) he detects quite a long period of continuous textual development from the material Samuel–Kings shares with Chronicles in (probably) the exilic period to final touches added to Samuel–Kings in the Hellenistic period.[76] Rightly (I think) he calls (some of) these final touches "Deuteronomic." Given this manifest continuity, should the shared beginnings also be termed "Deuteronomic"? I have resisted this in several publications. The Former Prophets narratives were called "Deuteronom(ist)ic," classically by Wellhausen and Noth (and followed by very many others), because they were held to have been influenced by (a form of) Deuteronomy. Person does share the judgment of Würthwein and myself that the (principal) direction of influence was the other way round: many themes now familiar within Deuteronomy were first presented within the developing national narrative. But he reckons that the organic continuity within the developing nar-

---

75. Auld, *I and II Samuel*, 625.
76. Person (*The Deuteronomic History and the Book of Chronicles*, 106, 141–43) is sympathetic to Adrian Schenker's view that Deuteronomic-like development is even more apparent in MT Samuel–Kings than in the LXX.

rative and between that developing narrative and the developing book of Deuteronomy justifies calling the whole process "Deuteronomic."

Hans Ausloos has come at this issue of the proper use of the term *Deuteronomistic* from trying to answer a different question: How can one "determine whether a relationship exists between a pericope [such as the conclusion to the Covenant Code in Exod 23:20–33] and the so-called Deuteronomistic canon"?[77] By that "canon" Ausloos means Deuteronomy through Kings plus Jeremiah. How are portions of Exodus and Numbers such as Exod 23:20–33 related to Deuteronomistic thinking, so defined? He proposes greater care in the use not only of "Dtr" but of "pre-Dtr," "proto-Dtr," and "post-Dtr"—he even advocates the introduction of "simili-Dtr." He notes, with obvious surprise, that "Person ... even argues that we should abandon the distinction between Deuteronomic and Deuteronomistic and only to [sic] use the notion Deuteronomic."[78] Continuity between the Book of Two Houses and the Deuteronom(ist)ic History is obvious. But unless we can specify that even a prototype of Deuteronomy or of Joshua or of Judges existed when the Book of Two Houses was composed, then we can hardly speak sensibly of even a proto-Deuteronom(ist)ic canon.

Person's second challenge concerns the deductions that should be drawn from the different placing of the same note or pericope in different versions of a synoptic text. I had proposed that a different location might indicate secondary material that had not found a secure agreed place within the narrative. But he found me inconsistent in applying this principle: the shared material should be even smaller than my reconstruction; I should have taken more strictly my own criterion about different order pointing to secondary addition. Drawing on a study by Julio Trebolle Barrera, Person asks whether even the solitary shared note about moving Pharaoh's daughter should be thought secondary because we find it in a different place in 1 Kgs 9 (LXX 3 Kgdms 9) from 1 Kgs 9:24 (MT) // 2 Chr 8:11.[79]

I think that Trebolle Barrera and Person need to distinguish here between two separate issues. That a note or a pericope is positioned differ-

---

77. Hans Ausloos, *The Deuteronomist's History: The Role of the Deuteronomist in Historical-Critical Research into Genesis–Numbers*, OTS 67 (Leiden: Brill, 2015), 285.

78. Ibid., 273 n. 48.

79. Person, *Deuteronomic History*, 127. See Julio Trebolle Barrera, "Kings (MT/LXX) and Chronicles: The Double and Triple Textual Tradition," in Rezetko, Lim, and Aucker, *Reflection and Refraction*, 483–501.

ently in each of three versions of (say) the Solomon story *may* (rightly, I still think) indicate that it was added to the developing narrative subsequent to those elements that share a fixed order in the tradition. On the other hand, that it is found in *all* three versions means that a prima facie case exists for its inclusion in any overview (or reconstruction) of the shared textual material. It was already available to each of the diverging, expanding traditions, even if it was not among the oldest of the elements they shared. We shall return to this issue when presenting the synoptic materials in the second part of the Solomon story. Of course, different locations within the text may also result from editorial decisions *within the development of the separate books* of Samuel–Kings and Chronicles. I have suggested in my Samuel commentary that at least some of Chronicles' ordering of the oldest elements of the David story may be more original than what we find in Samuel.[80] For example, two purposes may have been served by moving the list of David's heroes from near the beginning in 2 Sam 5 // 1 Chr 11 to their present position in 2 Sam 23. Removing a list of such powerful men from 2 Sam 5 helps to emphasize David's own key role in consolidating Jerusalem. Then within the balanced coda created in 2 Sam 21–24 this list is a counterpart to the exploits of David's heroes and Philistine giants (2 Sam 21:18–22 // 1 Chr 20:4–8), which were already reported adjacent to David's census (2 Sam 24 // 1 Chr 21).

1.3. Toward *Life in Kings*

The material shared by Samuel–Kings and Chronicles is far from "paltry" (*dürftig*), as de Wette called it. And the shared elements, though very varied, exhibit greater cohesion than first appears. Much of the basic research for this book has already been presented in a number of convergent recent studies. (1) A symposium in Jena in September 2012 considered evidence for post-Chronistic influence on the books of Samuel. My contribution concentrated on some texts shared by Samuel and Chronicles in which one could argue that Chronicles had preserved an earlier reading.[81] At the time, I had no idea that the present volume would become a

---

80. Auld, *I and II Samuel*, 10–11.
81. A. Graeme Auld, "The Text of Chronicles and the Beginnings of Samuel," in *Rereading the* relecture? *The Question of (Post)chronistic Influence in the Latest Redactions of the Books of Samuel*, ed. Uwe Becker and Hannes Bezzel, FAT 2/66 (Tübingen: Mohr Siebeck, 2014), 31–40.

second outcome of the days in Jena. (2) A volume celebrating the work of Philip Davies had already included a review of the usage of some temporal markers in Samuel–Kings and Chronicles.[82] (3) A study extending and correcting the results of both these papers appeared in *Revue biblique*, as a response to Kalimi's critique in that journal of my *Kings without Privilege* published some twenty years earlier.[83] (4) At the Prophecy Network Symposium in Utrecht in September 2013 on the topic of prophetic narratives, I contributed a study on God-king communication in narratives shared by Samuel–Kings and Chronicles.[84] (5) An invitation to contribute to a Festschrift for Hans Barstad stimulated a long-promised interaction with studies by the honorand and led me into surprising Baal territory.[85] (6) A symposium in Prague in April 2014 on kingship provided the opportunity to compare what is said about the kings of northern Israel within the story of Jerusalem's kings, as told in both Kings and Chronicles, with how they are presented in the interleaved connected account of the north in the book of Kings.[86] (7) At the 2015 Society for Old Testament Studies Summer Meeting in Edinburgh, I contrasted how Kings and Chronicles present the account by the Assyrian envoy of Hezekiah's reform.[87] (8) The 2015 symposium of the (Aberdeen) prophecy network in Göttingen heard

---

82. A. Graeme Auld, "Writing Time and Eternity in Samuel and Kings," in *Far from Minimal: Celebrating the Work and Influence of Philip R. Davies*, ed. Duncan Burns and John W. Rogerson, LHBOTS 484 (London: T&T Clark, 2012), 1–10.

83. A. Graeme Auld, "The Shaping of Israelite History in Samuel and Kings," *RB* 121 (2014): 195–216. In response to Isaac Kalimi, "Kings *with* Privilege: The Core Sources of the Parallel Texts between the Deuteronomistic and Chronistic Histories," *RB* 119 (2012): 498–517; essentially repeated in Kalimi, "Die Quelle(n) der Textparallelen zwischen Samuel-Könige und Chronik," in Becker and Bezzel, *Rereading the relecture?*, 11–30.

84. Auld, "Isaiah and the Oldest 'Biblical' Prophetic Narrative," 45–63.

85. A. Graeme Auld, "Elijah and the Prophets of Baal and of Asherah: Towards a Discussion of 'No Prophets?,'" in *New Perspectives on Prophecy and History: Essays in Honour of Hans M. Barstad*, ed. Rannfrid I. Thelle, Terje Stordalen, and Mervyn E. J. Richardson, VTSup 168 (Leiden: Brill, 2015), 7–16.

86. A. Graeme Auld, "Righting Israel's Kings: Israel's Kings in Synoptic Perspective," in *A King Like All the Nations? Kingdoms of Israel and Judah in the Bible and History*, ed. Manfred Oeming and Petr Sláma, Beiträge zum Verstehen der Bibel 28 (Berlin: LIT, 2015), 147–58.

87. "Did the Assyrian Envoy Know the *Venite*? What Did He Know? What Did He Say? And Should He Be Believed?," in *Torah and Tradition*, ed. Klaas Spronk, OTS 70 (Leiden: Brill, 2017), 42–53.

a fresh triangulation of the reports in Chronicles, Isaiah, and Kings about Hezekiah and Isaiah.[88] However, all of these studies have been rewritten—some partially, some more extensively—for this volume.

The material Samuel and Kings share with Chronicles, the synoptic material, constitutes some 20–25 percent of Samuel–Kings and some 40–45 percent of Chronicles. The core of the present enterprise is a demonstration that this synoptic material enjoys sufficient cohesion to have once stood alone. The rest simply follows up some of the consequences. After the pair of introductory case studies at the end of this chapter, the next chapters (2–5) present fresh and cumulative evidence that the shared or synoptic material within Samuel and Kings is substantially different from the rest of these books in wording and usage. The new evidence adduced gives support to many of the proposals made some twenty years ago in my *Kings without Privilege*, but stands quite independent of that earlier monograph. Chapter 6 offers an interim presentation of the synoptic material. Chapters 7–9 sketch the development from this Book of Two Houses to the books of Samuel and Kings: first in Davidic and pre-Davidic story, then in the creation of a connected history of northern Israel, and finally in the rewriting of the house of David from Solomon to the fall of Jerusalem. After a fresh account (ch. 10) of the relationships between the stories of Hezekiah and Isaiah in the books of Kings, Chronicles, and Isaiah, chapter 11 sketches some fresh questions. The final chapter offers a reconstruction of the synoptic material in Kings in both Hebrew and (rather literal) English translation. The whole volume offers a new perspective: if we view the developing book of Kings from the vantage point of what it shares with the book of Chronicles, fresh opportunities open up for understanding much of the material peculiar to Kings.

1.4. Words Sampled

Our starting point is in two seemingly unconnected pairs of texts. One pair relates to King Hezekiah and is told differently in Kings and Isaiah; the other relates to an action by King David that is told differently in Samuel and Chronicles. It turns out that there are important links between what Kings reports in addition to Isaiah, on the one side, and what Samuel

---

88. A. Graeme Auld, "Chronicles—Isaiah—Kings," in *Imperial Visions: The Prophet and the Book of Isaiah in an Age of Empires*, ed. Joachim Schaper (Göttingen: Vandenhoeck & Ruprecht, forthcoming).

reports in addition to Chronicles, on the other; and these "extras" will receive much closer scrutiny in the following chapters.

1.4.1. The Rabshakeh's Offer

We shall return again and again during this study to the three biblical accounts of King Hezekiah. It is all the more appropriate that our first example concerns two of these. Isaiah 36–39 and 2 Kgs 18–20 tell much the same story and mostly in very similar terms. There is, however, one large-scale difference between them: Isaiah includes a substantial poetic composition attributed to Hezekiah on his recovery from illness (38:9–20); and the material in the verses that surround this poem (38:7–8, 21–22) is differently arranged and more fully stated in 2 Kgs 20:7–11.[89] We shall return to these issues in chapter 10. Our present purpose is better served at an earlier stage in the story shared by Isaiah and Kings by comparing the two versions of the offer made by the envoy of the king of Assyria to those standing on the walls of besieged Jerusalem.

Isa 36:16b–18	2 Kgs 18:31b–33
עשו־אתי ברכה וצאו אלי ואכלו איש־גפנו ואיש תאנתו ושתו איש מי־בורו עד־באי ולקחתי אתכם אל־ארץ כארצכם ארץ דגן ותירוש ארץ לחם וכרמים	עשו־אתי ברכה וצאו אלי ואכלו איש־גפנו ואיש תאנתו ושתו איש מי־בורו עד־באי ולקחתי אתכם אל־ארץ כארצכם ארץ דגן ותירוש ארץ לחם וכרמים ארץ זית יצהר ודבש וחיו ולא תמתו

---

89. Admittedly, that summary understates the differences between the two accounts. ויחי is vocalized differently in each: in 2 Kgs 20:7 it reports the success of the treatment, but in Isa 38:21—after the king's long poetic prayer (38:9–20)—the treatment is still in prospect. See further Greg Goswell, "The Literary Logic and Meaning of Isaiah 38," *JSOT* 39 (2014): 182.

90. The phrase עשו־אתי ברכה is unusual and is often rendered freely. However, if it is not rendered literally, the link with the thought-world of Deut 7–8 is lost. The only near parallel to "a land of olive, oil, and honey" (2 Kgs 18:32) is in Deut 8:8, where we find the commoner שמן for יצהר. And when they enjoy the promised resources of the land (8:7–9), the people will "bless" Yahweh (8:10), just as he will "bless" the people and their crops and flocks if they obey him (7:12–14).

פֶּן־יַסִּית אֶתְכֶם חִזְקִיָּהוּ לֵאמֹר יְהוָה יַצִּילֵנוּ הַהִצִּילוּ אֱלֹהֵי הַגּוֹיִם אִישׁ אֶת־אַרְצוֹ מִיַּד מֶלֶךְ אַשּׁוּר	וְאַל־תִּשְׁמְעוּ אֶל־חִזְקִיָּהוּ כִּי־יַסִּית אֶתְכֶם לֵאמֹר יְהוָה יַצִּילֵנוּ הַצֵּל יַצִּילוּ אֱלֹהֵי הַגּוֹיִם אִישׁ אֶת־אַרְצוֹ מִיַּד מֶלֶךְ אַשּׁוּר
Do with me a blessing,[87] and come out to me, and eat each his vine and each his fig tree, and drink each the water of his well, until I come and take you to a land like your land, a land of grain and wine, a land of food and orchards,	Do with me a blessing, and come out to me, and eat each his vine and each his fig tree, and drink each the water of his well, until I come and take you to a land like your land, a land of grain and wine, a land of food and orchards, *a land of olive, oil, and honey—and live and you must not die—and do not listen to*
lest Hezekiah mislead you, saying, "It is Yahweh who will deliver you." Have the gods of the nations delivered each his land from the hand of the king of Assyria?[88]	Hezekiah, for he will mislead you, saying, "It is Yahweh who will deliver you." *Deliver!*—have the gods of the nations delivered each his land from the hand of the king of Assyria?

Although the total number of words by which these two texts differ is small, four distinct elements characterize the longer version of the Rabshakeh's offer; and not all of them need have been drafted together:

1. The list of familiar home comforts in Kings includes also אֶרֶץ זַיִת יִצְהָר וּדְבָשׁ ("a land of olive, oil, and honey").
2. The promise of these benefits is reinforced by a pair of commands, the first stated positively in the imperative וִחְיוּ ("live"), and the second negatively in the prohibition לֹא תָמֻתוּ ("you must not die"—לֹא with the imperfect).
3. The warning against Hezekiah is strengthened by repeating, "Do not listen to Hezekiah," from 2 Kgs 18:31a // Isa 36:16a (this time the prohibition is stated in the commoner jussive with אַל).
4. The use at the beginning of 2 Kgs 18:33 of the strengthening infinitive absolute הַצֵּל focuses even closer critical attention on Hezekiah's promise that Yahweh will deliver. By stating the question more fully, Kings asks the reader to ponder whether "deliver" is

---

91. Unless otherwise stated, all biblical translations are my own.

at all the right word to describe what other national gods have achieved.

If the longer form of the text (in 2 Kings) was original, at least two of these four elements, considered in and for themselves, could have been lost as a result of accident to help produce (what became) the shorter Isaiah version. Regarding the first element, after two phrases introduced by ארץ ("a land of …"), a copyist's eye could have skipped mistakenly over the third. In the fourth element, three forms of the same verb "deliver," set side by side (יצילנו ההצל הציל), could easily have led to another simplifying error. However, neither of these possible accidents helps explain the loss of the second element or the reduction in the force of the third. On the other hand, all four of these separate elements do tend in the same direction, even if they were not all drafted together. That each of them serves to reinforce the Assyrian invitation diminishes the likelihood of separate accidental loss of only two of them. It is very much more probable that the pluses in 2 Kgs 18:32–33 are secondary additions;[92] and this sends us to the longer version of David and Moab in 2 Sam 8:2.

1.4.2. David in Moab

Second Samuel 8 and 1 Chr 18 tell much the same story of how David secured his rule in Jerusalem by bringing all the neighboring peoples and their rulers into a subject role. These very closely related chapters contain several small differences within the different texts of Samuel and between any of these and Chronicles. But the most substantial difference between Samuel and the parallel text in Chronicles is in the second verse.

2 Sam 8:2	1 Chr 18:2
ויך את־מואב וימדדם בחבל השכב אותם ארצה	ויך את־מואב
וימדד שני־חבלים להמית ומלא החבל להחיות	
ותהי מואב לדוד לעבדים נשאי מנחה	ויהיו מואב עבדים לדוד נשאי מנחה

---

92. We shall find further examples in ch. 10 below.

And he struck Moab and measured them by line, making them lie down on the ground.	And he struck Moab.
And he measured two lines for putting to death and the full of the line for keeping alive.	
And Moab became servants for David bearing a gift.	And Moab became servants for David bearing a gift.

The Chronicler reports on David and Moab briefly, using only two clauses. Between these two, Samuel provides us with much greater detail. The text of Samuel above is the Masoretic Text—Greek texts of Samuel report that there were two lines for keeping alive as well as for putting to death. Josephus reports a third version of the life-death calculus: "the full of the *third* line," as noted by the editors of 4QSam^a; they follow his lead in their reconstruction of the appropriate Hebrew fragments. These fragments do not include the infinitive absolute השכב; however, in place of the next verbal form attested in the Masoretic Text and Septuagint, one fragment presents not the finite וימדד (MT), coordinate with the preceding ויך and וימדדם, but ומדד, which is presumably to be read as an infinitive absolute coordinate with השכב.[93] The clause structure of 2 Sam 8:2 (MT) can be expressed as follows:

And he struck Moab;
and he measured them by line,
    making them lie down on the ground;
and he measured two lines for putting to death and the full of the line for keeping alive;
and Moab became servants to David bearing tribute.

But the structure implied by ומדד in 4QSam^a is different:

And he struck Moab;
and he measured them by line,

---

93. The fragmentary 4QSam^a includes two other differences from MT:]היו in the synoptic portion attests ויהי as in Chronicles; and ומדד is immediately preceded not by MT ארצה but by רץ[. See Frank M. Cross et al., *Qumran Cave 4.XII: 1–2 Samuel*, DJD XVII (Oxford: Clarendon, 2005), 133.

> making them lie down on the ground,
> and measuring two lines for putting to death and the full of the [third] line for keeping alive;
> and Moab became servants to David bearing tribute.

Whatever the original structure of these clauses, several elements of the lengthy plus(es) in 2 Sam 8:2 are unique (and not just within Samuel–Kings).[94] Causative forms of the verbs מות ("die") and חיה ("live") are linked in just two other passages within Samuel–Kings. Hannah's song claims (1 Sam 2:6) that "Yahweh brings to death and makes alive" (יהוה ממית ומחיה). When asked by the king of Syria to assist the sick Naaman (2 Kgs 5:7), the unnamed king of Israel protests: "Am I God, to put to death and keep alive?" (האלהים אני להמית ולהחיות). Exultant Hannah and a worried king of Israel are very different witnesses, but they have a shared view of Yahweh. Both of them recognize life-giving and death-dealing to be divine prerogatives. Whether primary or secondary in the drafting of this text, it may be that the pairing of these words in 2 Sam 8:2 implies rather strong criticism of David overstepping even the royal mark. Certainly the treatment described there of defeated Moab is even more explicitly violent than the textually rather opaquely described treatment of Ammon in the synoptic 2 Sam 12:31 // 1 Chr 20:3. It is widely supposed that the Chronicler deleted the gruesome details in the case of Moab out of concern for David's reputation.[95] But it is equally possible that a later author of Samuel had added them, to bring David's ruthlessness into clearer relief. For any hope of arbitrating such a choice, the issues need to be set in a wider context.

1.4.3. Taking Stock

The plus in 2 Sam 8:2 vis-à-vis 1 Chr 18:2 and the pluses in 2 Kgs 18:32–33 vis-à-vis Isa 36:17–18 have two features in common. Both employ the

---

94. "Measure" (מדד) and "line/rope" (חבל) never again occur in the same context in the HB. מדד (*piel*) appears again only in Ps 60:8 = 108:8. The only other form of מדד used in the Former Prophets is ויתמדד in 1 Kgs 17:21, of Elijah "measuring/stretching himself" over the lad he was asked to heal.

95. Ralph Klein argues the case in *1 Chronicles*, Hermeneia (Minneapolis: Fortress, 2006), 391.

infinitive absolute, although not in the same way;[96] and both explicitly concern a choice between life and death. Read together as they stand, the more detailed 2 Sam 8:2 and 2 Kgs 18:32–33 point up a contrast between the claim by the Assyrian invader of future generosity to Hezekiah's people and the actual ferocity to a conquered people of his ancestor David. In no sense am I suggesting here that those who penned 2 Sam 8 and 2 Kgs 18 as they stand intended to make such a comparison (although we shall review a possibly related matter as soon as 2.1 below). But I am putting at least prima facie evidence on record that more frequent use both of the word חי/חיה ("live/life") and of the infinitive absolute were characteristic of later additions to Samuel and Kings.[97] It will be the business of the next two chapters to review both these usages more widely, to follow the words over Samuel–Kings as a whole.

---

96. In 2 Sam 8:2, the infinitive absolute is used independently and where a finite verb form would also have been possible; in 2 Kgs 18:33, an infinitive absolute is used alongside the cognate finite form of the verb and the doubling is emphatic. See further ch. 3 below.

97. When I presented some of this material orally at the SOTS Summer Meeting in 2013, Hugh Williamson observed critically that the infinitive absolute is not found in post-Biblical Hebrew. Perhaps so. Yet these pluses suggest that its use was still current among some scribes of the late biblical period.

2
LIFE

2.1. THE SYNOPTIC TEXTS

The whole cluster "life/live/living" (חי/חיה/חיים) is widely used in the Hezekiah narrative found in both Isa 36–39 and 2 Kgs 18–20. Four core instances are shared in 2 Kgs 19:4, 16; 20:1, 7 // Isa 37:4, 17; 38:1, 21. A fifth (2 Kgs 18:32, a plus) was discussed above (1.4.1); and there are seven further pluses in the poem unique to Isa 38:9–20.[1] However, this language of "life" is wholly absent from the regular synoptic parallel with 2 Kgs 18–20 in 2 Chr 29–32. From the familiar perspective, of Chronicles as a rewritten form of Samuel–Kings, this seems strange. And yet, when viewed from another direction, the phenomenon is much less surprising: indeed, members of this "life" word family make only eight appearances in all of Chronicles. Seven of these are straightforward from a synoptic point of view. Six of them are simply identical to Kings.[2] As for a seventh, the use of חיים ("[captured] alive") within nonsynoptic 2 Chr 25:12 belongs to the same broad context as the nearby synoptic pair 25:18, 25 (= 2 Kgs 14:9, 17), whether coincidentally or under their influence.

The eighth (in fact the first) and only remaining instance of this word cluster in the whole book of Chronicles forms part of a positive statement about David's general Joab at the end of 1 Chr 11:8, that he was "letting live" or "restoring to life" the remnant of Jerusalem (ויואב יחיה את־שאר העיר). This is of course only one of several differences between the reports of David's taking of Jerusalem in 2 Sam 5:6–9 and 1 Chr 11:4–8; but the others need not concern us here. I noted (1.1.2) that Wellhausen considered this note in

---

1. Isa 38:9, 11, 12, 16 (3x), 20.
2. 1 Kgs 8:40 // 2 Chr 6:31; 1 Kgs 12:6 // 2 Chr 10:6; 1 Kgs 22:14 // 2 Chr 18:13; 2 Kgs 11:12 // 2 Chr 23:11; 2 Kgs 14:9, 17 // 2 Chr 25:18, 25.

1 Chr 11:8 secondary and also understood "revived" figuratively ("restored/rebuilt"). In the opposite direction, I proposed that the author of Samuel had removed Joab from the report of taking Jerusalem to augment David's role, just as he delayed the list of David's many heroes from early in the David story (1 Chr 11) till late (2 Sam 23).³ If 1 Chr 11:8 does tell the older version of the story and is not a modification of 2 Sam 5:9, then 2 Chr 25:12 will supply the *only* instance of the Chronicler actually *adding* "live/living/life" to his source text. In any case, there is no talk of life or living in any text shared by Samuel–Kings and Chronicles after the synoptic 2 Kgs 14 // 2 Chr 25.

Of the synoptic passages listed above, at least three relate specifically to the life of a king:

- "while [Solomon] was still *alive*" (1 Kgs 12:6 // 2 Chr 10:6)
- "[long] *life* to the king!" (2 Kgs 11:12 // 2 Chr 23:11)
- "King Amaziah *lived* for fifteen years after the death …" (2 Kgs 14:17 // 2 Chr 25:25)

First Kings 8:40 may supply a fourth instance. Yahweh's "servant[s]" are mentioned in most of the individual petitions in Solomon's long prayer at the dedication of the temple;⁴ and it is likely that these "servants" were originally understood as royal עבדים (the kings as servants to Yahweh). These royal servants are not explicitly mentioned in the seventh petition, but may be assumed to be included among those who fear Yahweh "all the days that they *live* on the face of the land you have given to our fathers."⁵ The fifth is uttered by Micaiah ben Imlah, as he protests his integrity to the kings' messenger (1 Kgs 22:14). Micaiah is the only synoptic character to reinforce his words with "as Yahweh lives" (חי יהוה), just as Ahab is the only king who puts a prophet on oath (משבעך, 1 Kgs 22:16). חי יהוה never

---

3. *I and II Samuel*, 396–97.
4. 1 Kgs 8:23, 24, 25, 26, 28, 30, 36 // 2 Chr 6:14, 15, 16, 17, 19, 21, 27.
5. The grant to Israel of "life" on the land (as in Deut 12:1; 32:47) was analogous to life on the land for a reigning king. Two synoptic royal contexts (1 Kgs 9:7 and 2 Kgs 21:8) record warnings to (David and) Solomon not to expect continued existence on that land (אדמה) in the case of misbehavior; and that the first of these warnings is given almost immediately after 1 Kgs 8:40 may support the royal "servant" interpretation. We shall note in a later chapter (4.2) that synoptic texts apply the title "servant" (sg.) only to Yahweh's royal servants David and Solomon.

reappears in Chronicles; but it is common in both Samuel (17x)[6] and Kings (13x).[7] And this major discrepancy in usage between Samuel–Kings and Chronicles is entirely typical of the whole "life" cluster. The sixth shared instance at first seems hardly relevant, and is mentioned at this point for the sake of completeness: the parable in 2 Kgs 14:9 includes a wild animal (חית השדה, lit. "field *life*") from Lebanon.

It is when he is under pressure that Micaiah invokes the *living* Yahweh; and two others out of this small set of synoptic passages may also use the verb חיה in a sense that is not simply formulaic. When the supporters of the boy-king Joash wish their new king (long) *life* (יחי המלך), they are doing so in an unusual and particularly poignant context. The usurper Athaliah had just been overthrown. When taking power, she had had all the siblings of Joash put to death—Joash himself had been hidden from her for his first six years. Wishing life for him was more than a coronation formula. Then, when the narrator observes that Amaziah *lived* for a further fifteen years after the death of Jehoash of Israel, he may be underlining the oddity of this situation: the king who had lost in the war between Israel and Judah was long outliving the victor. Amaziah was a survivor, and his courtiers hoped that Joash would survive—we are told he went on to reign for forty years.

Amaziah survived because Jehoash of Israel allowed him to live on after defeating him. The Chronicler may well have had this rare synoptic report in mind when he expanded the earlier short report of Amaziah's victory in Edom (see further 12.3.14), and reported that Amaziah had had ten thousand men captured "alive" (חיים) tossed from the summit of Sela (2 Chr 25:12): Amaziah had not merited the lenient treatment he would receive from Jehoash. This mismatch of behavior and fate contributed by the Chronicler encourages us to detect another in the same portion of the earlier synoptic text. In the warning parable told by Jehoash to Amaziah, Jehoash may have reckoned himself as the wild animal or "field *life*" (חית השדה) who would trample Amaziah, the presumptuous thornbush. But paradoxically, as matters worked out, though he did trample Amaziah, it was Amaziah who "lived" on while he himself soon died.

---

6. 1 Sam 14:39, 45; 19:6; 20:3, 21; 25:26, 34; 26:10, 16; 28:10; 29:6; 2 Sam 2:27 (חי האלהים MT); 4:9; 12:5; 14:11; 15:21; 22:47.

7. 1 Kgs 1:29; 2:24; 17:1, 12; 18:10, 15; 2 Kgs 2:2, 4, 6; 3:14; 4:30; 5:16, 20.

2.2. Overview of "Live," "Life," and "Alive" in Samuel–Kings

Beyond the small synoptic core of six or seven instances and the thirty instances of חי יהוה ("as Yahweh lives") in the rest of Samuel–Kings just noted, nonsynoptic portions of these books contain no less than eighty further instances of the word cluster: (1) the adjective חי (pl. חיים) occurs thirty-one times;[8] forms of the verb חיה occur thirty-six times;[9] there are two nonsynoptic mentions of animal life (חית);[10] the phrase "the days of his life" (ימי חייו) is used in eight passages;[11] and there are three further miscellaneous uses of the noun חיים.[12] After the two synoptic instances in 2 Kgs 14:9, 17, the *only* occurrences of this cluster later in Kings are in the Hezekiah story (18:32; 19:4, 16; 20:1, 7) and at the very end of the book (25:29, 30).[13]

2.3. Swearing by Living Yahweh

The following persons within Samuel–Kings anticipate Micaiah in swearing by Yahweh's life, or by the living Yahweh: Saul and then his people, over whether Jonathan deserves death (1 Sam 14:39, 45); Saul agreeing with Jonathan that David should not die (19:6); David on the imminence of his own death (20:3); Jonathan's arrows signifying David's safety (20:21); Abigail and then David, on the latter being saved from shedding Saul's blood

---

8. 1 Sam 1:26; 2:15; 15:8; 17:26, 36, 55; 20:14; 25:26, 29; 2 Sam 11:11; 12:18, 21, 22; 14:19; 18:14; 19:7; 1 Kgs 3:25, 26 (2x), 27; 17:23; 20:18 (2x), 32; 21:15; 2 Kgs 4:16, 17; 7:12; 10:14; 19:4, 16.

9. 1 Sam 2:6; 10:24; 20:31; 27:9, 11; 2 Sam 1:10; 8:2; 12:3, 22; 16:16; 1 Kgs 1:25, 31, 34, 39; 17:22; 18:5; 20:31, 32; 2 Kgs 1:2; 4:7; 5:7; 7:4 (2x); 8:1, 5 (3x), 8, 9, 10, 14 (Ben-Hadad "living" from an illness); 10:19; 13:21; 18:32; 20:1, 7. (Illness and life are together in 1 Kgs 17; 2 Kgs 1; 13; Isa 38.)

10. 1 Sam 17:46; 2 Sam 21:10.

11. 1 Sam 1:11; 7:15; 1 Kgs 5:1; 11:34; 15:5, 6; 2 Kgs 25:29, 30 (4QSam[a] may have used the phrase in 1 Sam 1:22 but not in 1:11). When 80-year-old Barzillai protests that he should not accompany David to Jerusalem (2 Sam 19:35), he uses the longer phrase, "How many are the days *of the years* of my life?"

12. 2 Sam 1:23 (life and death); 15:21 (life and death); 18:18 (in his life[time]).

13. We should note in passing that these few instances within the final eleven chapters of Kings are all in texts shared with a book in the Latter Prophets: Isa 37:4, 17; 38:1, 21; Jer 52:33, 34. As already noted, "and live" (2 Kgs 18:32) is part of a complex plus not represented in Isa 36:16–17.

(25:26, 34); David to Abishai on Saul's death (26:10); David teasing Abner and his men for being "sons of death" (26:16); Saul assuring the woman at Endor that she runs no risk of capital punishment (28:10); Achish to David after his colleagues have warned him about danger from David (29:6); Joab complimenting Abner on his diplomatic warning of the sword devouring forever (2 Sam 2:27); David condemning Ish-boshet's assassins (4:9); David condemning the transgressor in the case brought to him by Nathan (12:5); David giving assurance to the woman of Tekoa about any potential blood avenger (14:11); Ittai swearing allegiance to David in life or death (15:21); David praising Yahweh for giving him victory over his enemies (22:47); David swearing to Bathsheba, just after those invited to Adonijah's coronation have shouted, יחי המלך אדניהו ("Long live King Adonijah," 1 Kgs 1:29); Solomon pronouncing sentence of death on Adonijah (2:24); Elijah threatening Ahab with no rain (17:1); the woman of Zarephath telling Elijah she is about to cook her last meal before dying with her son (17:12); Obadiah to Elijah, claiming veracity like Micaiah but in fear of his life (18:10);[14] and Elijah reassuring Obadiah that he will give Ahab no excuse to cause his death (18:15).

Only a few instances of the oath actually follow synoptic 1 Kgs 22 // 2 Chr 18: Elisha to Elijah three times in solemn promise, like Micaiah (2 Kgs 2:2, 4, 6); Elisha to the king of Israel, repeating Micaiah's role (3:14); the mother of a dead child to Elisha (4:30); Elisha to Naaman refusing the offer of a gift (5:16); Gehazi assuring himself that a gift should be accepted (5:20). Only these instances that *follow* Micaiah, only Elisha (and Gehazi), actually replicate Micaiah's situation of protesting his veracity under challenge. In all the earlier instances without exception, the explicit context is of life and death. Whether we render חי יהוה by "as Yahweh lives" or "by Yahweh's life," the wording of this oath corresponds to the life/death situation of the moment. The Elisha texts all occur close to 1 Kgs 22, and Elisha's role in 2 Kgs 3 seems actually to have been modeled on Micaiah's (see further 8.2).

This wording of an oath is attested outside the Bible, in ostraca from Lachish and Arad.[15] Within the Hebrew Bible, it is much more common in Samuel–Kings than elsewhere. It is never found in Genesis–Joshua, and only once in Judges (see 2.8). In the Latter Prophets, its use is restricted to

---

14. Obadiah repeats the very words uttered by the woman from Zarephath: חי יהוה אלהיך אם־יש.
15. *DCH* 3:203.

Jer 4:2; 5:2; 12:16; 16:14, 15; 23:7, 8; and Hos 4:15 (see further 9.11). As for the Writings, it is used only in Ps 18:47 // 2 Sam 22:47 and by Boaz in Ruth 3:13—yet note the similar חי אל in Job 27:2. In addition, and uniquely in Amos 8:14, חי is apparently used with two other divine names, חי אלהיך דן ("as your god Dan lives") and חי דרך באר־שבע ("as the way of Beer-sheba lives"). חי־אני ("as I live") attributed to Yahweh himself is a feature of Ezekiel (17x)[16] and occurs occasionally elsewhere.[17] In short, the single synoptic use of חי יהוה by Micaiah is much more typical of the density of usage in the Hebrew Bible as a whole than the thirty instances in the rest of Samuel–Kings. That no one else in Chronicles swears this way is typical rather than atypical of biblical usage.[18]

The issue of Yahweh as "alive" reappears in two related nonsynoptic passages where the people are under threat from an external foe, and this foe is mocking or scorning Yahweh (חרף יהוה). The first is the David and Goliath story, which uses the adjective in the plural: "living God" (אלהים חיים, 1 Sam 17:26, 36). The other is the Hezekiah and Isaiah story (2 Kgs 19:4, 16), where the adjective is singular (אלהים חי).[19]

2.4. The King's Life

The synoptic acclamation of the boy-king Joash (יחי המלך) is preceded several times in nonsynoptic Samuel–Kings. The new (would-be) kings in question are Saul (1 Sam 10:24), Absalom (2 Sam 16:16), Adonijah (1 Kgs 1:25), and Solomon (1 Kgs 1:34, 39). Saul and Absalom share Joash's short acclamation: "May the king live!" Adonijah and Solomon are named. The one remaining instance of the acclamation is doubly exceptional: it concerns a king at the end of his reign and not the beginning, and it is uttered by an individual and not a group. Those invited to Adonijah's investiture have just said, יחי המלך אדניהו, "May King Adonijah live!" (1:25). David

---

16. Ezek 5:11, 14, 16, 18, 20; 16:48; 17:16, 19; 18:3; 20:3, 31, 33; 33:11, 27; 34:8; 35:6, 11.

17. Num 14:21, 28; Isa 49:18; Jer 22:24; 46:18; Zeph 2:9; and cf. חי אנכי לעלם ("as I live forever") in Deut 32:40.

18. Not only does חי יהוה not reappear in Chronicles, but talk of "oath taking" (שבע) is restricted to 2 Chr 15:15–16; 36:13.

19. אלהים חי(ים) or חי אל is found six times elsewhere in the HB: Deut 5:23; Josh 3:10; Jer 23:36; Hos 2:1; Pss 42:3; 84:3. The corresponding Aramaic formula (אלהא חיא) is used in Dan 6:21, 27.

has just assured Bathsheba, on oath "by living Yahweh" (1 Kgs 1:29), that Solomon will replace him on the throne of Israel. She in turn responds by prostrating herself before him and saying (1 Kgs 1:31), "May my lord king David live forever!" (יחי אדני המלך דוד לעלם). The wording of her acclamation is also doubly novel. She adds the name David to "my lord king";[20] and the final "forever" has parallels within the Hebrew Bible only in the court language of the Aramaic narratives of Daniel.[21] "Forever" certainly trumps the fifteen years by which defeated Amaziah outlived victorious Jehoash (2 Kgs 14:17 // 2 Chr 25:25). The only other king of Israel or Judah said to have "lived" is Hezekiah, meaning that he "recovered [life]" after his illness (2 Kgs 20:7) with the benefit of Isaiah's ministrations (see more fully ch. 10 below). King Ahaziah of Israel, by contrast, made the mistake of approaching the wrong god after he was injured (2 Kgs 1:2); accordingly, as warned by Elijah, he did not survive (1:17).

"All the days of his life" (כל־ימי חייו) is a phrase used in nonsynoptic statements made and repeated about three of Jerusalem's kings: Solomon (1 Kgs 5:1; 11:34), Abijam (1 Kgs 15:5, 6), and Jehoiachin (2 Kgs 25:29, 30). Elsewhere in Samuel–Kings, it is used only of Samuel (1 Sam 1:11; 7:15), who as lifelong judge was something of a proto-king.[22] As already noted, the protest by the king of Israel that he is not a god able to cause death or life (2 Kgs 5:7) comes in the context of the extended tale of Naaman, commander of the king of Aram. Then 2 Kgs 8 concerns the (im)possibility of recovery for Ben-Hadad of Aram (vv. 8, 9, 10, 14).

---

20. In this respect, she will be followed almost immediately (1:37) by Benaiah. אדני המלך has a near-unique relationship with David: he addresses Saul at their final meetings as "my lord king" (1 Sam 24:9; 26:17, 19); and after this it is overwhelmingly he that is so addressed (2 Sam 3:21; 9:11; 13:33; 14:9, 12, 15, 17, 18, 19, 22; 15:15, 21; 16:4, 9; 18:31, 32; 19:20, 21, 27, 28, 31, 36, 38; 24:3, 21; 1 Kgs 1:13, 18, 20, 21, 27, 31, 36, 37). The few exceptions are 1 Kgs 2:38; 20:4; 2 Kgs 6:12, 26; 8:5; Jer 37:20; 38:9; Dan 1:10. The only synoptic instances are 2 Sam 24:3, 21 // 1 Chr 21:3, 23.

21. Dan 2:4; 3:9; 5:10; 6:7, 22.

22. "All the days of his/your/my life" is used in the law of the king (Deut 17:19), and in Josh 1:5 and 4:14 of another national leader or proto-king. Elsewhere we find it in the divine curses on the serpent and the man (Gen 3:14, 17), in the praise of the fine woman's care for her husband (Prov 31:12), of Israel or the Israelite (Deut 4:9; 6:2; 16:3), and of the psalmist (Pss 23:6; 27:4; 128:5). However, חיים ("life") is used most densely in Qoheleth (2:3; 3:12; 5:17, 19; 6:12; 8:15; 9:9). Corresponding to this density, seventeen other instances of the cluster are found in Qoh 2:17; 4:2, 15; 6:3, 6, 8, 12; 7:2, 12; 9:3, 4 (2x), 5, 9 (2x); 10:19; 11:8.

Oaths are taken not only on the life of a god but also on the life of the king, or at least a king-substitute, the current power-in-the-land: חי נפשך. This formula of swearing is peculiar in the Hebrew Bible to Samuel–Kings, and is never addressed to an actual king after David.[23] חי נפשך is used on its own by Hannah to Eli (1 Sam 1:26) and by Abner to Saul (1 Sam 17:55); and together with חי יהוה by David to Jonathan on being a step away from death (1 Sam 20:3), Abigail to David on him being saved from bloodguilt (1 Sam 25:26), Ittai to David (2 Sam 15:21[24]), Elisha to Elijah three times (2 Kgs 2:2, 4, 6), and the mother of a dead child to Elisha (2 Kgs 4:30).

2.5. God and King Together as Alive

The interplay of the "life" of Adonijah, Yahweh, David, and Solomon in 1 Kgs 1 has just been noted (2.4). A similar theme is elaborated more extensively in 2 Kgs 18–20 // Isa 36–39, where we find two pairs of identical instances. One pair (in 2 Kgs 19:4, 16 // Isa 37:4, 17) concerns the Assyrians scorning the "living God"; and the other (in 2 Kgs 20:1, 7 // Isa 38:1, 21) concerns whether King Hezekiah will die or live. But in each book there are instances additional to this already significant usage. We have observed (1.4.1) that "and live" (וחיו) is part of a small Kings plus (or set of pluses) in 2 Kgs 18:32–33 as compared with Isa 36:17 (in each parallel, LXX attests the same text as we find in MT). And in the opposite direction, the verb *live* and the noun *life* are both very prominent (together 9x) in the large Isaiah plus (38:9–20) found between the synoptic instances in Isa 38:1 and 21 noted above. Yet none of this concentrated interest in "life"—or in the Deity adding to the "days" of the king (2 Kgs 20:6 // Isa 38:5)[25]—is reflected at all in 2 Chr 32. These data will be set in a wider context below (ch. 10).

---

23. In the only instance in the HB outside Samuel–Kings, Joseph swears twice (Gen 42:15, 16) to his brothers by the life of Pharaoh (חי פרעה). The "live/life/alive" cluster is found in Genesis mostly in the primeval narratives (Gen 1–11) and in the Joseph story (Gen 39–50).

24. Here not וחי נפשך but the unique וחי אדני המלך.

25. That expression can be found (only?) in Ps 61:7 and Prov 10:27. The Chronicler uses "days" in his Hezekiah narrative only in (the synoptic) 2 Chr 32:24 and 26.

2.6. Nonroyal Human Life

Two other characters in nonsynoptic Kings "recover [life]," and so help to put the Hezekiah tradition in context. As with that king, a prophetic figure is also involved. One is the son of the widow from Zarephath for whom Elijah prayed (1 Kgs 17:22); and the other, the dead man thrown into Elisha's grave who "revived" on contact with the prophet's bones (2 Kgs 13:21).[26]

2.7. Animal Life

For the sake of completeness, we can simply note that "field life," as in synoptic 2 Kgs 14:9 // 2 Chr 25:18, makes just two further appearances. David threatens to give over Philistine corpses to the birds and wild animals (1 Sam 17:46)—Goliath's prior threat (17:44) has used not the standard חית השדה but בהמת השדה.[27] And Rizpah preserved the bodies of her exposed relatives from birds by day and wild animals by night (2 Sam 21:10).

2.8. Life/Live in Joshua–Judges and Deuteronomy

The "life" cluster is very much less common in the other books of the Former Prophets: only twelve times in Joshua[28] and five times in Judges.[29] Half of the instances in Joshua concern the special status of foreigners allowed to live on (survive) within the community of Israel.[30] Then two of the instances in Judges clearly anticipate the royal ambience of Samuel and Kings. According to Judg 8:22–32, his grateful people offer the victorious Gideon sole rule ("monarchy") that will pass to his son. Immediately beforehand, we have seen an already very kinglike Gideon dealing with the kings of Midian. The latter have talked of their victims (8:18) as "like the form of the king's sons" (כתאר בני המלך). Gideon's reply (8:19) opens with the sole use in Judges of the oath "by Yahweh's life" (חי יהוה), and

---

26. Beyond Samuel–Kings, we can compare Samson (Judg 15:19) and Job (42:16).
27. Elsewhere in the HB (Deut 28:26; Isa 18:6 [2x]; Jer 7:33; 15:3; 16:4; 19:7; 34:20), בהמה ("beast") is construed with ארץ ("earth"), not שדה ("field").
28. Josh 1:5; 2:13; 3:10; 4:14; 5:8; 6:17, 25; 8:23; 9:15, 20, 21; 14:10.
29. Judg 8:19 (2x); 15:19; 16:30; 21:14.
30. Josh 2:13; 6:17, 25; 9:15, 20, 21.

continues: "Had you kept them alive, I had not slain you" (לו החיתם אותם לא הרגתי אתכם). Just like Boaz in the book of Ruth (see 2.3), which is set in the same judges period, Gideon is speaking just as we would expect a king to speak in the book of Samuel. On the other hand, adjective,[31] verb,[32] and noun[33] are more prominent in Deuteronomy but are concentrated in a few portions: sixteen times in Deut 4:1–8:3 (but not elsewhere in 1–11); only once in 12–15; six times in 16–20; never in 21–27; and thirteen times in 28–33.

---

31. חי and חיים (adj.) are used in Deut 4:4, 10; 5:3, 26; 12:1; 31:13, 27; 32:40.

32. Deut 4:1, 33, 43; 5:24, 26, 33; 6:24; 8:1, 3 (2x); 16:20; 19:4, 5; 20:16; 30:16, 19; 32:39; 33:6.

33. חיים is used in Deut 4:9; 6:2; 16:3; 17:19; 28:66 (2x); 30:6, 19, 20; 32:47.

3
More Words

3.1. Counting Time

As documented in the last chapter, nonsynoptic portions of Samuel and Kings use "live," "life," and "living" very much more often than either synoptic portions or Chronicles as a whole. Synoptic usage of these words is much more typical of Chronicles than of Samuel–Kings. When we move to words and phrases that mark time, the situation is very similar.

3.1.1. Remarkable Stability

Samuel–Kings on the one side and Chronicles on the other exhibit minimal variation over the terms in which chronology is expressed in synoptic portions. I have demonstrated elsewhere that the shared tradition has been preserved with quite remarkable fixity.[1] The less surprising aspect is that Kings and Chronicles supply the same information about the ages of all the kings of Jerusalem at their accession and the length of their reigns in the headers to the individual reports—and in exactly the same terms. Much more surprising is the stability of temporal markers within each report, given the amount of rewriting that we can observe there. Stability and flexibility can both be inspected in the presentation of much of the synoptic material at the end of this volume (ch. 12).

My survey of some seventy synoptic instances demonstrates almost complete unanimity. The expressions range from "on the morrow," "at that time," "now," "then," "afterward," and many such, to several phrases based on "day," such as "on that day," "all the days," "from the day that…," "until

---

1. "Writing Time and Eternity"; and "Shaping of Israelite History."

this day." There were only two differences: "in the fourteenth year of King Hezekiah" (2 Kgs 18:13) instead of the simple "after this" (2 Chr 32:9), and "at that time" (2 Kgs 24:10) instead of "at the turn of the year" (2 Chr 36:10).

Those who wrote or rewrote Kings and Chronicles may have exercised considerable freedom in some matters. But they appear to have left intact the chronological structure they inherited. I shall have much more to say below about one of the two unusual exceptions, Hezekiah's fourteenth year (10.5.1). Ray Person has sought to explain the differences between Samuel–Kings and Chronicles as resulting from different oral performances of shared material.[2] However, almost complete constancy in both Kings and Chronicles over their separate reporting of the synoptic chronological record may instead suggest scribal fidelity.

3.1.2. Surprising Variation

This constancy permits confidence in our reconstruction of the shared chronology. However, there are large differences of usage between synoptic and nonsynoptic portions of Samuel–Kings and Chronicles. Most remarkable are those relating to phrases including יום ("day"). "Day" is used twenty-four times in synoptic passages and twenty-six times in nonsynoptic Chronicles—so there is a similar density of usage throughout Chronicles. However, nonsynoptic Samuel–Kings use "day" more than 210 times—some four times as densely as synoptic portions.[3] Two expressions are particularly notable. The first is the complete absence from Chronicles of היום הזה ("this day"), which we find nineteen times in Samuel–Kings, but never in a synoptic context. Then היום ("today") occurs only twice in Chronicles (1 Chr 29:5; 2 Chr 35:21), but sixty-two times throughout Samuel–Kings. Three of these instances are in synoptic contexts and so require brief discussion.

1. Pleased with the terms of Solomon's message, Hiram of Tyre responds in 1 Kgs 5:21: ברוך יהוה היום אשר נתן לדוד בן חכם ("Blessed be Yahweh *today*, who has given David a wise son"). Synoptic 2 Chr 2:11, though much fuller, lacks "today": ברוך יהוה אלהי ישראל אשר

---

2. *Deuteronomic History*, 94–129.
3. I set out the details in "Shaping of Israelite History," 206–9.

עשה את־השמים ואת־הארץ אשר נתן לדוד המלך בן חכם יודע שכל ובינה ("Blessed be Yahweh, *God of Israel, who has made the heaven and the earth,* who has given *King* David a wise son, *knowing discretion and understanding*"). Since Chronicles does use "today" twice in nonsynoptic contexts, it seems unlikely that the term was deliberately omitted from a sentence that was also being much expanded.

2. In 1 Kgs 8:28, Solomon asks Yahweh to hear "the cry … that your servant is praying before you *today*." The synoptic parallel (2 Chr 6:19) closes without היום in the Masoretic Text, though "today" is attested in the Septuagint. The following word in both books, להיות shares three letters in the same order; and this could have led to a scribe overlooking היום. But equally, להיות could have triggered the insertion into 1 Kgs 8:28 of this commonest of temporal expressions in Samuel–Kings. The issue deserves mention in more than a footnote because it illustrates a rule observed in this study, of arguing routinely on the basis of data shared in Samuel–Kings (MT) and Chronicles (MT).

3. Rehoboam's more senior courtiers respond to him differently in Kings and Chronicles: אם־היום תהיה־עבד לעם הזה ועבדתם ועניתם ("If *today* you will be *servant* to this people, *and serve them and answer them*," 1 Kgs 12:7); אם־תהיה לטוב לעם הזה ורציתם ("If you will be *for good* to this people, *and please them*," 2 Chr 10:7). As in the second instance, the first two letters of היום early in 1 Kgs 12:7 anticipate the middle two letters of the following תהיה, which could have led to accidental miscopying. But here, as in the first example, it is not a case of one simple addition to or deletion from a shared text, but of repeated alterations to an older text, and Kings' "today" plus is simply one of these.

It cannot cause surprise that any given quarter of Samuel–Kings should exhibit a smaller lexical range than the remaining three-quarters. But that the quarter of Samuel–Kings that marks time much less than the average is the same as the quarter of Samuel–Kings in which no character may originally have said "this day" or "today" and that these chapters are also the quarter of Samuel–Kings that is shared with Chronicles—all that is very surprising within the consensus view that the Chronicler worked from something like our familiar text of Samuel–Kings. Is it really likely that a Chronicler working from Samuel–Kings would end up making such a series of untypical excerpts, whether aware or unaware of what he was doing? The many expressions preserved in synoptic portions, though not repeated in nonsynoptic material, provide strong even if negative testimony to the Chronicler's fidelity to inherited material. By comparison, only one expression of time used in Chronicles (item 25 in the published list) is not repeated in Samuel–Kings.[4]

3.2. Widening the Front

We have seen that synoptic portions of Samuel–Kings are very much less concerned with "life" than nonsynoptic portions. The differences over temporal expressions, and especially "today" and "this day," are quite as striking. And other markers of the distinctiveness of the synoptic material within Samuel–Kings deserve brief mention here.

3.2.1. יֵשׁ ("There Is/Are")

Quite simply, the little word יֵשׁ is completely absent from the texts shared by Samuel–Kings and Chronicles, but it is used in nonsynoptic portions of all three books.[5] In Kings, it is used only in the central third of the book, the chapters that focus on the work of Elijah and Elisha.[6] Three of the four instances in Chronicles are in speeches by a prophet or a "man of God,"[7] and in the fourth David is speaking.[8] The usage in Samuel is distinctive in another way.[9] In my commentary on Samuel, I argued on quite other grounds that the earliest chapters in the book were the synoptic material, and that 1 Sam 1–8, 25–30, and 2 Sam 1–4 were among the latest additions.[10] If this argument proves reliable, יֵשׁ will have been absent from the earliest and latest strata of that book: it will only have been included in the linguistic repertoire of the author(s) of the first substantial rewriting of the story of Saul and David, but not of the second.

Elsewhere in the Hebrew Bible, this little word is used most often in "wisdom" books: in Proverbs (13x), in Job (12x), and still more densely in the shorter book of Qoheleth (16x). If we set the density of usage in

---

4. See my "Shaping of Israelite History," 208, for item 25; items 1, 10, 13, 17a, 17b, 18a, 20b-e, 21a, and 26–27 are among the 53 items separately listed (204–11).

5. It is found in 1 Sam 9:11, 12; 14:39; 17:48; 20:8; 21:4, 5, 9; 23:23; 2 Sam 9:1; 14:19, 32; 19:29; 1 Kgs 17:12; 18:10; 2 Kgs 2:16; 3:12; 4:2, 13; 5:8; 9:15; 10:15 (3x), 23; 1 Chr 29:3; 2 Chr 15:7; 16:9; 25:8.

6. 1 Kgs 17:12; 18:10; 2 Kgs 2:16; 3:12; 4:2, 13; 5:8; 9:15; 10:15 (3x), 23.

7. 2 Chr 15:7; 16:9; 25:8.

8. 1 Chr 29:3.

9. 1 Sam 9:11, 12; 14:39; 17:46; 20:8; 21:4, 5, 9; 23:23; 2 Sam 9:1; 14:19, 32; 19:29.

10. *1 and 2 Samuel*, e.g., 9–14.

Samuel (13x) and Kings (12x) alongside the Torah and the rest of the Former Prophets, only Judges is comparable (6x),[11] while the usage in Genesis is still higher, with the greatest density (12 of 21x) in the Joseph story.[12] It is absent from Leviticus and Joshua, used in Exodus only in 17:7, and found a few times in Numbers (4x)[13] and Deuteronomy (3x).[14] In the Latter Prophets, it is used in Isa 43:8, 44:8, and Jeremiah (9x),[15] but never in Ezekiel; and, within the Twelve, only in Mic 2:1; 6:10; Jonah 4:11; and Mal 1:14. There are a few remaining instances.[16]

3.2.2. נאם יהוה ("Utterance of Yahweh")

No synoptic text uses יש, and Huldah (2 Kgs 22:19 // 2 Chr 34:27) is the only synoptic character to reinforce a report of divine speech with נאם יהוה—this phrase is never used again in Chronicles.[17] We noted above (2.1) that Micaiah is similarly the only synoptic character to reinforce his prophetic words with "as Yahweh lives" (חי יהוה)—and this phrase too is never repeated in Chronicles. But there the comparison ends: while נאם יהוה is one of the most frequently used formulae throughout the books of the Latter Prophets (it is absent only from Habakkuk and Jonah), חי יהוה is much more prominent in Samuel and Kings; and, as we have seen (2.3), its use in these books is part of a wider phenomenon. (On synoptic Huldah, see further 5.3.1.4.)

3.2.3. ניר ("Fief/Land")

ניר occurs only once in Chronicles (2 Chr 21:7 // 2 Kgs 8:19) but is twice anticipated in nonsynoptic 1 Kgs 11:36; 15:4. Some think it should be rendered "lamp" (as if this נִיר were a simple alternative to the commoner נֵר); and others have argued that the metaphor is developed from land that

---

11. Judg 4:20; 6:13, 36; 18:14; 19:19 (2x).
12. Gen 18:24; 23:8; 24:23, 42, 49; 28:16; 31:29; 33:9, 11; 39:4, 5 (2x), 8; 42:1, 2; 43:4, 7; 44:19, 20, 26; 47:6.
13. Num 9:20, 21; 13:20; 22:29.
14. Deut 13:4; 29:14, 17.
15. Jer 5:1; 14:22; 23:26; 27:18; 31:6, 16, 17; 37:17 (2x).
16. Pss 7:4; 14:2 // 53:3; 58:12; 73:11; 135:17; Ruth 1:12; 3:12; Lam 1:12; 3:29; Ezra 10:2, 44; Neh 5:2, 3, 4, 5; Esth 3:8.
17. Samuel-Kings use נאם יהוה on five further occasions (see further below).

should be worked or managed (as illustrated in identical instructions in Jer 4:3 and Hos 10:12—נירו לכם ניר, "till for yourselves tillage"). Either way, it clearly denotes Yahweh's special grant of Jerusalem and Judah to the house of David.[18]

3.2.4. אך ("However")

אך appears synoptically only once (1 Kgs 22:44 // 2 Chr 20:33). The previous verse has assessed the reign of King Jehoshaphat favorably. But אך introduces the limiting remark that the במות ("high places") had not been removed. Previously, in the shared 1 Kgs 15:14 // 2 Chr 15:17, a similar note had been introduced by the simple connective ו ("and"). Then in 2 Kgs 12:4; 14:4; 15:4, 35 (but *not* the synoptic parallels in Chronicles), we find the same critical qualification introduced with רק ("only") rather than אך ("however").[19] Nonsynoptic Chronicles uses אך only twice more (1 Chr 22:12; 2 Chr 30:11), but Samuel fourteen times[20] and Kings fourteen times.[21] Five of these twenty-eight pluses in Samuel–Kings are found within synoptic contexts.

1. The first of them, at the end of 2 Sam 23:10, is probably original—the much shorter parallel in 1 Chr 11:14 may result from haplography.

2. אך opens a note in 2 Kgs 12:14–16, within a report of temple reconstruction, which ends with a statement about accounts not being required of the skilled workers.[22]

3. A plus introduces the similar but shorter note in 2 Kgs 22:7 about honest artisans of whom no financial accounts were required.[23]

---

18. It will be significant that these two nonsynoptic occurrences are in immediate proximity to "all the days of his life," discussed at 2.2 and 2.4.

19. See further 6.2.

20. 1 Sam 1:23; 8:9; 12:20, 24; 16:6; 18:8, 17; 20:39; 21:5; 25:21; 29:9; 2 Sam 2:10; 3:13; 23:10.

21. 1 Kgs 9:24; 11:12, 39; 17:13; 22:32; 2 Kgs 5:7; 12:14; 13:6; 18:20; 22:7; 23:9, 26, 35; 24:3.

22. 2 Kgs 12:9–16 is broadly parallel to 2 Chr 24:8–14, but the latter says nothing about accounting.

23. אך is found again in 2 Kgs 23:9. On Josiah's dealings with the priests of the במות, see Kucová, "Common Source Theory," 135–39—the במות themselves were the topic of (the original?) 1 Kgs 22:44 // 2 Chr 20:33. And אך is used once more in the Josiah narrative: 2 Kgs 23:26 may well depend on Jer 2:35.

4. In 1 Kgs 22:32, but not in the parallel 2 Chr 18:31, a plus opens the (mis)identification of Jehoshaphat as "king of Israel." In Chronicles, the chariot officers of the king of Aram say simply, "It is the king of Israel"; however, in Kings, "*But* it is the king of Israel."

5. A plus is part of a text-critical puzzle relating to the move of the daughter of Pharaoh to quarters in Jerusalem:

1 Kgs 9:24 MT: אַךְ בת־פרעה עלתה ("*However*, the daughter of Pharaoh went up")

3 Kgdms 9:9*: אָז העלה שלמה בת־פרעה ("*Then* Solomon brought up the daughter of Pharaoh")

2 Chr 8:11: וְאֶת־בת־פרעה העלה ("*And* the daughter of Pharaoh he brought up")

Both אַךְ ("however") and אָז ("then") are regularly used to add fresh information to an existing context—and of course the simple connective ו ("and") even more often. There is another twist in the puzzle: in both (broadly) synoptic 2 Chr 8:17 and nonsynoptic 1 Kgs 22:50, אָז ("then") introduces a note about Solomon or Jehoshaphat visiting Ezion-geber. Presumably, just as in the case of the infinitive absolute, heavy usage of אָז in nonsynoptic Samuel and Kings will have influenced the redrafting of some synoptic passages.[24]

3.2.5. הנה ("Look/Behold")

הנה is used only minimally (some 10x) in synoptic texts,[25] more often (38x) by the Chronicler, and much more frequently in nonsynoptic Samuel (126x) and Kings (97x).

---

24. The moving of the daughter of Pharaoh will be reviewed further in 12.3.2 (synoptic reconstruction).

25. 2 Sam 5:1 // 1 Chr 11:1; 1 Kgs 8:27 // 2 Chr 6:18; 1 Kgs 10:7 // 2 Chr 9:6; 1 Kgs 15:19 // 2 Chr 16:3; 1 Kgs 22:13, 23, 25 // 2 Chr 18:12, 22, 24; 2 Kgs 11:14 // 2 Chr 23:13; 2 Kgs 22:16, 20 // 2 Chr 34:24, 28 (these and the following totals include והנה and all the suffix forms). An eleventh synoptic instance of הנה is probably to be recognized in 1 Chr 17:1 (MT and LXX) // 2 Sam 7:2 (LXX), although 2 Sam 7:2 (MT) reads

3.3. Infinitive Absolute

Our final example is not of a word used here but not there, or more here and less there, but of an unusual form of the Hebrew verb—unusual at least from the perspective of English and most other European languages. The infinitive absolute is employed quite differently across the Hebrew Bible, both in frequency and in purpose. This uninflected form of the verb performs different functions in a Hebrew sentence. In the opening chapter (1.4) we saw the infinitive absolute in two of its distinct roles: in the Samuel plus (2 Sam 8:2), it was used where a finite form of the verb could also have been used; and in the Kings plus (2 Kgs 18:33), it was used to underline or strengthen the idea expressed in the immediately adjacent and cognate inflected finite verb. Alongside reinforcing or replacing finite forms, the other commonest functions can be loosely described as resuming, instructing, and (adverbially) modifying.[26]

The frequency of usage is also very widely varied throughout the Hebrew Bible. It appears most densely of all in Haggai and least often in Ezra (only once).[27] And because both Haggai and Ezra are relatively late biblical books, this fact suggests immediately that variation in frequency is more a matter of authorial preference than of the date of the book in question. If we limit the overview to bigger books, the spectrum stretches from Jeremiah (where it is used almost as densely as in Haggai) to Chronicles (where it is just not quite as infrequent as in Ezra). Among the books of the Former Prophets, the heavier usage in Samuel comes closest to Jeremiah, with 1 Samuel even closer than 2 Samuel. However, this difference between 1 Samuel and 2 Samuel disappears if we bracket out synoptic material—nonsynoptic Samuel uses the infinitive absolute much more densely than synoptic Samuel.

Most of the separate functions are found in Chronicles (of the five mentioned above, only instructing is absent); and of the eighteen instances

---

ראה. On הנה הכית in 2 Chr 25:19, when synoptic 2 Kgs 14:10 reads the very similar הכה הכית, see 3.3.1 below.

26. Aaron Hornkohl operates with just four categories: paronomastic, substitutionary for finite verbal forms, imperatival, and general adverbial (*Ancient Hebrew Periodization and the Language of the Book of Jeremiah: The Case for a Sixth-Century Date of Composition*, SSLL [Leiden: Brill, 2014], 266).

27. If Ezra-Nehemiah were counted as a single book, Song of Songs (with also only one instance) would represent the end of the spectrum.

of infinitive absolute in Chronicles, eight belong to synoptic contexts while ten do not. Since synoptic material represents some 40 percent of the text of Chronicles, the shared contexts are broadly typical of that whole book in level of infinitive absolute usage. Of the eight in synoptic contexts, six are simply identical to their parallels in Samuel–Kings: 1 Chr 11:9 (2x) // 2 Sam 5:10 (2x); 1 Chr 21:24 // 2 Sam 24:24; and 2 Chr 18:27, 29 (2x) // 1 Kgs 22:28, 30 (2x). In the case of 2 Chr 32:13 // 2 Kgs 18:33, there has been redrafting in one direction or the other; but the use of the cognate reinforcing infinitive absolute has been maintained although with a different verb. The one remaining case (1 Chr 21:17 and 2 Sam 24:17) will be considered below (3.3.2).

In Samuel–Kings the infinitive absolute is found 124 times—as many as 50 times in 1 Samuel, and 74 in 2 Samuel–2 Kings. Of the latter 74, 15 are found in synoptic contexts: the 7 shared with Chronicles and 8 more (2 Sam 5:19; 8:2; 24:12; 1 Kgs 8:13; 9:6, 25; 2 Kgs 11:18; 14:10).

3.3.1. Infinitive Absolute in Samuel–Kings but Not Chronicles

Of the eight passages just listed, 2 Sam 8:2 // 1 Chr 18:2 has already been discussed (1.4.2). Four of the other seven are similar to it: in each case, the infinitive absolute is only one of several pluses in the Samuel–Kings version of the shared tradition.

2 Sam 5:19	1 Chr 14:10
עלה כי נתן אתן את־הפלשתים בידך	עלה ונתתים בידך
Go up; *for* I shall *in fact* give *the Philistines* into your hand.	Go up, and I shall give them into your hand.

The divine answer to David's query is longer and more emphatic in Samuel: it adds the causal "for," includes the strengthening cognate infinitive absolute, and specifies the object of the divine grant as "the Philistines." The third addition is unnecessary, because this enemy has been repeatedly mentioned in the previous verses, but its presence may be editorially significant. Samuel (MT) normally (in many dozens of cases) calls (the) Philistines פלשתים (without the article), and only seven times reads הפלשתים.[28] Only this instance occurs in a synoptic context, and that fact

---

28. 1 Sam 4:17; 7:13; 13:20; 17:51, 52; 2 Sam 5:19; 21:12.

suggests the activity of a different and secondary hand—the hand that may also have made the other additions to the verse, including the infinitive absolute.

2 Sam 24:11–12	1 Chr 21:9–10
ודבר יהוה היה אל־גד הנביא חזה דוד לאמר הלוך ודברת אל־דוד	וידבר יהוה אל־גד חזה דויד לאמר לך ודברת אל־דויד
And Yahweh's word came to Gad the prophet, David's seer, saying, "*Go* and say to David...."	And Yahweh spoke to Gad, David's seer, saying, "*Go* and say to David...."

The difference between the parallel Hebrew words underlined above does not show up in translation. Chronicles uses the simple imperative, while Samuel uses the infinitive absolute to start the command. Chronicles nowhere expresses a command with the infinitive absolute, and so could be claimed to have replaced it here with the imperative. On the other hand, nine instructions in Jeremiah are expressed like Samuel here,[29] and we have noted how similar Samuel is to Jeremiah in density of infinitive absolute usage. Each variant, therefore, fits its context well. Our decision about priority may fairly be influenced by our decision about the previous clause. There the shorter and more direct note in Chronicles about Yahweh speaking seems to have been carefully restated in Samuel, and the title "prophet" (also an oft-repeated feature of Jeremiah) added to "seer." Changing לך ("go") to הלוך would be a natural editorial consequence.

Again, in the case of 1 Kgs 9:6 // 2 Chr 7:19, the presence or absence of the infinitive absolute is not the only difference between these verses:

1 Kgs 9:6	2 Chr 7:19
ואם־<u>שוב</u> תשבון אתם <u>ובניכם מאחרי</u> <u>ולא תשמרו</u> מצותי חקתי	ואם־ תשובון אתם <u>ועזבתם</u> חקותי ומצותי
And if you yourselves *and your sons really* turn *from following me* and do not keep my commands and my decrees	And if you yourselves turn and abandon my decrees and my commands

---

29. Jer 2:2; 3:12; 13:1; 17:19; 19:1; 28:13; 34:2; 35:13; 39:16.

The cognate infinitive absolute שוב in 1 Kgs 9:6 is only one of the three pluses when compared with the opening words of 2 Chr 7:19. The subject of "turn" in the shorter text is "you yourselves," but "you yourselves *and your sons*" in Kings; and Kings also specifies the turning as being "away from me." The next two differences seem less substantial: in place of "and abandon" in Chronicles, Kings has "and do not keep"; and "my decrees" and "my commands," the object of these verbs, appear in reverse order. Though less substantial in themselves, these further two differences add to the already clear evidence that the presence or absence of the infinitive absolute at the beginning did not result from accidental duplication or simplification of the text, but was simply one part of a substantial rewriting of the whole conditional clause in one direction or the other.

First Kings 9:25b is distinctive both textually and orthographically. The sentence concludes a large portion of the Solomon story in the Masoretic Text (9:15–25a) the whole of which is attested much earlier in the Septuagint (although without the puzzling אתו אשר near the end).[30]

1 Kgs 9:25b	2 Chr 8:12
והעלה שלמה שלש פעמים בשנה	אז העלה שלמה
עלות ו<u>שלמים</u>	עלות ליהוה
על־המזבח אשר בנה ליהוה	על־מזבח יהוה אשר בנה
והקטיר <u>אתו אשר</u> לפני יהוה	לפני האולם
And Solomon offered up *three times a year*	*Then* Solomon offered up
holocausts *and* שלמים *sacrifices*	holocausts to Yahweh
on the altar that he built to Yahweh	on the altar of Yahweh that he built
and burned incense with it that was before Yahweh	before the vestibule

The cultic theme introduced here is much more fully developed in 2 Chr 8:13–16a, ahead of the conclusion in synoptic 8:16b // 1 Kgs 9:25b (these two half-verses are clearly related, but not identical). Most of the additional material in Chronicles relates to a fresh subtopic, the role of

---

30. At 3 Kgdms 2:35g (Rahlfs), which is the same as 1 Reyes 2:7 in *El Texto Antioqueno de la Biblia Griega* II *1–2 Reyes*, ed. Natalio Fernández Marcos and José Ramón Busto Saiz, TECC (Madrid: Instituto de Filología del CSIC, 1992).

priests and Levites (a frequent concern of that book, but not of Samuel–Kings). However, while שלש פעמים בשנה ("three times per year") at the beginning of 1 Kgs 9:25 is also more fully explained (2 Chr 8:13), neither שלמים sacrifices nor הקטיר ("burned incense") in 1 Kgs 9:25b plays any part in the Chronicler's longer version, although each term is familiar elsewhere in Chronicles. David offering שלמים on bringing the ark into Jerusalem (2 Sam 6:17, 18[31]) and including them among his sacrifices after the census (2 Sam 24:25) has also been reported in the synoptic 1 Chr 16:1, 2; 21:26. Similarly Solomon has offered them as part of the culmination of his dedication of the temple in synoptic 1 Kgs 8:64 // 2 Chr 7:7. Two further synoptic contexts in Samuel–Kings in addition to 1 Kgs 9:25 use שלמים where it is not found in Chronicles: 1 Kgs 8:63 and 64 mention שלמים three times, while synoptic 2 Chr 7:7 has it only once; and 1 Kgs 3:15, but not the shorter parallel in 2 Chr 1, reports both holocausts and שלמים sacrifices at the end of Solomon's vision at Gibeon. On the other hand, שלמים is found in four nonsynoptic passages later in Chronicles.[32] Given all this variation in both directions, it is hard to see any reason for the Chronicler to have deleted from his source an otherwise acceptable sacrificial term when he was actually engaged in expansively rewriting that very source: 1 Kgs 9:25 expanded to 2 Chr 8:12–16.

The situation of הקטיר ("burned [incense]") is different. Unlike the שלמים sacrifices that do sometimes feature in synoptic texts, the *hiphil* theme of קטר is always attested in *different* contexts in Kings and Chronicles *and never synoptically*.[33] As vocalized, this is an instance of an infinitive absolute replacing a finite form. Indeed, in the context of this verse, the consonants הקטיר would be (grammatically) ambiguous if unvocalized: they could also be read as perfect/*qatal* ("offered incense"). In addition, הקטיר in 1 Kgs 9:25 is the only *hiphil* in the Masoretic Text of Samuel–Kings–Chronicles that is both written plene (with *yod*) and vocalized as an infinitive absolute.[34] And yet, although this verb form stands isolated

---

31. It is argued on the basis of vertical alignment that there was not space in 4QSam[a] to repeat ושלמים in 6:18.

32. 2 Chr 29:35; 30:22; 31:2; 33:16.

33. We shall discuss later (chs. 5–6) the synoptic instances of קטר *piel*. The *hiphil* predominates in the Pentateuch. In (nonsynoptic) Samuel–Kings, it is attested only in 1 Sam 2 (3x) and in 1 Kgs 3:3; 9:25; 11:8; 12:33; 13:1, 2; 2 Kgs 16:13, 15.

34. The almost standard *hiphil* infinitive absolute without *yod* is found at 1 Sam 3:12; 6:3; 8:9; 10:16; 12:25; 14:28; 15:23; 17:16 (2x); 22:22; 25:26, 33; 27:12; 30:8 (2x);

3. MORE WORDS

within Samuel–Kings–Chronicles, Jeremiah (MT) does provide three comparators for the traditional vocalization in 1 Kgs 9:25. In each of Jer 3:15, 10:5, and 23:32, the context requires reading the *hiphil* forms written with *yod* as infinitives absolute.

In the final two cases, the differences between Kings and Chronicles are less substantial. Second Chronicles 23:17 already catches the enthusiasm with which the Jerusalem crowd destroyed images of Baal after the fall of Athaliah by reading שברו as *piel*, "shattered," rather than simply as *qal*, "broke"; and 2 Kgs 11:18 simply adds the adverbial infinitive absolute היטב ("well"; see 12.3.12). Then הכה הכית ("you have certainly struck," 2 Kgs 14:10) looks so similar to הנה הכית ("look, you have struck," 2 Chr 25:19) that a scribal slip could easily have been made in either direction.

In the one remaining case of divergence, of Samuel–Kings using an infinitive absolute but Chronicles not, we must compare three versions of the text and not simply two.

1 Kgs 8:12b–13 MT	3 Kgdms 8:53 retroverted	2 Chr 6:1b–2 MT
יהוה	שמש הכיר בשמים יהוה	יהוה
אמר לשכן בערפל	אמר לשכן בערפל	אמר לשכון בערפל
בנה בניתי בית זבול לך	בנה ביתי בית זבול לך	ואני בניתי בית זבול לך
מכון לשבתך עולמים	...	ומכון לשבתך עולמים
Yahweh	Yahweh recognized sun in the heavens.	Yahweh
spoke of dwelling in deep darkness:	He spoke of dwelling in deep darkness	spoke of dwelling in deep darkness:
"I have surely built a princely house for you,	"Build my house, a princely house for yourself."	"It is I who have built a princely house for you
an establishment for you to live in forever."	...	and an establishment for you to live in forever."

---

2 Sam 8:2; 1 Kgs 3:26, 27; 20:37; 2 Kgs 4:43; 11:15, 18; 14:10; 18:30, 33; 1 Chr 21:17; 2 Chr 2:9; 31:10, 15; Jer 4:10; 7:5, 9, 13, 18, 25; 9:24; 11:7 (3x), 12; 19:13; 22:19; 25:4; 26:5, 19; 29:19; 32:33, 44; 35:14, 15; 36:16, 23; 38:15; 44:4, 17, 18, 19, 25; 49:23.

It is widely recognized that the differently placed verse in the Septuagint has preserved the original three opening words of this perhaps more ancient fragment, an opening that has been lost, or suppressed for ideological reasons, from Kings (MT) and Chronicles.[35] More relevant to our purpose are the variants at the beginning of the third line above. Whatever these differences, the object of the building, stated in the second half of this line, is undisputed: "a princely house for you[rself]." In Kings (MT), we read the infinitive absolute with a following cognate perfect/ *qatal* of "build": "I have assuredly built." In Chronicles, we also read "I have built" in second place; but the first word accentuates the subject, not the verbal idea: "I myself have built." Kingdoms (LXX) opens with the command "Build"; but the Hebrew attested in this version has "my house" (ביתי) in second position, not "I have built" (בניתי): "Build my house, a princely house for yourself." The Greek imperative represents Hebrew בנה, but could have interpreted this either as a standard imperative or as an infinitive absolute with the force of a command. Given that בנה בניתי בית and בנה ביתי בית share so many letters and differ only over the presence or absence of one of them (נ), it seems unwise to pronounce on which of these variants is closest to the original text.

3.3.2. Infinite Absolute in Chronicles but Not Samuel–Kings

Possibly the most significant divergence between Samuel–Kings and Chronicles over the use or nonuse of the infinitive absolute is the one case where we *do* find this verbal form in 1 Chr 21:17 but *not* in synoptic 2 Sam 24:17. אני־הוא אשר־חטאתי והרע הרעותי ואלה הצאן מה עשו ("I am the one who has sinned and I have done very wrong. But these sheep: what have they done?") provides an important contrast to the profiles just sketched of much heavier infinitive absolute usage in Samuel–Kings than in Chronicles. Here instead, an infinitive absolute is used in Chronicles but not—or not with complete certainty—in any available text of the parallel in 2 Sam 24:17. Two texts of the Samuel parallel do preserve or attest to a consonantal text very similar to what we read in Chronicles. What we read in the Lucianic text (LXX[L]), "I the shepherd have done wrong," is an

---

35. Following Wellhausen's lead, Noth (*Könige*, 172) pronounced it *so gut wie sicher* ("as good as certain") that the longer text was original. Many commentators agree, but not Sweeney (*I and II Kings*, 132): "The obscurity of the MT suggests that it is the original text, which the LXX attempts to clarify."

appropriate translation of what is written in 4QSam^a; and הרעה הרעותי only differs from the Chronicler's והרע הרעותי by the repetition of one consonant (ה).³⁶ These two forms of the text are clearly related, but which is more original?³⁷ David follows up his taking the blame on himself by exclaiming, according to all our available texts, "But these sheep—what have they done?" The resulting correspondence of shepherd/sheep attested in 2 Sam 24:17 (LXX^L and possibly 4QSam^a) is effective rhetorically, but need not represent the original drafting of the verse. The comparative data on the usage of the infinitive absolute already reviewed encourage giving preference to Chronicles, and should make us look for further arguments. Some are available in linkages with earlier passages of the book of Samuel, and will be reviewed below (7.4).

3.3.3. Interim Review

The Chronicler's reputation as a remover of infinitives absolute *whenever possible* from his inherited text is clearly not deserved; indeed, 1 Chr 11:9 (// 2 Sam 5:10) exemplifies his fidelity to inherited material, for he nowhere reuses the "linking" or "resumptive" infinitive absolute in his own drafting.³⁸ Additionally, in the one divergence over infinitives absolute between 2 Kgs 18–20 and Isa 36–39, it is again Kings that offers a longer text than synoptic Isaiah. The synoptic portions of Samuel–Kings–Chronicles make only small use of infinitives absolute; and the Chronicler's additional nonsynoptic usage is similarly sparse. The infinitive absolute is used much more frequently in the nonsynoptic portions of Samuel and Kings, as already noted.

Given that we find infinitives absolute much more often in Samuel and Kings than in Chronicles *within synoptic portions* of these books, we should reckon that this represents an adjustment toward the much greater use of infinitives absolute that Samuel–Kings exhibit generally. In 2 Sam 8:2, 24:12, and 1 Kgs 9:25 (all examples of independent or noncognate

---

36. In MT, followed by LXX^B, we read a different verb (העויתי), preceded by neither infinitive absolute nor a similar participle.

37. We cannot be certain that הרעה in 4QSam^a was not intended to be read as an infinitive absolute.

38. One may suggest that fidelity over preserving the infinitive absolute in 11:9 may add to the likelihood that the Chronicler has equally faithfully preserved חיה *piel* in 11:8 (as proposed in 2.1 above).

infinitive absolute), as well as in 2 Sam 5:19, 1 Kgs 8:13, and 9:6 (all cognate infinitives absolute), the differences from the synoptic passages in Chronicles relate to more than the use or nonuse of the infinitive absolute.[39] The addition of infinitives absolute had been simply one element in later, more extensive rewriting.

3.4. Retrospect

In these early chapters I have attempted to review only ideologically neutral indicators of word usage—terms that are *not* indicative of the religious predispositions of Samuel–Kings and Chronicles. The varied evidence so far accumulated in chapters 2–3 permits two preliminary conclusions.

1. The synoptic portions are quite *untypical* of Samuel–Kings as a whole:

- יש ("there is") together with quite the commonest expressions for time in Samuel–Kings ("today" and "this day") are completely absent.
- Otherwise common terms or phrases such as אך and נאם יהוה feature only once,[40] as does ניר.
- The somewhat more frequent occurrences of infinitives absolute, of הנה, and of the cluster "life-live-living," while important within synoptic texts, are still relatively few in number.

The synoptic material, when set against Samuel–Kings as a whole, has something of a negative footprint: on these indicators, it is more distinctive by what it lacks than by what it contains.

2. The Chronicler emerges as more faithful to his (synoptic) source material, in this respect at least: in a large number of cases he preserves the wording he finds, even though he does not use this wording again in what he himself drafts.

Those who wish to maintain the consensus view that the Chronicler worked from some form of the text of Samuel–Kings must at least concede that he made his selection from portions of his base text that were highly untypical of the whole. That the Chronicler should have homed in on such

---

39. I discuss 2 Sam 5:19, 24:12, and 1 Kgs 8:13 all in "Text" (19 n. 81 above).

40. Or twice in the case of אך ("however"), if 2 Sam 23:10 is accepted as more original than 1 Chr 11:14.

unusual chapters to excerpt from and build on is surprising enough. But it must be no less surprising that such untypical clusters of text are to be found within Samuel-Kings in the first place, *unless they also formed its relatively unchanged core.* This alternative continues to seem preferable: a base document more or less coextensive with the synoptic *and untypical* material was differently expanded—in one direction toward Samuel and Kings, and in another toward Chronicles. Isaac Kalimi has used the fact that (nonsynoptic) Chronicles is aware of some portions of nonsynoptic Samuel-Kings as an argument for his continued privileging of Samuel-Kings.[41] But that is to assume the substantial unity of "the Chronicler" and to overlook the quiet warning in the second sentence of the preface to Arno Kropat's classic study: "Hierbei ist es ohne Belang, dass 'der Chronist' aller Wahrscheinlichkeit nach nicht ein einzelnes Individuum war, sondern als Sammelname zu verstehen ist."[42] Neither "the Chronicler" nor "the author" of Samuel-Kings was an individual. The Jena Symposium mentioned above (1.3) discussed several examples of plausible influence in the opposite direction: from Chronicles on Samuel-Kings.[43] In any scrutiny of mutual influence between these two developing corpora, it is important to seek to define first what they had shared at the outset.

3.5. Afterword

Infinitives absolute occur not only more rarely in synoptic Samuel-Kings than in nonsynoptic Samuel-Kings, but always singly. In nonsynoptic Samuel-Kings, but never in synoptic texts, cognate infinitives absolute are often paired responsively. In 1 Sam 14:43–44, Jonathan confesses "Taste!—I did taste" (טעם טעמתי), and his father immediately responds "Die!—you shall die" (מות תמות). Similarly, within 2 Sam 12:14, Nathan announces to David, "Scorn!—you have scorned" (נאץ נאצת), with the result for his baby son, "Die!—he shall die" (מות ימות). In each case the double pairing underscores the correlation of cause and effect.

---

41. Kalimi, "Kings *with* Privilege."

42. Kropat, *Die Syntax des Autors der Chronik verglichen mit der seiner Quellen: Ein Beitrag zur historischen Syntax des Hebräischen*, BZAW 16 (Giessen: Töpelmann, 1909), v.

43. "The symposium's theme asks whether chronistic or postchronistic influences can be identified in the most recent revisions of the Books of Samuel" (cited from the preface to Becker and Bezzel, *Rereading the* relecture?, v).

The infinitive absolute is used in still larger (nonsynoptic) patterns. The two accounts of David sparing King Saul's life when he had him in his power (1 Sam 24 and 26) are very closely related; and each includes two of the linguistic or stylistic features under review, infinitives absolute and markers of time. First Samuel 26:8 corresponds to 24:11 as does 26:21 to 24:20 in their use of "today" (היום). Then, in 1 Sam 26, both verses 23 and 24 repeat "today" as they restate and reinforce verse 21. In each chapter, the sentence including the climactic היום (24:20 and 26:24) is immediately followed by a sentence including an infinitive absolute. In the first account, Saul insists doubly that David will be king: מלך תמלוך וקמה בידך ממלכת ישראל ("King you surely shall be, and the kingdom of Israel will come up into your hand," 24:21). Then, in the second, he insists doubly that he will have sure success—and in this second case not one but both verbs are emphasized by a cognate infinitive absolute: גם עשה תעשה וגם יכל תוכל (26:25).[44] This use of the infinitive absolute in 1 Sam 26, where it echoes the infinitive absolute in 1 Sam 24 but uses different verbs, is analogous to the relationship between 2 Kgs 18:30 and 2 Chr 32:13 already discussed (3.3). In both cases, substantial rewriting has taken place. However, in whichever direction the rewriting has occurred,[45] the linguistic feature infinitive absolute + cognate verb has been retained, even though a different verb has been used within this linguistic idiom. A similar feature can be observed at the end of Genesis, where it seems that several features (including infinitives absolute) from the end of 2 Sam 24 have been anticipated.[46] The stylistic featuring of infinitives absolute goes still further toward the end of 1 Samuel, and will be discussed in 7.1.

Expressions of time (all including "day") are also juxtaposed with infinitives absolute in 1 Sam 14:28, 30, 43–45; 20:27–28; 22:15–16; and 2 Sam 6:20, resulting in a total of at least ten such pairings across 1–2 Samuel. This is an oft-repeated feature in nonsynoptic Samuel but wholly absent from the synoptic texts: the contrast is complete. Neither in the five synoptic contexts in Samuel, nor indeed in the eight synoptic contexts reviewed

---

44. It is very hard to convey in English the dynamics of the Hebrew. Saul is equally convinced that David will act and that he will have the ability to act successfully.

45. While most scholars consider 2 Chr 32 a reworking of 2 Kgs 18, there is much more debate over the priority of 1 Sam 24 and 26.

46. Graeme Auld, "Reading Genesis after Samuel," in *The Pentateuch*, ed. Thomas B. Dozeman, Konrad Schmid, and Baruch J. Schwartz, FAT 78 (Tübingen: Mohr Siebeck, 2011), 468–69.

above in Kings,[47] is there any marker of time anywhere near an instance of the infinitive absolute. I have argued above that the infinitive absolute was not original to all fourteen synoptic passages; but, even if it had been, it would not have been associated with any expression including "day," or indeed any other specification of time.

3.6. Outlook

Before we proceed to the second main section of our study, it is important to be clear just what we may deduce and what we should not deduce from the data assembled so far. Three clusters of quite different sorts have been inspected:

- verb, noun, and adjective forms of "live"
- a wide spectrum of expressions used to measure or mark the passage of time
- all five different ways in which the infinitive absolute is employed

In each case we found that the synoptic texts employ items within these clusters very much less frequently than Samuel–Kings as a whole. We also found that Samuel–Kings and Chronicles, within the texts that they broadly share, exhibit minimal difference over the "life" and "time" clusters. By contrast, Samuel–Kings uses the infinitive absolute more often than Chronicles in synoptic contexts, though still much less densely than in nonsynoptic portions of Samuel–Kings. These data relating to quite diverse clusters have been complemented by plotting the usage of five single terms. The most striking of these is שׁי: though used several times in Chronicles and much more often in Samuel–Kings, it is completely absent from synoptic contexts. It may be that some of these features, whether singly or in combination, point to different authorial or editorial hands. For example, both of the worked examples of the emphatic infinitive absolute itself reinforced by association with expressions built on "day" were taken from 1 Sam 25–30 (see 3.5); and I have argued elsewhere that these chapters form part of the latest main stratum of Samuel. On the other hand, they certainly do not all belong to the same editorial strand. For

---

47. When counting contexts rather than individual instances, 2 Sam 5:10 (2x) and 1 Kgs 22:30 (2x) are each counted as one.

example, not one of the instances of יש is found in these chapters at the end of 1 Samuel, or indeed in any part of this late stratum. The data discussed so far permit and even require a fresh perspective on the relationship between Samuel–Kings and Chronicles—and, possibly even more important, on the writing of Samuel–Kings itself. Some of this reconsideration may turn out to be relevant to the contemporary discussion of the history of Biblical Hebrew. But that is not my purpose. My prime concern is to note divergent preferences and usages, not to date them.

The synoptic materials are far from typical of Samuel–Kings as a whole. The indicators we have reviewed are very different from one another. That they each—and quite separately from one another—characterize one and the same subset of Samuel–Kings as distinctive within the whole makes a strong case for further examination. In some respects, these synoptic materials are more typical of Chronicles. And of course, viewed from the familiar critical perspective, such continuity with nonsynoptic Chronicles would be unsurprising, if the Chronicler had started with his own partisan selection from Samuel–Kings. But it is hardly plausible that he started with such an untypical selection from his main source. Divergence from a synoptic core toward both Samuel–Kings and Chronicles seems at least equally plausible, and therefore deserves further consideration. The next chapters sample portions of nonsynoptic Samuel–Kings as development from synoptic texts.

4
God-King Communication in Jerusalem

We have seen in the several comparisons undertaken so far that the differences in usage between synoptic Samuel–Kings on the one hand and nonsynoptic Samuel–Kings on the other are even greater than the differences between the shared material and the Chronicler's own. This makes it advisable to develop further tests of the hypothesis that Samuel–Kings and Chronicles are alternative appropriations and expansions of a shorter and older shared narrative. Accordingly, the following chapters have a different focus. Instead of scrutinizing individual linguistic features, they concentrate on topics. The first reviews prophecy or divination, in the widest sense of these terms. The next reviews altar and "high place" throughout the royal narratives. Chapter 6 draws some conclusions about the emerging synoptic narrative.

4.1. Overview

This chapter offers a first test of the internal coherence of the synoptic texts. The following shared texts report divine/human communication, with or without a mediator.[1]

2 Sam 5:19, 23	David asks for divine guidance before attacking Philistines
2 Sam 7	Nathan on building a house, and David's prayer
2 Sam 24	Gad and David's choice among three punishments
1 Kgs 3:4–15	Solomon's vision at Gibeon

---

1. The parallels in Chronicles to these passages are 1 Chr 14:10, 14; 17; 21; 2 Chr 1:3–13; 6:12–39; 7:12–22; 10:15; 11:2–4; 18; 32; 33:9–10; 34:20–28.

1 Kgs 8:22–50a	Solomon prays at the dedication of the Jerusalem temple
1 Kgs 9:1–9	Solomon's vision in Jerusalem
1 Kgs 12:15	confirmation of a word spoken by Ahijah the Shilonite
1 Kgs 12:22–24	oracle spoken by Shemaiah
1 Kgs 22	Micaiah and the prophets with Jehoshaphat and the king of Israel
2 Kgs 18–20	Isaiah and Hezekiah
2 Kgs 21:9–10	Manasseh
2 Kgs 22:14–22	Huldah the prophetess and Josiah

4.2. Patterns

Several general observations follow from the listing above. Communication from or with the Deity is reported in synoptic texts in connection with:

- the founding kings, David and Solomon
- the first kings of separated Israel and Judah, Jeroboam and Rehoboam
- the first kings of Israel and Judah who mount joint action, Ahab and Jehoshaphat
- the good kings of surviving Judah who come under acute external threat, Hezekiah and Josiah
- wicked Manasseh

Against such a background, the absence of any such explicitly reported communication during the restoration of Joash after his grandmother Athaliah's usurpation of power seems to constitute a remarkable break in pattern.[2]

It is almost always the king who takes the initiative in communication between king and Deity (2 Sam 5; 7; 1 Kgs 3; 8; 9; 22; 2 Kgs 22). Only once (in 2 Sam 24) is it certainly the Deity, while the two reports in 1 Kgs 12 are so brief as to be ambiguous on the issue.

---

2. It may be considered implicit in the guiding role of Jehoiada the priest.

4. GOD-KING COMMUNICATION IN JERUSALEM

Most of the intermediaries (from Nathan to Huldah) are termed נביא(ה) ("prophet[ess]"). Of the three exceptions, Gad is a חזה ("seer"); synoptic Ahijah is simply "someone from Shiloh"; and Shemaiah is "the man of God" (איש האלהים). Only Gad is termed חזה ("seer," 2 Sam 24:11), but the related abstract noun חז[י]ון ("vision") concludes the summary of the whole communication mediated to David through Nathan: ככל־הדברים האלה וככל־החז[י]ון ("according to all these words and all the vision," 2 Sam 7:17). Within the synoptic texts, חזה ("seer") and its cognate חז[י]ון ("vision") are used only in the David narratives.[3] The participial form of ראה ("seer") is never found in synoptic texts; but other forms of this verb are used in visionary contexts: *qal* in 1 Kgs 22:17, 19, 25; and *niphal* in 1 Kgs 3:5; 9:2. And these in turn may have influenced the wording in 2 Sam 7:2 (MT) of David's request to Nathan (ראה נא)—the parallel in 1 Chr 17:1 reads simply הנה, and that is also attested by the Septuagint in both verses.[4] In synoptic texts, only David and Solomon are called Yahweh's "servant," whether by calling themselves עבדך ("your servant") in their prayers[5] or by being described as עבדי ("my servant") in divine speech to them through a prophet.[6] The sole exception—or extension—to this is found in 2 Kgs 8:19, where the narrator writes, למען דוד עבדו ("for the sake of David his servant").[7] Correspondingly, only David (2 Sam 7:18) and Solomon (1 Kgs 8:22) out of all the kings and intermediaries reported on are explicitly described as speaking directly to Yahweh.

Despite the broadly synonymous use of שאל ("ask") and דרש ("inquire") in, for example, Isa 30–31,[8] the synoptic narrative seems to deliberately distinguish between these two verbs. שאל ("ask") is used to describe the *direct* approach of David and Solomon to Yahweh (these are also the kings who are said to "speak" to Yahweh), and דרש ("seek/

---

3. חזון is anticipated in 1 Sam 3:1, while חזה reappears in 2 Kgs 17:13. By contrast, Chronicles uses חזה 9x in addition to 1 Chr 21:9, and uses חזון again in 2 Chr 32:32.

4. Samuel is styled "the seer" (הראה) in 1 Sam 9:9, 11, 18, 19; 1 Chr 9:22; 26:28; 29:29; as is Hanani in 2 Chr 16:7, 10. Elsewhere in the HB, ראה is found only in Isa 28:7; 30:10.

5. 2 Sam 7:19, 20, 21, 25, 26, 27, 28, 29; 24:10; 1 Kgs 8:28, 29, 30.

6. 2 Sam 7:5, 8.

7. However, it must be noted that synoptic 2 Chr 21:7 offers a slightly different text that includes covenant making, but not the title "servant": למען הברית אשר כרת לדויד.

8. ואת־יהוה לא דרשו (31:1) and ופי לא שאלו (Isa 30:2) make essentially the same point.

inquire") refers to the inquiries made *about* the divine will by Jehoshaphat and the king of Israel (1 Kgs 22) and by Josiah (2 Kgs 22), and in each case *through* prophets (Micaiah and Huldah). One may add that it is only in these two "prophetic" narratives that הנה ("look/behold") is used, twice each by Micaiah and Huldah, and once by a royal messenger.[9]

First Kings 22:8 and 2 Kgs 22:15 also share a significant use of איש where a title, "prophet" or "king," might have been expected. Asked if there is no other "prophet of Yahweh" (1 Kgs 22:7), the king of Israel responds impatiently that there is another *individual* (איש) by whom they may inquire of Yahweh, but he hates him. Then Huldah, when approached by the emissaries sent by King Josiah, replies: "Tell the *individual* who sent you to me …"—the individual, not the king. It is as if the prophetess is repaying the king of her own much later time for the slighting terms in which an earlier king had spoken of Micaiah.

If we can assume that the distinction made in the root text between שאל ("ask") and דרש ("seek") was noticed by those who extended the text as they wrote the book of Samuel, then it gives greater poignancy to the wordplay in the earlier chapters about first Hannah boldly anticipating David and Solomon by "asking" Yahweh for a son, and then the people "asking" Yahweh for a king—a king who turned out to be named "Asked-for" (שאול) or "Saul." (Nonsynoptic) Samuel uses דרש ("seek") only of Saul consulting Samuel (1 Sam 9:9; 28:7)—apart, that is, from David's presumably nonoracular inquiry about Bathsheba (2 Sam 11:3). And we find "seek" (דרש) in a few nonsynoptic contexts in Kings (1 Kgs 14:5; 2 Kgs 1 [5x]; 3:11; 8:8). In Chronicles, by contrast, דרש ("seek") is very much more common, some thirty-five times from Saul (1 Chr 10:13–14) onward. Rannfrid Thelle, in her careful overview of such issues,[10] notes that שאל ("ask") is used mainly in Judges and Samuel, and דרש ("seek") in Kings. The present discussion explores the roots of these preferences.

---

9. As already noted, הנה introduces David's words to Nathan in 1 Chr 17:1 and in synoptic 2 Sam 7:2 (LXX), while only 2 Sam 7:2 (MT) uses ראה.

10. Rannfrid Thelle, "Reflections of Ancient Israelite Divination in the Former Prophets," in *Israelite Prophecy and the Deuteronomistic History: Portrait, Reality, and the Formation of a History*, ed. Mignon R. Jacobs and Raymond F. Person, AIL 14 (Atlanta: Society of Biblical Literature, 2013), 7–33.

4.3. Shifts in Perspective

The issue of context and appropriate perspective is particularly important for correct understanding of the brief reports in 2 Sam 5:19 and 23. Read in traditional canonical order, these "askings" by David come at the end of a long series.[11] In each of the fifteen previous askings, as in 2 Sam 5 // 1 Chr 14, the Hebrew idiom is שאל ב- ("ask of"). In Judg 18:5; 20:18; 1 Sam 14:37; 22:13, 15,[12] as in synoptic 1 Chr 14:10, 14, it is "the Deity" that is consulted (שאל באלהים); in the other passages it is Yahweh (שאל ביהוה), as in the synoptic parallels 2 Sam 5:19 and 23. The attendant circumstances of half of these briefly described consultations are as opaque as in the synoptic pair. But six of them (Judg 18:5; 1 Sam 14:37; 22:10, 13, 15; 30:8) mention the involvement of a priest. The still more detailed Judg 20:27–28 includes talk of the ark and of Phinehas ministering before it, but does not explicitly state that this priest helped to secure the divine response. Then 1 Sam 28:6 reports that Yahweh made no response by any one of three methods to Saul's inquiry: not by dreams, not by Urim, and not by prophets.

The relevance of context is this. When read as the final members of a long series, the circumstances of David's inquiries in 2 Sam 5:19, 23 // 1 Chr 14:10, 14, just like the other less detailed and hence more opaque reports within the series, may be clarified by the other more detailed members of the set: even where it is not stated, the mediating role of a priest may be fairly intuited. Read on their own, however, or rather as part of a different series—in the broader context of the synoptic texts under review in this paper, where several features invite us to pair David with Solomon over against the following kings—David's askings, like Solomon's, may instead imply unmediated access to the Deity by these early kings.

As reported in 1 Chr 14, David's asking of the Deity follows the first stage in his collection of the ark (1 Chr 13). It is neither stated nor denied that there is a link between his first recovering this potent symbol of divine presence and his then asking for guidance. However, divine irruption (פרץ) is a key element in both narratives (2 Sam 5:20 // 1 Chr 14:11 and 2 Sam 6:8 // 1 Chr 13:11). And the author of Judg 20:27–28 may have intuited from these David narratives such a link between ark and divination.

---

11. Judg 1:1; 18:5; 20:18, 23, 27; 1 Sam 10:22; 14:37; 22:10, 13, 15; 23:2, 4; 28:6; 30:8; 2 Sam 2:1.

12. And also in 22:10 (LXX and 4QSam[a]).

On the other hand, there is no explicit priestly role in the account of the ark's return.

4.4. One Claim of Incoherence Disputed

Instances of God-king communication (4.1) are reported synoptically at very different length. Among these, Ahijah is mentioned only once, in a single verse. First Kings 12:15 // 2 Chr 10:15 notes that Yahweh had been instrumental in Rehoboam's refusal to listen to his people: למען הקים את־ דברו אשר דבר יהוה ביד אחיה השילני אל־ירבעם בן־נבט ("in order to establish his word that Yahweh had spoken by the hand of Ahijah the Shilonite to Jeroboam son of Nebat"). This note gives no information about the content of the word spoken by Ahijah; and it has been urged that such a reference out of the blue to a message by agency of Ahijah from Shiloh would have made no sense to a reader who did not know the (nonsynoptic) narrative featuring Ahijah in 1 Kgs 11. Stated differently: when we read this lone synoptic verse in the context of 2 Chr 10, we are able to understand it (only) because we are already familiar with the encounter of Jeroboam and Ahijah in the (supposed) parent text in 1 Kgs 11:29–39.[13] As already noted (1.2), Ray Person supposes that an early reader of such a lone text would have been familiar with oral versions of other stories about Ahijah.

However sensible this objection about the lack of written synoptic background on Ahijah may seem at first sight, two strong arguments can be advanced against it. First, the familiar book of Kings includes two analogous situations in nonsynoptic material. In the cases of both Jehu ben Hanani (1 Kgs 16:7, 12) and Jonah ben Amittai (2 Kgs 14:25), we find an oracle mentioned but no content reported. One reader of an earlier draft of this section objected that these two cases are more out of the blue. And yet that is just the point: if we can tolerate notes from the blue in Kings as it stands, why not also in an earlier (synoptic) draft? Second, Ahijah is named differently in the synoptic verse from his other mentions in Kings. Only in 1 Kgs 12:15 // 2 Chr 10:15 is he called simply "Ahijah the Shilonite."[14] At the beginning of each of the other (nonsynoptic) narratives in which he features, *both before and after 1 Kgs 12:15*,

---

13. Steven L. McKenzie, "The Chronicler as Redactor," in Graham and McKenzie, *Chronicler as Author*, 83.

14. אחיה השילני in 1 Kgs 12:15 and אחיהו השלוני in 2 Chr 10:15.

he is instead (re)introduced with a title, whether "the prophet" or "his [Yahweh's] servant" or both together: אחיה [השילני] הנביא ("Ahijah [the Shilonite] the prophet") in 1 Kgs 11:29; 14:2; עבדו אחיה השילני ("his servant Ahijah the Shilonite") in 15:29; and עבדו אחיהו הנביא ("his servant Ahijah the prophet") in 14:18. The admittedly puzzlingly brief synoptic note is in fact no more puzzling than the (nonsynoptic) notes about Jehu and Jonah. And the narrative in 1 Kgs 11:29–39 may well have been written precisely to supply the content of the word spoken by agency of Ahijah, and so satisfy the curiosity of readers puzzled by 1 Kgs 12:15 // 2 Chr 10:15.[15]

4.5. Exceptions

Within these synoptic contexts, three areas of divergence must be noted. The smallest one relates to Gad and Manasseh, the next to Solomon, and quite the largest to Hezekiah. The verb דבר ("speak") commonly has "Yahweh" as subject in synoptic portions, but almost always within reported speech.[16] It is normally the synoptic characters who claim that Yahweh has spoken. However, the actual narrator does claim Yahweh as speaker at three points. Only one of these is straightforward, and was discussed above: "in order to establish his word that he/Yahweh had spoken by the hand of Ahijah the Shilonite" (1 Kgs 12:15 // 2 Chr 10:15).[17] Within the narrative of David's census, however, we find textual variety: in Chronicles, Yahweh simply *speaks* to Gad, David's seer; but in Samuel, it is Yahweh's *word* that *comes* to Gad—and he is no longer simply David's "seer" but is first called "the prophet" as well:

---

15. It is unnecessary here to rehearse the divergent traditions about Jeroboam and Ahijah (and Shemaiah too) in 1 Kings and 3 Kingdoms. Even where Jeroboam does not himself feature in the report of Rehoboam at Shechem (as in some Greek versions), the word of Yahweh "by the hand of Ahijah" is spoken concerning him.

16. The speakers are David (2 Sam 7:7, 19, 25 [2x], 28), Solomon (1 Kgs 8:15, 20 [2x], 24 [2x], 26; 9:5), Shemaiah (1 Kgs 12:24), and Micaiah (1 Kgs 22:23, 28).

17. Although straightforward, the form of words attested in 1 Kgs 12:15 // 2 Chr 10:15 is strictly unique within synoptic texts. It is used of "prophetic" mediators (including Moses) in 1 Sam 28:15; 2 Sam 12:25; 1 Kgs 8:53, 56; 14:18; 15:29; 16:7, 12, 34; 17:16; 2 Kgs 9:36; 10:10; 14:25; 17:13, 23; 21:10; 24:2; and in 1 Chr 11:3; 2 Chr 33:8; 34:14; 35:6; 36:15. Only at 2 Kgs 21:10 and 2 Chr 33:8 is there a near-overlap (see below).

2 Sam 24:11	1 Chr 21:9
ודבר יהוה היה אל־גד הנביא חזה דוד	וידבר יהוה אל־גד חזה דויד
And Yahweh's word came to Gad the prophet, David's seer	And Yahweh spoke to Gad, David's seer

Third, and similarly, Chronicles suggests unmediated address by Yahweh to Manasseh and his people (unless he is suggesting that he spoke to Manasseh too through the Mosaic legislation), while Kings reports the role of "his servants the prophets" in Yahweh's declaration of judgment.

2 Kgs 21:9–10	2 Chr 33:9–10
ולא שמעו	
ויתעם מנשה לעשות ...	ויתע מנשה את־יהודה וישבי ירושלם לעשות ...
וידבר יהוה ביד־עבדיו הנביאים	וידבר יהוה אל־מנשה ואל־עמו
	ולא הקשיבו
... and they did not hear.	
And Manasseh misled them to do ...	And Manasseh misled Judah and the inhabitants of Jerusalem to do ...
And Yahweh spoke by the hand of his servants the prophets.	And Yahweh spoke to Manasseh and his people.
	And they did not pay attention.

Assessment of this second divergence is complex: neither ולא שמעו ("and they did not hear") of Kings nor ולא הקשיבו ("and they did not pay attention") of Chronicles is attested anywhere synoptically;[18] and "his servants the prophets" is a theme of Kings never found in Chronicles. Second Kings 17:13–14 anticipates both expressions from 21:9–10.

Discussion of the very different Hezekiah narratives will occupy chapter 10 below, after some further observations about word usage. The differences between Kings and Chronicles over Solomon's two visions are much less; I will note Chronicles' substantial plus in the second (at 5.3.2.2), and the role of hearing in Kings' version of the first (at 9.2.2). But, before pass-

---

18. In fact, הקשיב is used in the narrative books only in 1 Sam 15:22 and 2 Chr 20:15; 33:10.

ing on, I should note that Yahweh's "word" is attested in synoptic narratorial contexts only in 2 Sam 24:11 (but not 1 Chr 21:9); 1 Kgs 12:15 // 2 Chr 10:15; and 1 Kgs 22:5, 19 // 2 Chr 18:4, 18.

4.6. Focus on Huldah

Huldah's response to King Josiah's emissaries is the final element in this series; and we have already noted some links between this and earlier reports of God-king communication (4.2). What she has to say about the behavior of first people and then king helps us understand the religious rhetoric of more of the synoptic material. It also provides further examples of terms retained by the Chronicler but not further developed in his work. Yahweh's anger will be kindled against the people and not quenched, because they have (2 Kgs 22:17 // 2 Chr 34:25):

1. "abandoned me": עזב has been used previously synoptically only in the report of Solomon's second vision (1 Kgs 9:9).
2. "made offerings": קטר *piel* has been used previously synoptically only in the narrator's introduction to wicked King Ahaz (2 Kgs 16:4).
3. "to other gods": אלהים אחרים are again shared synoptically only in Solomon's second vision (1 Kgs 9:6, 9).
4. "provoking me": הכעיס is a complaint that had been made only against Manasseh (2 Kgs 21:6).
5. "with all the work of their hands": while בכל מעשי ידיהם is unique within synoptic texts, it recalls עשה in connection with sacred objects Manasseh should not have "made" (2 Kgs 21:3, 7 // 2 Chr 33:3, 7).

Solomon had already been warned of what could happen and what its consequences would be; but the people had followed the perverse example of wicked kings Ahaz and Manasseh. As for Josiah, he had softened his heart, humbled himself before Yahweh, torn his clothes, and wept before Yahweh. Only the tearing of clothes had previously been mentioned synoptically: first, of Athaliah's response to seeing the boy-king Joash in the temple (2 Kgs 11:14), and then of Josiah's own response to hearing the words of the book found in the temple (2 Kgs 22:11).

It may have been in part to distinguish Josiah's reactive behavior from Athaliah's that Huldah glossed her king's tearing his clothes as accompanied by his heart becoming soft (רך־לבבך), humbling himself before Yahweh (ותכנע), and weeping before Yahweh (ותבך). However, by choosing these three phrases, Huldah also distinguishes Josiah from every other character in synoptic texts. Reacting to the unique quality of Josiah's responses, Huldah promises the king that he himself will not see the coming disaster. The role Athaliah plays as foil to Josiah is a further indication that the Athaliah-Joash episode should after all be considered within the set describing God-king communication. While Josiah's rending was accompanied by regret and tears, Athaliah had protested, "Conspiracy! Conspiracy!"

Neither Chronicles nor Samuel–Kings uses רך־לבבך again. No one else in Chronicles weeps; and Athaliah is the only other there to tear her clothes. But several other characters in Chronicles humble themselves before Yahweh, or before their god.[19] By contrast, only Ahab does so in Kings (1 Kgs 21:29), while many others in Samuel–Kings tear their clothes (18x)[20] or weep (27x).[21]

The great majority of the synoptic reports of communication between God and king provide on the one side a further example of the very high degree of textual stability in shared portions of Samuel–Kings and Chronicles. On the other, they demonstrate just how exceptional the reports of Hezekiah and Isaiah are. As we shall see (in ch. 10 below), the synoptic links are far from obvious and have to be retrieved painstakingly from the unusually divergent texts.

---

19. 2 Chr 7:14; 12:6, 7, 12; 30:11; 32:26; 33:12, 19, 23 (2x).

20. 1 Sam 4:12; 15:27; 2 Sam 1:2, 11; 3:31; 13:19, 31 (2x); 15:32; 1 Kgs 11:30; 21:27; 2 Kgs 2:12; 5:7, 8 (2x); 6:30; 18:37; 19:1.

21. 1 Sam 1:7, 8, 10; 11:4, 5; 20:41; 24:17; 30:4; 2 Sam 1:12, 24; 3:16, 32 (2x), 34; 12:21, 22; 13:36 (2x); 15:23, 30 (2x); 19:1, 2; 2 Kgs 8:11, 12; 13:14; 20:3.

5
Cultic Matters: The Synoptic Tradition

5.1. Religious Constructions by Jerusalem's Kings

The shared cultic story in Samuel–Kings and Chronicles is essentially simple in its main lines. David's own last act had been to build an altar in Jerusalem; and the sacrifices on his altar after the plague that followed his census did prove acceptable to Yahweh (2 Sam 24:18, 21, 25 // 1 Chr 21:18, 22, 26). The synoptic narrative of Solomon starts with a vision at the Gibeon במה (1 Kgs 3:4-15 // 2 Chr 1:3-13). After the completion of the temple, reported at the heart of the Solomon narrative, a special space had to be consecrated for the massive celebratory sacrifices: the regular bronze altar (מזבח) was too small (1 Kgs 8:64 // 2 Chr 7:7). A second vision followed Solomon's building of the temple, this time in Jerusalem (1 Kgs 9:1-9 // 2 Chr 7:11-22); and sacrifice (of "whole burnt offerings," עלות) was offered at the Jerusalem altar (1 Kgs 9:25 // 2 Chr 8:12).[1] The guards for young Joash ahead of his installation were stationed near altar and "house" (2 Kgs 11:11 // 2 Chr 23:10). Yahweh's temple in Jerusalem is routinely called his "house" (בית); and it is called היכל (lit. "palace") in synoptic texts or contexts only in relation to its construction by Solomon (1 Kgs 6–7 // 2 Chr 3–4) and to actions by Hezekiah (differently reported in 2 Kgs 18:16 and 2 Chr 29:16).[2]

Solomon's altar reappears several times in his story. We might expect that the inauguration of this altar adjacent to the divine "palace," taken together with the fact that his second vision happened in Jerusalem and not again in Gibeon, should have combined to delegitimate the Gibeon

---

1. The texts are discussed at 3.3.1 above.
2. This makes a further link between Hezekiah and the founding kings: praying directly to Yahweh was noted in 4.2. Yahweh's היכל features also in (nonsynoptic) 1 Sam 1:9; 3:3; 2 Kgs 23:4; 24:13; 2 Chr 26:16; 27:2.

במה and perhaps any other such cult place. The first synoptic mentions of במות (pl.) occur in 1 Kgs 15:14; 22:44 // 2 Chr 15:17; 20:33, where we are informed that, even under good kings such as Asa and Jehoshaphat, these cultic installations were not removed. Examples of במות were still around when Ahaz became king (2 Kgs 16:4 // 2 Chr 28:4), and he also built (other?) illicit shrines. Hezekiah removed/pulled down these "high places" (2 Kgs 18:4; 2 Chr 31:1) and was credited with declaring the unique status of an altar in Jerusalem (2 Kgs 18:22 // 2 Chr 32:12).[3] Manasseh brought back the במות and even introduced several new altars within the sacred Jerusalem precinct (2 Kgs 21:3, 4, 5 // 2 Chr 33:3, 4, 5). And these in turn were removed during the reform instituted by Josiah (but here the texts are not identical).

Achieving a synoptic overview of Ahaz, Manasseh, and Josiah is somewhat easier than in the case of Hezekiah. And some (at least partial) results can be found below (12.3.17, 19, 21). What I shall do here is sketch the synoptic situation in each of the three, and concentrate comments on what they report about altars and "high places."

5.2. "High Places" (במות)

Though they differ over what they report about Ahaz and altars, Kings and Chronicles jointly present this king's enthusiasm for "high places" as the climactic element of their summary of his wicked behavior.

2 Kgs 16:2b–3a, 3b–4		2 Chr 28:1b–2a, 2b–3a, 3b–4
כדויד	ולא־עשה הישר בעיני יהוה אלהיו כדוד אביו	ולא־עשה הישר בעיני יהוה אביו
	וילך בדרך מלכי ישראל	וילך בדרכי מלכי ישראל
		וגם מסכות עשה לבעלים
		והוא הקטיר בגיא בן־הנם
	וגם את־בנו העביר באש כתעבות הגוים	ויבער את־בניו באש כתעבות הגוים
	אשר הוריש יהוה אתם מפני בני ישראל	אשר הריש יהוה מפני בני ישראל

---

3. See further 10.4: the report is in the mouth of the Assyrian envoy.

5. CULTIC MATTERS: THE SYNOPTIC TRADITION

ויזבח ויקטר בבמות ועל־הגבעות	ויזבח ויקטר בבמות ועל־הגבעות
ותחת כל־עץ רענן	ותחת כל־עץ רענן

And he did not do what was right in the eyes of Yahweh [his God] like David his father. And he walked in the way[s] of the kings of Israel. And even [cast images did he make for the Baals; and he himself burned incense in the valley of the son of Hinnom] his son[s] did he pass through the fire[4] like the abominations of the nations that Yahweh had dispossessed before the sons of Israel. And he enthusiastically sacrificed and burned incense at the high places and on the heights and under every green tree.[5]

As already noted, "high places" (במות) are only mentioned twice in synoptic texts between the time of Solomon's early visit to the במה at Gibeon and the period of oscillating changes that started with Ahaz. Both times they appear in passages that concern good kings, Asa and Jehoshaphat. The relevant note on Asa (1 Kgs 15:14 // 2 Chr 15:17) immediately follows his total destruction of a cultic installation associated with his mother in honor of Asherah:

1 Kgs 15:14	2 Chr 15:17
והבמות לא סרו	והבמות לא סרו <u>מישראל</u>
רק לבב־אסא היה שלם <u>עם־יהוה</u>	רק לבב־אסא היה שלם
כל־ימיו	כל־ימיו

The nonremoval of the "high places" is not held against Asa: "his heart had been perfect [with Yahweh] all his days."[6] (The pluses "with Yahweh" in Kings and "from Israel" in Chronicles appear to have no great significance.) There is greater divergence over what is said of Jehoshaphat:

---

4. Chronicles MT (ויבער) actually means "and he burned [his sons in fire]," but some Hebrew MSS and the ancient versions attest ויעבר ("made pass").

5. Additional material in Chronicles is set in square brackets.

6. לבב is construed with שלם several times more (1 Kgs 8:61; 11:4; 15:3; 2 Kgs 20:3; 1 Chr 12:39; 28:9; 29:9, 19; 2 Chr 16:9; 19:9; 25:2), but never again synoptically.

1 Kgs 22:44	2 Chr 20:33
אך הבמות לא סרו	אך הבמות לא סרו
עוד העם מזבחים ומקטרים בבמות	ועוד העם לא־הכינו לבבם לאלהי אבתיהם

Again no blame is imputed for the continuing presence of the "high places." But this time, instead of a note about the "heart" of the king, attention is directed to the people. Chronicles says that they "still had not set their heart to the God of their fathers," while Kings notes that they "still were sacrificing and burning [incense] at the high places."

In fact, it is only in their shared introduction to bad king Ahaz (2 Kgs 16:4 // 2 Chr 28:4) that Kings and Chronicles state in unison that the king *himself* "sacrificed and offered [incense] at the high places and on the heights and under every green tree." This summary is quite remarkable from a synoptic perspective:

- 2 Chr 28:4 is the only verse in Chronicles to use either גבעה ("height") or עץ רענן ("green tree").
- The *piel* of זבח ("sacrifice enthusiastically") is found in shared texts only twice, at 1 Kgs 8:5 // 2 Chr 5:6 and 2 Kgs 16:4 // 2 Chr 28:4.
- The *piel* of קטר ("offer incense") occurs synoptically only twice, at 2 Kgs 16:4 // 2 Chr 28:4 and 2 Kgs 22:17 // 2 Chr 34:25.[7]

The two synoptic pairings should remind us of both Athaliah and Josiah tearing their clothes (see 4.6 and, more fully, 6.3). Given such links, it cannot be fanciful to hear echoes of synoptic Solomon in this introduction to Ahaz. First, the very location of his sacrificing בבמות ועל־הגבעות ("at the high places and on the heights") can hardly fail to recall Solomon's multiple sacrifices at a במה ("high place") located precisely at גבעון; and Gibeon by its very name is the epitome of such a "height." Second, the energy of the sacrificing (signified in the *piel* stem of זבח) contrasts Ahaz's false enthusiasms with the enthusiastic sacrificial beginnings at the new Jerusalem temple. Solomon (if not always his people) had moved on from worship at the במה in Gibeon to worship at the temple in Jerusalem. By

---

7. I noted (3.3.1) that the *hiphil* stem of קטר, which appears to be used in much the same sense as the *piel*, is never attested synoptically, though relatively common in each of Kings (8x) and 2 Chronicles (11x).

5. CULTIC MATTERS: THE SYNOPTIC TRADITION

contrast, instead of giving up "high places" on heights like Gibeon, Ahaz concentrated his enthusiastic sacrificing at such במות. To repeat: it is only with reference to the behavior of bad king Ahaz that all these terms are found massed in the same *synoptic* text.

The Chronicler is a prime witness to how the במות theme had been handled synoptically. At first sight, this claim seems simply tautologous, since "synoptic" is defined as what appears at the same place in both Samuel-Kings and Chronicles. However, unlike the author(s) of Kings, the Chronicler normally only adds *further* detail about "high places" to individual reports that *already* mention these shrines. As noted, synoptic 2 Chr 15:17 and 20:33 record at the end of each report the continuing presence of במות under Asa and Jehoshaphat. The Chronicler adds 2 Chr 14:2, 4, and 17:6 to his introductions to each king. These notes claim that both these *good* kings had made efforts toward their removal. By contrast, his additional notes about במות in 2 Chr 28:25 and 33:19 reinforce the critique of *bad* kings Ahaz and Manasseh already offered in synoptic 2 Chr 28:4 and 33:3.

The immediate successors of Asa and Jehoshaphat were Jehoram and Ahaziah, who followed the (bad, but unspecified) example of the kings of Israel (2 Kgs 8:18, 27 // 2 Chr 21:6; 22:3). Nonsynoptic 2 Chr 21:11 provides the single exception to Chronicles' normal practice: Jehoram making במות is an added example of his leading Jerusalem and Judah into apostasy.[8]

The four kings who came after them and preceded Ahaz were all deemed "straight" (ישר) in Yahweh's eyes. Synoptic texts admit that the "high places" had not been removed even in the time of good kings Asa and Jehoshaphat; and they were clearly still there when Ahaz succeeded to the kingship. The readers of these shared texts could fairly have assumed that במות had been tolerated by all of the intervening good kings (Joash, Amaziah, Azariah, and Jotham). However, it is only the book of Kings that makes this explicit (2 Kgs 12:4a; 14:4a; 15:4a, 35a). In each of these four introductions, Kings turns into a cliché what had first been reported synoptically of Jehoshaphat (1 Kgs 22:44a)—only its opening word is altered; and, after all, it is rare in synoptic texts (see 3.2.4). Instead of אך הבמות לא

---

8. Cf. Ralph W. Klein, *2 Chronicles*, Hermeneia (Minneapolis: Fortress, 2012), 406.

סרו ("However, the high places did not cease"), we find the commoner רק הבמות לא סרו ("Only the high places did not cease").⁹

A limitation introduced by רק לא was apparently already part of the synoptic context in 2 Kgs 14:3b // 2 Chr 25:2b, where Amaziah's straightness in Yahweh's eyes is downplayed on other grounds, though differently in Kings and Chronicles: "*only not* like David his father …" (2 Kgs 14:4), or "*only not* with a complete heart" (2 Chr 25:2), in a modification of synoptic 1 Kgs 15:14 // 2 Chr 15:17. No similar limitation is reported of synoptic Joash before him, or of Azariah/Uzziah after him. However, both Kings and Chronicles make additions to their shared positive report on Jotham:

2 Kgs 15:35   רק הבמות לא סרו   עוד העם מזבחים ומקטרים בבמות
"*Only* the במות did *not* disappear; *still the people* were sacrificing"

2 Chr 27:2   רק לא־בא אל־היכל יהוה   ועוד העם משחיתים
"*Only* he did *not* come to Yahweh's palace; and *still the people* were acting destructively"

Kings simply repeats the limiting formula familiar from the introductions to the three previous kings of Judah. But in Chronicles, while both clauses begin the same way as in Kings, the first clause reports what the king did not do; and the second, what the people did do. From the perspective of the consensus view of the relationship of Chronicles to Kings, the Chronicler has retained the outer shell of the qualification in the text he inherited but supplied his own new content. However, seen from a synoptic perspective, the situation appears rather different. The behavior of several kings is compared with their immediate father's.¹⁰ In this case, Chronicles (but not Kings) had reported an incursion by Uzziah into the temple, resisted by the priests (2 Chr 26:16). The comparison introduced by רק לא in 2 Chr 27:2 is to the *benefit* of Jotham's reputation and not its detriment: unlike his father, he had *not* entered the temple to offer sacrifice. The people, however, were still "acting destructively." Unlike their own king—but like his father Uzziah, who had "raised his heart to the point of acting destructively" (2 Chr 26:16) and entered the temple—the people were continuing to flirt with danger.

---

9. רק is used synoptically in 1 Kgs 8:9, 19, 25; 15:14; 22:16; 2 Kgs 14:4; 15:35; 21:8.
10. Jehoshaphat (1 Kgs 22:43 // 2 Chr 20:32), Azariah/Uzziah (2 Kgs 15:4 // 2 Chr 26:4), Jotham (2 Kgs 15:34 // 2 Chr 27:2), and Amon (2 Kgs 21:20 // 2 Chr 33:22).

5. CULTIC MATTERS: THE SYNOPTIC TRADITION

Viewing the topic of "high places" from a synoptic standpoint helps make sense of the very different usage of במות in Kings and Chronicles. The authors of each book had reinforced quite differently a feature that was already significant in what they inherited. With the exception of 2 Chr 21:11 (on Jehoram), the Chronicler only added mention of במות to the reports of four kings where these shrines were already part of the (synoptic) source: to explain that two earlier good kings (Asa and Jehoshaphat) had made efforts to remove them, and to reinforce the criticism of two later bad kings (Ahaz and Manasseh) who had cultivated them. The author of Kings, by contrast, made no changes to the "high places" element he inherited in the reports of these same four kings. One set of his additions made a simple deduction explicit: if במות were still available for bad king Ahaz to frequent (2 Kgs 16:4), then they could not have been removed by any of the four good kings who preceded him (2 Kgs 12:4; 14:4; 15:4, 35). He also employed "high places" within his rhetorical repertoire for blackening the reputations of still earlier kings Rehoboam (1 Kgs 14:23) and Solomon (1 Kgs 3:3; 11:7); and the result was that a large number of Jerusalem's rulers became tarred in Kings with this same במות brush.

From a synoptic perspective, it is easy to trace the development of the במות theme from small shared beginnings to what we read in either Kings or Chronicles. It is much harder to trace a plausible line of development directly from Kings to Chronicles. The account just offered is very different from any explanation of the growth of this prominent theme in the book of Kings that is based only on that book itself. To take just one example from several attempts: Iain Provan opted quite reasonably—but probably mistakenly—for the priority of the series of almost identical notes that started in 1 Kgs 3:3 and were concentrated between 1 Kgs 15 and 2 Kgs 15; and he argued that Hezekiah's reform (2 Kgs 18:4) offered a more original conclusion to that series than Josiah's (2 Kgs 23:8).[11] This initial decision led him to assign a reworked 2 Kgs 16:4 to a later stratum of the book, associated with 1 Kgs 14:22-24 and 2 Kgs 17:7-17. From our synoptic perspective, the "linguistic affinities" he mentions between the latter pair of passages and 2 Kgs 16:4 are to be explained instead as

---

11. *Hezekiah and the Books of Kings: A Contribution to the Debate about the Composition of the Deuteronomistic History*, BZAW 172 (Berlin: de Gruyter, 1988), 82–85.

5.3. "The Place" (המקום)

Reading "place" synoptically in Samuel–Kings and Chronicles also brings a clearer view. In principle, at least three groups of texts should be inspected separately; and in this case we must add a fourth.

5.3.1. Strictly Synoptic

5.3.1.1. The David Story

In the David story, we find it certainly three times: בעל־פרצים (Baal-perazim, 2 Sam 5:20 // 1 Chr 13:11) and פרץ־עזה (Perez-uzzah, 2 Sam 6:8 // 1 Chr 14:11) are so named because Yahweh had burst out destructively (פרץ) at both: each is accordingly a "place" (מקום) associated with divine activity. A third "place" that features in the synoptic record of David (in nearby 2 Sam 7:10 // 1 Chr 17:9) relates to activity of Yahweh that is rather more benign: he will appoint a "place" for his people Israel and plant them to "dwell" (שכן) there. And a possible fourth example will be discussed separately (5.3.3).

5.3.1.2. The Jerusalem Temple

The Jerusalem temple is intimately associated synoptically with "place." When the building was completed, the priests brought the divine ark "to its place" (אל־מקומו) in the innermost sanctum where the cherubim spread their wings over "the place of the ark" (מקום הארון).[12] It then has an important role in Solomon's prayer at the dedication of the temple. "Place" occurs four times in the opening portion,[13] as Solomon asks for Yahweh's full attention to whatever his servant prays "toward this house, toward the place of which you said, 'My name shall be there'" (אל־הבית

---

12. 1 Kgs 8:6, 7 // 2 Chr 5:7, 8.
13. 8:29 // 6:20 2x; 8:30 // 6:21 2x. The first three refer to the inner sanctum *within* the house.

5. CULTIC MATTERS: THE SYNOPTIC TRADITION

הזה אל־המקום אשר אמרת יהיה שמי שם). It then reappears in the third of the specific petitions, and in the same sense.[14]

5.3.1.3. The Royal Throne

The royal throne is the context for one further user of "place" in the Solomon story. The description of this seat includes "and arm[rest]s on this side and that of the sitting place" (וידות מזה ומזה אל־מקום השבת).[15]

5.3.1.4. Words of Huldah

In the words of Huldah, "place" makes its next and only reappearance within synoptic material. Answering Josiah's servants (twice each in both of her responses[16]), she reports Yahweh's determination to bring disaster אל־המקום הזה ועל־ישביו ("to this place and upon its [rulers? inhabitants?]"). The final ישביו is ambiguous, as the verb ישב can mean both "sit" (on the throne as ruler) or "inhabit"; and each option enjoys support from one previous synoptic passage. מקום השבת ("the place of sitting [enthroned]")[17] points in the first direction, and a place for Yahweh's people to be planted and dwell[18] points in the other. However, before pressing the second option, we need to note that the divine promise through Nathan to David uses the unambiguous שכן ("dwell") rather than the ambiguous ישב. In short, Huldah could be talking about the temple/palace complex in Jerusalem and the kings who preside there ("to this place and on its rulers"), or about the city or the land and those who live there ("to this place and on its inhabitants").

5.3.1.5. Summary

To sum up: where the wording in Samuel–Kings and Chronicles is identical (or nearly so)—in synoptic portions in the strictest sense—"place" is only used of a location where something of the Deity has been invested,

---

14. 1 Kgs 8:35 // 2 Chr 6:26.
15. 1 Kgs 10:19 // 2 Chr 9:18.
16. 2 Kgs 22:16, 17, 19, 20 // 2 Chr 34:24, 25, 27, 28.
17. 1 Kgs 10:19 // 2 Chr 9:18.
18. 2 Sam 7:10 // 1 Chr 17:9.

whether that be destructive force or more benign choice and commitment. It is never just an ordinary place, but always a special one.

5.3.2. Broadly Synoptic

There are a few additional cases within synoptic contexts. In all but one of these, "place" has a sacred dimension.

5.3.2.1. David

In 1 Chr 21:22, 25 David acquires not simply "the threshing floor" for his altar to Yahweh as in 2 Sam 24:21, 25, but *"the place* of the threshing floor" (מקום הגרן). And in a psalm included in the celebrations of the arrival of the ark (1 Chr 16:27), "place" signifies the temple in Jerusalem.

5.3.2.2. Solomon

Before his prayer, Solomon recalls how Yahweh had fulfilled his promise (1 Kgs 8:20 // 2 Chr 6:10): he had succeeded his father and had built a house for the name of Yahweh, the God of Israel. The following verse in Kings includes two pluses vis-à-vis Chronicles: "And I have set there *a place for* the ark, in which is the covenant of Yahweh that he made with the people of Israel/*our fathers when he brought them out of the land of Egypt.*" Similarly, but in a different position, Chronicles has a large plus early in the report of the king's second (Jerusalem) vision (2 Chr 7:12b–15): it includes "place" at start and finish. The promise at the end, of open eyes and attentive ears to what is prayed in this place (7:15), both assents to Solomon's repeated plea (6:20, 40[19]) and again sets "place" in close association with the synoptic "house," which Yahweh has chosen and consecrated (7:16 // 1 Kgs 9:3).

But the beginning of this large plus, "And I have chosen this place for myself for a house of sacrifice" (ובחרתי במקום הזה לי לבית זבח), goes two steps further: (1) the explicit combination of "place" and "choose" (2 Chr 7:12b) is a stock link in Deuteronomy, but is never found in Samuel–Kings; and (2) nowhere else in the Hebrew Bible is the combination בית זבח ("a house of sacrifice") used.[20] Earlier (2 Chr 3:1), Chronicles notes in

---

19. At the end of Solomon's long prayer, 2 Chr 6:40 repeats the wording of synoptic 6:20 (// 1 Kgs 8:29).

20. Chronicles' characterization of the temple as a "house of sacrifice" is reminis-

a similar vein that the house of Yahweh that Solomon began to build was at the "place" David had designated at the threshing floor. In the one exceptional case (1 Kgs 5:23), Hiram promises to send timber "as far as the place about which you will send to me" (עד־המקום אשר־תשלח אלי); however, in 2 Chr 2:15 he simply specifies Jaffa (יפו).

5.3.2.3. Hezekiah

The Assyrian envoy asks Hezekiah (2 Kgs 18:25): "Is it without Yahweh that I have come up against this place to destroy it?" He anticipates the disaster of which Huldah would speak (5.3.1.4); and his words are similarly ambiguous.

5.3.2.4. Summary

"Place" (מקום) and "house" (בית) are already intimately associated in a strictly synoptic text (where the wording of Samuel–Kings and Chronicles are identical or nearly so); and these key terms are repeated together in broadly synoptic portions of the Solomon story: once in 1 Kgs 8:20–21, and twice in 2 Chr 7:12–16. Second Chronicles 7:12b is the only occasion in the narrative books in the Hebrew Bible where מקום ("place") is the object of the verb בחר ("choose"), while that very combination is a stock theme of Deuteronomy (22x). In this respect, Chronicles appears more Deuteronomic than Kings.[21]

5.3.3. Ambiguously Synoptic?

The end of the story of David bringing the ark into Jerusalem deserves closer attention. If we compare 2 Sam 6:17 (MT), "they brought in the ark of Yahweh and set it *in its place* inside the tent that David had pitched for it," only with the otherwise identical 1 Chr 16:1 (MT), we find that Chronicles lacks the italicized phrase.[22] The description of David's action in Samuel *explicitly* anticipates the movement of the ark into the most holy locus in

---

cent of Isa 56:7, where sacrifice accepted on the altar is part of being "a house of prayer for all nations."

21. Kalimi usefully notes how often Chronicles adjusts the synoptic text toward the relevant portion of Deuteronomy (*Geschichtsschreibung*, 113–27).

22. Rezetko usefully surveys the textual variations in *Source and Revision*, 183–86.

the temple under Solomon (5.3.2.2); but this is not the case in 1 Chr 16:1. The preliminary conclusion must be that במקמו ("in its place") is an exegetical expansion in Samuel. However, Chronicles' substantial additional chapter (1 Chr 15) is largely taken up with appropriate preparations by David for receiving the ark in Jerusalem in "the place" prepared (explicitly so in 15:1, 3, 12). I have to pose a cautionary question. Does the repeated mention of "the place" in 1 Chr 15 count as evidence that Chronicles had found "in its place" in its "synoptic" source (2 Sam 6:17 // 1 Chr 16:1)? Or should we reckon both the modest plus "in its place" (2 Sam 6:17) and the more largely described preparation of "the place" in 1 Chr 15 as separate but parallel extensions of (strictly[23]) synoptic 1 Chr 16:1?

5.3.4. Nonsynoptic

More than half (24x) of the nonsynoptic instances of "place" occur in 1 Sam 1–30, and hence before the synoptic material begins. A few of these do have cultic associations: where Eli or Samuel is located at Shiloh (3:2, 9), the statue of Dagon at Ashdod (5:3, 11), or where the ark should return (6:2). But the remainder[24] bear a wide range of senses. Bethel of course has (problematic) sacral associations (1 Kgs 13:8, 16, 22). But the other instances in 2 Samuel–2 Kings (18x)[25] are as varied as those in 1 Samuel. The few instances in nonsynoptic Chronicles[26] are also varied.

5.4. Sacred Objects and Actions

5.4.1. Asa

Most of the report in 1 Kgs 15:9–24 about good king Asa is repeated almost verbatim within the much longer 2 Chr 14–16. He stripped his mother of her role as "first lady" because of a מפלצת she had made for Asherah—the offending idol was cut up and burned by the Kidron. He

---

23. Strictly synoptic, because the wording actually shared in Samuel and Chronicles does not include במקמו ("in its place").

24. 1 Sam 2:20; 7:16; 9:22; 12:8; 14:46; 20:19, 25, 27, 37; 21:3; 23:22, 28; 26:5 (2x), 13, 25; 27:5; 29:4; 30:31.

25. 2 Sam 2:16, 23; 11:16; 15:19, 21; 17:9, 12; 19:40; 1 Kgs 5:8; 20:24; 21:19; 2 Kgs 5:11; 6:1, 2, 6, 8, 9, 10.

26. 2 Chr 20:26; 24:11; 25:10 (2x).

also brought to Yahweh's house gold, silver, and utensils, dedicated by his father and himself.²⁷ But the objects of his actions reported in 1 Kgs 15:12 are not repeated in Chronicles. Neither קדשים (normally understood to have been cult prostitutes) nor גלולים (some sort of idols) are ever mentioned in Chronicles. However, Chronicles seems to have been fully aware of 1 Kgs 15:12 and to have rewritten it very substantially in 2 Chr 14:2–15:15. Both verbs denoting removal are repeated: ויעבר (1 Kgs 15:12a) in 2 Chr 15:8, and ויסר (1 Kgs 15:12b) in 2 Chr 14:2, 4.²⁸ In 2 Chr 15:8 the scandalous קדשים are replaced by שקוצים ("abominations"). By contrast, 2 Chr 14:2–4 turns the removal of גלולים into a clichéd report of thoroughgoing cultic reform. גלולים reappear once in a synoptic context (2 Kgs 21:21, where 2 Chr 33:22 has הפסילים).²⁹

5.4.2. Joash

The future boy-king Joash spent his earliest years hidden in the temple, after being saved from Athaliah's purge: he was "in Yahweh's house" while she reigned "over the land" (2 Kgs 11:1–3). Her overthrow was coordinated by the priest of the temple; and, after she was put to death, the people sacked "the house of Baal": ויבאו כל־העם בית הבעל ויתצהו את־מזבחתיו ואת־צלמיו שברו ואת־מתן כהן הבעל הרגו לפני המזבחות—"and all the people came to the house of Baal and they pulled it down: its altars and its images they shattered, and Mattan the priest of Baal they slew in face of the altars" (11:18). Baal has not been mentioned synoptically since the David story. It is clearly implied that Baal worship had been encouraged by Athaliah, who was daughter or niece to Ahab.

5.4.3. Ahaz

Bad king Ahaz, in addition to his enthusiastic sacrifice at במות, "made even his son pass through fire" (וגם את־בנו העביר באש, 2 Kgs 16:3). Although what this involved is much debated, the context is cultic.

---

27. 1 Kgs 15:13, 15 // 2 Chr 15:16, 18.

28. Apart from the neighboring 1 Kgs 15:13 // 2 Chr 15:16, there is only one further synoptic use of סור hiphil: 2 Kgs 18:22 // 2 Chr 32:12.

29. They reappear also several times in nonsynoptic Kings (1 Kgs 21:26; 2 Kgs 17:12; 21:11; 23:24). They are found also in Lev 26:30; Deut 29:16; Jer 50:2; and most often in Ezekiel (39x), but never in Chronicles.

5.4.4. Hezekiah

The reports about good king Hezekiah in Kings and Chronicles differ more than the accounts of any successor of David and Solomon in Jerusalem, and these will be assessed separately below (ch. 10).

5.4.5. Manasseh

The critique of bad king Manasseh is the most extensive of all. The start (2 Kgs 21:1-2 // 2 Chr 33:1-2) and finish (2 Kgs 21:17-18 // 2 Chr 33:18-20) of the reports of Hezekiah's son are largely formulaic and need not concern us here.

Topic	Nonsynoptic Kings	Synoptic Kings	Synoptic Chronicles	Nonsynoptic Chronicles
Shared critique		21:3-9	33:3-9	
Further critique	21:10-16			
Punishment and penitence				33:10-17

Verses 3-9 in each chapter are also transcribed from the shared text. Small and not very significant differences over the wording of verses 3a and 4 can be readily detected in the synoptic presentation below. But the larger divergences are in verse 3b: whether Baal and Asherah should be singular (Kings) or plural (Chronicles), and whether Kings has added or Chronicles deleted the cross-reference to Ahab. If the shorter text is preferred as more original, we should read singular Baal and Asherah with Kings, but not the comparison with Ahab.

2 Kgs 21:3-5	2 Chr 33:3-5
3a He rebuilt the במות that his father Hezekiah had *destroyed* [אבד],	3a He rebuilt the במות that his father Hezekiah had *torn down* [נתץ],
3b and he raised altars to *Baal* and made *an Asherah, as Ahab king of Israel had done,*	3b and he raised altars to *the Baals* and made *Asherahs*

and prostrated himself to all the host of heaven and served them.	and prostrated himself to all the host of heaven and served them.
4 And he built altars in the house of Yahweh, of which Yahweh had said, "In Jerusalem shall *I set* my name."	4 And he built altars in the house of Yahweh, of which Yahweh had said, "In Jerusalem shall my name *be forever.*"
5 And he built altars to all the host of heaven in the two courts of the house of Yahweh.	5 And he built altars to all the host of heaven in the two courts of the house of Yahweh.

This first set of complaints about Manasseh brings together his cultic promotion of Baal, Asherah, and the host of heaven. Each of these three has appeared only once before in the synoptic narrative; and none of them has been linked earlier with either of the others. Indeed, when previously mentioned in the Micaiah story (1 Kgs 22:19), the host of heaven was part of Yahweh's retinue. Then, in the case of Asa and his mother, the problem may not have been Asherah herself but the making of a מפלצת; in addition, there is extrabiblical evidence in support of the view that Asherah had been Yahweh's consort.[30] Here, in the critique of Manasseh, not only are the three brought together for the first time, but two of them are also problematized—only Baal had certainly been a problem before, in the synoptic narrative of the restoration of Joash (2 Kgs 11).[31] Now, at the first mention of Asherah within the critique of Manasseh (21:3), she is rendered guilty by association with Baal: as with the host of heaven, the problem may have been veneration of Yahweh's close associates instead of simply Yahweh himself.[32] Altars in the plural (21:4–5) and the image of Asherah (21:7) are here held to infringe the rights of Yahweh, whose name had been set in the temple (21:4, 7). Read in synoptic context, Manasseh

---

30. Most notably the inscription at Kuntillet ʿAjrud, not far from Kadesh-barnea, that identifies a male and female pair as "Yahweh and his Asherah."

31. Earlier in the royal story even Baal had been an acceptable part of place names (2 Sam 5:20) and personal names associated with David (his son's name Baal-iada [NRSV Beeliada] in 1 Chr 14:7 may be more original than El-iada in synoptic 2 Sam 5:16).

32. Steve A. Wiggins notes (*A Reassessment of Asherah: With Further Considerations of the Goddess*, Gorgias Ugaritic Studies 2 [Piscataway, NJ: Gorgias, 2007], 219–20) that, wherever she is mentioned across the ancient Near East, "her relationship to the chief deity appears to be a constant character trait."

was ignoring the divine warning to Solomon in his second vision (1 Kgs 9:6, 9) not to *prostrate oneself* to "other gods." The link is achieved by the verb השתחוה, which is very uncommon in synoptic texts. However Asherah and the heavenly host (even if not Baal) may have been related to Yahweh in narratives about earlier times, Manasseh's prostration to them is presented here as the veneration of *other* gods.

5.4.6. Amon

Amon continued Manasseh's wicked ways: he served the גלולים ("idols"), last mentioned synoptically when Asa removed them.[33]

5.4.7. Josiah

The cultic reform of good king Josiah, while it is the key element in the narrative in the eyes of modern scholars since de Wette, is not (straightforwardly, at least) a part of the text that Kings and Chronicles share. The synoptic text amounts to more than half of the Kings report and about half of that in Chronicles. But the similarities go still further.

Topic	Kings +	Kings Book of Two Houses	Chronicles Book of Two Houses	Chronicles +
standard introduction		22:1–2	34:1–2	
initial reforms				34:3–7
temple repairs		22:3–7	34:8–12a	
Levitical responsibility				34:12b–13
law book discovered		22:8–10	34:15–18	34:14
Josiah's response		22:11–23:3a	34:19–31	
people's response		23:3b	34:32*	
cultic reforms	23:4–20			34:33

---

33. Here synoptic 2 Chr 33:22 describes them as פסילים ("images").

5. CULTIC MATTERS: THE SYNOPTIC TRADITION

Passover		23:21a, 22–23	35:1a, 18–19	35:1b–17
perfect, *but* Manasseh …	23:24–27			
standard ending		23:28, 30b	35:26–27	
death at Megiddo		23:29–30a	35:20, 24	35:21–23, 25

Two verses in Chronicles separate synoptic Josiah's covenant making from his reform of Passover. Second Chronicles 34:32 is an expansive rewriting of (the presumably original) ויעמד כל־העם בברית ("and all the people *stood* in the *covenant*") in 2 Kgs 23:3b. In Kings, the verb ויעמד is read as *qal* ("stood"). The king had stood when making the covenant (2 Kgs 23:3a // 2 Chr 34:31), and the people's action corresponded exactly: he led and they followed. In Chronicles, the verb is read as causative *hiphil* with the king as subject; and "everyone found in Jerusalem and Benjamin" (replacing "all the people") become the object rather than the subject of ויעמד: "and he *caused* everyone found in Jerusalem and Benjamin *to stand*, and they acted according to the divine *covenant*" (2 Chr 34:32). The following statement ("He removed all the abominations [התועבות] from all the lands belonging to the sons of Israel," v. 33) corresponds to the lengthy report in 2 Kings (23:4–20) that immediately follows synoptic 23:3b. If 2 Chr 34:32 has expanded 2 Kgs 23:3b, the relationship between 2 Chr 34:33 and 2 Kgs 23:4–20 is quite the other way round. Its opening verb ("remove") and principal object ("abomination") are both used in the longer text: "all the houses of the במות he removed" (2 Kgs 23:19), and "Milcom the abomination of the sons of Ammon" (23:13). However, it is far from clear in which direction any influence had been working.

Much of the nonsynoptic material is quite specific to either Kings or Chronicles. Second Kings 23:24–27 insists, with no counterpart in Chronicles, that Josiah's positive achievements were beyond compare—and yet even they could not undo the entail of what Manasseh had done. Second Chronicles 34:12a shares with 2 Kgs 22:7b the note that those working on the restoration of the temple operated fairly; but then the Chronicler adds (34:12b–13) that Levites had provided oversight. And the brief synoptic report on Josiah's Passover (2 Kgs 23:21–23) is very substantially extended in 2 Chr 35:1b–17. Equally, other cultic reforms are handled much more fully in Kings.

Each book as it stands presents this king as a reformer who took things back to where they were at an ideal beginning. For the Chronicler, Josiah's reforming effort was concentrated on Passover (2 Chr 35:1–19). The synoptic text had already noted that no previous king had managed this festival properly; and Josiah took the matter in hand with the aid of the Levites. On Passover the author of Kings more or less simply repeats what his source had said (2 Kgs 23:21–23). The principal attention of his extended portrait of Josiah was directed toward a whole plethora of other cultic problems (2 Kgs 23:4–20). However, the synoptic text (strictly defined) presents this exemplary king as a promoter of temple repairs who responded appropriately to a book found during these repairs and carried out a reformed celebration of Passover.

The other reforming actions of Josiah are very differently reported in Kings and Chronicles, and will be discussed later (see 9.10). However, the manner in which his career is dated is a feature of the Passover report and should be reviewed immediately. The unusual dating formula used synoptically in 2 Kgs 23:23 // 2 Chr 35:19—בשמנה עשרה שנה למלך/למלכות יאשיהו ("In year 18 of the king[dom of] Josiah [… this Passover was 'done' in Jerusalem]") is found in Chronicles only at this one synoptic point. "In year x of …" (שנה ל- x-ב) is most prominent within Ezek 26–33 (7x)[34] and is also used to introduce two major sections of the book of Ezekiel (1:1; 40:1). In the book of Jeremiah too it is used at start (1:2) and finish (52:31), and also in 39:2 (where it notes the beginning of the end of Jerusalem).

While unique synoptically to the Passover report, it does mark a few key stages in the narrative of the book of Kings:

- 1 Kgs 6:1, "In year 480 of the exodus from Egypt … Solomon built the temple."
- 2 Kgs 18:13, "In year 14 of King Hezekiah … King Sennacherib came up."
- 2 Kgs 22:3, "in year 18 of King Josiah … the king sent to the temple."
- 2 Kgs 25:27 // Jer 52:31, "in year 37 of the exile of Jehoiachin king of Judah … Evil-merodach … raised the head of Jehoiachin."

---

34. Ezek 26:1; 29:17; 30:20; 31:1; 32:1, 17; 33:21.

5. CULTIC MATTERS: THE SYNOPTIC TRADITION

The first and fourth of these examples introduce substantial Kings pluses;[35] the second will be reviewed more fully later (10.4.1). The third underlines that the renewal of the temple by Josiah belonged to the same year as the Passover he celebrated without parallel since Israel's early days in its land; and it seems likely that this was an original feature of the Josiah report and was altered by the Chronicler.[36] It seems likely that 2 Kgs 22:3, as well as 23:23, represents the original text in stressing that temple renewal, finding the book, and Passover belonged within a single year, his eighteenth. If so, it may be more likely that the Chronicler altered the date formula in 2 Chr 34:8 when adding new material in 34:3–7.

---

35. Furthermore, I noted above that 2 Kgs 25:29–30 pairs significant markers (3 and 7) in כל־ימי חייו.

36. Although Chronicles also sets the start of Josiah's temple repairs in the same eighteenth year, he states the date in a different way: instead of בשמנה עשרה שנה למלך יאשיהו, we find ובשנת שמנה עשרה למלכו ("and in the year of eighteen of his reigning"). The final element resumes part of the formula he uses to introduce Josiah's initial reforms (2 Chr 34:3): ובשמנה שנים למלכו והוא עודנו נער ("and in eight years *of his reigning*, he being still a lad")—but the opening ובשמנה שנים appears to be a unique formulation within the HB. As for למלכו, it is never used synoptically, and is apparently always late: 2 Kgs 24:12 (+); 25:1 (= Jer 52:4); Jer 1:2; 51:59; 52:4; Esth 1:3; Dan 9:2; 2 Chr 16:13 (+); 17:7 (+); 29:3 (+); 34:3, 8.

6
Toward the Synoptic Narrative

6.1. The Problem

In the previous chapters I have urged recognizing a novel standpoint from which to view the development of the book of Kings, and recommended seeing its literary history in fresh perspective. It is time now to flesh out these proposals. The principal "source"—the principal *immediate* source—from which the book of (Samuel and) Kings was written was neither archival nor legendary, but was an already integrated history of Jerusalem throughout the time of David's house. This earlier history had doubtless had its own prehistory, but I make no attempt to probe that here. That would be the business of another study. But of course it is sensible to reapply to the proposed synoptic source the remark by Baruch Halpern and André Lemaire about the finished book of Kings: "To sentient scholars ... it is clear that the ... authors ... enjoyed access to sources or to previous editions whose authors had already applied themselves to and therefore prepared information from sources."[1]

Admittedly we do not possess the synoptic source history in its pristine form, but only as differently preserved in Kings and Chronicles: a word or phrase changed here, a paragraph recast there, and the trace of the original almost lost in substantial rewriting as in the case of Hezekiah, or even of David's census.[2] Attempting a reconstruction can only be provisional and incomplete, as the attempt at the end of this volume amply

---

1. "The Composition of Kings," in *The Books of Kings: Sources, Composition, Historiography and Reception*, ed. Baruch Halpern and André Lemaire, VTSup 129 (Leiden: Brill, 2010), 136–37.

2. I showed in "David's Census: Some Textual and Literary Links," in *Textual Criticism and Dead Sea Scrolls Studies in Honour of Julio Trebolle Barrera: Florilegium Complutense*, ed. Andrés Piquer Otero and Pablo A. Torijano Morales, JSJSup 158

demonstrates. Three preliminary questions about this partially obscured text suggest themselves immediately:

1. Distinctiveness: Is the shared material sufficiently different from its wider context(s)?
2. Coherence: Does any common element clearly not belong within the shared whole?
3. Meaning: What is this whole glimpsed text about?

6.2. Distinctiveness Sampled

Several key features of the earlier history have been discussed in previous chapters.

- Its chronological framework can be read off the successor books of Kings and Chronicles, almost to the last detail (3.1.1).
- It never uses יש; it uses אך, בכה, חי יהוה, נאם יהוה, and ניר, only once each, and הנה seldom (3.2 and 4.2); and unlike (Samuel and) Kings, none of its characters ever says "today" or "this day."
- Its account of God-king communication in Jerusalem can also be read almost unchanged in the successor books. But here there is one major exception: the Hezekiah story and the role within it of Isaiah the prophet (chs. 4 and 10).
- It talked about "life" very much more sparingly than the books of Samuel and Kings, and with consequent emphasis when it did so (ch. 2).
- It used the infinitive absolute similarly sparingly, while Samuel and Kings are large-scale users of this verb form (3.3).
- While its main concern was with the house of David and the cult in Jerusalem, it also mentioned nine of the successors of David and Solomon in northern Israel, and blamed the house of Ahab for malign influence on Jerusalem's kings (ch. 8).
- It depicts Ahaz as the first king since Solomon who actively resorted to a "high place," and suggests (though only through

---

(Leiden: Brill, 2012), 32–34, that, even after secondary growth in both 2 Sam 24 and 1 Chr 21 has been identified, the base text in each is different.

words uttered by an Assyrian envoy) that it was Hezekiah who ordained a unique role for the Jerusalem altar (5.3.2.3).

6.3. Meaning Suggested

A network of more than two dozen pairings allows us to evaluate comparisons and contrasts in the shared narrative. (The detailed references are provided in the table that follows this overview.) *Philistines* bring Saul's house to an end; but David defeats them and establishes a centuries-long dynasty, while they do not reappear in the story (except as a boundary point when describing Solomon's empire, 1 Kgs 5:1 // 2 Chr 9:26). *Israel's elders* have an explicit role only when David is anointed and when the ark is brought into Solomon's temple in Jerusalem. *Ramoth-gilead* is the goal of a joint venture of Judah and Israel under both Jehoshaphat and Azariah. Joash is *anointed* like David, each anointing marking a fresh start;[3] and each of these fresh dynastic starts is accompanied by making a *covenant* (ברית).[4] Only David and Solomon *ask* the Deity, and only they preside over movement of the *divine ark*. Assyrians resemble Philistines in *scorning* Israel and its God, and only in narratives relating to these enemies is *deliver* (הציל) used.[5] Only the Hittite Ornan/Araunah practices *prostration*, and only the Assyrian envoy describes Hezekiah's centralizing demand as "prostration" before Jerusalem's altar. Both appearances of *Yahweh's envoy* (מלאך יהוה) involve deliverance for Jerusalem. Only in connection with *good* Asa and Jehoshaphat are we told that the *high places* did not disappear. Ahaz's *vigorous sacrificing* (זבח piel) at "high places" polemically recalls Solomon first at Gibeon and then in Jerusalem. Only the bad behavior of Ahaz and Manasseh is compared with "the *abominations* of the nations that Yahweh drove out before the sons of Israel." The divine warning in Solomon's second vision about prostration before other

---

3. משח is found once more in a synoptic context, in most versions of the "king-ing" of Jehoahaz on the death of his father Josiah (2 Kgs 23:30 // 2 Chr 36:1) but crucially not in 2 Chr 36:1 (MT). Ralph Klein provides detail about the text-critical debate (*2 Chronicles*, 530).

4. David with the elders before Yahweh at Hebron (2 Sam 5:3 // 1 Chr 11:3) and Jehoiada with Joash and the people in Jerusalem (2 Kgs 11:17 // 2 Chr 23:16), as earlier with the guards (2 Kgs 11:4 // 2 Chr 23:1). Josiah is the only other king associated with such covenant making.

5. The synoptic theme of Philistine "scorn" is developed in the David and Goliath story (1 Sam 17:26, 36) with "deliver" nearby (17:35, 37).

gods is cited against Manasseh; and the divine warning about abandoning Yahweh is cited against the inhabitants of Jerusalem. After Solomon, only Azariah had dealings with the southern port of *Elat*. Josiah includes the *elders*, while Rehoboam had rejected their advice; and Josiah, like Jehoshaphat and the king of Israel, *inquires* of Yahweh through a prophet. Both Jehoram and Ahaziah of Judah follow in the way of the house of *Ahab*. Only Amaziah and Amon were *conspired* against by their "servants." Huldah describes *offerings* to other gods using a verb (קטר *piel*) previously associated only with wicked Ahaz. The *host of heaven* pay court to Yahweh in Micaiah's vision, but are themselves worshiped by Manasseh. Huldah alludes to Manasseh when she speaks of *vexing* Yahweh by means of what was handmade. Only Athaliah and Josiah *tear their clothes*, but with different motivation.[6]

Philistines	Saul: 1 Sam 31	David: 2 Sam 5, 8, 21
elders of Israel	David: 2 Sam 5:3	Solomon: 1 Kgs 8:1
משח ("anoint")	David: 2 Sam 5:3	Joash: 2 Kgs 11:12
שאל ("ask")	David: 2 Sam 5:19, 23	Solomon: 1 Kgs 3:4–15
divine ark	David: 2 Sam 6	Solomon: 1 Kgs 8
חרף ("scorn")	Philistines: 2 Sam 21:21	Assyrians: 2 Kgs 19 (4x)
יציל ("deliver")	Philistines: 2 Sam 23:12	Assyrians: 2 Kgs 18–20
מלאך יהוה ("Yahweh's envoy")	David: 2 Sam 24	Hezekiah: 2 Kgs 19
השתחוה (foreigner)	Araunah: 2 Sam 24	Rabshakeh: 2 Kgs 18
במה/גבעה	Solomon: 1 Kgs 3:4	Ahaz: 2 Kgs 16:4
שפט ("rule")	Solomon: 1 Kgs 3:9; 8:32	Jotham: 2 Kgs 15:5
זבח *piel*	Solomon: 1 Kgs 8:5	Ahaz: 2 Kgs 16:4
השתחוה (to other gods)	Solomon: 1 Kgs 9:6, 9	Manasseh: 2 Kgs 21:3
עזב	Solomon: 1 Kgs 9:9	Huldah: 2 Kgs 22:17
Elath port	Solomon: 1 Kgs 9:26	Azariah: 2 Kgs 14:22

---

6. Of course not all significant synoptic connections come in pairs; for example, "rejoicing" (שמח[ה]) accompanies David bringing the ark to Jerusalem (2 Sam 6:12), the dispatch of the people after Solomon's great assembly (1 Kgs 8:66), and the establishment of young Joash as king (2 Kgs 11:14, 20).

6. TOWARD THE SYNOPTIC NARRATIVE 93

elders	Rehoboam: 1 Kgs 12:6, 8, 13	Josiah: 2 Kgs 23:1
Ramoth-gilead	Jehoshaphat: 1 Kgs 22	Ahaziah: 2 Kgs 8:28
דרש ("seek")	Micaiah: 1 Kgs 22:5, 7, 8	Huldah: 2 Kgs 22:13, 18
like house of Ahab	Jehoram: 2 Kgs 8:18	Ahaziah: 2 Kgs 8:27
קטר piel	Ahaz: 2 Kgs 16:4	Huldah: 2 Kgs 22:17
הבמות לא סרו	Asa: 1 Kgs 15:17	Jehoshaphat: 1 Kgs 22:44
Asherah	Asa: 1 Kgs 15:13	Manasseh, Josiah?: 2 Kgs 21:3, 7
Baal	Athaliah/Joash: 2 Kgs 11:18	Manasseh: 2 Kgs 21:3
host of heaven	Micaiah: 1 Kgs 22:19	Manasseh: 2 Kgs 21:3
tear clothes	Athaliah: 2 Kgs 11:14	Josiah: 2 Kgs 22:19
conspiracy	Amaziah: 2 Kgs 14:19	Amon: 2 Kgs 21:23
כתעבות הגוים	Ahaz: 2 Kgs 16:3	Manasseh: 2 Kgs 21:2
הכעיס	Manasseh: 2 Kgs 21:6	Josiah: 2 Kgs 22:17
בכל מעשי ידיהם	Hezekiah: 2 Kgs 19:18	Josiah: 2 Kgs 22:17

Doubtless further relevant links will be added to the interlocking patterns within the synoptic narrative already noted. Significantly, some of these pairs also come in pairs, such as "anoint" (משח) and "covenant" (ברית), or "scorn" (חרף) and "deliver" (הציל). A very strange pairing not included above relates to the city of Lachish: Judah's second city is mentioned synoptically only in the reports of kings Amaziah (2 Kgs 14:19 // 2 Chr 25:27) and Hezekiah (2 Kgs 18:17 // 2 Chr 32:9). My discussion of Hezekiah's recovery (10.5.2) will note how the author of Kings was attentive to the synoptic pairing of that king with Amaziah and developed it further. An additional surprising factor is that both of these kings are reported as acceding to the throne aged 25 and as reigning for 29 years. Of the seventeen kings for whom an age at accession is given,[7] as many as four are said to be 25 years old when they become king (but neither of the others reigned for 29 years!); two are 22, and the other eleven all accede at different ages: 41, 35, 32, 23, 21, 20, 18, 16, 12, 8, and 7 years.

---

7. None is provided for Rehoboam's immediate successor, Abijam (1 Kgs 15:1–2).

As many as four out of seventeen sharing the same accession age already appears improbable without the added detail of two reigning for the same period. It was under Joash and Josiah, the two kings who were youngest at their accession (7 and 8 years), that the temple was repaired; and Manasseh (aged 12 on accession) was the most prolific cultic wrongdoer. There is another unusual pattern: the final four kings of Judah are reported as reigning for 3 months, 11 years, 3 months, and 11 years. Suffice it to say that it will be unwise to suppose that all of these dates are to be taken at face value.

The language of Josiah's inquiry of Huldah and her response resonate with many other strands of the synoptic narrative:

- עזב ("abandon") echoes Solomon's second vision.
- Josiah "seeking" (דרש) recalls the two kings' approach to Micaiah.
- Burning incense (קטר) recalls the complaint about Ahaz.
- Josiah tearing his clothes recalls Athaliah.
- Vexing Yahweh reminds us of Manasseh.
- "All the work of their hands" also recalls the idols made by Manasseh.

The accumulation of these echoes from Solomon to Manasseh signals that with Josiah we are approaching the culmination of the narrative.

6.4. Independence Plus?

We are not able to reconstruct every detail of the shared text. But we can inspect enough of its shape and its detail to realize that we are dealing with more than simple distinctiveness over against the two texts in which it is now embedded, and also more than basic coherence. The extensive pairings just sampled provide sufficient documentation of composition that is artistic. On the one side, we are provided with directions toward understanding; but on the other, much is left almost provocatively open.

Some verbal links are less precise, more allusive, and hence admittedly more in the eye of their readers. But still the words deserve to be followed. On only three occasions in the Book of Two Houses are kings of Judah and Israel reported in some sort of joint participation.[8] In each

---

8. Baasha's threat against Judah (1 Kgs 15:17–22 // 2 Chr 16:1–6) is not included:

6. TOWARD THE SYNOPTIC NARRATIVE

case, part of the action is described using the *hithpael* form of the verb, a form that suggests reflexivity or mutuality. (1) Before a first battle with the Aramaeans (1 Kgs 22:30 // 2 Chr 18:29), the king of Israel proposes to Jehoshaphat that he "disguise himself" (התחפש). (2) After a later defeat by Aram (2 Kgs 8:29 // 2 Chr 22:6), Joram of Israel goes to Jezreel in an unsuccessful attempt to "heal himself" (התרפא) and is visited there by Ahaziah of Judah, his relative and partner. (3) As Amaziah of Judah subsequently provokes trouble with Joash of Israel (2 Kgs 14:8, 11 // 2 Chr 25:17, 21), his challenge or invitation is that they should "see each other in the face." Here התראה פנים is not simply the third in a series of three reflexive *hithpael*s. Other characters in the Hebrew Bible practice disguise; but both "heal oneself" and "see each other in the face" are unique expressions.[9] And assonance helps the reader become aware that a significant link is in play: ראה ("see") shares two letters of רפא ("heal"); and the one it does not share (פ) becomes the first letter of פנים ("face"), its integral complement. Within the total context of meaningful pairings, the novel usage of each of these otherwise familiar verbs, accentuated by their similarity, assists the reader to notice the intended contrast in relationship, from a solicitous visit to the sick king to military challenge. The first of these co-operative ventures is reported in almost unchanged terms (1 Kgs 22:4–35 // 2 Chr 18:3–34); but the introductions in 1 Kgs 22:1–3 and 2 Chr 18:1–2 to the two otherwise identical versions are different. Whichever is more original, the reflexive *hithpael* התחתן ("intermarried with") in 2 Chr 18:1 offers a thoroughly appropriate start to this triad of episodes.

Even where Kings and Chronicles diverged in presenting the "same" text, their authors (or their underlying texts) continued to seek out the most appropriate pairing. A nice example comes in the report of Solomon using the labor of the other nations that had survived in the land (1 Kgs 9:21 // 2 Chr 8:8). Chronicles says that Israel "had not finished them off" (לא כלום), using a verb found elsewhere synoptically only in the Micaiah story, where Zedekiah's iron horns symbolized finishing off the Aramaeans (1 Kgs 22:11 // 2 Chr 18:10). Kings says, "had not been able to put them to the ban" (לא יכלו להחרימם), using a verb found elsewhere

---

Judah bought help from Aram and battle with Israel was not joined (the note in 1 Kgs 15:16 about perpetual war between Asa and Baasha is an addition to the Book of Two Houses).

9. התראה does occur once more in the HB (in Gen 42:1), but without פנים as complement.

synoptically only in the Hezekiah story: according to the Assyrian envoy, Assyria's kings used to put all enemies to the ban (2 Kgs 19:11 // 2 Chr 32:14). Given the qualities of their shared inheritance, no wonder that the authors of Samuel–Kings and Chronicles took up the challenge of closer examination and further development with great enthusiasm.

6.5. Implied Historical Outlook

David as king and commander of Israel is successor to Saul, and Solomon's building of the temple in Jerusalem is preceded by sacrifice and a vision at Gibeon. No background information is provided in synoptic material about Saul or Gibeon: Saul and Gibeon are simply the backdrop for David's reign and Jerusalem's temple. Like the Philistines, neither Saul nor Gibeon will be mentioned again. David, and Saul and Solomon too, are all kings of *Israel*, not of a united kingdom of Judah and Israel: there is no separate role for Judah in the synoptic account of the first kings. Equally, neither Hebron, where Israel comes to anoint David as king, nor Shechem, where his grandson goes to have his kingship recognized by Israel, will feature again in the shared texts.

There is no hint of an earlier Israel as a (twelve-)tribal structure. Of the tribal names familiar from biblical books, Asher, Gad, Issachar, Joseph, Manasseh, Reuben, Simeon, and Zebulun go unmentioned. Levites (1 Kgs 8:3-4 // 2 Chr 6:4-5) are not part of the shorter Septuagint version in 3 Kgdms 8, and will have entered Kings (MT) from Chronicles (see 12.2 below). Ephraim is the name of one of Jerusalem's city gates (2 Kgs 14:13 // 2 Chr 25:23). Naphtali is a "land" (1 Kgs 15:20) or "city" (in synoptic 2 Chr 16:4) among the conquests by Aram in northern Israel. The "Dan" that also features in this list of conquests is probably the city that has already defined Israel's northern extremity in David's instruction to count all his people (2 Sam 24:2 // 1 Chr 21:2). It is noted three times (1 Kgs 8:16; 14:21; 2 Kgs 21:7 // 2 Chr 6:6; 12:13; 33:7) that Jerusalem—not Judah!—was Yahweh's choice out of all the שבטי ישראל. But שבט in this context should be translated "staff" or "scepter" (as already in LXX) rather than "tribe": "out of all Israel's authorities."[10]

---

10. In the only other possibly relevant synoptic context, 2 Sam 7:7 has Yahweh strongly questioning whether he had ever addressed "one of the שבטי ['tribes/scepters'] of Israel" on the subject of shepherding his people, while in 1 Chr 17:6 it is "one of the שפטי ['judges'] of Israel."

Benjamin is the exception. But even Benjamin is only once given separate synoptic mention: immediately after the division of Israel, when Rehoboam failed to win the support of Israel at Shechem and sought to regain by force what he had lost by ill-advised words. Exactly how the original report was drafted is not easy to recover (it presents a neat microcosm of the bigger issue). We have four principal versions of how the first author described the forces Rehoboam assembled and the enemy he sought to tackle.[11]

1 Kgs 12:21	3 Kgdms 12:21	3 Kgdms 12:24x	2 Chr 11:1
את־כל־בית יהודה ואת־שבט בנימין	את־כל־איש יהודה ושבט בנימין	את־כל־איש יהודה ובנימין	את־בית יהודה ובנימין
the whole house of Judah and the שבט of Benjamin	every man of Judah and the שבט of Benjamin	every man of Judah and Benjamin	the house of Judah and Benjamin
להלחם עם־בית ישראל	להלחם עם־בית ישראל	להלחם עם־ירבעם	להלחם עם־ישראל
to fight with the house of Israel	to fight with the house of Israel	to fight with Jeroboam	to fight with Israel

We also have four versions of how Shemaiah addressed the southerners and named their northern opponents.

1 Kgs 12:23	3 Kgdms 12:23	3 Kgdms 12:24y	2 Chr 11:3
כל־בית יהודה ובנימין	כל־בית יהודה ובנימין	כל־בית יהודה ובנימין	כל־ישראל ביהודה ובנימין
the whole house of Judah and Benjamin	the whole house of Judah and Benjamin	the whole house of Judah and Benjamin	all Israel in Judah and Benjamin
עם־אחיהם בני ישראל	עם־אחיהם בני ישראל	עם־אחיהם בני ישראל	עם־אחיהם
with their brothers the sons of Israel	with their brothers the sons of Israel	with their brothers the sons of Israel	with their brothers

---

11. The retroversions into Hebrew of the two LXX versions in the two central columns below are straightforward and uncontroversial.

It can hardly come as a surprise that, at the very point in the narrative they inherited where the old unity of Israel (as depicted under Saul, David, and Solomon) was breaking down, later authors/editors were unable to agree over how to label Judah, Benjamin, and Israel. But more important than the detail of the descriptors is the explicit presence of Benjamin, alongside Judah and jointly with Judah over against Israel, at the very beginning of the separate existence of the two kingdoms. Whatever their other differences at the beginning of the report, two of the four witnesses simply pair "Judah and Benjamin," and the same is true of all four witnesses to Shemaiah's words. Hence it seems unwise to accept 1 Kgs 12:21 and 3 Kgdms 12:21 as original, when they distinguish between "all the house/men of Judah" and "the שבט ['tribe'?] of Benjamin."

Benjamin will never be mentioned synoptically again. Presumably its mention here says something about the social/political setting (after the fall of Jerusalem?) within which the synoptic narrative was composed.[12] And conceivably this unexplained and unique mention of Benjamin at the earliest relevant point in the narrative is also related to the similarly unexplained introductions of Saul (the Benjaminite) and Gibeon (a sanctuary within Benjamin).

Philistines, Moab, Ammon, Edom, and several Aramaean states became subject to David (2 Sam 5, 8, 23). Philistines and Moab are never mentioned again synoptically, and Ammon only as the home of Rehoboam's wife; but both אדם (Edom) and similar-looking ארם (Aram) reappear several times and are sometimes confused.[13] The king of Tyre assists both David and Solomon with their building operations, but neither Tyre nor Sidon appears again. There is no suggestion in any shared narrative that these surrounding nations posed any religious threat to Judah and Jerusalem. Rehoboam's wife was from Ammon, but she is not blamed for his failings. Asa's mother loses her formal role as queen mother over devotion to Asherah, but there is no suggestion that she is foreign. Kings of Israel, not other neighbors, are blamed synoptically for religious lapses in Jerusalem and Judah. Intermarriage with the house of Ahab had led to

---

12. It goes without saying that dating the earliest draft of the history is closely related to deciding where that draft ended. Halpern and Lemaire note some overlap between my earlier work and Halpern's preference for a much earlier (Hezekian) date ("Composition of Kings," 144).

13. Edom in 2 Kgs 8, 14, 16; and Aram in 1 Kgs 10:29; 15:18; 22; 2 Kgs 8:28, 29; 16.

the building of a house for Baal in Jerusalem and the crisis of Athaliah's usurpation of power.[14]

The demands of the more distant Assyrians were another matter. Ahaz is the first king of Judah whose religious policies are described in any detail: he is blamed in general for following in the path of Israel's kings and indulging in reprehensible practices of former inhabitants, but in particular for the religious implications of accepting Assyrian help against Israel. And this greater detail about Ahaz is replicated in the reports of Hezekiah, Manasseh, and Josiah. Whether and how the older shared narrative reported the fall of Samaria to the Assyrians is unclear. The fall and deportation is reported (2 Kgs 18:9–12) after the extended introduction to Hezekiah (18:1–8); but the Chronicler simply notes Hezekiah's invitation to "the remnant of you who have escaped from the hand of the king of Assyria" to come to Jerusalem for Passover (2 Chr 30:5–6).

It seems clear that the author of the older synoptic material had been most interested in—or had had most information about—these four kings closer to his own time. However, in each case, the differences between Kings and Chronicles are too great to permit detailed reconstruction of the underlying shared text. While Kings adds materially to the synoptic critique of Manasseh, Chronicles reports that he turned to Yahweh when he came under pressure. By contrast, when Ahaz came under pressure, he did worse and worse (2 Chr 28:22). I detailed above (5.2) the very different handling of the במות in Kings and Chronicles.

6.6. Implied Evaluation

The report of almost every king in Jerusalem after Solomon includes an introductory overall judgment: he did what was either straight (ישר) or bad (רע) in Yahweh's eyes—or sometimes straight but with a qualification.[15] However, much of what underlies or fleshes out these judgments

---

14. The impending trouble is signaled in the use of התחתן at the start of the Micaiah story in Chronicles (2 Chr 18:1). This verb is not used at the opening of synoptic 1 Kgs 22—typically Kings sets the start of the intermarriage problem earlier, at the beginning of the Solomon story, in connection with his marriage with (the house of) Pharaoh (1 Kgs 3:1).

15. Abijam/h is the exception. Both his own name and his mother's name are recorded differently in 1 Kgs 15:1–2 from 2 Chr 13:1–2. Puzzlingly both 1 Kgs 15:2b and 15:10b report Maacah daughter of Abishalom as mother to Abijam and Asa "his

is indicated in the comparisons and contrasts sampled above (at 6.4). The operative norms are not—or at least not explicitly—imposed from outside the narrative. Instead, it is by comparing some kings and contrasting others that a picture is gradually built up of what constitutes behavior acceptable or unacceptable to Yahweh.[16] Biblical scholars almost routinely label these introductory judgments "Deuteronomistic"; but our discussion makes this long-standing habit doubly problematic. (1) It is the book of Kings—if not the book as we know it, then at least what can be recognized as an earlier version of the familiar book—that is held to be the culmination of the history compiled by the so-called Deuteronomists. However, the almost-standard introductions to each Jerusalem reign were already integral to the synoptic source material: they existed prior to the familiar synchronous history of Israel plus Judah that constitutes the book of Kings. The author of Kings (whether he was a "Deuteronomist" or not) may have reused them in his introductions to the kings of Israel, but they were not created by him. (2) It is far from clear that the judgments invited by the narratives shared by Kings and Chronicles had been drawn from a preexisting normative text such as Deuteronomy.[17]

6.7. Fresh Questions

The pattern of relationships noted at 6.4 almost invites a series of interesting historical questions. Three can serve as illustrations:

- Why are Philistines depicted as finished off by David, never to be mentioned again, when we know that they continued to play an important role on the Mediterranean coast for many centuries?

---

son." And the following reports diverge widely: 1 Kgs 15:3–5 is brief and negative, while 2 Chr 13:3–21 is longer and positive. There is nothing in the latter to suggest that the Chronicler was aware of anything like 1 Kgs 15:3–5, which in any case appears to be a patchwork of quotations: v. 3a from Ezek 18:14; v. 3b from 1 Kgs 15:14 // 2 Chr 15:17; v. 4a from 2 Kgs 8:19 // 21:7—and v. 5 refers to the story of David and Bathsheba, which itself was developed from the synoptic David story (see 7.2).

16. The elaboration of norms in the synoptic narrative is not unlike the argument of the opening chapters of Amos, but on a grand scale.

17. Outside Kings and Chronicles, הישר ("the straight") is the object of עשה ("do") only in Exod 15:26; Deut 6:18; 12:8, 25, 28; 13:18; 21:9; Judg 17:6; 21:25; Jer 34:15.

6. TOWARD THE SYNOPTIC NARRATIVE

- Only David and Joash are reported as having been anointed; and their reigns did mark fresh starts after the death of Saul or the overthrow of Athaliah. But was it only in such abnormal circumstances that a new king in Jerusalem would be anointed?
- Each of the few mentions of prostration (השתחוה) has an alien element: it is practiced by an alien (Araunah/Ornan), spoken of by an alien (the Assyrian envoy), and Israel is warned against practicing it in worship of alien deities.[18] Are we to suppose that, in the worldview of this narrative, prostration was not (yet) practiced in honor of Israel's God or king?[19]

And the pattern, clearly demonstrable in Kings, of projecting religious critique back to earlier situations, makes one ponder in turn the original historical locus of the critique attached to synoptic Ahaz and Manasseh.

---

18. If 2 Kgs 21:21 does represent the older shared tradition (see 12.3.20), then Amon is described as prostrating himself before "idols" (גלולים).

19. The shared text that describes the dedication of Yahweh's "palace" portrays Solomon standing as he blesses his standing people, and standing before the altar as he prays (1 Kgs 8:14, 22 // 2 Chr 6:3, 12). Only nonsynoptic portions of Samuel–Kings and Chronicles describe kneeling or prostrating oneself before Yahweh. Ezekiel 8:16 depicts renegade worshipers, with their backs to the altar, prostrating themselves eastward to the sun.

7
SAMUEL REVISITED

7.1. ACHISH

Saul *insists* (end of 1 Sam 26), using the first of a series of cognate infinitives absolute (see 3.3), that David will enjoy success as king (גם עשה תעשה וגם יכל תוכל); and David, in deep distrust of Saul, responds immediately (start of 1 Sam 27) that escape to Philistine territory is *imperative* for him (המלט אמלט). David's behavior there leads Achish to deduce that Israel must be *utterly* disgusted (הבאש הבאיש) by David (end of 1 Sam 27); and Achish goes on to state (start of 1 Sam 28) that David must be left *in no doubt* (ידע תדע) of his welcome among Philistine forces. At the end of this series, the correspondence of the final pair of cognate infinitives is further emphasized by juxtaposed temporal markers. It is because he reckons David's behavior to the south of Judah to be *continual* (כל־הימים, 27:11) that Achish decisively assesses David to be an *absolute* stinker (infinitive absolute) among his own people (27:12). He then immediately (28:1) leaves David *in no doubt at all* (infinitive absolute) about his new status; and that role will involve no less than being bodyguard *continually* (כל־הימים) to his Philistine patron (28:2). Within each pair of verses, the presence of a temporal marker serves to reinforce the emphasis already explicit in the balancing infinitives absolute. Employing the identical temporal marking in the outer verses (27:11 and 28:2) serves to reinforce the correspondence in the inner pair (27:12 and 28:1) between how Achish judges the situation and what he says emphatically to David. At the very heart of this *abba* structure (כל־הימים, infinitive absolute, infinitive absolute, כל־הימים) are two variations (c^1 and c^2) on the temporal expression:

a	This was [David's] justice *all the days* (27:11)	כה משפטו <u>כל־הימים</u>
b	*Stink—he has become stinking* among his people (27:12a)	<u>הבאש הבאיש</u> בעמו
c¹	He has become my servant *eternally* (27:12b)	היה לי לעבד <u>עולם</u>
c²	*In those days* Philistines assembled (28:1a)	<u>בימים ההם</u> ויקבצו פלשתים
b	*Know—you must know* that with me you shall go out (28:1b)	<u>ידע תדע</u> כי אתי תצא
a	Guard of my head I shall set you *all the days* (28:2)	שמר לראשי אשימך <u>כל־הימים</u>

In one variation (c¹), the sense of the *a* phrase is intensified in the last word of 1 Sam 27, where "continual" (lit. "all the days") becomes "perpetual" or "eternal" (עולם). In the other (c²), the wording of the *a* phrase is modified from כל־הימים to בימים ההם ("all the days" becomes "in those days"), so making the force of the structural correspondence explicit. Anticipating key language from the chapter on the dynastic oracle (2 Sam 7), where Nathan will report Yahweh calling David "my servant" and promising him an "eternal house," Achish ironically promises that David will be his "eternal servant."

It is striking to realize that 27:11 actually begins by noting grimly that the sort of "justice" practiced habitually by David made it its business to take *life* from others indiscriminately. These balancing expressions of time and infinitives absolute (3.3) are introduced by a statement about life (ch. 2)! The link thus achieved between 27:11 (the opening element of the rhetorical structure) and 28:2 (the balancing final element) should make us readers immediately aware of what Achish is unknowingly doing—he is taking a big risk with his *life* when he chooses David as his bodyguard:

    a   Neither man nor woman did David *let live* ... so was his justice *all the days* (27:11)
        b   *Stink—he has become stinking* among his people (27:12a)
            c¹   He has become my servant *eternally* (27:12b)
            c²   *In those days* Philistines assembled (28:1a)
        b   *Know—you must know* that with me you shall go out to war (28:1b)
    a   Guard of my head I shall set you *all the days* (28:2)

We saw earlier (2.1) that the Chronicler may have preserved the older version of David taking Jerusalem when he notes that Joab "let live" (חיה *piel*) the remnant of the city. If so, the contrasting note in 1 Sam 27:11 that "neither man nor woman did David let live [חיה *piel*]" becomes all the more eloquent. And in its turn, this climactic statement of David's standards corresponds to the longer version of his treatment of Moab (2 Sam 8:2), which we have already discussed (1.4.2).[1]

But there is more. When the author of the David/Achish narrative in 1 Sam 27:1–28:2 puts the rare phrase עבד עולם ("servant forever")[2] at the heart of his conclusion, he deploys two words in combination, each of which is used (separately) more densely in synoptic 2 Sam 7 // 1 Chr 17 than anywhere else in the Hebrew Bible. Such deliberate drawing on the shared narrative makes it likely that Achish's perception of the results of David's cruelty is also stated in language borrowed from nearby synoptic 2 Sam 10 // 1 Chr 19—the Ammonite realization that their mistreatment of his ambassadors had made them "stink" in David's nose. The author of 1 Sam 25–30 deployed a wide range of resources from synoptic texts to create an alibi for David. Those familiar with the older synoptic narrative were aware that Israel, when they approached David to become their king, had reminded him that he used to lead them out to battle when Saul was king (2 Sam 5:1–2); and these readers presumably also wondered why he was absent when Saul died. The answer contrived at the end of the book of 1 Samuel was that he had had to flee for his life from Saul and take refuge with the ancestral enemy—but all the time he was successfully manipulating Achish of Gath, and he managed to be in neither army on Mount Gilboa. Expressions of time, using infinitives absolute for emphasis, interest in "life"—all are known synoptically, but never in such dense combination as here, and nowhere else combined with keywords from the prime text of Davidic royal ideology.

7.2. Bathsheba

Bathsheba plays her famous role at the heart of 2 Samuel almost wordlessly. Indeed, in all of two chapters (2 Sam 11:2–12:25) only two Hebrew words are attributed to her, her message to King David: הרה אנכי ("I am pregnant"). But the elaborate story in which she features offers a prime

---

1. I treat these issues more fully in *I and II Samuel*, 318–19.
2. It is found also in Job 40:28.

sample of how an author of this book has used and reused words that were already highly significant in his principal source. The synoptic narrative of David, shared between the books of Samuel and Chronicles, had left readers with several problems to ponder, and it also provided a suitable setting for narrative reflection. As we saw in chapter 4, the shared story of David depicts divine-human communication only at beginning (2 Sam 5, 7) and end (2 Sam 24).

Apart from his own anointing by Samuel (1 Sam 16) and his later flight to that prophet-statesman (1 Sam 19), this story about David, Bathsheba, Uriah the Hittite, Joab, and Nathan the prophet is the only element of the whole nonsynoptic David narrative in the book of Samuel that includes a prophet. (Of course, Nathan, Bathsheba, and David will feature together again in 1 Kgs 1.) And Bathsheba herself is the only character in her story not directly drawn from synoptic material.[3] Appropriately, the problems on which this famous story reflects are posed by the only episodes of the older synoptic David narrative in which a prophet (Nathan in 2 Sam 7 // 1 Chr 17) or seer (Gad in 2 Sam 24 // 1 Chr 21) has appeared. In the first of these earlier substantial episodes, Nathan assures David of a divine promise to establish his house—his dynasty—"forever" (2 Sam 7:13); and David responds in direct prayer to Yahweh, taking up Nathan's "forever" repeatedly (7x).[4] In the second episode, after insisting on a count being made of his whole people, David admits to Yahweh that this had been a very sinful mistake (2 Sam 24:10). Here the role of Gad, his seer, is simply to convey to David three divine options of punishment, each of which will bear heavily on his people (24:12–13). David protests that the error has been his and not his people's: it is his house, and not they, that should suffer (24:17). However, no divine response to this protest is reported in 2 Sam 24 // 1 Chr 21; and nowhere within the continuing synoptic narrative do we find explicit—or seemingly even implicit—reflection on whether or how David's later sinful mistake may have impacted on the earlier divine undertaking through Nathan.[5]

---

3. Her father Eliam and her husband Uriah are both listed among David's warriors (2 Sam 23:34, 39).

4. 2 Sam 7:16 (2x), 24, 25, 26, 29 (2x).

5. 2 Sam 24 is the culmination of a balancing coda to the book of Samuel (2 Sam 21–24) and is often thereby assumed to be part of a later addition to the book. However, the census narrative, like the list of David's warriors and the account of some of

7. SAMUEL REVISITED

It is the interpretive challenge of this divine silence that the author of the Bathsheba and Nathan story takes up. By setting the new story within the older account of David's Ammonite campaign (2 Sam 10:1–11:1 // 1 Chr 19:1–20:1 + 2 Sam 12:26–31 // 1 Chr 20:2–3), he has David take his fateful opportunity when his forces are in the field. By the device of filling a small gap in the old story of the war with Ammon, he ponders in the new story the larger issues of divine promise and royal blame posed in the same older synoptic account of David's census.[6] The illicit taking of Bathsheba and killing of her husband here corresponds to the illicit counting of Israel there. The death of their first child here corresponds not only to the death of many of David's people there but also to David's admission there that the divine hand should be against himself and his own family. The threat—"a sword shall not turn from your house forever" (2 Sam 12:10), uttered here by the same Nathan as had earlier uttered the dynastic promise, combines the impending divine sword of 24:16 with his previous promise "forever" of 7:13 and includes the "house" of David, which is part of both original contexts.

Christophe Nihan writes with seeming impatience that I have been deaf (my words, not his) to criticism "consistently" voiced to my reconstruction over some thirty years.[7] I confess to similar disappointment that my critics have been seemingly blind to the essential ambiguity of key pieces of evidence, *especially when these are taken each for themselves*. My commentary draws attention more than seventy times to ambiguity in the book of Samuel.[8] If we stand where most critics have stood for two centuries, it makes good sense to observe that David's stay in Jerusalem in 2 Sam 11:1 simply "serves to introduce the Bathsheba account in the rest of chap. 11."[9] And yet, read in the light of the immediately preceding campaign reports in 2 Sam 10 // 1 Chr 19 and without the (inserted) Bathsheba account, the verse simply continues a pattern. Sometimes Joab commanded the army in the field alone, and sometimes, where necessary, David took command. Only David could be crowned in Rabbah, and it was necessary for him to

---

their battles with Philistines, are shared with Chronicles and should be regarded as primary. For fuller discussion see Auld, *I and II Samuel*, 9–11, 565.

6. For fuller discussion, see ibid., 447–73.

7. "Samuel, Chronicles, and 'Postchronistic' Revisions: Some Remarks of Method," in *Rereading the* relecture?, 60.

8. Within the Bathsheba story (*I and II Samuel*, 447-73), esp. 453 and 472.

9. "Samuel, Chronicles, and 'Postchronistic' Revisions," 61.

cross to Ammon once Joab's campaign had succeeded. In this case, there are two different *right* ways of reading the evidence.

Similarly, it has been argued that, when the Chronicler drastically shortened 2 Sam 11–12 into 1 Chr 20:1–3, he sourced ויהרסה ("and tore through it") at his new end of the opening verse from the very middle of the long narrative he omitted (2 Sam 11:25)—and thereby proved that the omission was no accident.[10] And yet, looked at the other way round, the teller of the new story in Samuel, who makes such a feature of "sending," rebuilds the simple statement of his source into an instruction sent by David to his commander in the field.

And similarly again, read *after* a list in 2 Sam 3:2–5 of sons and mothers from David's Hebron days, the statement that "David took *more* wives … and *more* sons and daughters were born to David" (5:13) makes obvious sense. Standing in de Wette's shoes and reading the synoptic 1 Chr 14:3, we naturally judge that the Chronicler has been careless in twice retaining "more" (עוד) from his source. Yet the synoptic verse also makes perfect sense when read in and for itself. How could we think that the David who under Saul had been leading Israel out and in (2 Sam 5:2 // 1 Chr 11:2) did not already have wives and offspring? That he should add "more" to their number after establishing himself in Jerusalem is simply unremarkable. If "more" were not included in the text, we might deduce that he was marrying in Jerusalem for the first time. Happily, Nihan is fully open to the good sense of the Chronicler's testimony in the synoptic contexts of Saul's death (1 Sam 31 // 1 Chr 10) and David's taking Jerusalem (2 Sam 5:6–9 // 1 Chr 11:4–8).[11] I shall discuss further similar cases in chapter 8. I agree with Ray Person that Chr may allude to stories already being told orally but not yet in the written tradition shared with Sam.[12] However, Sam also developed new stories on the basis of that shared tradition.

7.3. SAUL

The older synoptic narrative had left its hearers with several questions about Saul. As prelude to the David story, it told us only about Saul's death

---

10. So, for example, Ralph Klein, *1 Chronicles*, 407.

11. "Samuel, Chronicles, and 'Postchronistic' Revisions," 63–65.

12. Raymond F. Person Jr., "The Problem of 'Literary Unity' from the Perspective of the Study of Oral Traditions," in *Empirical Models Challenging Biblical Criticism*, ed. Raymond F. Person Jr. and Robert Rezetko, AIL 25 (Atlanta: SBL Press, 2016), 229–35.

in a battle with Philistines: he had died with all his sons, and so there was no one from his house to succeed. When Israel's representatives came to make David their king, they noted he used to lead them in battle. And yet he had not been there when Saul died with his sons. Why was this so? And, more important, what wrong had Saul done? A similar-minded author of the book of Samuel as had crafted the David and Bathsheba story had made much the same point earlier in the narrative, again drawing on the same synoptic texts (2 Sam 7 and 24). He reported Samuel voicing Yahweh's displeasure at Saul (1 Sam 13:13–14): "You have been *foolish*. You *have not kept Yahweh's command*.... Yahweh established your reign over Israel *forever*. But now your reign shall not stand." We learn early in the book of Samuel that foolish *kingly disobedience* to divine commands can trump even *divine undertakings* to kings. In the Bathsheba episode, crafted for this new and expansive retelling of the David story, Nathan's threat about the sword in David's house becomes all the more compelling: Nathan echoes what Samuel had said to Saul, and what Samuel said to Saul had already been confirmed in what happened to Saul and his sons (1 Sam 31).

7.4. Samuel

The fresh presentation of the role of Samuel in the latest strata of the book that bears his name has its culmination in 1 Sam 12.

7.4.1. Deuteronomistic Samuel

Within a book where manifest Deuteronomistic features are widely recognized as scarce, this chapter may have suffered more than any other from the prevailing Deuteronomistic History thesis.[13] First Samuel 12 is held to be an exception to the rule. And, for Martin Noth, it actually constituted one of the key pillars supporting the whole Deuteronomistic historical presentation. Samuel's speech, like those of Moses and Joshua before him

---

13. Although it has appeared in several footnotes, I have avoided the contentious term *Deuteronomistic* in the main text till this point. A very clear account of the issues is available in Römer's cautiously titled *So-Called Deuteronomistic History*, esp. ch. 2 (13–43). Key issues in the Samuel debate have been thoroughly reviewed in Cynthia Edenburg and Juha Pakkala, eds., *Is Samuel among the Deuteronomists? Current Views on the Place of Samuel within a Deuteronomistic History*, AIL 16 (Atlanta: SBL Press, 2013).

and of Solomon after him, was held to have been drafted by the historian to mark up the significance of the transition from one major period to the next—in Samuel's case, from the period of the judges to that of the kings.[14] Here again the position from which we view the material may predetermine what we actually see. Read after the book of Deuteronomy and the end of the book of Joshua, we may expect a major speech of Samuel to mark an end or a major transition: Samuel and kingship, like Moses and Torah, or Joshua and promised land. Indeed, there are several suggestive links between 1 Sam 12 and Joshua: (1) The theme of Samuel's advanced age (1 Sam 12:2) is resumed from 1 Sam 8:1, like Joshua's in Josh 23:1 from 13:1, although שבתי (1 Sam 12:2 MT) is unique. (2) Yahweh and his anointed are witnesses (12:5), corresponding to the people as witness in Josh 24:22 and the stone playing the same role in Josh 24:27. (3) "Fearing Yahweh and Samuel" (1 Sam 12:18b) echoes "fearing Yahweh and Joshua" (Josh 4:14)—and reminds readers of "believe in Yahweh and Moses" (Exod 14:31) and "believe in Yahweh and his prophets" (2 Chr 20:20). (4) חלילה לי מ־ ("Perish the thought that I might …," 1 Sam 12:23) uses the same idiom as Josh 24:16. (5) "Serve Yahweh *in truth*" (1 Sam 12:24) recalls Josh 24:14 (though באמת is paired differently in each). There are certainly links between the two major speeches, but it is not clear which is the direction of influence. Possibly more significant, however: while the speeches of Moses (in much of Deuteronomy) and of Joshua (in Josh 23 and 24) are set at the *end* of their lives, this is not true of 1 Sam 12.[15] Quite apart from his first and second denunciations of Saul (1 Sam 13, 15) that follow soon afterward, Samuel still has to anoint David (1 Sam 16), and will himself die much later in the narrative (1 Sam 25:1; 28:3), and only shortly before Saul (1 Sam 31).

7.4.2. Samuel in Synoptic Context

When we read 1 Sam 12 within the more immediate context of Samuel-Kings rather than all of Deuteronomy-Kings, we receive a quite different impression of the chapter. As demonstrated in the table below, this key chapter is yet another portion of nonsynoptic Samuel with close links to several significant elements of the synoptic narrative of Israel's

---

14. Noth, *Deuteronomistic History*, 42, 47–50.
15. Wellhausen had also drawn attention to links between 1 Sam 12 and (Deuteronomistic) Judg 12:9–11 (*Composition*, 246).

kings, shared by Samuel–Kings and Chronicles. Among these elements, Solomon's lengthy prayer at the dedication of the temple has particular resonance. Set at the heart (1 Kgs 8)—not the culmination—of the report of Solomon's reign (1 Kgs 3–11), its first three specific petitions (1 Kgs 8:31–32, 33–34, 35–36) provide not only structure and example for 1 Sam 12, but several keywords as well. And as we have noted in other younger portions of Samuel, we also find anticipations in 1 Sam 12 of both 2 Sam 7 and the story of David's census. Then one phrase unique in the Hebrew Bible may best be explained as recombining elements of the response by the prophetess Huldah to King Josiah.

1 Sam 12	Topic	Synoptic source
1–5	Solemn claim of innocence	1 Kgs 8:31–32 // 2 Chr 6:22–23
8	ישב ("dwell") and מקום ("place") combined	2 Kgs 22:16, 19 // 2 Chr 34:24, 27
9–15	Restoration following a defeat attributed to "sin" (אויב + חטא)	1 Kgs 8:33–34 // 2 Chr 6:24–25
14–15 + 25	"you" + "people"	1 Kgs 8:36 // 2 Chr 6:27
16–18	"Rain" (מטר)	1 Kgs 8:35–36 // 2 Chr 6:26–27
22	Divine "pleasure" (הואיל)	2 Sam 7:29 // 1 Chr 17:27
23b	"the good [and right] way"	1 Kgs 8:36 // 2 Chr 6:27
25	Combination of רעע + infinitive absolute and ספה	1 Chr 21:17 and 21:12

Solomon's second petition (1 Kgs 8:33–34) seeks to establish a principle: if sin against Yahweh leads to defeat before an enemy, but is then followed by the people confessing allegiance to Yahweh and pleading with him, then they should be restored to the land granted to their fathers. Samuel applies this principle in telling the story of his people's repeated forgetting and forsaking Yahweh, defeat by neighbors, confessing guilt, and Yahweh acceding to the appeals for restoration (1 Sam 12:9–15).

In the first seven examples tabled above, the synoptic nature of the links is unambiguous: the shared texts compared with 1 Sam 12 have been preserved (virtually) identically in Samuel–Kings and Chronicles. But in the final example, the links are between 1 Sam 12:25 and elements of David's census story according to the version found not in 2 Sam 24 but in the corresponding 1 Chr 21. Samuel's long speech warning his people over the institution of kingship comes to this rousing conclusion: אִם־הָרֵעַ תָּרֵעוּ גַּם־אַתֶּם גַּם־מַלְכְּכֶם תִּסָּפוּ ("If you do real evil, both you and indeed your king will be swept away"). At least three significant elements link 1 Sam 12:25 with the version of the census story in Chronicles, and so constitute a strong argument for deliberate allusion.

1 Sam 12:25	1 Chr 21:17, 12
אִם־<u>הָרֵעַ תָּרֵעוּ</u>	וַאֲנִי־הוּא אֲשֶׁר־חָטָאתִי <u>וְהָרֵעַ הֲרֵעוֹתִי</u> וְאֵלֶּה הַצֹּאן מֶה עָשׂוּ
גַּם־אַתֶּם גַּם־מַלְכְּכֶם <u>תִּסָּפוּ</u>	אִם־שָׁלוֹשׁ שָׁנִים רָעָב וְאִם־שְׁלֹשָׁה חֳדָשִׁים <u>נִסְפֶּה</u> מִפְּנֵי־צָרֶיךָ

1. The reinforcing use of the infinitive absolute הרע is found in the Hebrew Bible only twice, at 1 Sam 12:25a and 1 Chr 21:17.
2. ספה *niphal* is part of both contexts (1 Sam 12:25b and 1 Chr 21:12).
3. In both contexts, the threat of being "swept away" is directed at the king, or at least specifically includes the king.

But in which direction is the allusion operating? A threat made first against a king (in the census story) but then generalized to include the people with their king (1 Sam 12) would represent a readily understandable exegetical development. On the other hand, ספה is found nowhere else in Chronicles: "be swept away" is not part of the Chronicler's regular vocabulary, and this sole use in 1 Chr 21:12 could result from—and indeed help to identify the presence of—deliberate allusion to an earlier portion of the book of Samuel. However, that may be too precipitate a conclusion, for ספה is hardly more common elsewhere; and the three cases in 1 Samuel (presumably related to one another) are the only instances of this verb anywhere in the Former Prophets. After Samuel's warning to Saul and people (1 Sam 12:25), the verb is used next in David's warning to Abishai to leave Saul to his fate (1 Sam 26:10), and very soon afterward in his fear for himself (27:1). In each of these other cases, even more clearly than in Samuel's generalized warning, the threat is either to the present king (Saul) or the intended king (David). ספה is used nowhere else in Samuel; and the broad contexts in Samuel and Chronicles are identical. It follows that the direction of allusion cannot be settled by appealing to "sweep away" as a unique usage within Chronicles.

There are other significant links between nonsynoptic Samuel and the text of synoptic portions preserved in Chronicles but not Samuel. I noted one such analogy at the end of 7.1 above: David's ruthlessness in not leaving (any) man or woman alive (1 Sam 27:11) made a contrast with Joab leaving alive the remnant of the populace of Jerusalem (1 Chr 11:8), a (possibly original) detail that now goes unreported in the Samuel parallel.

There is another memorable example of a synoptic comparator no longer present in the Masoretic and Septuagint texts of 2 Sam 24. The hapless Absalom stranded in a tree "between heaven and earth" (2 Sam 18:9) anticipates the divine agent observed by David "stationed between heaven and earth" (2 Sam 24:16 [4QSam^a] // 1 Chr 21:16): Absalom suspended wordlessly reminds us that he too had been an agent divinely ordained to punish his father. It may even be that another verbal "coincidence" (though in this case unstated) was instrumental in leading Samuel's train of thought from "rain" (1 Kgs 8:35, 36) and "the good way" (1 Kgs 8:36) to the consequences of David's census. Solomon's third petition (1 Kgs 8:35–36 // 2 Chr 6:26–27) starts with עצר niphal: "when [the heavens] are *closed off*"; and the only other synoptic use of this uncommon verbal form is part of the climax of the census story: "and the plague will be *closed off* from the people" (2 Sam 24:21 // 1 Chr 21:22). Uwe Becker has doubted on quite other grounds whether it is wise to continue reading 1 Sam 12 as a contribution of "Deuteronomists," whether early or late, and has argued that its concept of kingship is close to how the Chronicler portrays David.[16] If the author of 1 Sam 12 was familiar with (at least an early draft of) the book of Chronicles, that could readily explain his knowledge and use of the census story as 1 Chr 21 reports it. However that may be, it is sufficient for my purpose to suppose that 1 Chr 21 preserved (in some of its wording at least) an older version of the census story than we read now in 2 Sam 24.

Samuel has already given a significant clue a couple of sentences earlier, when he says, "and I shall teach you in the good and straight way" (1 Sam 12:23b). "You will teach them the good way" is part of Solomon's long prayer at the dedication of the temple (1 Kgs 8:36).[17] As Samuel

---

16. "Wie 'deuteronomistisch' ist die Samuel-Rede in I Sam 12?" in *Rereading the relecture?*, 131–45.

17. The association of divine instruction with the Jerusalem temple is also made in Mic 4:2.

alludes to it, he also has in mind Ps 25:8,[18] "Good and straight is Yahweh; accordingly he will teach sinners in the way." First Kings 8:35–36 is the third of Solomon's requests to his God. Solomon there is quite explicit, as is Ps 25, that it is "sinners" who need to be taught the good way.[19] However, this third element of Solomon's long prayer is of still wider relevance to Samuel. For it starts with the heavens shut up and no rain, and moves on to call people to pray toward this place and turn from sin, and then to Yahweh forgiving the sins "of your servants and of your people Israel," teaching them the good way, and giving rain again. The rain with which the petition starts is also a spectacular feature at the heart of 1 Sam 12: just as the heavens could be shut up in season (1 Kgs 8:35–36), they could also be opened up out of season (1 Sam 12:16–18). And Solomon linking "your servants" (the kings) and "your people Israel" as joint sinners (1 Kgs 8:36) lends further authority to Samuel's repeated linking of "both you and your king": not just at the climax of his speech (12:25) but already in verses 14 and 15, immediately before the storm spectacle.

7.4.3. Samuel Relaunched

How we read Samuel's speech in 1 Sam 12 is again a matter of context. As we have noted, it has long been customary for readers who come to Samuel after Moses and Joshua to describe 1 Sam 12 as Samuel's farewell address: further to the establishment of the monarchy in Israel, his leadership was no longer required. However, seen for itself, and seen in the light of its sources, Samuel's speech is hardly a farewell: far from anticipating his retirement or death, it actually inaugurates a relaunch of his career. His radical claim for ongoing "prophetic" oversight has authority, first, because it draws on words of David and Solomon (the founding kings, and the only kings apart from Hezekiah who address the Deity directly); and second, because it reuses words of recognized intermediaries (Gad the seer and the prophetess Huldah). And even if kingship, so recently established, may have to be dispensed with (12:25), in that case too Samuel "will teach [his people] in the good and straight way" (12:23). His God may have assured him that, in asking for a king like all the nations, his people

---

18. Ps 25:11 (and elsewhere in Psalms only 103:3) echoes Solomon's key verb סלח ("forgive"): 1 Kgs 8:30, 34, 36, 39, 50.

19. As verb or noun, "sin" recurs throughout Solomon's prayer—some ten times in 1 Kgs 8:31–50.

were rejecting their God and not Samuel, who had been their judge (8:7). However, Samuel himself gives no sign of awareness that his own claim (to the divine teaching role) might be a similar usurpation.

Samuel's argument may have influenced the dynamics of the provision in Deut 16–18 for leadership roles, where kingship is only *permitted* (17:14–18) but prophecy is *promised* (18:15–22). However, the specifics of his rhetoric are hardly drawn from that book. The key movement marked in 1 Sam 12 is not a shift in historical era, from a period of judges to a period of kings, but an ideological or religious shift from leadership and intermediation by kings to leadership and intermediation by prophets.

7.5. Summary

The fateful interaction of David with Bathsheba, Uriah, Joab, and Nathan (7.2) was inserted within the parameters of the older David story; and Achish and David (7.1), Saul rejected (7.3), and Samuel rebranded (7.4) were all created as part of a fresh introduction to that older story. In each case, these narratives drew on characters and language from the synoptic material, and were crafted to help illumine some of its themes. Indeed, each of them drew on at least two portions of the shared text. All of them drew on the dynastic oracle and David's response to it in 2 Sam 7 // 1 Chr 17.[20] The first also drew on the embassy to Ammon (2 Sam 10 // 1 Chr 19), and the other three of them on the census narrative in 2 Sam 24 // 1 Chr 21. The following chapters will explore analogous developments within the book of Kings from the material shared by Samuel–Kings and Chronicles.

---

20. As always in this study, "2 Sam 7 // 1 Chr 17" is shorthand for "the synoptic material shared by 2 Sam 7 and 1 Chr 17." Chapters such as this and 1 Kgs 8 // 2 Chr 6 (Solomon's prayer) are almost certainly layered compositions; and much of 1 Kgs 8 is often ascribed to a second Deuteronomistic author. Be that as it may, this study proposes that the penultimate draft (shared with 2 Chr 6) influenced the author of 1 Sam 12.

8
Prophets and Kings in Israel

8.1. Prophets of Asherah

Asherah and Baal (and the host of heaven too) are found together synoptically for the first time in the critique of Manasseh. As the book of Kings was being developed on the basis of the older shared narrative, Asherah together with Baal was retrojected into earlier history in two contexts. Second Kings 17 includes a very detailed explanation of the religious reasons that had led to the demise of northern Israel; and, within that review, verses 16b–17 blame the northern kingdom for the same wicked practices that the synoptic history (21:3b–7a) had associated with Manasseh: "They made [an] Asherah,[1] and they prostrated before all the host of heaven, and they served Baal. And they passed their sons and their daughters through fire; and they practiced divination and augury; and they made themselves over to doing evil in Yahweh's eyes—to vexing him." In 2 Kgs 17, as throughout Deuteronomy, the people are blamed. Second Kings 21:1–9 // 2 Chr 33:1–9 represents the earlier view, according to which the king had been responsible.[2] Second Kings 17 is discussed more fully below (8.7).

The other nonsynoptic mentions of Asherah alongside Baal are still earlier, in connection with King Ahab in Israel (1 Kgs 16:32–33a): ויקם

---

1. The first synoptic instance of Asherah is in 1 Kgs 15:13 // 2 Chr 15:16. While 2 Kgs 21:3 and 7 also read Asherah (sg.), synoptic 2 Chr 33:3 has the plural and 33:7 replaces פסל האשרה by פסל הסמל.

2. Ehud Ben Zvi, "The Account of the Reign of Manasseh in II Reg 21,1–18 and the Redactional History of the Book of Kings," ZAW 103 (1991): 362–63. The language in which the critique of Manasseh is expressed in 2 Kgs 21:2–9 is usefully discussed in Percy S. F. van Keulen, *Manasseh through the Eyes of the Deuteronomists*, OTS 38 (Leiden: Brill, 1996), 89–122.

מזבח לבעל בית הבעל אשר בנה בשמרון ויעש אחאב את־האשרה ("He erected an altar for Baal in the house of Baal, which he built in Samaria. And Ahab made the Asherah"). Large purges of prophets of Baal are reported in 1 Kgs 18:40 at the instigation of Elijah and in 2 Kgs 10:18–27 at the instigation of Jehu. But only the opening of the report of the spectacular contest involving Elijah mentions Asherah as well: Ahab is asked to gather at Mount Carmel "the four hundred fifty prophets of Baal and the four hundred prophets of Asherah who eat at Jezebel's table" (את־ נביאי הבעל ארבע מאות וחמשים ונביאי האשרה ארבע מאות אכלי שלחן איזבל, 1 Kgs 18:19). In the remainder of that story, only prophets of Baal are mentioned (1 Kgs 18:22, 25, 40). Similarly, the report of the Jehu purge talks only of "prophets of Baal" (2 Kgs 10:19) and "those who serve Baal" (10:19, 21, 22, 23), but makes no mention of Asherah.[3] I suggested (5.4) that mention of Ahab in 2 Kgs 21:3 (but not the parallel 2 Chr 33:3) was an addition to that older synoptic report where Baal and Asherah had first been linked. It seems likely that we find in 1 Kgs 18:19 a reciprocal cross-reference—את־נביאי הבעל ארבע מאות וחמשים ונביאי האשרה ארבע מאות אכלי שלחן איזבל ("the prophets of Baal [450] and the prophets of Asherah [400] who eat at Jezebel's table"). The linking of "prophets" and "Asherah" here is unique in the Hebrew Bible, and will have been simply a literary invention.

8.2. Elisha and the Three Kings

Within the synoptic narratives, נביא ליהוה ("prophet of Yahweh") is found only once—in 1 Kgs 22:7 // 2 Chr 18:6, where Micaiah is identified as a "prophet of Yahweh" through whom the kings of Israel and Judah may seek Yahweh. This phrase makes only three further appearances in the Hebrew Bible: in 1 Kgs 18:22, of Elijah; in 2 Kgs 3:11, of Elisha, and in 2 Chr 28:9, of Oded. "Prophet of Yahweh" is only one of several links between the synoptic narrative about Micaiah and an early narrative of Elisha—the latter is entirely a nonsynoptic figure.

---

3. We find Asherah (sg.) also in nonsynoptic 1 Kgs 16:33; 2 Kgs 13:6; 17:16; 18:4; 23:4, 6, 7, 15; and plural in 1 Kgs 14:15, 23; 2 Kgs 17:10; 23:14. In 2 Kgs 23:4–5, Baal is also mentioned twice.

1. In both 2 Kgs 3:7 and 1 Kgs 22:4 // 2 Chr 18:3, the king of Israel of the time[4] invites the corresponding king of Judah[5] to join with him in military action eastward to regain territory to which he makes a claim.
2. The Judahite partner responds in identical terms (כמוני כמוך כעמי בעמך כסוסי כסוסיך, "I am as you are, my people as your people, my horses as your horses") in 2 Kgs 3:7 and 1 Kgs 22:4, although the synoptic parallel in 2 Chr 18:3 (כמוך וכעמך עמי כמוני), "I am as you are and your people as my people") presents two differences: "your people" and "my people" are in reverse order, and horses go unmentioned.
3. ונדרשה את־יהוה מאותו ("of whom we may seek Yahweh") in 2 Kgs 3:11 is closely related to both ונדרשה מאותו ("of whom we may seek") in 1 Kgs 22:7 and עוד איש אחד לדרש את־יהוה מאתו ("there is one other individual of whom to seek *Yahweh*") in the answering 1 Kgs 22:8, and may be a conflation of the wording of both.

Like the shared "prophet of Yahweh," each of these three expressions is very rare within the Hebrew Bible; and the combination of all four is unique to Micaiah in 1 Kgs 22 // 2 Chr 18 and Elisha in 2 Kgs 3. In addition, reports of common purpose by Israel and Judah are very unusual. Such a remarkable set of links demands explanation. From our synoptic perspective, the Elisha story will depend on the Micaiah one—not least because Jehoshaphat's response in 2 Kgs 3:12 includes the little word יש (see 3.2.1): יש אותו דבר־יהוה ("Yahweh's word is with him.") The repetition in 2 Kgs 3 of key details from a synoptic narrative is reminiscent of our samples from the book of Samuel (ch. 7), or Hezekiah's "fifteen [extra] years" of "life" (see 10.4.1). Further, if 2 Kgs 3 is rooted in 1 Kgs 22, it becomes much less surprising that a story of a northern prophet includes (2 Kgs 3:14) a complimentary remark about the southern king ("Had I not regard for Jehoshaphat king of Judah, I would neither look at you nor see you").[6]

---

4. Ahab and Jehoram.
5. Jehoshaphat in both cases according to the MT, while LXX[L] attests Ahaziah as partner to Jehoram.
6. John Gray commented on 2 Kgs 3:14 that "Elisha's respect for the king of Judah certainly suggests a secondary source, the Judaean revision of the original North Isra-

Other elements of the story of Elisha and the three kings have close verbal links with features of the whole Elijah-Elisha cycle. When Elisha redirects the king of Israel to the prophets of his father and mother (such prophets had also featured in the synoptic 1 Kgs 22), his opening words (2 Kgs 3:13) deny any commonality with that king, using terms last met in the retort of the widow of Zarephath to Elijah: מה־לי־ולך ("What have I in common with you?"; 1 Kgs 17:18).[7] When the king of Israel replies that it is Yahweh that has brought three kings to their present pass, Elisha starts his response (2 Kgs 3:14) by repeating exactly the claim of authority used in Elijah's very first words to Ahab (1 Kgs 17:1) and then in his reassurance to Obadiah (1 Kgs 18:15): חי יהוה אשר עמדתי לפניו ("As Yahweh lives, before whom I stand").

"Before whom I stand" is used always and only as reinforcement to חי יהוה ("as Yahweh lives"), and is uttered just once more in the Hebrew Bible: by Elisha when he solemnly refuses any gift from the Syrian Naaman (2 Kgs 5:16). If this phrase had been a well-established self-referential prophetic formula in real life, it would be surprising that we meet it only in the book of Kings.[8] However, as used there by Elijah and Elisha, it may also have synoptic roots—and again, in Micaiah's report of his vision (1 Kgs 22:21). When Micaiah was advised by the royal messenger to agree with the other prophets, his response included the only synoptic use of the oath חי יהוה ("as Yahweh lives," 22:14). When his

---

elite matter" (*I and II Kings*, 3rd ed., OTL [London: SCM, 1977], 486). Mordechai Cogan and Hayim Tadmor observe more appropriately that the role of the king of Judah is as pivotal in 2 Kgs 3 as in 1 Kgs 22 (*II Kings: A New Translation with Introduction and Commentary*, AB 11 [Garden City, NY: Doubleday, 1988], 49). Ernst Würthwein reckons 2 Kgs 3:9b–17 as a secondary insert into the original story (*1. Kön.17–2. Kön.25*, vol. 2 of *Die Bücher der Könige*, ATD 11.2 [Göttingen: Vandenhoeck & Ruprecht, 1984], 285–86); and Marvin Sweeney, 2 Kgs 3:10–19 (*I and II Kings*, 280). These portions include most of the explicit word links with 1 Kgs 22, but not the formula that 2 Kgs 3:7 shares with 1 Kgs 22:4. Cogan and Tadmor (*II Kings*, 48) treat 2 Kgs 3:6–25 as a prophetic narrative set in a new framework of vv. 4–5 and 26–27; and Rachelle Gilmour (*Juxtaposition and the Elisha Cycle*, LHBOTS 594 [London: Bloomsbury T&T Clark, 2014], 108) finds that "the episode in 2 Kgs 3:4–27 is self-contained and can be read coherently ... with a beginning, middle, and ending to the story."

7. Variants of this formula reappear in 2 Sam 16:10; 19:23 (sons of Zeruiah: Abishai and Shimei); 2 Chr 35:21; cf. also 2 Kgs 9:18, 19; Ps 50:16 (as read by Peshitta).

8. It is used in narrative at the very beginning of Kings, of the search for a young woman who "will stand before the king" (1 Kgs 1:2).

first words were challenged by the king (22:16), he responded with a first vision (22:17). Then, after the king of Israel's comments to Jehoshaphat (22:18), he responded with a second vision (22:19–22) that includes the words "One [spirit] spoke this way and another was speaking that way. And a spirit went out *and stood before Yahweh* and said, 'I—I shall make a fool of him.'" The earlier oath is a response to unwelcome advice. The second vision is a response to a royal challenge. From the perspective of this synoptic resource, we should read Elijah's self-introduction (1 Kgs 17:1) as a novel combination of Micaiah's oath with a key element of his second vision. The import of Elijah's first words to Ahab will be this: "As Yahweh lives, I am like the spirit who volunteered to entice you and was dispatched by Yahweh to do so."

8.3. Prophets of Baal

In reviewing four narratives from the book of Samuel (ch. 7), I noted that each could sensibly be read as having drawn on two or more portions already shared by Samuel–Kings and Chronicles. This is also the case with the expansive account of Hezekiah and Isaiah (ch. 10). And this again seems to be true of the *only two* narratives in Kings that feature the prophets (or servants) of Baal.

The synoptic narrative has included two substantial accounts relevant to the northern kings Omri and Ahab. In the first (1 Kgs 22 // 2 Chr 18), King Ahab of Israel had enjoyed support (but support that proved fatal to him!) from a large number of prophets (presumably prophets *of Yahweh*, since nothing different is stated or suggested about their allegiance). In the second (2 Kgs 11 // 2 Chr 23), Judah was saved from the intrigues of a queen descended from Omri (בת־עמרי, 2 Kgs 8:26) at the initiative of the priest of Yahweh's temple (2 Kgs 11:4–12); and the aftermath of this restoration of the male line of David included sacking the temple of Baal and killing the priest of Baal (11:18).

8.3.1. Elijah at Carmel

The famous new story crafted in 1 Kgs 18 can be read as having blended elements from both of these accounts in synoptic Kings and Chronicles:

1. The wicked woman has become Ahab's wife Jezebel rather than his daughter or niece Athaliah.

2. Yahweh's champion, Elijah, who bears a name honoring Yahweh (אֵלִיָּהוּ) and who presides at a sacrifice, shares characteristics with both Micaiah (מִיכָיְהוּ), lone faithful prophet of Yahweh from 1 Kgs 22 // 2 Chr 18, and Jehoiada (יְהוֹיָדָע), priest of Yahweh in 2 Kgs 11 // 2 Chr 23.
3. The band of *prophets* opposing Micaiah have become *prophets of Baal* opposing Elijah; and when they are finally slaughtered en masse, they anticipate corporately the fate of Mattan, priest of Baal, in the other older story (2 Kgs 11:18 // 2 Chr 23:17).
4. The king who asks (1 Kgs 22:16 // 2 Chr 18:15), "How many times am I making you swear [מַשְׁבִּעֶךָ] that you will speak to me only truth in Yahweh's name?" becomes the king who made every kingdom and nation swear (הִשְׁבִּיעַ)[9] that they did not know the whereabouts of Elijah (1 Kgs 18:10).

In addition to these links, יש ("there is"; see 3.2.1) is also used in 1 Kgs 18:10 (as also in 2 Kgs 3:12; see 11.1). I proposed above (end of 8.1) that "prophets of Asherah" were a literary invention; and it appears now that this is also true of "prophets of Baal." Marvin Sweeney's observations about the links between Elijah's sacrificing on Carmel and the holocaust sacrifice appropriate for Sukkot are well taken. But he seems to be on much weaker ground when he argues that Elijah would have been acceptable as a priest in northern Israel. He claims on the basis of the Samuel story that the first son of a mother could function as a priest.[10] However, Elijah's priestly credentials did not derive *literally* from his (unknown) place among his (unknown) mother's sons. They were instead inherited *literarily* from Jehoiada.

8.3.2. Fate of Jezebel and Baal's Prophetic Servants

Prophets of Baal make a second appearance in the Jehu story where Jezebel also meets her fate (2 Kgs 9–10), but they are found nowhere else in

---

9. שבע *hiphil* is also used in nonsynoptic Samuel-Kings in 1 Sam 14:27-28; 20:17; 1 Kgs 2:42; and, in a synoptic context, in 2 Kgs 11:4, where the shared covenant theme is developed differently from 2 Chr 23:1–3. It is also found in nonsynoptic 2 Chr 36:13. Neither שבע *niphal* ("swear") nor שבועה ("oath") is found in synoptic texts.

10. Marvin A. Sweeney, "Prophets and Priests in the Deuteronomistic History: Elijah and Elisha," in Jacobs and Person, *Israelite Prophecy and the Deuteronomistic History*, 37–39.

the Hebrew Bible.[11] As further evidence that this second literary-historical proposal about the background to Baal's prophetic servants is not mistaken, 2 Kgs 9–10 also has significant linguistic links with both 1 Kgs 22 // 2 Chr 18 and 2 Kgs 11 // 2 Chr 23.

1. As the newly anointed Jehu and his officers discuss the significance of a lone prophetic "madman," the word שקר ("lie, falsehood") has its only other outing in the book of Kings (1 Kgs 22:22, 23; 2 Kgs 9:12).
2. In both narratives (1 Kgs 22:34; 2 Kgs 9:24) the luckless king of Israel is in a chariot and his assailant uses a bow (קשת).
3. חדר בחדר ("in an inner room") is used outside 2 Kgs 9:2 and 1 Kgs 22:25 only in the neighboring 1 Kgs 20:30.
4. The combination הפך יד- ("turn the hand") is used only in 1 Kgs 22:34 and 2 Kgs 9:23, both times preparatory to flight.
5. Only in 1 Kgs 22:34 and 2 Kgs 9:17 do we find רכב (voiced *rakkāb*) used for a charioteer.[12]
6. מזבח ("altar") is the object of שבר piel ("shatter") in 2 Kgs 11:18 // 2 Chr 23:17 and 2 Kgs 10:27 (and also 23:7).
7. בית is the object of נתץ ("tear down") only in 2 Kgs 11:18 // 2 Chr 23:17 and 2 Kgs 10:27; and in both cases the "house" is specified as "Baal's house" (בית הבעל)!
8. Royal guards called "runners" (רצים) are encountered in northern Israel only in 2 Kgs 10:25, immediately before their synoptic appearance in Jerusalem in 2 Kgs 11:13 // 2 Chr 23:12.[13]

Again, to this large number of quite explicit links, we should add that יש is used in 2 Kgs 9:15; 10:15 (3x), 23, but of course *not* in synoptic 1 Kgs

---

11. Gray (*I and II Kings*, 537) finds the unity of 2 Kgs 9:1–10:31 "imposed by a compiler"; and Würthwein (*1. Kön.17–2. Kön.25*, 328–43) finds several layers in the narrative. However, both Cogan and Tadmor explicitly (*II Kings*, 117–22) and Sweeney implicitly (*I and II Kings*, 328–40) read it as a sustained narrative, the longest in Kings.

12. I am indebted to Omer Sergi ("Die Schlacht von Ramot-Gilead und der Niedergang der Omriden-Dynastie: Versuch einer historischen Rekonstruktion," in Oeming and Sláma, *King Like All the Nations*, 43–44) for 4 and 5. The combination in 4 occurs only once more in the HB (Lam 3:3), but there without the connotation of flight.

13. Their other synoptic appearance is in 1 Kgs 14:27–28 // 2 Chr 12:10–11.

22 // 2 Chr 18. Such a pattern of word associations is very similar to what was just described above in relation to 2 Kgs 3 and 1 Kgs 22. In neither case is it a matter of simply replicating whole blocks of the narrative. In this second example, by incorporating so many elements from 1 Kgs 22 and 2 Kgs 11 that happen to be otherwise unique in the Hebrew Bible, the author of 2 Kgs 9 brings his report of the end of "the house of Ahab" into correspondence with the end of King Ahab himself.

Drawing on these and other links, Julius Wellhausen had classified 1 Kgs 20; 22; 2 Kgs 3; 6:24–7:20; and 9–10 as a group of northern narratives.[14] Against his view that these were mainly of political character, Mordechai Cogan and Hayim Tadmor make the sensible observation that "it is the prominent place of the prophetic word and its effect which permits associating 2 Kings 9–10 with 1 Kgs 22 and perhaps 20."[15] The stories about Elijah and Elisha and Jehu and the prophets or servants of Baal are often reckoned to belong to a special *northern* prophetic source or stratum, distinct from the record of the *northern* kings. Many of them, however, turn out instead to be significantly rooted in the older and *southern* synoptic narrative. We shall observe below that the same is true of the whole integrated record of the northern kings. It is worth tabulating just how many elements of synoptic 1 Kgs 22 (// 2 Chr 18) and of synoptic 2 Kgs 11 (// 2 Chr 23) are reused in 1 Kgs 18 and 2 Kgs 3, 9–10.

1 Kgs 22:4	2 Kgs 3:7		invitation made and accepted
1 Kgs 22:7–8	1 Kgs 18:22; 2 Kgs 3:11	נביא ליהוה + דרש מן	("inquire of" + "prophet of Yahweh")
1 Kgs 22:14	1 Kgs 18:15	חי יהוה	("as Yahweh lives")
1 Kgs 22:16	1 Kgs 18:10	השביע	("make swear")
1 Kgs 22:21	1 Kgs 18:15	עמד לפני	("stand before")
1 Kgs 22:22, 23	2 Kgs 9:12	שקר	("lie")
1 Kgs 22:25	2 Kgs 9:2	חדר בחדר	("in the innermost room")

---

14. Wellhausen, *Composition des Hexateuchs*, 282–87.
15. *II Kings*, 119.

1 Kgs 22:34	2 Kgs 9:17	רכב	("charioteer")
1 Kgs 22:34	2 Kgs 9:23	הפך יד	
1 Kgs 22:34	2 Kgs 9:24	קשת	("bow")
2 Kgs 11:13	2 Kgs 10:25	רצים	("runners")
2 Kgs 11:18	2 Kgs 10:27	שבר מזבח + נתץ בית	("tear down house" + "shatter altar")

Just as 1 Kgs 18 and 2 Kgs 9–10 draw on key elements of synoptic 1 Kgs 22 + 2 Kgs 11–12, so too the epilogue on the northern kingdom in 2 Kgs 17 draws heavily on synoptic 2 Kgs 21:1–9.[16]

8.3.3. Conclusion

Mount Carmel may have represented a long-standing natural frontier between the heartland of Israel and coastal Phoenicia. However, many important features of the story of Elijah and the prophets of Baal (and of Asherah) and of Jehu and Baal's prophet-servants have their origins in two (or three) other stories, all of them elements of a synoptic narrative written in a period after the end of northern Israel. Baal was part of the synoptic story (2 Kgs 11), as were multiple prophets in the time of Ahab (1 Kgs 22)—but not multiple "prophets of Baal." Ehud Ben Zvi is somewhat misleading when he writes of the Chronicler's "explicit exclusion of reference to the worship of Baal (or Ashera) in northern Israel."[17] The Chronicler certainly does not *explicitly describe the practice* of such northern worship. On the other hand, without deviating from his source in the older southern narrative, he does associate the worship of Baal in Jerusalem under Athaliah with her connections with the north.

It is uncontroversial, when reviewing the composition of the book of Kings, to observe that the (longer) story of the southern kingdom supplied the base text into whose pages the story of northern Israel's kings and prophets was interleaved. But the account of Jerusalem's kings and

---

16. As detailed in 8.1 above.

17. "The House of Omri/Ahab in Chronicles," in *Ahab Agonistes: The Rise and Fall of the Omri Dynasty*, ed. Lester L. Grabbe, LHBOTS 421 (London: T&T Clark, 2007), 50.

prophets shared by Kings and Chronicles also turns out to have been much more than simply the framework into which other source material was inserted. From a synoptic perspective, it must now be recognized as itself the source and inspiration for the writing of many of these interleaved pages. The next step must be to extend our review to include the connected account in the book of Kings of all the kings in northern Israel.

8.4. David's Twenty Successors

In this section of the argument, patterns of word usage are less relevant.[18] On the other hand, a different sort of patterning is rather important. The final king in each successor kingdom, Hoshea in the north and Zedekiah in the south, is the twentieth after David.

Rehoboam	Jeroboam
Abijam/h	Nadab
Asa	Baasha
Jehoshaphat	Elah
Jehoram	Zimri
Ahaziah	Omri
Joash	Ahab
Amaziah	Ahaziah
Azariah/Uzziah	J(eh)oram
Jotham	Jehu
Ahaz	Jehoahaz
Hezekiah	J(eh)oash
Manasseh	Jeroboam
Amon	Zechariah
Josiah	Shallum
Jehoahaz	Menachem

---

18. The infinitive absolute is never used in the many brief reports of northern kings, but only in stories of Elijah and Elisha. Joash of Israel "weeps" on hearing of Elisha's illness (2 Kgs 13:14); but that too may be categorized as prophetic story. אך is used in the reflection on Jehoahaz ben Jehu (2 Kgs 13:6); and 2 Kgs 9:26 has Jehu use נאם יהוה twice when tying the end of Ahab's house to Elijah's verdict on Ahab (1 Kgs 21), so aligning *King* Jehu with the unnamed "man of God" in 1 Sam 2:30 and with Isaiah in 2 Kgs 19:33! These few usages may be part of the more favorable attitude in Kings to the house of Jehu.

Jehoiakim	Pekahiah
Jehoiachin	Pekah
Zedekiah	Hoshea

Jeroboam and Rehoboam are the first of Solomon's nineteen successors in each of Israel and Judah. Then, as if David having 2 × 10 successors in each part of his divided kingdom were not enough, there is a wicked queen at the same point in both successions: Jezebel and Athaliah.[19] Jeremy Schipper offers usefully convergent evidence when he notes in his study of significant generational patterns that Ahaziah of Judah, murdered by Jehu, had been David's seventh successor.[20] And we can add that Jehu does not just found a new dynasty: he himself is the first of David's second set of ten successors in the north.[21] It seems probable is that we are dealing with historical patterning rather than documentary evidence.

Rehoboam	Jeroboam
Abijam/h	Nadab
Asa	Baasha
Jehoshaphat	Elah
Jehoram	Zimri
Ahaziah	Omri
ATHALIAH	JEZEBEL
Joash	+ Ahab
Amaziah	Ahaziah
Azariah/Uzziah	J(eh)oram
———	———
Jotham	Jehu
Ahaz	Jehoahaz
Hezekiah	J(eh)oash

---

19. Graeme Auld, "Reading Kings on the Divided Monarchy: What Sort of Narrative?" in *Understanding the History of Ancient Israel*, ed. Hugh G. M. Williamson, Proceedings of the British Academy 143 (Oxford: Oxford University Press, 2007), 340.

20. "Hezekiah, Manasseh, and Dynastic or Transgenerational Punishment," in *Soundings in Kings: Perspectives and Methods in Contemporary Scholarship*, ed. Mark Leuchter and Klaus-Peter Adam (Minneapolis: Fortress, 2010), 83.

21. The question השלום is asked more persistently in 2 Kgs 9 (5x), as Jehu drives toward the two kings, than elsewhere in the HB; and it has hardly been heard in Samuel–Kings since problems were noted about the succession to David (2 Sam 18:32; 1 Kgs 2:13).

Manasseh	Jeroboam
Amon	Zechariah
Josiah	Shallum
Jehoahaz	Menachem
Jehoiakim	Pekahiah
Jehoiachin	Pekah
Zedekiah	Hoshea

Nine of the nineteen northern kings from Jeroboam to Hoshea receive at least a mention in the synoptic southern record. These nine are contemporaries of the first twelve kings of separate Judah (from Rehoboam to Hezekiah). It may be hardly surprising that these are also the northern monarchs for whom the book of Kings reports the longest reigns, with the single and signal exception of Jeroboam II (see below).

- Jeroboam I (first) succeeds when Rehoboam is rejected at Shechem (1 Kgs 12:1–19; 15:1 // 2 Chr 10:1–19; 13:1).
- Baasha (third) made war against Asa of Judah (1 Kgs 15:17–22 // 2 Chr 16:1–6).
- Omri (sixth) was an ancestor of Athaliah (2 Kgs 8:26 // 2 Chr 22:2).
- Ahab (seventh) made war along with Jehoshaphat of Judah (1 Kgs 22 // 2 Chr 18); Athaliah (his daughter or niece) was wife to Jehoram of Judah (2 Kgs 8:18 // 2 Chr 21:6), and mother and counselor to Ahaziah (2 Kgs 8:26–27 // 2 Chr 22:2–3).
- Joram (ninth) was joined by Ahaziah in war against Aram (2 Kgs 8:28–29 // 2 Chr 22:5–6); and Ahaziah's visit to the wounded Joram led to his own death at the hands of Jehu (2 Kgs 9:21, 27 // 2 Chr 22:7–9).
- Jehu (tenth) killed the confederate kings of Israel and Judah as just noted, and was grandfather of King Joash (2 Kgs 14:8 // 2 Chr 25:17).
- Jehoahaz (eleventh) was father of King Jehoash (2 Kgs 14:8 // 2 Chr 25:17).
- Jehoash (twelfth) met a challenge from Amaziah of Judah with a warning proverb, then defeated him and damaged the wall of Jerusalem (2 Kgs 14:8–14 // 2 Chr 25:17–24); but after the death of Jehoash, Amaziah lived a further fifteen years (2 Kgs 14:17 // 2 Chr 25:25).

- Pekah (eighteenth) made war against Ahaz of Judah, with differently reported results (2 Kgs 16:5 and 2 Chr 28:6).

8.5. Writing Israel's Kings

When the author of Kings created the familiar synchronic portrayal of the kings of Israel and Judah, much of the material for their presentation of the north was already to hand in the synoptic narrative that had its focus on Jerusalem:

- The names of half of the northern kings and several details about them were already in the synoptic narrative.
- The number of the successors of David and Solomon in the north was simply made to equal those in the south, by adding mostly insignificant figures. As already noted, Menahem (2 Kgs 15:17–22) is the only northern king who *is not* mentioned in Chronicles but *is* attested in an external inscription.
- The introductions and conclusions to most individual reports about northern kings largely followed the southern model.
- The large attention paid in the central third of the (nonsynoptic) book of Kings to the house of Ahab (the narratives that fill all of 1 Kgs 16 through 2 Kgs 10 except for 1 Kgs 22:1–35 and 2 Kgs 8:16–29) simply develops, even if massively, a theme already present in the shared history.
- Near the beginning and end of this large middle section we read major accounts of the destruction of large numbers of Baal's prophetic servants. This literary creation of a prophetic party hostile to Yahweh draws on key details from episodes in the older history that dealt (separately) with blameworthy prophets and a purge of Baal worship. At least one of the central narratives (2 Kgs 3) also reworks a major element of the older history (see 8.2).

Israel Finkelstein has contributed a very attractive synthesis of evidence available for understanding northern Israel, which he calls *The Forgotten Kingdom*.[22] As his subtitle makes clear, Finkelstein's quest is

---

22. Israel Finkelstein, *The Forgotten Kingdom: The Archaeology and History of Northern Israel*, ANEM 5 (Atlanta: Society of Biblical Literature, 2013).

a historical one. Mine, although it may have implications for history writing, is an exploration of how the book of Kings was written: it is literary history, rather than archaeologically informed history, although of course these two historical exercises overlap. Finkelstein reminds us that no writing has been found (in Israel) from the "Omride" period[23] (broadly the first half of the ninth century BCE); that daily administration is not documented there (in the Samaria ostraca) till the first half of the eighth century; and that, in between these dates, we have some political information in the Mesha Stela and the Tel Dan inscription. (We should remember, however, that neither of these inscriptions is Israelite: the former is from Moab and the latter is Aramaean.) If all this is as he states, Finkelstein's thinking may be rather wishful, that an Israel king list including pre-Omride names but written a full century later became available to the southern scribes who compiled the book of Kings.[24] In support of this claim, Finkelstein adduces the view of Frank Moore Cross and others, who have dated the first edition of the Deuteronomistic History only one century after the fall of Samaria.[25] I am not sure that even the prior synoptic Jerusalem narrative is as old as that—the first edition of the book of Kings with its north/south synchronisms will be much more recent.

This hypothesis seems both improbable and unnecessary: improbable because of the overall pattern just documented, and unnecessary because an alternative source was available to the authors of Kings. I review below how little is reported about the other ten northern kings. Indeed, it becomes more sensible to suppose that the most reliable information about the kings in the north had come to the authors of Kings *not* from a supposed ancient king list emanating from Samaria, but from the shared southern narrative. Whatever supplementary information they may have possessed, there is no need to suppose that the authors of Kings had access to a list of northern kings that had made its way from the palace in Samaria to a Jerusalem archive.

Finkelstein, with many other archaeologists and historians, advocates an archaeologically tested reconstruction of the relations between Israel

---

23. Ibid., 115. This terminology is indebted to Assyrian usage, which knew (northern) Israel as "the house of Omri" even after the last royal descendant of Omri had been supplanted.

24. Ibid., 64–65.

25. *Canaanite Myth and Hebrew Epic*, 287–89.

and Judah that portrays Israel from the period of the house of Omri as the culturally senior partner. Developments in architecture and artifacts normally followed in Judah half a century later. My reconstruction of the writing of the biblical record in no way opposes this. In fact, by recognizing the impact on Judah and Jerusalem from northern Israel since the time of Ahab and his sons, the developing narrative continuous from the synoptic source to the developed book of Kings is fully convergent with the prevailing archaeological paradigm.

8.6. Redrawing Jeroboam

The book of Kings does add something completely new when it presents the *whole* northern monarchy as almost uniformly "sinful." In his influential study of the Deuteronomistic History, Cross defined the original sin of Jeroboam as one of the two main themes of the first edition of Kings,[26] along with the dynastic promise to David. However, only the dynastic promise to David plays the same role in the synoptic narrative as in the familiar books of Samuel–Kings. Jeroboam I had been a neutral figure in that synoptic narrative—there the house of Ahab, *not Jeroboam*, was the source of evil. Once Jeroboam's sin came to be blamed in Kings in the report of every one of his northern successors, that older story is certainly given a new theological spin. But it must be the business of another study to probe whether this familiar evaluation of Jeroboam was integral to the first *synchronic* presentation of the kings of Judah and Israel—the first edition of the book of Kings—or was added later.

Kings introduces Jeroboam as the third of three named refugees in flight from Solomon. Yahweh had already declared judgment on Solomon but had stated (1 Kgs 11:9–13) that he would limit his punishment out of respect for David. Each of the three had led revolts against the king. Jeroboam's managerial skills had been noted by Solomon, who had put him in charge of the rebuilding work in Jerusalem (1 Kgs 11:27–28). Ahijah meets him as he escapes; in an acted parable, he assures him of kingship over most of Israel because of Solomon's service of Ashtoreth (NRSV Astarte), Chemosh, and Milcom (11:34–36). He then promises on behalf of Yahweh that, if Jeroboam keeps divine instructions as David did,

---

26. Ibid., 279–81.

"I will be with you, and will build you an established house [בית נאמן]²⁷ as I built for David, and I will give Israel to you."

Ahijah promises him "an established house" (1 Kgs 11:38), like Nathan promised David in synoptic 2 Sam 7:16. Synoptic David had also been in the service of the previous king: he had commanded Saul's army (2 Sam 5:2 // 1 Chr 11:2). Just as nonsynoptic Kings makes Jeroboam a refugee from Solomon, so nonsynoptic Samuel makes the younger David a refugee from Saul (1 Sam 27:1; see 7.1 above), so increasing the similarity with Jeroboam.

Sometime after Israel made Jeroboam their king, he feared that continuing resort to sacrifice in Jerusalem would lead to his people defecting to Rehoboam. He set up golden calves in Bethel and Dan (1 Kgs 12:26–29); "and this thing came to be a sin" (ויהי הדבר הזה לחטאת, 12:30a).²⁸ And synoptic David also had to confess to "sin" (2 Sam 24:17). Placing priests of his own making in Bethel and setting his own sacred calendar (1 Kgs 12:31–33) simply made matters more deplorable. Jeroboam's visit to the altar at Bethel (12:33b) provides the opportunity for the lengthy tale (13:1–32) of the man of God from Judah and the prophet of Bethel (with its links to Amos 7:10–17) that reinforces the divine warning "against the altar in Bethel and all the houses of the high places that are in the cities of Samaria" (1 Kgs 13:32). A recapitulatory note follows (13:33–34): Jeroboam did not turn from his evil way but created priests of his own for his "high places"; and this "sin" led to the utter destruction of Jeroboam's house.

The first stage of the threatened destruction is reported immediately (1 Kgs 14:1–18), in a narrative reminiscent in several respects of (nonsynoptic) 2 Sam 11–12 (see 7.2). The divine threat against Jeroboam's house is directed first against his son Abijah. This story also involves both the child's

---

27. This formulation is reminiscent of the divine promise to David conveyed first by synoptic Nathan (2 Sam 7:16) and "later" anticipated by Abigail (1 Sam 25:28). It also evokes the promised establishment of a priestly house (1 Sam 2:35). The different formulation in the synoptic parallel 1 Chr 17:14 (והעמדתיהו בביתי ובמלכותי עד־עולם, "and I shall have him stand firm in my house and in my kingdom forever") is almost certainly secondary: עמד hiphil is widely used in later biblical books; and, while it is found in a few other synoptic contexts (2 Chr 9:8; 18:34; 33:8 [// 1 Kgs 10:9; 22:35; 2 Kgs 21:8]), the Kings variant is always preferable.

28. לחטאת is often used in Leviticus (16x) and Numbers (18x), and also twice in Ezekiel, meaning "for a sin offering." The only nonsacrificial usage apart from 1 Kgs 12:30 (and its near-repetition in 13:34) is in Prov 10:16, where חטאת is contrasted with חיים ("life").

mother and the same Ahijah the prophet as had uttered the divine promise to Jeroboam. The unusual twist in the prophetic oracle is that only this dying child, of all the house of Jeroboam, will be buried "because something good has been found in him."[29] Accordingly, no burial is reported for Jeroboam, though we are told (14:20) that "he lay with his fathers"—in the case of Nadab his successor, not even that is reported (15:31).

8.7. Evaluating Northern Israel

All but two of Jeroboam's successors in the northern kingdom are said in almost identical terms to have followed in his sinful ways.[30] This stereotypical complaint is more unrelenting than anything in the synoptic record. Four of David's successors in Jerusalem have their behavior likened to their own *immediate* father.[31] On the other hand, in the shared tradition, only Ahaz, Hezekiah, and Josiah are compared with the father *of the dynasty*—Ahaz negatively, Hezekiah and Josiah positively.[32] Although in these three cases the founder of the dynasty is favorably remembered, David's own record had included the "sin" of counting Israel. The consequences of this sin had blighted his whole people; and that memory contributed to the reshaping of Jeroboam, who "had made Israel sin."

Manasseh of Jerusalem is also clearly in the mind of the authors of the integrated story of northern Israel in Kings. In the assessment of most of the earlier kings of Israel (from Jeroboam to Ahaziah), the stock complaint that they caused Israel to sin is supplemented by the remark, "vexing Yahweh God of Israel by their 'nonentities'" (להכעיס את־יהוה אלהי ישראל בהבליהם).[33] The synoptic narrative had first directed this critique of vexing Yahweh against King Manasseh (2 Kgs 21:6), although Huldah (22:17) went some way to generalize the complaint and include her people in the blame. In the global judgment against the northern people (17:7–

---

29. "All Israel" burying and mourning this (innocent) child (1 Kgs 14:18) may be an implicit comment on David not mourning his first child with Bathsheba (2 Sam 12:20–23).

30. Elah (1 Kgs 16:8) and Zimri (16:9–12). In fact, Elah and his father Baasha are blamed for their own sins in 16:13.

31. Jehoshaphat (1 Kgs 22:43), Azariah (2 Kgs 15:3), and Jotham (2 Kgs 15:34) are all praised; and Amon (2 Kgs 21:21) is blamed.

32. 2 Kgs 16:2; 18:3; 22:2.

33. 1 Kgs 15:30; 16:2, 7, 13, 26, 33; 21:22; 22:54.

17), it is repeatedly the details of Manasseh's sins from the shared story (21:2–7) supplemented by Ahaz's sin (16:3–4) that are listed against them:

- בחקות הגוים אשר הוריש יהוה מפני בני ישראל ("by the norms of the nations that Yahweh had dispossessed before the sons of Israel," 17:8) < הוריש יהוה מפני בני ישראל כתועבת הגוים אשר ("like the abominations of the nations that Yahweh had dispossessed before the sons of Israel," 16:3; 21:2)
- ויבנו להם במות ("and they built themselves high places," 17:9) < ויבן את־הבמות ("and he built the high places," 21:3)
- על כל־גבעה גבהה ותחת כל־עץ רענן ("on every high hill and under every green tree," 17:10) < על־הגבעות ותחת כל־עץ רענן ("on the hills and under every green tree," 16:4)
- וישתחוו לכל־צבא השמים ויעבדו את־הבעל ("and they prostrated to all the host of heaven and served the Baal," 17:16) < וישתחו לכל־צבא השמים ויעבד אתם ("and he prostrated to all the host of heaven and served them," 21:3)
- ויעבירו את־בניהם ואת־בנותיהם באש ("and they made their sons and their daughters pass in the fire," 17:17) < והעביר את־בנ[ו]ו[ן] באש ("and he made his son[s] pass in the fire," 21:6)
- וינחשו ... לעשות הרע בעיני יהוה להכעיסו ("and they divined ... doing evil in Yahweh's eyes, vexing him," 17:17) < ונחש ... לעשות הרע בעיני יהוה להכעיסו ("and he divined ... doing evil in Yahweh's eyes, vexing him," 21:6)

We shall find in a later discussion that this comprehensive stocktaking of northern Israel does not just draw on the synoptic reports of wicked Ahaz and Manasseh (not forgetting David). Two elements of the (synoptic) Hezekiah story also make a significant contribution to 2 Kgs 17.[34] The key verb "deliver" (הציל), used many times in both versions of the Hezekiah story, is found just once more in Kings—close to the end of the long,

---

34. While noting many of the same links between 2 Kgs 17 and the Hezekiah narrative, Michael Press draws a different literary-historical conclusion: "The sudden first appearance of these words in 2 Kgs 17, followed by their repetition in the notice on Hezekiah's reign and dramatically in the speech of the Rabshakeh, signals that both chapters are part of a unified literary composition" ("'Where Are the Gods of Hamath?' [2 Kings 18.34 // Isaiah 36.19]: The Use of Foreign Deities in the Rabshakeh's Speech," *JSOT* 40 [2015]: 215).

8. PROPHETS AND KINGS IN ISRAEL

critical peroration on the north (2 Kgs 17:39), and hence immediately before the account of Hezekiah. Similarly "have faith in" (האמין) of 2 Chr 32:15 (but not the parallel in Kings as we now read it) is found in Kings only once (2 Kgs 17:14). Significantly, each of הציל and האמין in 2 Kgs 17 is in close proximity to "but they did not listen" (ולא שמעו).[35] These indicators invite the suggestion that האמין, a significant element of Isa 7:9 and 28:16 now attested only in the Chronicler's version (2 Chr 32:15), had been original to the Hezekiah story but was overwritten by the synonymous בטח ("trust"), when that verb became much more prominently used in the Kings/Isaiah version.

The usage of השתחוה in the rest of Kings as a whole is largely consistent with what we can observe in the synoptic texts. Referring to prostration before a deity, it is found in 1 Kgs 11:33 of the worship of Ashtoreth of Sidon and several other gods of surrounding peoples; in 1 Kgs 16:31 and 22:54 of Ahab and then his son worshiping Baal; in 2 Kgs 5:18 of Naaman worshiping in the house of Rimmon once he returns home to Aram; in 2 Kgs 17:16 of the sons of Israel anticipating Manasseh and worshiping the whole host of heaven; in 2 Kgs 19:37 of the king of Assyria worshiping in the house of Nisroch his god; and in 2 Kgs 21:21 of Amon son of Manasseh worshiping the גללים that his father had served.[36]

Second Kings 17 provides the sole passage in Kings where we find this verb explicitly related to worship of Yahweh. First of all, verse 35 reaffirms in a fourfold prohibition the long-held (synoptic) situation forbidding prostration to other gods:

You shall not fear other gods	לא תיראו אלהים אחרים
and you shall not prostrate yourselves to them	ולא תשתחוו להם
and you shall not serve them	ולא תעבדום
and you shall not sacrifice to them	ולא תזבחו להם

Then verse 36 identifies Yahweh as the God of the exodus from Egypt, and continues in a crisp threefold enjoinder:

---

35. שמעו may itself have been drawn from synoptic 2 Kgs 21:9; but where this clause is found in synoptic contexts in Kings (2 Kgs 21:9; 22:13), Chronicles uses a different verb: הקשיבו in 2 Chr 33:10 and שמרו in 34:21.

36. Unless this should be regarded as synoptic (see 12.3.20).

Him you shall fear	אתו תיראו
and to him you shall prostrate yourselves	ולו תשתחוו
and to him you shall sacrifice	ולו תזבחו

Translation catches only half of the rhetorical flourish, as "not ... to them" gives way before "to him." But it cannot hear how the opening negative לא ("not") is subtly transmuted into the opening emphatic לו ("to him"), which sounded identical (lō).[37]

The theme of prostration to Yahweh is more widespread in Chronicles (1 Chr 16:29; 29:20; 2 Chr 7:3; 20:18; 29:28, 29, 30). In two of these five contexts, the purpose of the additional material may be corrective. One of these "corrections" (2 Chr 7:3) is placed significantly close to and ahead of Solomon's second vision (7:12–22), while three more (29:28–30) report part of Hezekiah's cultic reform ahead of the report of the Assyrian embassy. My discussion of 2 Kgs 18:22 (see 10.2) will show that similar clarification was required in 2 Kgs 17:36. Prostration to a human is reported in the book of Kings only during the transition from David to Solomon[38] and on two occasions where Elisha is similarly saluted.[39]

8.8. Overview of Israel's Kings

8.8.1. Contemporaries of Asa

According to 1 Kgs 15–16, Asa of Judah overlaps with no less than seven kings of Israel; and four of these are known from the synoptic record. (1) Jeroboam had outlived both Rehoboam and Abijam, and died in Asa's second year. (2) Baasha (15:33–16:7) is credited with the longest (24 years) of the five northern reigns within the still longer reign of Asa (41 years), on whom he had made war. (3) The reign of Omri (16:23–28), whose name is attested in both Assyrian and Moabite inscriptions, is also

---

37. The balance in Deuteronomy is similar: warnings against prostration *to* other gods are repeated in 4:19; 5:9; 8:19; 11:16; 17:3; 29:25; and 30:17; and the sole positive command to prostrate oneself *before* Yahweh('s altar) is in 26:10.

38. 1 Kgs 1:16, 23, 31, 47, 53; 2:19.

39. 2 Kgs 2:15; 4:37. I noted (end of 2.4) that the oath חי נפשך is normally sworn on a king's life, the sole exceptions being in the same two chapters of 2 Kings. Elisha's "anointing" in place of Elijah is announced alongside the succession of two royal figures. This "prophet" had a quasi-royal status.

wholly included within Asa's; but, apart from the early civil strife (see below), all we are told about him is that he moved the capital from Tirzah to Samaria. (4) The long reign of Ahab (16:29–22:40) overlapped with the final years of Asa.

Three names are added. (1) From the report on Nadab (15:25–32), we learn only that Baasha overthrew him in his second year. (2) Baasha was succeeded by Elah, his own son (16:8–14); but (3) he in turn was overthrown in his second year by Zimri, who lasted only seven days (16:15–20). Both Baasha (15:27) and Zimri (16:15) launched their revolts when Israel was encamped against Gibbethon, controlled by Philistines. The troops besieging Gibbethon rejected Zimri's claim to the throne, and both Omri and Tibni were claimants to follow him (16:21–22). Though he lasted only seven days before being ousted, Zimri is counted as having been king, but Tibni is not. It is hard not to believe that a succession has been manufactured from very little information, with at least one key element (the army at Gibbethon) recycled.

The wording of 16:24 about Omri first buying the site for Samaria suggests imitation of synoptic David (2 Sam 24:24 // 1 Chr 21:24–25).

8.8.2. Cooperation and Intermarriage: The House of Ahab

Omri's name is known in Assyrian inscriptions; and these continued to term northern Israel "the house of Omri" even after his own dynasty had fallen. Within the Hebrew Bible, however, not only Kings and Chronicles but the book of Micah as well speaks not of "Omri's house" but of Ahab's (בית אחאב). Ahab's twenty-two-year reign overlaps very substantially with Jehoshaphat's (25 years); and their co-operation against the Aramaeans is backdrop to one of the longest episodes recounted in the synoptic record (1 Kgs 22:1–35 // 2 Chr 18). The brief summary in Kings of Ahab's reign reports only his marriage to the daughter of Ethbaal, king of Sidon, his erection of an altar to Baal in the temple of Baal he had built in Samaria, and his fabrication of an Asherah (1 Kgs 16:31–33). No spouse (or mother) of any previous king of northern Israel had been listed in Kings; and the implication seems clear: Ahab's marriage into a family associated with Baal resulted in a substantial cultic entail. The consequences of his marriage are much more fully elaborated in the Elijah stories in 1 Kgs 17–19 and 21 (we already discussed 1 Kgs 18 in 8.3.1).

The close association of the two royal houses is mirrored in the names of the next two kings of each. Jehoshaphat was succeeded by his son

Jehoram (who married a daughter of Ahab), and he in turn by his son Ahaziah. In the same period, Ahab is reported as succeeded by a short-lived Ahaziah (who does not feature in the synoptic story), and he by his brother J(eh)oram since he had no son. The latter pair, Ahaziah and Joram, cooperated in a military adventure against Aram at Ramoth-gilead, like Ahab and Jehoshaphat before them; and both lost their lives to Jehu when he usurped the northern throne.

8.8.3. A Synchronistic History

It is a feature of the book of Kings that the accession of almost every king of Israel after Solomon is dated by the regnal year of the king of Judah of the time, and vice versa. Three synchronisms, stated or implied, had been provided in the synoptic record. (1) The reigns of Solomon's successors, Rehoboam and Jeroboam, had started more or less together. (2) Ahaziah and Joram died within a short time of each other. (3) Despite being worsted in his challenge to the northern Jehoash, Amaziah outlived the victor by fifteen years: ויחי אמציהו בן־יואש מלך יהודה אחרי מות יהואש בן־יהואחז מלך ישראל חמש עשרה שנה (2 Kgs 14:17 // 2 Chr 25:25). "Live" and "life" are used very sparingly in synoptic narrative (as already reviewed in 2.1): some special significance may be intended. It is of course possible that "Long live the king" (יחי המלך) was shouted at every royal accession; but it is reported only once synoptically (2 Kgs 11:12 // 2 Chr 23:11) at the installation of the boy-king Joash of Judah, all of whose siblings had been murdered by Athaliah. Perhaps it was the very surprise of Amaziah's "survival" that occasioned this third (implied) synchronic note that he "lived for fifteen years after the death of King Jehoash."

Unfortunately this apparently straightforward note is surrounded by a series of chronological issues in the book of Kings. First of all, the death of Jehoash of Israel and the succession of his son Jeroboam (II) is reported twice, in very similar terms. On the first occasion, the concluding formula for J(eh)oash (2 Kgs 13:12–13) immediately follows the introductory formula (13:10–11). On the second, his concluding formula (14:15–16) follows the detailed report of his success against Amaziah of Judah (14:8–14). On the first occasion, the concluding formula seems to be placed too soon; there is still more to tell about Joash: not only victories over Aram (13:24–25) but the success over Judah as well. On the second occasion, the formula appears to interrupt the account of Amaziah of Judah (14:1–14, 17–20). Matters are further complicated. The second half of the possibly intrusive 14:15–16 ends unremarkably: וישכב יהואש עם־אבתיו ויקבר בשמרון עם־מלכי ישראל וימלך ירבעם בנו תחתיו ("and Jehoash lay with his fathers and was buried in Samaria with the kings of Israel, and Jeroboam his son became king in his place"). On the other hand, the earlier 13:13 reports quite uniquely, וישכב יואש עם־אבתיו וירבעם ישב על־כסאו ויקבר יואש בשמרון עם־מלכי ישראל ("and Joash lay with his fathers, and it was Jeroboam that sat on his throne, and Joash was buried in Samaria with the kings of Israel"). The syntax of the central clause about Jeroboam is disjunctive, appropriate for a note that interrupts the report about the burial of Joash; and successor Jeroboam is not said to be son of the dead king. Furthermore, Zimri is the only other king (since Solomon) reported as sitting on the throne of his predecessor—and he had overthrown Elah son of Baasha (1 Kgs 16:11).

This Jeroboam is something of an elephant in the room of the synchronic account of Samaria. Jeroboam II is credited in 2 Kgs 14:23–29 with a reign of forty-one years during the final fifteen years of Joash of Judah and the first half of the reign of Azariah/Uzziah; and two of the notes about him in Kings report territorial advances (14:25, 28). On the other hand, while the Chronicler makes no mention of Jeroboam within his reports on Joash (2 Chr 24), Uzziah (2 Chr 25–26) or indeed Jotham (2 Chr 27) in Jerusalem, 1 Chr 5:17 has reported that Transjordanian clans were enrolled in genealogies "in the days of King Jotham of Judah and in the days of King Jeroboam of Israel." This alternative to 2 Kgs 14, this synchronism between Jeroboam II and a later king of Judah, can claim support in Hos 1:1: "The word of Yahweh that came to Hosea son of Beeri in the days of Uzziah, Jotham, Ahaz, Hezekiah, the kings of Judah, and in the days of Jeroboam son of Joash, the king of Israel."[40]

Whichever dating is appropriate, some of his achievements seem to have become reattributed to the earlier Jeroboam. Finkelstein notes that "the description in 1 Kgs 12:29 of the establishment of an Israelite cult place at Tel Dan probably depicts eighth-century realities,"[41] and reports the (negative) archaeological evidence that Bethel was unoccupied in Early Iron IIA.[42] This is not to say that the description dates from the eighth

---

40. Two details of this title verse in Hosea link it with Chronicles' version of the royal record: calling the first of the Jerusalem kings Uzziah rather than Azariah, and using (as also in Mic 1:1) a longer Hebrew form of Hezekiah's name (יחזקיה).

41. *Forgotten Kingdom*, 129.

42. Ibid., 75.

century, as it had required some fair elapse of time before situations relating to eighth-century Jeroboam II could be reattributed to tenth-century Jeroboam I.

The title verse of the book of Amos dates his visionary work to the days of Uzziah and of Jeroboam II; and the book mentions Bethel critically several times (3:14; 4:4; 5:5–6) and Dan once (8:14). The short narrative in 7:10–17 about Amaziah, priest of (the royal sanctuary at) Bethel, and the troublesome Amos, a seer from Judah, is even more important for this issue. As noted at least since the work of Wellhausen,[43] the language and situation of the Amos story have several unique links with the very much longer tale in 1 Kgs 13 (set in the time of the earlier Jeroboam) about a "man of God" from Judah sent to Bethel with an oracle against its altar and his dealings there first with Jeroboam I and then with the old prophet in Bethel. The relationship between these two stories mirrors that between the shorter 2 Kgs 11 and the longer 1 Kgs 18 (discussed at 8.3.1). In both pairs, the role played by a priest in the older, shorter narrative is taken over by a prophet in the longer tale.

8.8.4. Final Decades in Samaria

Reported between the summary synoptic treatment of Azariah/Uzziah (2 Kgs 15:1–7) and of Jotham (15:32–38), and reigning during the exceptionally long 52-year reign of Azariah, we find five kings in Samaria: Zechariah (15:8–12), Shallum (15:13–16), Menahem (15:17–22), Pekahiah (15:23–26), and Pekah (15:27–31). Menahem, credited with ten years, is the only king of Israel who *does* appear in the external inscriptional record but is *not* also mentioned in Chronicles. The usurper Pekah son of Remaliah is mentioned in Isaiah (7:1) as well as in 2 Chr 28:6. But the others (Zechariah, Shallum, and Pekahiah) go without mention in any biblical book other than Kings. Pekah himself falls to Hoshea, the final king of northern Israel (2 Kgs 15:30; 17:1–6), who is also otherwise unknown. These four further unknowns mirror the earlier Nadab, Elah, and Zimri, who have the very short reigns around the time of Baasha.

---

43. *Composition des Hexateuchs*, 280.

9
Rewriting Judah's Kings

9.1. The Synoptic House of David

There is no explicit assessment in shared texts of David's son and successor. Nothing discreditable is reported; Solomon's record is left to speak for itself. He received two divine visions, built Jerusalem's temple, and received congratulations from two foreign monarchs. Rehoboam was foolish in not heeding good advice from his more senior advisers, but the summary assessment of his reign is very differently reported. Abijam/h is very differently reported in Kings and Chronicles, and not explicitly assessed in either. Asa is credited with several positive reforms. Jehoshaphat is said to have followed in his father's footsteps (despite having made common cause with the king of Israel). Only Chronicles reports that he intermarried with the house of Ahab: nothing is said in Kings of his own wife, though his son Jehoram was married to a daughter of Ahab and is blamed for walking in the way of the kings of Israel. Jehoram's son Ahaziah is similarly blamed, and he too joined the current king of Israel in a campaign against Aram.

Ahaziah's mother, Athaliah, usurped the throne on his death. When she was ousted by Jehoiada, the priest of Yahweh, in favor of the infant Joash, the cult of Baal in Jerusalem was destroyed and its priest put to death. Under Joash, who is assessed positively, the Jerusalem temple was repaired; he himself was killed in a conspiracy. Amaziah is also assessed positively and was also killed in a conspiracy. Azariah (known also as Uzziah) also "did right in Yahweh's eyes," but became "leprous." Ahaz "walked in the ways of the kings of Israel" and was enthusiastic in his abominable practices. His son Hezekiah, by contrast, "did right in Yahweh's eyes" and was compared with David. He instituted cultic reforms; and, when Judah was occupied by the Assyrians, Jerusalem itself was saved from Assyrian assault.

With Manasseh, the pendulum swung back again toward Ahaz—and beyond: Manasseh's cultic malpractices are the most fully reported of all the kings of Judah. The brief reign of his son Amon was no improvement, and he was killed in a conspiracy. Josiah's introduction outdoes Hezekiah's: he was not only like David, but did not deviate to right or left. He behaved appropriately when hearing the words of the book found during temple repairs, and presided over a restored Passover. No assessment is given of Jehoahaz, who reigned for only three months before being deposed by the king of Egypt. His three final successors were all rated negatively, but without explanation.

9.2. Solomon Re-presented

The shared account of King Solomon opens with his vision at Gibeon and his request there for wisdom (1 Kgs 3:5–15 // 2 Chr 1:7–13), and closes with demonstrations of the riches and power promised him at Gibeon by Yahweh (1 Kgs 10 // 2 Chr 9). The intervening synoptic material about building and dedicating "Yahweh's palace" (היכל יהוה) in Jerusalem portrays him positively. But there is much additional (nonsynoptic) material in the book of Kings; and this brings Solomon much less credit. Of course the book of Samuel embodies an even greater expansion of the synoptic traditions about Saul and David.[1]

9.2.1. A New Outer Framework

Between the first note about his succession on the death of David (1 Kgs 2:12) and its recapitulation that states for a second time the establishment of the kingdom in his hands (2:46b), we read of the assassination of a series of potential rivals. The remark in 1 Kgs 3:1 (MT),[2] that Solomon had brought his Egyptian wife into David's city, prepares for the synoptic note (1 Kgs 9:24a // 2 Chr 8:11) that she later moved from David's city to her own house. In turn, the related Kings pluses about Solomon building the Millo (1 Kgs 9:15, 24b)[3] prepare for the narrative about Jeroboam as corvée master to Solomon (1 Kgs 11:26–40).

---

1. Auld, *I and II Samuel*, 622–30.
2. The corresponding note in LXX is at 3 Kgdms 2:35c.
3. Synoptic tradition reports only David as Millo builder (2 Sam 5:9 // 1 Chr 11:8).

9. REWRITING JUDAH'S KINGS

Both introductions to the report of Solomon's first vision at Gibeon that have come down to us do betray some embarrassment. On the other hand, the reports of Solomon offering vast numbers of animals in sacrifice during the visit to the preexisting "great במה" suggest an earlier form of that story that had been quite devoid of any embarrassment. A first prefatory verse in 1 Kings (3:2) concerns his people: "they were sacrificing enthusiastically at the high places, because a house for Yahweh's name had not been built up to these days" (העם מזבחים בבמות כי לא־נבנה בית לשם יהוה עד הימים ההם). And a second (3:3) tells us that "Solomon *loved* Yahweh, walking by the norms of David his father—but it was at the high places that *he was sacrificing enthusiastically and offering incense*" (ויאהב שלמה את־יהוה ללכת בחקות דוד אביו רק בבמות הוא מזבח ומקטיר). King and people were resorting to במות ("high places") as places for sacrifice simply because the temple for Yahweh had not yet been built. For the Chronicler too, sacrifice at Gibeon was not improper: not because Jerusalem still lacked suitable facilities, but more positively because the Mosaic divine tent of meeting was located there in addition to the bronze altar constructed by Bezalel, also from the wilderness period.

When we view it in double retrospect from 1 Kgs 11, this early note becomes much more menacing. The nonsynoptic conclusion opens (11:1–8) by charging Solomon with the religious implications of intermarriage with many alien women in addition to the daughter of the Egyptian pharaoh. The first and last words of 3:3 are reused at beginning and end of this opening portion, the report about his wives: והמלך שלמה אהב נשים נכריות רבות ("But King Solomon *loved* many foreign women," 11:1) and מקטירות ומזבחות לאלהיהן ("they were *offering and sacrificing* to their gods," 11:8). Some of the gods for whom he built sanctuaries are named: עשתרת אלהי צדנים ("Ashtoreth, god of Sidonians," 11:5); מלכם שקץ עמנים ("Milcom, abomination of Ammonites," 11:5), presumably the same as מלך שקץ בני עמון ("Molech, abomination of the sons of Ammon," 11:7); כמוש שקץ מואב ("Chemosh, abomination of Moab," 11:7). There is also a more distant but quite as important an echo with the start of 1 Kgs 3: בחקות ("by the norms," 3:3) will introduce an implied comparison in only one further biblical context, in 2 Kgs 17 (see 8.7).[4]

Yahweh's punishment for the king who had enjoyed the privilege of two divine visions (11:9), but had failed to heed the instruction about

---

4. In 2 Kgs 17:8, Israel is blamed for following the norms of "the nations"; and in 17:19, Judah is similarly blamed for following the norms of Israel.

foreign gods, was the loss of his kingdom. However, there were two limitations on the punishment, both of them out of respect for his father, David: the loss would be delayed till the time of Solomon's son; and it would not be total—one שבט ("scepter" or "tribe") of Israel would remain for David's house (11:13). Building shrines for foreign gods had led to the divine verdict that much of his kingdom would pass to one of his servants, not to his son. Two potential candidates for the throne of Israel, refugees from his own kingdom, would cause difficulties for Solomon at divine instigation (11:14–22, 23–25) before a third, Jeroboam, the actual successor, was identified (11:26–40). See further 8.7.

We noted earlier (3.5) that temporal markers and infinitives absolute, though never adjacent in synoptic texts, are linked in at least ten contexts in nonsynoptic Samuel–Kings. Others among the words that we followed in chapters 2–3 are combined in 1 Kgs 11. "Day" and "life" are never adjacent in synoptic texts; but we find כל־ימי חייו ("all the days of his life") in 1 Sam 1:11; 7:15; 1 Kgs 5:1; 11:34; 15:5, 6; 2 Kgs 25:29, 30 (// Jer 52:33, 34).[5] Similarly אך ("however") introduces a temporal expression including "days" in both 1 Kgs 11:12 and 39. And ניר ("tillage" or "lamp") is a key part of the argument in both 1 Kgs 11:36 and 15:4, where nonsynoptic Solomon and Abijam benefit like synoptic Jehoram from the divine promise to David, despite following the example of the house of Ahab. "All the days" (כל־הימים) had been part of the original Jehoram context in 2 Kgs 8:19. Such an open-ended divine commitment could only be maintained if it applied to Solomon, like each of David's successors, "all the days of his life" (כל־ימי חייו).

9.2.2. Early Solomon Report Supplemented

Between Solomon's inaugural vision (1 Kgs 3:5–15 // 2 Chr 1:7–13) and the start of his building works (1 Kgs 6–7 // 2 Chr 3–4), Kings is much longer than Chronicles. Solomon's judgment in the case of the two women and one (living) child (1 Kgs 3:16–28) and the list of his officials (1 Kgs 4:1–19) both develop themes of the vision. The judgment is a first and striking illustration of the wisdom he had requested; and the enumeration

---

5. They are also linked in Deut 17:19; Josh 4:14; Qoh 5:17, 19; 8:15 (cf. כל־ימי חייך in Gen 3:14, 17; Deut 4:9; 6:2; 16:3; Josh 1:5; Ps 128:5; כל־ימי חייה in Prov 31:12; and מספר ימי חייהם in Qoh 2:3). Other close links in Deuteronomy include 4:4, 10: 5:3; 30:20; 31:13, 27.

of his principal courtiers suggests the scope of the wealth bestowed on him as a bonus by Yahweh. Neither the narrative nor the list corresponds to anything in Chronicles, and both can readily be assessed as additions to Kings from a source distinct from the synoptic tradition. However, the relationship between what follows in 1 Kgs 4:20–5:32 and synoptic material on Solomon is more complex.

The much shorter space in Chronicles between vision and building is occupied by just two elements. Second Chronicles 1:14–17 anticipates the synoptic 1 Kgs 10:26–29 // 2 Chr 9:25–28 and offers a third version of this largely shared material. And 2 Chr 2:1–17 corresponds to one section of 1 Kgs 4:20–5:32—it offers a somewhat different version from 1 Kgs 5:15–26 of the deal done between Solomon and Hiram of Tyre: he had been an ally of David, and would now provide material and craftsmen for Solomon's building works.

1. First Kings 4:20–5:8 continues from 4:1–19 the theme of Solomon's officials and the needs of his court that they had to supply.

- 1 Kgs 5:1a and 5:6 make summary statements about the extent of Solomon's empire and the numbers of his cavalry that appear in Chronicles only at the end of the Solomon story (2 Chr 9:26, 25a).
- 1 Kgs 5:4 restates 5:1a in rather different terms.
- 1 Kgs 5:5 and 4:20 offer similar judgments about the prosperity of Judah and Israel under Solomon.

Thus 4:20–5:5 presents a chiastic pattern: a (4:20) b (5:1) c (5:2–3) b (5:4) a (5:5).

2. If 4:20–5:8 extends the theme of Solomon's officials and their duties, 5:9–14 returns to the theme of his unparalleled wisdom already illustrated in his judgment of the rival women. Here again there are links with the end of the shared Solomon story. The triple statement of his wisdom in 5:9 (חכמה, תבונה, רחב לב, "wisdom, discernment, expansive heart") corresponds to Hiram's master craftsman in 1 Kgs 7:14 (דעת, תבונה, חכמה, "wisdom, discernment, knowledge") and 2 Chr 2:12 (איש חכם יודע בינה, "a man wise and knowing discernment"). A large amount of wisdom comparable with the sand by the sea links the theme of Solomon's wisdom to Israel's numbers. The comparison of his wisdom with that of the east[6]

---

6. קדם in the sense of "east" is not known elsewhere in Samuel–Kings–Chronicles.

and of Egypt (1 Kgs 5:10) restates synoptic ויגדל המלך שלמה מכל מלכי הארץ לעשר וחכמה ("And King Solomon was greater than all the kings of the earth for wealth and wisdom," 1 Kgs 10:23 // 2 Chr 9:22). The verb חכם ("be wise") in 1 Kgs 5:11 ("He was wiser than all humankind") never appears again in Samuel-Kings-Chronicles—its usage is late and mostly in Proverbs; and hence it is hardly surprising that 1 Kgs 5:12-13 goes on to report Solomon's wide knowledge of songs and proverbs. As for the five potential competitors in 5:11 for the crown of wisdom, Ethan the Ezrahite is named at the head of Ps 89, and Heman at the head of Ps 88; Calcol is named again in 1 Chr 2:6, but Darda and Mahol are otherwise unknown. First Kings 5:14 extends and restates 10:24 // 2 Chr 9:23. Indeed, this whole paragraph in 1 Kgs 5:9-14 could be described as an expansive exposition of synoptic 10:24 // 2 Chr 9:23.

3. Much of 1 Kgs 5 is expansive repetition of themes from the final synoptic summaries on Solomon (including larger totals of cavalry, etc.). However, there are two important novelties in this enhanced introduction. One is the double mention of Judah separate from Israel: Judah and Israel can hardly be counted (4:20), and they extend "from Dan to Beer-sheba" (5:5). In each case, the account of David's census (2 Sam 24:1-9 // 1 Chr 21:1-5) is the synoptic source being drawn on. And the other is Solomon's raising of forced labor from the people of Israel themselves (1 Kgs 5:27).

Synoptic traditions relating to the first three kings in Jerusalem are quite clear in what they say about corvée:

- There is no mention of it among David's officials (2 Sam 8:15-18 // 1 Chr 18:14-17).
- Solomon did not impose forced labor on Israelites (1 Kgs 9:23 // 2 Chr 8:9).
- Forced labor was clearly part of the regime of foolish Rehoboam, and A/Hadoram was the official responsible (1 Kgs 12:18 // 2 Chr 10:18).

Chronicles has no more to say on the matter, but pluses in Samuel-Kings push the issue back to the time of David:[7]

---

7. One can also argue that David dealing separately with Judah in some late portions of the book of Samuel (1 Sam 30; 2 Sam 2-4) is a further instance of pushing back to his time a division between Judah and Israel that earlier synoptic tradition attributed to Rehoboam.

- The second list of David's officials, a recapitulation of 2 Sam 8:15–18 after the major additions in 2 Sam 9–20, includes "Adoram in charge of the forced labor" (20:24).
- Adoniram, whether the same person or different, has the same role among Solomon's officials (1 Kgs 4:6).
- Solomon appointed Jeroboam over the corvée in Ephraim (1 Kgs 11:28).

First Kings 5:27 contradicts synoptic 9:23 // 2 Chr 8:9 quite explicitly when it reports that Solomon raised a corvée out of all Israel, with Adoniram specified (1 Kgs 5:28b) as being in charge.[8] And 1 Kgs 5:30 shares with 9:23 the plus העשים במלאכה ("those working on the project").[9]

If we read 1 Kgs 4:20–5:32 from a synoptic perspective and explore parallels within the Hebrew Bible for some of the pluses, several elements of the text become much less affirming of Solomon than appears from first reading:

- שמח ("rejoice") is a benign term in synoptic 2 Sam 6:12 // 1 Chr 15:25; 1 Kgs 8:66 // 2 Chr 7:10; and 2 Kgs 11:14, 20 // 2 Chr 23:13, 21; but אכלים ושתים ("eating and drinking") is never synoptic, and occurs elsewhere in the Hebrew Bible only in nonsynoptic Samuel–Kings (1 Sam 30:16; 1 Kgs 1:25; 4:20) and in Job (1:13, 18), and only there in situations of disaster waiting to happen.
- מגשים מנחה ("bringing an offering near," 1 Kgs 5:1b) is a combination paralleled only in Mal 2:12 and 3:3 of offerings brought to Yahweh's table, while the participle עבדים ("serving") reappears in Kings only in 2 Kgs 17:33, 41, where the service is false worship. The suggestion may be that Solomon is being served like a god. And we noted in the previous section that "all the days of his life" is a nonsynoptic combination.
- נסע hiphil ("remove," 1 Kgs 5:31) is uncommon, and only once more construed with אבנים ("stones"): מסיע אבנים יעצב בהם ("whoever 'quarries' stones will be hurt by them," Qoh 10:9); the verse is not in the Septuagint.

---

8. Sweeney suggests that Israel performed forced labor in building Yahweh's house, but "Canaanites work on 'secular' projects" (*I and II Kings*, 145).

9. See further in 12.3.2.

- The verb פסל ("carve," 1 Kgs 5:32) is used positively in Exod 34:1, 4 // Deut 10:1, 3 of Moses preparing tablets for the commandments; but it occurs elsewhere only in Hab 2:18, of making an idol.

The synoptic account of Solomon is often said to evoke a golden age. Insofar as this is so, these observations suggest that nonsynoptic 1 Kgs 5 sets out to deconstruct such an impression well before we reach the long-recognized, more up-front critique of Solomon in 1 Kgs 11.

9.3. Rehoboam

Both 3 Kgdms 14:22a and 2 Chr 12:14 note that this king "did evil in Yahweh's eyes," but 1 Kgs 14:22a (MT) has "Judah" as the subject of the verb "did evil" (ויעש יהודה הרע). Chronicles offers no further explanation of the negative judgment; however, 1 Kgs 14:22b–24 (both MT and LXX) set the behavior of Judah or Rehoboam in a much wider context.

22b: ויקנאו אתו ב/מכל אשר עשו אבתם בחטאתם אשר חטאו, "And they made him more jealous than all that their fathers had done by their sins that they sinned" (MT); or "And they made him jealous by all that their fathers had made, by their sins that they sinned" (LXX). The Septuagint is reminiscent of Deut 32:21: הם קנאוני בלא־אל ("they have made me jealous by a non-god").

23: ויבנו גם־המה להם במות ומצבות ואשרים על כל־גבעה גבהה ותחת כל־עץ רענן, "And they too built themselves במות and cultic pillars and Asherahs on every high hill and under every green tree." The verb בנה ("build") refers throughout the Solomon story to the Jerusalem temple until 11:7, where Solomon builds a במה to Chemosh (referred to in 2 Kgs 23:13). In 1 Kgs 16:32 it is used of Ahab building in Samaria a house for Baal. The language of 1 Kgs 14:23b is drawn from (synoptic) 2 Kgs 16:4 (Ahaz).

24: וגם־קדש היה בארץ עשו ככל התועבות הגוים אשר הוריש יהוה מפני בני ישראל, "And even a cult prostitute was in the land. They made like all [the abominations] the nations that Yahweh expropriated in face of the sons of Israel." The first part of this note provides background for their removal by Asa (explicit in 1 Kgs 15:12 but hidden in synoptic 2 Chronicles). Nonsynoptic 1 Kgs 22:47 credits Jehoshaphat with completing Asa's task; and Josiah pulled down their houses (2 Kgs 23:7). The second part is also indebted to the synoptic critique of Ahaz (2 Kgs 16:3b).

In sum, Rehoboam (or Judah) continues the building work of (bad) Solomon, leaves untouched something with which Asa would have to deal, and anticipates the abominations of Ahaz and the sin of Manasseh.

9.4. Abijam and Asa

Abijah in 2 Chr 13 is a loyal warrior against Jeroboam. But in 1 Kgs 15:1–8 Abijam follows Solomon as a paradigm case of Yahweh's loyalty to Jerusalem and his promise to David against the odds, again (1 Kgs 15:5 like 11:36) anticipating wicked Jehoram (2 Kgs 8:19). The synoptic report on Asa in 1 Kgs 15:9–24 is repeated almost verbatim within the much longer 2 Chr 14–16.

9.5. Jehoshaphat, Jehoram, and Ahaziah

A brief plus in 1 Kgs 22:47 has Jehoshaphat complete his father's suppression of the קדשים (cult prostitutes). Kings adds nothing to the unspecific synoptic dismissal that both his successors had walked in the way of the house of Ahab.

9.6. Athaliah and J(eh)oash

There are small differences in how Kings and Chronicles report the management of Athaliah's removal and the subsequent repairs to the temple in Jerusalem. Levites have a role in both 2 Chr 23 and 24, but not in 2 Kgs 11 and 12 even where these chapters mention priests. The note about the honesty of the artisans repairing the temple (2 Kgs 12:15–16) may even be a response to any suggestion that they needed Levitical supervision. Second Kings 12:4 is the first of four linked Kings pluses about the nonremoval of "high places."

9.7. Amaziah, Azariah/Uzziah, and Jotham

The second, third, and fourth of four linked Kings pluses about the nonremoval of "high places" are found in 2 Kgs 14:4; 15:4, 35. There is a partially related text to the fourth in 2 Chr 27:2.

9.8. Ahaz

While sharing the content inserted in the standard outer structure of their reports, Kings and Chronicles deal differently with the struggle between Judah and Israel, with Judah's appeal to Assyria for help, and also with altar construction.

Topic	Nonsynoptic Kings	Synoptic Kings	Synoptic Chronicles	Nonsynoptic Chronicles
Standard introduction		16:2–3a, 3b–4	28:1–2a, 3b–4	
Cultic critique				28:2b–3a
Syro-Ephraimite war	16:5–6			28:5–8
Oded intervenes				28:9–15
Appeal to Assyria	16:7–9			28:16–23
Great Assyrian altar	16:10–16			
Clippings	16:17–18			28:24–25
Ending		16:19–20	28:26–27	

It was from the single, significant, synoptic, summary introduction to Ahaz that "hills" and "green trees" became part of the critique of others in the book of Kings: of Rehoboam at the start of the separate story of Judah (1 Kgs 14:23), and of northern Israel as that kingdom came to an end (2 Kgs 17:10).[10] Solomon had moved on from Gibeon and its במה. According to 2 Kgs 16:10–16, without a parallel in Chronicles, Ahaz compounded his errors at the במות by displacing Solomon's altar in favor of a new one constructed from an Assyrian model. Shortly before the standard concluding formula, 2 Chr 28:24 records simply that Ahaz had made altars (pl.) in every corner of Jerusalem. In complete contrast, 2 Kgs 16:10–16, nearer the heart of the account of this king, uses the term מזבח

---

10. The only other instances of "under every green tree" are in Deut 12:2; Isa 57:5; Jer 2:20; 3:6, 13; Ezek 6:13; they are linked with גבעות in Deut 12:2; with גבעה גבהה in Jer 2:20 and הר גבה in Jer 3:6; and with גבעה רמה in Ezek 6:13.

(sg.) as many as eleven times as it describes how the old main "altar" in Jerusalem was moved aside in favor of a copy in Damascus of an Assyrian altar, and yet was retained for some functions.[11] Jacob Wright repeats de Wette's claim[12] that the Chronicler deleted this report to exonerate the priests from complicity with Ahaz.[13] But it is no less likely that an author of Kings willingly implicated the priests in step-by-step complicity with this wicked king. The very massing of the keyword *altar* resembles the manifold repetition of בטח ("trust") in the secondary expansion of the Hezekiah story (2 Kgs 18).

9.9. Manasseh

The varied grounds for blame assembled in 2 Kgs 21:3–9 // 2 Chr 33:3–9 had already justified Manasseh's reputation as the most wicked king in the synoptic record. In the sections that immediately follow, Kings and Chronicles are completely divergent. However, within their summaries ("and the remainder of his deeds …") both books mention his "sin" (2 Kgs 21:17; 2 Chr 33:19). While Chronicles reports the repentance of this once very wicked king (2 Chr 33:10–17), Kings notes how his behavior corrupted Judah and sealed its fate. It adds a very eclectic set of complaints and arguments in 2 Kgs 21:11–16, which help explain the shared summary mention of his sin and its national consequences. Two precise statements of just how Manasseh made his people sin (vv. 11, 16) frame a divine speech declaring judgment on Jerusalem and Judah (vv. 12–15).

In the opening synoptic account of Manasseh (vv. 1–9), the first complaint against him (v. 2) had been that "he did evil … like the abominations of the nations that Yahweh had dispossessed" (ויעש הרע כתועבת הגוים אשר הוריש יהוה). The start of the new material (v. 11a) opens by restating two elements of this before linking them with "sin" from the sum-

---

11. This new "great altar" of Ahaz (2 Kgs 16:15) may be alluded to in the Hebrew (MT) version of the intriguing story in Josh 22, while the "great במה" of the Greek (LXX) version of that Joshua episode will have in mind the location at Gibeon of Solomon's first vision. For further discussion, see A. Graeme Auld, "Re-telling the Disputed 'Altar' in Joshua 22," in *The Book of Joshua*, ed. Ed Noort, BETL 250 (Leuven: Peeters, 2012), 281–93.

12. See Rogerson, *W. M. L. de Wette*, 57.

13. Jacob L. Wright, *David, King of Israel, and Caleb in Biblical Memory* (Cambridge: Cambridge University Press, 2014), 120.

mary (v. 11b): "Because Manasseh ... did/made these abominations, he did more evil than the Amorites had done" (יען אשר עשה מנשה התעבות האלה הרע מכל אשר־עשו האמרי). (1) We find "abominations" (תעבות) construed with "do/make" (עשה) only in a few pentateuchal texts.[14] (2) "The nations" have become "the Amorites." As for "he made even Judah to sin by his idols [בגלוליו]," "sin" anticipates the synoptic conclusion on Manasseh (2 Kgs 21:17 // 2 Chr 33:19) and "idols" the short synoptic report on Amon his son. Elsewhere in Kings (15x), only Israel is the object of החטיא ("made to sin"), but here "even Judah."[15] Idols and Amorites and acting abominably are also linked in the critique of Ahab (1 Kgs 21:26),[16] with whom Manasseh has been compared in 2 Kgs 21:3 (Kings plus).

The following divine judgment is stated in a miscellany of phrases mostly from the Latter Prophets. The opening statement of the severity of the threat (2 Kgs 21:12) is shared with 1 Sam 3:11 and Jer 19:3. ונטיתי ("And I shall stretch") introduces a divine threat seven times in the Latter Prophets.[17] There, what is stretched is always "my hand" (ידי), but here (2 Kgs 21:13a) "the measure of Samaria and the plumb line of the house of Ahab" (את־קו שמרון ואת־משקלת בית אחאב).[18] "And I shall wipe Jerusalem" (ומחיתי את־ירושלם, v. 13b) is reminiscent of "I shall wipe [Israel's] name off the face of the earth" and "wipe the memory of Amalek" in Deuteronomy.[19] משסה (v. 14) is a term for "booty" five times in the Latter Prophets.[20] And all these threats are appropriate because they (Judah) have been "vexing me" (מכעסים אתי) from the day of the exodus till this day (v. 15). Like החטיא ("make to sin"), הכעיס ("vex") mostly has Israel as subject in nonsynoptic Kings, but Judah here.[21]

After the threats (vv. 12–15), we return to and add to the charge against Manasseh (v. 16): גם דם נקי שפך מנשה הרבה מאד עד אשר־מלא את־ירושלם פה לפה לבד מחטאתו אשר החטיא את־יהודה לעשות הרע

---

14. Lev 18:27; 20:13; Deut 12:31; 13:15; 17:4.

15. Outside Kings, the objects of החטיא are "you" (Exod 23:33; Qoh 5:5), "the land" (Deut 24:4), "Judah" (Jer 32:35), and Solomon (Neh 13:26).

16. ויתעב מאד ללכת אחרי הגללים ככל אשר עשו האמרי ("and he acted very abominably, going after the idols as all that the Amorites had done").

17. Jer 51:25; Ezek 6:14; 14:9, 13; 25:13; 35:3; Zeph 1:4.

18. Citing קו and משקלת from Isa 28:17.

19. Deut 9:14; 29:19; and 25:19.

20. Isa 42:22, 24; Jer 30:16; Hab 2:7; Zeph 1:13; in Isa 42:22, as here, combined with the commoner בז.

21. The verb is synoptic in 2 Kgs 21:6; 22:17.

בעיני יהוה, "Even innocent blood did Manasseh shed in very great quantity until he filled Jerusalem side to side—apart from his sin that he made Judah sin, doing evil in Yahweh's eyes." Manasseh's sin had already been established on other grounds; and the guilt of shedding innocent blood was distinct from it.

This new complaint against him is repeated in 24:3b–4a: בחטאת מנשה ככל אשר עשה וגם דם־הנקי אשר שפך וימלא את־ירושלם דם נקי, "by the sins of Manasseh according to all that he did, and also the blood of the innocent that he shed, and filled Jerusalem with innocent blood." This theme has echoes in different books in the Hebrew Bible;[22] but the closest parallel comes in Jer 19:4, which speaks of the kings of Judah "filling this place with innocent blood." I cited Jer 19:3 above in connection with 2 Kgs 21:12; and links with other themes in this study are concentrated in the same chapter (Jer 19:1, 6, 7, 8, 13).

9.10. Josiah

Our earlier discussion of synoptic Josiah (5.4) suggested positively that a prior account had included some cultic reform between covenant making and Passover, and negatively that Chronicles had moved forward its main statement about cultic reform. Although they are differently placed within the total report—between royal covenant and Passover in 2 Kgs 23:4–20 and at the very start in 2 Chr 34:3–7—there is some common ground over the content of Josiah's reforms. A few terms are shared, and both books report activities in the north as well as the south. Defiling sacred places with human bones and tombs with dust of burned *sacra* is pervasive in each account,[23] but novel to Chronicles and reported elsewhere only in 1 Kgs 12–13.

In more recent scholarly debate, both Ernst Würthwein and Walter Dietrich have drawn attention to the importance of the distinction Theodor Oestreicher made in 1923 between the narrative in 2 Kgs 22:1–23:3 and the list of reforming actions in 23:4–20, while Christoph Levin has sought to undercut this distinction by proposing a very brief original draft on Josiah that included elements of both: 2 Kgs 22:1–2; 23:8a, 25, 28–30.[24]

---

22. Deut 19:10, 13; 21:8, 9; 27:25; 1 Sam 19:15; Isa 59:7; Jer 2:34; 7:6; 19:4; 22:3, 17; 26:15; Joel 4:19; Jonah 1:14; Pss 94:21; 106:38; Prov 6:17.

23. 2 Kgs 23:4, 6, 12–14, 16, 20; 2 Chr 34:4, 5.

24. Würthwein, "Die Josianische Reform und das Deuteronomium," in *Stu-

W. Boyd Barrick has argued attractively that many details in 2 Kgs 23:4–20 (and especially the seven actions introduced by "*waw*-conjunctive + perfect") were not part of the reform narrative available to the Chronicler.[25] It may be unwise to argue that this usage of the Hebrew verb is only late; however, that it is only used in portions of 2 Kgs 23:4–20 not represented in Chronicles does appear significant. Lauren Monroe has drawn renewed attention to the amount of material within 2 Kgs 23:4–20 that is related more to "holiness" issues in Leviticus and Numbers than to so-called Deuteronomistic concerns.[26] Her solution is to posit a late monarchic stratum in the report representing these "holiness" concerns, and a postexilic edition aligned to Deuteronomy. Julia Rhyder, however, has presented a brief but powerful critique of her monograph.[27] In common with most of her predecessors, but notably not Boyd Barrick, Monroe appears not to have considered the Chronicler's report in her analysis.

There is much repetition—or supplementation—in the Kings version:

1. "Altar" is mentioned three times in relation to Jerusalem and Judah (23:9, 12 [2x]) and five times in connection with Josiah's reforms in Bethel and the north (vv. 15 [2x], 16, 17, 20). Altars made by Ahaz and by Manasseh were torn down (v. 12), as was the altar beside the במה at Bethel constructed by Jeroboam (v. 15).

2. A few verses in 2 Kgs 23:4–20 resume recent elements in the synoptic narrative:

- Wrongs done by Manasseh (2 Kgs 21:3–7) are righted (v. 4), although he himself is not explicitly mentioned till later (v. 12).
- Ahaz is mentioned along with Manasseh (v. 12).
- בית יהוה ("the house of Yahweh") appears four times in the Kings report of Josiah's cultic reform (vv. 6, 7, 11, 12), but never in the corresponding shorter text in Chronicles.

---

dien zum deuteronomistischer Geschichtswerk, 192; Dietrich, "Josia und das Gesetzbuch (2 Reg. XXII)," *VT* 27 (1977): 13–15; Levin, "Joschija im deuteronomistischen Geschichtswerk," *ZAW* 96 (1984): 371.

25. *The King and the Cemeteries: Toward a New Understanding of Josiah's Reform*, VTSup 88 (Leiden: Brill, 2002), 106–11.

26. Lauren Monroe, *Josiah's Reform and the Dynamics of Defilement: Israelite Rites of Violence and the Making of a Biblical Text* (Oxford: Oxford University Press, 2011).

27. "Holiness Language in II Kings 23? A Note on a Recent Proposal," *ZAW* 127 (2015): 497–501.

3. Other verses in 2 Kgs 23:4–20 relate to passages in the nonsynoptic material earlier in Kings:

- כהני הבמות ("the priests of the high places," v. 9) have appeared previously only in 1 Kgs 13:33.
- Cultic installations built east of Jerusalem by Solomon for some of his wives (1 Kgs 11:5, 7) are defiled (2 Kgs 23:13–14).
- Bethel and Jeroboam (1 Kgs 12:25–33) are specified (2 Kgs 23:15).
- The long tale in 1 Kgs 13 about the man of God from Judah and the prophet from Bethel has its sequel (2 Kgs 23:16–18).

4. כמרים (v. 5), a term for some sort of "priest" found only in Hos 10:5 and Zeph 1:4, is unique within Kings,[28] and is the object of one of the "*waw*-conjunctive + perfect" verbs.

5. The note in 2 Kgs 23:14, at the end of a list of cultic items Josiah destroyed, that "he filled their *place* with human bones" (וימלא את־מְקוֹמָם עצמות אדם) may even correspond to "the *places* on which [Manasseh] built במות" (וְהַמְּקֹמוֹת אשר בנה בהם במות) in 2 Chr 33:19.

6. Some further portions of the extended reform narrative are unique within the Hebrew Bible as a whole:

- מזלות, listed after sun and moon and before all the host of heaven (2 Kgs 23:5), is taken to refer to (zodiacal) constellations
- Women weaving for Asherah (v. 7) and horses for the sun (v. 11)

Second Chronicles 34 mentions purges of sanctuaries not only in Judah and Jerusalem (34:3b–5) but also among named northern tribes (34:6–7). In both south and north, "altars" (מזבחות) were "torn down" (נתץ); and, as part of the purification of Judah and Jerusalem, the bones of priests were burned on their altars (34:5). These "purifications" are reported *ahead of* the work on the Jerusalem temple (34:9–13), and the finding of the book (34:14–18). Nowhere in 2 Chr 34–35 is there any mention of Ahaz, Manasseh, Bethel, or Jeroboam.

טהר ("purify") is a key verb in the Chronicler's report (2 Chr 34:3, 5, 8), resuming a theme from his report on Hezekiah's temple reform (2 Chr 29:15, 16, 18). The term is prominent in Leviticus, Numbers, and Ezekiel,

---

28. However, the regular term for priests (כהנים) is used in vv. 4, 8, 9, 20.

and in some (other) late books, but rare elsewhere. Kings uses it only in relation to the cleansing/healing of Naaman. The opposite ritual term טמא ("defile") is, however, key to the Josiah report in Kings (2 Kgs 23:8, 10, 13, 16). Widespread in the very books where טהר is also common, it is unique here in the Former Prophets, and is found just once in Deuteronomy (21:23). The emphasis in Kings is on taking over illicit installations and rendering them impure, while Chronicles is concerned with returning to purity those installations that had been defiled.

Kings glosses Josiah's cultic actions with the negative ritual term (טמא), but Chronicles with the positive one (טהר). Yet these books do share (2 Kgs 23:6, 15; 2 Chr 34:4, 7) a rare term relating to the *process* of defilement: דקק hiphil ("pulverize"). Paradoxically, this term is *not* used in Leviticus–Numbers or Ezekiel, where טהר and טמא are common. In 2 Kgs 23:6, the Asherah is removed from Yahweh's house and taken outside Jerusalem to the Kidron, where it is burned and crushed to dust, and the dust "thrown" (שלך hiphil) on human tombs. In 2 Chr 34:4, Asherahs (pl.) are among a list of objectionable objects crushed and "scattered" (זרק) "on the face of the tombs those sacrificing to them" (*sic*: the Hebrew in MT appears ungrammatical). Then 2 Kgs 23:15 and 2 Chr 34:7 both relate to actions in the north. They share mention of "altar(s)" (מזבח[ות]), "tear down" (נתץ), "crush" (הדק), and Asherah. While not impossible, it is difficult to portray 2 Chr 34:3–7 (or 34:32–33) as based on 2 Kgs 23:4–20; yet the few common features call for explanation.

Lydie Kucová's attempt at a reconstruction underlines how hard it is to achieve.[29]

1[30] 2 Kgs 23:6a // 2 Chr 33:15

ויצא/ויסר את־האשרה/הסמל מבית יהוה

2[31] 2 Kgs 23:6a // 2 Chr 33:15

וישלך מחוץ לירושלם/חוצה לעיר אל־נחל קדרון

---

29. "Common Source Theory," 121.
30. הסמל has already replaced האשרה in 2 Chr 33:7.
31. Neither השליך ("cast") nor the general directional phrases for "outside Jerusalem/the city" are ever used synoptically. The more precise direction אל־נחל קדרון ("to the Kidron Valley") is used synoptically, but only once: in 1 Kgs 15:13 // 2 Chr 15:16, in the report of Asa's removal of something related to Asherah. This phrase is not part of 2 Chr 33:15 but is used twice in the Chronicler's report on Hezekiah's reforms (2 Chr 29:16; 30:14).

9. REWRITING JUDAH'S KINGS   157

3³²   2 Kgs 23:8aβ // 2 Chr 34:3b

ויטמא את־הבמות

4³³   2 Kgs 23:12a // 2 Chr 34:4aα

וי[נ]תץ את מזבחות הבעל

5³⁴   2 Kgs 23:14aβ // 2 Chr 34:4

ויגדע/ויכרת את־האשרים וישבר את־המצבות/הפסלים

6³⁵   2 Kgs 23:6aβ-b // 2 Chr 34:4

וידק ויזרק על־פני הקברים

7³⁶   2 Kgs 23:16aα // 2 Chr 34:5

וישרף עצמות על־המזבח ויטמאהו

8³⁷   2 Kgs 23:19 // 2 Chr 34:6

את־כל־בתי הבמות אשר בערי שמרון הסיר/בער יאשיהו וגם

9³⁸   2 Kgs 23:20b // 2 Chr 34:7b

וישב ירושלם

10³⁹ 2 Kgs 23:24a // 2 Chr 34:33a

ויסר/ויבער יאשיהו את־כל־התועבת מן־הארץ

My own hunch is to propose an even shorter original:

---

32. 2 Chr 34:3b does not report "defiling" the "high places" as in 2 Kgs 23:8, but "purifying" Judah and Jerusalem from them.

33. This parallel is among the most secure.

34. 2 Chr 34:4 uses both the verb גדע and the noun אשרים but not in the same clause.

35. "Crush" and "on tombs" are shared, making another secure parallel.

36. "Burn," "bones," and "altar" are again all shared.

37. The Chronicler's שמעון may be simply a corruption of שמרון; however, there are no בתי הבמות in 2 Chr 34:6.

38. The return to Jerusalem (וישב ירושלם) is reminiscent of 2 Sam 24:9 // 1 Chr 21:5, reporting the end of a landwide operation, though ויבא ("came") is the verb used there.

39. ארצות/ארץ ("land[s]") is the only term in common.

4	And he tore down the Baal's altars	וי[נ]תץ את מזבחות הבעל
5	and hacked the Asherahs and shattered the standing stones	ויגדע/ויכרת את־האשרים וישבר את־המצבות
6	and ground them on top of the tombs	וידק על־פני הקברים
7	and burned bones on the altar	וישרף עצמות על־המזבח
8	and even all the high places in the cities of Samaria did Josiah remove	וגם את־כל־הבמות אשר בערי שמרון הסיר יאשיהו
9	and returned to Jerusalem	וישב ירושלם

The reform notices in both books relate to actions in the north as well as south. This may relate to another issue. Yahweh's adjunct title "the God of Israel" (אלהי ישראל) is used remarkably seldom synoptically, and only certainly in relation to Solomon and Josiah/Huldah.[40] It is also found within the David[41] and Hezekiah[42] narratives, but not at exactly the same points. After David and Solomon, this title of Yahweh is not found in synoptic contexts until the fall of the northern kingdom in the time of Hezekiah. It was only under (Hezekiah and) Josiah that the national God worshiped in Jerusalem regained an all-Israel perspective.

9.11. Review

I have chosen to set the detailed sampling of the synoptic Hebrew text at the end of this study. The inevitable result is that the volume goes out with the proverbial whimper rather than a bang. A satisfactory reconstruction of a shared report on Jerusalem's last four kings has so far proved elusive. Certainly Kings and Chronicles had already followed quite divergent paths

---

40. 1 Kgs 8:15, 17, 20, 23, 25, 26 // 2 Chr 6:4, 7, 10, 14, 16, 17; and 2 Kgs 22:15, 18 // 2 Chr 34:23, 26.

41. 2 Sam 7:27 and 1 Chr 17:24 (which corresponds instead to 2 Sam 7:26).

42. 2 Kgs 18:5; 19:15, 20; and 2 Chr 32:17 (which corresponds instead to 2 Kgs 19:4). The objects of חרף ("scorn") in 2 Chr 32:17 ("the God of Israel") and 2 Kgs 19:4 ("living God") are similarly related to its objects in 2 Sam 21:21 // 1 Chr 20:7 ("Israel") and 1 Sam 17:26, 36 ("the battle lines of living God").

in retelling the immediately preceding kings: Ahaz, Hezekiah, Manasseh, Amon, and Josiah; but in each case a basic substratum remained visible.

In short, the main changes in Jerusalem and elsewhere made by "bad" Ahaz, "good" Hezekiah, "bad" Manasseh, and "good" Josiah were to religious structures known or believed to have been constructed by David and Solomon in ancient times. The only altar or temple construction by David or Solomon that is reported synoptically is within Jerusalem. We shall return to Josiah as reformer (see 11.3).

Most of nonsynoptic Judah is developed out of the resources of synoptic Judah—but influence also from the Latter Prophets generally, especially Jeremiah. Several sections of our discussion have noted that Samuel–Kings has closer links with the book of Jeremiah than with any other part of the Hebrew Bible. Ancient readers attributed the authorship of Kings to Jeremiah; and modern readers have argued that Jeremiah is no less "Deuteronomistic" a book than Kings. Samuel–Kings and Jeremiah start alike: Samuel and Jeremiah are both prophets from the womb; and the books of Kings and Jeremiah share the same final chapter. Both feature Yahweh's "servants the prophets" more than any other biblical book (5x each, and only 5x elsewhere in the Hebrew Bible). The presentation of Manasseh in nonsynoptic Kings neatly develops mention of "his servants the prophets" (2 Kgs 21:10) using materials shared with the Latter Prophets (21:12–14). As with nonsynoptic Josiah, some of the language is also shared with Leviticus.

The presentation of northern Israel in the book of Kings draws on more than what was available within the synoptic tradition; and some of these resources are to be found in Jeremiah. "They went after the insubstantial and became insubstantial" (וילכו אחרי ההבל ויהבלו) is a clause found only in 2 Kgs 17:15 and Jer 2:5. Play on noun and verb forms of הבל is present also in Ps 62:10–11 and Job 27:12; and these poetic analogies encourage giving priority to Jer 2:5 over 2 Kgs 17:15. Just as the golden calves are mentioned at start, middle, and end of the northern story, so הבל as a derogatory put-down of empty alien deities, as insubstantial as a breath of wind, is placed both early in the story (relating to the second and third kings found in the synoptic record, Baasha in 1 Kgs 16:13 and Omri in 1 Kgs 16:26) and at its conclusion.

In the book of Kings, as in Jer 3:11, the failed history of (northern) Israel is offered as a warning, or what should have been a warning, to (southern) Judah. Judah should have seen itself as it contemplated the story of Israel—should have seen itself and drawn the necessary consequences in good time. Of course it has been commonplace in biblical scholarship to remark that Israel's story has been (re)told from Judah's point of view. However, viewed from the fresh perspective proposed in this study, the matter has to be stated more radically. The Israel portion of the synchronous narrative in Kings had been largely created out of (material about Israel in) the Judah portion: even in origin, it was never Israel's own story about itself. We are dealing with something rather like a hall of mirrors. Judah should have been able to recognize itself in the story of Israel; after all, the Israel story it told was simply a reflection of its own. As we have just observed, nowhere is this truer than in the extensive peroration on the fall of the northern kingdom in 2 Kgs 17.

Of the several indicators deployed earlier in our study, the infinitive absolute occurs more often in Jeremiah than in any other large book of the Hebrew Bible; and נאם יהוה is used very much more often in Jeremiah than in any other book. יש is used more often in Jeremiah (10x) than in the rest of the Latter Prophets together (only 6x); and אך is used almost as often in Jeremiah (15x) as in the rest of the Latter Prophets (18x). On the other hand, in the Latter Prophets, the use of חי יהוה (an unusually prominent feature of Samuel–Kings) is restricted to four passages in Jeremiah[43] and to Hos 4:15.[44] Developing the implications of these observations would require a separate project. There are significant cross-currents. As just noted, to take one example, we find יש more often in Jeremiah than in the rest of the Latter Prophets together; however, the blocks at the beginning and end of Samuel–Kings (1 Sam 1–8 and 2 Kgs 18–25), where we have found significant links with Jeremiah, are among the יש-free zones within the narratives of the monarchy.

In the study of Hezekiah and Isaiah (10.4.2), we will note a cluster of expressions that we find again together within Samuel–Kings only close to the start, in 1 Sam 2:27–36. These include: (1) כה אמר יהוה (1 Sam 2:27) used in 2 Kgs 19:6, 32; 20:1, 5; (2) נאם יהוה (1 Sam 2:30) in 2 Kgs 19:33; (3) התהלך לפני (1 Sam 2:30, 35) in 2 Kgs 20:3; (4) הנה ימים באים (1 Sam 2:31) in 2 Kgs 20:17; and (5) וזה־לך האות (1 Sam 2:34) in 2 Kgs 19:29 and 20:9. All but the third are found in Jeremiah.[45] The first two have both

---

43. Jer 4:2; 5:2; 12:16; 16:14, 15 (= 23:7, 8 in MT only).

44. The context is Beth-aven and Gilgal; and in Amos 5, resort to (the sanctuaries in) these towns is contrasted with the offer of "life"!

45. Elsewhere in the HB התהלך לפני is found only in Gen 17:1; 24:40; 48:15; 1 Sam 12:2 (2x); Pss 56:14; 116:9.

9. REWRITING JUDAH'S KINGS

been used in synoptic passages, and are very common in Jeremiah.[46] הנה ימים באים (4) is also found some fifteen times in Jeremiah, and is often reinforced there by נאם יהוה.[47] And וזה־לך האות (5), apart from the parallels to 2 Kgs 19:29 and 20:9 in Isa 37:30 and 38:8, occurs only in Exod 3:12, 1 Sam 14:10, and Jer 44:29.

These several links between the stories of the unnamed man of God near the beginning of Samuel and of the prophet Isaiah near the end of Kings, and between both of them and Jeremiah, are reminiscent of the "tingling ears" triangle that links the beginning of Samuel (1 Sam 3:11), the end of Kings (2 Kgs 21:12), and the book of Jeremiah (19:3).[48] The Jeremiah counterparts to these two relationships near the start and close of Samuel–Kings overlap at Jer 19:3, 6; and the relevance of this observation may be confirmed in the adjacent Jer 19:7. For we find there the unique parallel in the Hebrew Bible to the pairing of והפלתיו בחרב ("and I shall have him fall by the sword") in 2 Kgs 19:7 // Isa 37:7. Yet in the present case we are not dealing with a second "triangle," since הנה ימים באים is also found in a fourth biblical context: Amos 4:2; 8:11; 9:13 (again always in proximity to נאם יהוה).[49] The unnamed man of God at the end of 1 Sam 2 anticipates the Isaiah of the nonsynoptic Hezekiah story (2 Kgs 19–20); and the young Samuel of 1 Sam 3 anticipates Yahweh's "servants the prophets" of the nonsynoptic portion of the Manasseh story (2 Kgs 21:10–15). Such coincidences may repay further study.

---

46. The usage of נאם יהוה was noted in 3.2.2 above; and כה אמר יהוה is found at 2 Sam 7:5, 8 (Nathan); 24:12 (Gad); 1 Kgs 12:24 (Shemaiah); 22:11 (Micaiah); 2 Kgs 22:15, 16, 18 (Huldah).

47. Jer 7:32; 9:24; 16:4; 19:6; 23:5, 7 (MT); 30:3; 31:27, 31, 38; 33:14; 48:12; 49:2; 51:47, 52.

48. See A. G. Auld, "Jeremiah—Manasseh—Samuel: Significant Triangle? Or Vicious Circle?" in *Prophecy in the Book of Jeremiah,* ed. Hans M. Barstad and Reinhard G. Kratz, BZAW 388 (Berlin: de Gruyter, 2009), 1–9.

49. And Amos 7:10–17 has already been discussed in connection with 1 Kgs 13 (see 8.8.3).

10
Isaiah and Hezekiah

10.1. Overview

The Hezekiah narratives have received attention again and again throughout this study.[1] My first synoptic comparison identified four linked pluses (vis-à-vis Isaiah) in the Kings version of the appeal by the Assyrian envoy (1.4.1). One of these was his recommendation to Jerusalem to choose life and not death; and my next chapter then noted two related pairs of pluses in Kings over against Chronicles: Yahweh described as "living God," and Hezekiah continuing to "live" after a near-fatal illness (2.3–5). Several other expressions found in synoptic texts were absent from Chronicles' Hezekiah account but present in profusion in Kings (3.2). An unusual difference between Kings and Chronicles was over the temporal markers that introduce the Assyrian campaign (3.1); on the other hand, the use of reinforcing cognate infinitives absolute at the same stage in the envoy's speech (even where different verbs were used) testified to the underlying stability of the tradition (3.3). When compared with the minimal variation elsewhere in the synoptic record over shorter notes and longer accounts of divine-human communication, the large-scale differences over the Hezekiah (and Isaiah) narratives are wholly exceptional (4); and that makes it

---

1. The scholarly literature on the Hezekiah chapters is huge, and only a very few studies are mentioned below. There is excellent discussion of much of the secondary literature in Song-Mi Suzie Park, *Hezekiah and the Dialogue of Memory*, Emerging Scholars (Minneapolis: Fortress, 2015), although her results are very different from those presented below. In the present chapter I have reworked three published contributions: "Prophetic Narrative"; "Chronicles—Isaiah—Kings," in *Imperial Visions: The Prophet and the Book of Isaiah in an Age of Empires*, ed. Joachim Schaper (Göttingen: Vandenhoeck &Ruprecht, forthcoming); and "Did the Assyrian Envoy Know the *Venite*? What Did He Know? What Did He Say? And Should He Be Believed?," in *Torah and Tradition*, ed. Klaas Spronk, OTS 70 (Leiden: Brill, 2017), 42–53.

even harder to recover synoptic Hezekiah than synoptic Ahaz or Josiah (5). My sketch of synoptic interconnections noted three links between kings Amaziah and Hezekiah: both became king aged 25, they were the only two kings who reigned for 29 years, and Lachish featured in both their stories (6.3). In what follows, we shall find that 2 Kgs 18–20 shares a great deal with the narratives we have reviewed in nonsynoptic Samuel (7) and Kings (8). If the other stories about divine-royal communication are preserved with less rewriting than the average in Samuel–Kings and Chronicles, quite the opposite is true of Hezekiah and Isaiah.

10.2. Cultic Reform

The two narrators' accounts of Hezekiah's reforms are not only very different in extent, but they resemble each other in their wording in less than a single verse:

2 Kgs 18:4a

הוא הסיר את־הבמות ושבר את־המצבת וכרת את־האשרה

"He it was removed the במות and shattered the pillars and cut the Asherah."

2 Chr 31:1aα

וישברו המצבות ויגדעו האשרים וינתצו את־הבמות ואת־המזבחת

"And they shattered the pillars and hacked the Asherahs and tore down the במות and the altars."

- Kings and Chronicles use the same verb *shatter* for the destruction of the pillars.
- They have "pillars" next to Asherah, but with different verbs.
- Kings mentions במות at the start.
- Chronicles adds "altars" to במות at the end.

Most of the rest of 2 Kgs 18:4–8 simply praises the king. He also crushed the bronze serpent made by Moses (v. 4b), trusted Yahweh incomparably (v. 5), clung to him (v. 6),[2] was successful in all his ventures (v. 7a),

---

2. In contrast to the later Solomon (1 Kgs 11:2); see further 9.2.1.

rebelled against the king of Assyria (v. 7b),³ and struck down Philistines (v. 8). Hezekiah in 2 Chr 29–31 concentrates on undoing what Ahaz had done (starting by reopening the temple doors), with an emphasis on Passover reform that anticipates Josiah's in 35:1–17.

The resemblances between 2 Kgs 18:4a and 2 Chr 31:1aα may just be sufficient to claim shared origin. Cultic pillars are a novelty in a shared report: מצבות have never before been mentioned in synoptic texts. In 1 Kgs 14:23 Judah in the time of Rehoboam is blamed for "building" them, as also other abominations that anticipate synoptic Ahaz; and Asa is credited in 2 Chr 14:2 with shattering them.⁴ Elsewhere in nonsynoptic Kings, מצבת (cultic pillars) are associated only with the north.⁵ While both note the removal or destruction of "high places" (במות), the Asherah, and cultic pillars (מצבות), they share only one verb: "shatter" (שבר piel). Removal of "high places" is an expected response to Ahaz's enthusiastic use of them (see 5.2).

Sennacherib's envoy scorns any attempt by Hezekiah to have his people trust Yahweh to deliver them from an Assyrian siege. Hezekiah, he says, had just taken away Yahweh's altars and "high places" around Judah, and commanded worship before one identified altar in Jerusalem (2 Kgs 18:22 // Isa 36:7 // 2 Chr 32:12). But how credible a witness is he?

There is broad agreement among the three versions of the majority tradition (in MT at least); and yet there are small differences in the way they present the Assyrian's account of Hezekiah's unwise centralizing instruction:

2 Kgs 18:22	לפני המזבח הזה תשתחוו בירושלם
Isa 36:7	לפני המזבח הזה תשתחוו
2 Chr 32:12	לפני מזבח אחד תשתחוו ועליו תקטירו

"Before *this* altar you shall prostrate yourselves" is read in Kings (and Isaiah) but "Before *one* altar …" in Chronicles. The continuation "in Jerusalem" (2 Kgs 18:22) is found also at Isa 36:7 in the Great Isaiah

---

3. The Assyrian envoy juxtaposes the rebellion (2 Kgs 18:7) with a question about whom Hezekiah is relying on (v. 5a) in his opening words (v. 20).

4. This correspondence between nonsynoptic Kings and Chronicles mirrors another noted above (5.2), where 2 Chr 33:19 mentions "the places on which [Manasseh] built "במות אשר בנה בהם במות"); and at the end of a list of cultic items Josiah destroyed, we read in 2 Kgs 23:14 that "he filled their place with human bones" (וימלא את־מקומם עצמות אדם).

5. 2 Kgs 3:2; 10:26, 27; 17:10.

Scroll (1QIsa^a) from the Dead Sea,[6] though marked on the scroll as a parenthesis. And the Chronicler continues differently: "and on it shall you offer [incense]."[7] In the light of our earlier discussion of Hezekiah, it would be unwise simply to privilege the version in Kings.[8] In any case, two further factors must be considered.

The first is text-critical. The Greek text (LXX) of Isa 36:7-8 is considerably shorter: "But if you say, 'On the Lord our God we have put our trust,' now be [joined] with my lord the king of Assyria, and I shall give you…." The shorter Greek text simply does not represent Isa 36:7b (MT + 1QIsa^a) // 2 Kgs 18:22b; it makes no mention of cultic reformation at all. The resultant shorter text, especially when the divine name is rendered by the standard Greek euphemism κύριος ("lord"), does make for a rhetorically attractive alternative: "You do have a lord in whom you trust, but I can introduce you to a more effective lord." In Kings and Chronicles, the Assyrian envoy's added parenthetical comment about Hezekiah as (unwise) reformer echoes what the narrator has already told us, in brief at the beginning of 2 Kgs 18 and at length in 2 Chr 29–31. But there is no such previous report in Isaiah.

The second is literary. In 2 Kgs 18:4, the narrator has reported in a brief *note* (hardly a "report"): הוא הסיר את־הבמות ושבר את־המצבת וכרת את־האשרה וכתת נחש הנחשת, "he it was removed the high places and shattered the pillars and cut the Asherah and crushed the bronze snake." But the envoy in 18:22 says more: הלוא־הוא אשר הסיר חזקיהו את־במתיו ואת־מזבחתיו ויאמר לפני המזבח הזה תשתחוו בירושלם, "Was it not [Yahweh[9]] whose high places and whose altars Hezekiah removed and said, 'Before this altar you shall prostrate yourselves in Jerusalem'?" In Kings, altars were *not* included in the narrator's list of four destructions practiced by Hezekiah. But by contrast, the envoy makes a *feature* of altars being *removed* and *this* altar chosen.

---

6. Donald W. Parry and Elisha Qimron, eds., *The Great Isaiah Scroll (1QIsa^a): A New Edition*, STDJ 32 (Leiden: Brill, 1999), 58–59.

7. I noted earlier (3.3.1) that Chronicles and Samuel–Kings never use this verb (הקטיר) in the same context.

8. Würthwein attributes 18:22 to DtrN and the latest expansion of its context (*1. Kön.17–2. Kön.25*, 421).

9. As in the similar-sounding authoritative claims אני יהוה ("I am Yahweh") and אני הוא ("I am he"), we may be dealing here with a play on יהוה/הוא.

10. ISAIAH AND HEZEKIAH

The situation in Chronicles is different. In his account of King Hezekiah, the Chronicler offers quite the longest reform report anywhere in the histories of the monarchies since David and Solomon. Much ground is covered in 2 Chr 29–31; but it is widely agreed[10] that there is one key summary statement in 31:1, closely related to 2 Kgs 18:4, of action taken by "all Israel who were present" (at the Festival of Passover and Unleavened Bread just celebrated): וישברו המצבות ויגדעו האשרים וינתצו את־הבמות ואת־המזבחת, "and they shattered the pillars and they hacked the Asherahs and they tore down the high places and the altars." And there is no conflict between the Chronicler's statement and what he later reports the envoy as saying (2 Chr 32:12): הלא־הוא יחזקיהו הסיר את־במתיו ואת־מזבחתיו ויאמר ליהודה ולירושלם לאמר לפני מזבח אחד תשתחוו ועליו תקטירו: "Is he not the one whose high places and whose altars Hezekiah removed and said to Judah and Jerusalem, 'Before one altar you shall prostrate yourselves and on it make offerings'?"

The envoy certainly passes over what was done to the pillars and the Asherahs. And by talking of simply "removing" the במות and altars he concentrates on the king's policy decision rather than the enthusiastic shattering and hacking and pulling down by the crowds. Then Hezekiah's final instruction (ועליו תקטירו, "and on it make offerings"), according at least to the Assyrian outside the walls, rights what the king had said was wrong at the very start of his reform: "[our fathers] have put out the lamps, and have not offered incense or made burnt offerings in the holy place to the God of Israel" (2 Chr 29:7).

In the context of Chronicles' much longer report, one detail in 2 Chr 31:1 is quite explicit: the action against pillars, and Asherahs, and במות, and altars was taken across Judah and Benjamin, and Ephraim and Manasseh as well; and people "went out" (יצאו) in order to shatter, and hack, and tear down. Chronicles is describing action not in Jerusalem but elsewhere. However, the very similar actions recounted in 2 Kgs 18:4 appear to belong in Jerusalem. For Chronicles, the Jerusalem cult had been sufficiently repaired in 2 Chr 29–30.

In Chronicles, envoy (2 Chr 32:12) and narrator (31:1) appear to agree about Hezekiah's reforms. Hezekiah's people had torn down altars as well as "high places," and Hezekiah had given instructions about rever-

---

10. So, for example, Sara Japhet, *I and II Chronicles*, OTL (Louisville: Westminster John Knox, 1993), 961–62.

ence to be shown before a particular altar. But the envoy in Kings (2 Kgs 18:22) adds to the note by the narrator (18:4), who has not mentioned altars. Is the narrator now using the envoy to spell out what he has already reported? Or is the narrator giving the envoy some independence? What does the envoy know? And, if he is at all independent, is the envoy a credible witness: whether to what Hezekiah has done, or to how Jerusalem did worship at the time? It is the business of politicians and diplomats to be cleverly economical with the truth.[11] The more the Assyrian envoy is seen to be a realistic character, the less perhaps we should believe him.[12] At least we should examine what he actually says.

His words repay closer attention: neither "before this altar" nor "before one altar" is found elsewhere in the Hebrew Bible; no one else in the Hebrew Bible links prostration with an altar; and indeed, לפני ("before/ in front of") and מזבח ("altar") are surprisingly seldom combined:[13] the link occurs in three other synoptic verses, in a fourth very nearby, and only once outside the narrative books.[14] Each other occurrence in Kings is relevant to the interpretation of Hezekiah's words:

1. "Before Yahweh's altar" (לפני מזבח יהוה) in 1 Kgs 8:22 // 2 Chr 6:12 defines Solomon's own location—he is standing—at the start of his prayer at the dedication of the temple.
2. In 1 Kgs 8:31 // 2 Chr 6:22, in the first of his seven specific petitions, he uses the same phrase to define the place where a self-exculpating oath should be uttered.
3. "Before the altars" is where Mattan, priest of Baal, is slaughtered (2 Kgs 11:18 // 2 Chr 23:17), after the altars of Baal's "house" had been torn down and its images smashed.
4. Nonsynoptic 1 Kgs 8:54 is part of a large Kings plus in 8:50b–61. It reports that after his long prayer Solomon "rose from before

---

11. Rannfrid Thelle also characterizes the envoy's words "as propagandistic, even derisive," in *Approaches to the "Chosen Place": Accessing a Biblical Concept*, LHBOTS 564 (London: T&T Clark, 2012), 144.

12. In Isaiah, unlike Kings or Chronicles, we are not offered any prior reform report—we have nothing against which to assess the envoy's words, apart from out natural skepticism.

13. These issues are more fully explored in Auld, "Assyrian Envoy."

14. Zech 14:20 predicts that, on that day, "the cooking pots in the house of Yahweh shall be as holy as the bowls in front of the altar."

Yahweh's altar from crouching [כרע] on his knees." This plus sets at the end of Solomon's prayer the same "correction" as Chronicles makes at the beginning (2 Chr 6:13–14): Solomon, after first standing, "kneels [ברך] on his knees," as urged by Ps 95:6 (and nowhere else in the HB[15]). The older shared text had reported that king and people "stood" throughout. Later liturgical practice had led to modifications of the account in each familiar book.

It appears that the Assyrian envoy's words suggest an implicit comparison of Hezekiah with both Solomon (again[16]) and the reform in Jerusalem after the fall of Athaliah.

Irrespective of my remarks about the plus in 1 Kgs 8:54, focus on השתחוה ("prostrate oneself") in synoptic perspective encourages a further observation. Solomon's second vision had warned against prostration to "other gods" (1 Kgs 9:6, 9 // 2 Chr 7:19, 22), and Manasseh draws criticism for doing just that (2 Kgs 21:3 // 2 Chr 33:3). Araunah/Ornan the Hittite in face of David (2 Sam 24:20 // 1 Chr 21:21) is the only synoptic character to prostrate himself to another human;[17] and the Assyrian envoy is the only other user of this verb (2 Kgs 18:22 // 2 Chr 32:12): "Before this/one altar shall you prostrate yourselves." The verbs קדד ("bow down"), כרע ("crouch"), and ברך ("kneel"), from the same semantic family, are never used in synoptic contexts; and the generic נפל ("fall") is used in synoptic texts only of falling into someone's hands (2 Sam 24:14 // 1 Chr 21:13) or falling in battle (1 Kgs 22:20 // 2 Chr 18:19; 2 Kgs 14:10 // 2 Chr 25:19). Prostration to *other* gods is forbidden, an *alien* Hittite prostrates himself to David, and an *alien* Assyrian talks about prostration before (Yahweh's) altar. But no synoptic text either prescribes prostration to Yahweh or describes such a practice among his people.[18] Importantly, Solomon, when addressing Yahweh in front of his altar, was standing (1 Kgs 8:22 //

---

15. In Hebrew at least—in the Aramaic portion of Daniel, the hero also kneels (6:19). In Ps 95:6, the LXX followed by the Latin Psalter may attest not נברכה but ונבכה ("and let us weep").

16. As already noted (5.1), the use of היכל ("palace") to denote the temple in Jerusalem is restricted in synoptic texts to reports about Solomon and Hezekiah.

17. Lydie Kucová developed some implications of this observation for the reading of Samuel, in "Obeisance in the Biblical Stories of David," in Rezetko, Lim, and Aucker, *Reflection and Refraction*, 241–60.

18. This synoptic situation may reflect a period in which prostration appeared as strange in Jerusalem as it later would to Alexander's Macedonian nobles when he

2 Chr 6:12). Given this total context, we have to ask: Does the Rabshakeh misrepresent Hezekiah? And, if so, is his mistake accidental or deliberate? The Rabshakeh is hardly a disinterested reporter of Hezekiah's policy.

In Greek Isaiah, as we have noted, even the envoy does not offer a reform report. He first disposes of Pharaoh as a credible ally; and then says, "But if you say, 'On the Lord our God we have put our trust,' then [try] my lord, the king of Assyria.'" Whether or not this shorter text is more original, I suspect that the Greek rendering of a key element of the text provides a clue about the envoy's character, his truthfulness. His recommendation runs as follows: התערב נא את־אדני המלך אשור (so MT in Isa 36:8; 2 Kgs 18:23a concludes, את־אדני את־מלך אשור). This has been widely rendered "Make a wager with my lord."[19]

David Clines offers anything from three to six lenses for inspecting verbal forms with the radicals ערב: ערב I: "mix"; ערב II: "stand surety"; ערב III: "be pleasant"; ערב IV: "be evening"; ערב V: "offer"; ערב VI: "enter."[20] This is not the place for a full review. "Make a wager" is explained on the basis of ערב II.[21] A *hithpael* form התערב is found just five more times in the Hebrew Bible: Ps 106:35; Prov 14:10; 20:19; 24:21; Ezra 9:2. There is no doubt about the meaning of the first and fifth instances. Psalm 106:35 talks of unwelcome "mixing" of Israel with other nations: ויתערבו בגוים וילמדו מעשיהם ("and they mixed among the nations and learned their deeds"); and Ezra 9:2a adds explicit mention of intermarriage: כי־נשאו מבנתיהם להם ולבניהם והתערבו זרע הקדש בעמי הארצות ("and they took of their daughters for themselves and their sons; and they, the holy seed, became mixed among the nations of the earth"). The Septuagint in Ps 105:35 (106:35 MT), as in both 2 Kgs 18:23 and Isa 36:8, renders התערב by μείγνυμι (passive: "be mixed"), but in 2 Esd 9:2 by παράγω (passive: "be diverted"). The Greek verb μείγνυμι corresponds to ערב I. It can be used literally of sexual mixing, and also in metaphors that take off from that literal sense. התערב is often rendered "share" in Prov 14:10, which could derived from ערב I or VI. "Associate with" (Prov 20:19) could also relate

---

began to accept Persian-style veneration (Arrian, *Anabasis Alexandri* 4.10–12, trans. E. Iliff Robson, LCL [London: Heinemann, 1929], 370–79).

19. So RSV, NRSV; James A. Montgomery, *A Critical and Exegetical Commentary on the Books of Kings*, ed. Henry Snyder Gehman, ICC (Edinburgh: T&T Clark, 1951), 487; Sweeney, *I and II Kings*, 405; similarly "bet" (CEV) and "bargain" (NEB).

20. *DCH* 6:546–49

21. *DCH* 6:548.

to I or VI.²² Whether he said, "Make a bet with my lord" or "Get into bed with my lord, the king of Assyria," the envoy would be marked out as a figure of fun. He would be speaking more like a stock false prophet than a serious diplomat.²³

A fresh and interesting proposal by Ronnie Goldstein about התערב has the envoy inviting Judah to become auxiliary or mercenary troops of his master.²⁴ He suggests that *urbi* (^LÚ urbī), used in three Akkadian texts, two of them inscriptions that record campaigns of Sennacherib, bears the sense of "auxiliary forces" and is related to the root ערב with the basic meaning "to enter," as in Akkadian *erēbu*. (The term is apparently of West Semitic origin, and it is probably used also in several passages within the Hebrew Bible, e.g., Jer 50:37.) התערב נא would accordingly be rendered, "Become an auxiliary force [to my lord …]." And Goldstein notes that the cognate בני התערבות in 2 Kgs 14:14 // 2 Chr 25:24 (obviously some sort of human "booty" carried off from Jerusalem to Samaria by Jehoash of Israel in addition to the gold and silver plundered from Yahweh's house and the royal treasury in Jerusalem) could also refer to such forces. Given the many links between synoptic Amaziah and Hezekiah—and even more between synoptic Amaziah and the developed Hezekiah of the Hezekiah/Isaiah legend in 2 Kgs 18–20 (see 10.4.1)—I find it highly likely that the author of nonsynoptic התערב נא in the Hezekiah/Isaiah legend had been influenced by synoptic בני התערבות, found in 2 Kgs 14:14 // 2 Chr 25:24 (a verse we shall meet again in 10.5.1).

If no one else anywhere in the Hebrew Bible ever describes or specifies prostration before an altar—not even sinking or falling or bowing or kneeling in front of an altar—is this another obvious mistake put into the mouth of the envoy? How were the earliest readers—or even the supposed hearers on Jerusalem's walls—intended to react to his words? In Kings/Isaiah, though not in Chronicles, there is one other instance of השתחוה in the Hezekiah story (2 Kgs 19:37 // Isa 37:38): Sennacherib was killed by his sons as *he* prostrated himself in the house of his god Nisroch. His envoy

---

22. In Prov 24:21, LXX implies a different consonantal text from MT.

23. A similar point is made on other grounds by Michael Press in "Where Are the Gods?," 217–21.

24. "On Treaties, Military Assistance and Divine Support in Isaiah 1-39," in *Imperial Visions: The Prophet and the Book of Isaiah in an Age of Empires*, ed. Joachim Schaper (Göttingen: Vandenhoeck & Ruprecht, forthcoming).

to Jerusalem would naturally have supposed that Hezekiah had prescribed worship like his own master practiced at home in Nineveh.

Prostration before a single altar does go beyond anything the narrator has told us about Hezekiah. But we tend to believe Chronicles' envoy—he has been well informed and fair about everything else. And it fits the contrast between Hezekiah and his father Ahaz. Previous kings in Jerusalem—even good ones—may have *failed* to remove the במות; but Ahaz was *enthusiastic* in cultivating them (note *piel*s in 2 Chr 28:4). He also "shut up the doors of Yahweh's house and made himself altars in every corner of Jerusalem" (28:24). "One altar" is Hezekiah's response to his father's "altars in every corner." The Septuagint reads "this altar" like the book of Kings, and may be more original. But, in a context of the son undoing the father's multiple mistakes, the difference between מזבח אחד and המזבח הזה may be immaterial: "one" simply clarifies "this."

Whether misrepresentation or not, what does the Assyrian envoy mean? The first part of his statement about Jerusalem's king is that Hezekiah had removed (Yahweh's) "high places" and altars: הסיר את־במתיו ואת־מזבחתיו. The shared text had mentioned a plurality of "high places" in connection with Asa, Jehoshaphat, and Ahaz, but made no mention of other altars. Has the envoy conflated the two, or misunderstood the situation? In the brief note in 2 Kgs 18:4, the narrator speaks only of "high places" and makes no mention of Hezekiah removing altars. In Kings too the envoy's words may direct us more precisely to what Hezekiah's father had done. According to 2 Kgs 16:10–16, Ahaz had made a large new altar displacing Solomon's. "Before *one* altar" (as in Chronicles) will have been intended as a critique of Ahaz's "altars in every corner in Jerusalem."[25]

On the other hand, "before *this* altar" (as in Kings/Isaiah) is ambiguous. If it is taken to imply "*this* and not *any* other," then the words carry much the same force as effective centralization. But if "before *this* altar" is heard as implying "but not before *that* one," then the envoy may have been making two quite distinct points: that Hezekiah was alienating many of his own people by removing the local "high places," and at the same time alienating the king of Assyria by favoring the old Jerusalem altar over his father's recent copy of an Assyrian model.

---

25. The lengthy reform report in 2 Chr 29–31 mentions Ahaz explicitly (29:19) and starts by opening "the doors of the house of Yahweh" (29:3) that Ahaz had shut up (28:24).

I drew attention earlier (8.7) to the skilfully worded formulation in 2 Kgs 17 that moves from prohibiting prostration before other gods (v. 35) to commanding prostration before Yahweh (v. 36). A further novelty in that passage is the close link between prostration and sacrifice in both the negative and the positive verse, whether to other gods or to Yahweh. Neither in Deuteronomy nor in Kings have השתחוה and זבח ever before appeared in the same context, let alone the same sentence.[26] It is natural to suppose that the author had in mind the words of the Assyrian envoy: לפני המזבח הזה תשתחוו ("before this altar [lit. 'sacrifice place'] you shall prostrate yourselves"). Like the Chronicler, the author of 2 Kgs 17 had taken the Assyrian at face value. And like the author of many other nonsynoptic portions of Samuel–Kings, he had thought together the Assyrian's synoptic report and the synoptic prohibition of prostration to other gods. Once prostration to Yahweh had been explicitly ordered (2 Kgs 17:36), no "misunderstanding" of the subsequent words of the Assyrian envoy (18:22) is possible. Spoken in the earlier synoptic context, the report was ambiguous: the foreigner could have been mistaken or mischievous. Spoken in the new context of Kings, the ambiguity was much reduced: prostration to Yahweh was required, and prostration and sacrifice to Yahweh could be spoken of together.

10.3. Triangulation

When mapping physical terrain, observations recorded from at least three known positions permit more accurate reconstruction. Each of the separate accounts in the books of Kings, Isaiah, and Chronicles about Hezekiah and the Assyrians,[27] Hezekiah's illness,[28] and Hezekiah and the visit of messengers from Babylon[29] is unusual in its own immediate context. And each is sufficiently different from the others, although of course Kings and Isaiah are much closer to each other in length and detail than either is to Chronicles. In Kings, the very large role played by the prophet Isaiah is without parallel in the narratives about Jerusalem's kings. In Isaiah, no other piece of prose narrative is nearly so extensive. And in Chronicles, no

---

26. The only other context in the Former Prophets where we do find them together is the (equally late) introduction to Samuel–Kings in 1 Sam 1–2.
27. 2 Kgs 18:13–19:37 // Isa 36–37 // 2 Chr 32:9–23.
28. 2 Kgs 20:1–11 // Isa 38:1–22 // 2 Chr 32:24–26.
29. 2 Kgs 20:12–19 // Isa 39:1–8 // 2 Chr 32:27–31.

other royal report is quite so different from—or so much shorter than—its synoptic parallel in Kings. However, comparisons between them permit reconstructions of their development that are more secure than if we possessed only two of these accounts instead of all three.

In Kings/Isaiah, there are two royal prayers (2 Kgs 19:15-19 // Isa 37:15-20; 2 Kgs 20:2-3 // Isa 38:2-3) with an answer to each (2 Kgs 19:20-34 // Isa 37:21-35; 2 Kgs 20:5-6 // Isa 38:5-6); and the two situations of national and royal distress are also closely and explicitly linked (2 Kgs 19:34 // Isa 37:35; 2 Kgs 20:6 // Isa 38:6). The precise dating in Kings/Isaiah is part of this linkage. In Chronicles, too, the king prays twice (2 Chr 32:20, 24), but no link is made between the situations of a city under threat from Assyria and a king in peril of death. However, Chronicles, like Kings/Isaiah, does link the Babylonian embassy with the king's illness (and recovery): in Kings/Isaiah (2 Kgs 20:12 // Isa 39:1) Babylon had heard that Hezekiah had been sick (though not that he had surprisingly revived), while in Chronicles they had come to inquire about the (unspecified) מופת ("portent") done in the land (2 Chr 32:24, 31)—in both versions Hezekiah had great riches. Does Chronicles preserve a witness to the textual situation before the link between the first two topics was made explicit in Kings/Isaiah? Or had Chronicles disentangled into its original elements what Kings/Isaiah may only secondarily have put together?

Most scholars consider Chronicles irrelevant to the study of the development of 2 Kgs 18–20 // Isa 36–39, and this for two reasons. The first is the more general one: Chronicles is "known" to be a reworking of Samuel and Kings. The second is more particular. Most scholars accept the division by Bernhard Stade of 2 Kgs 18:13 + 18:17–19:37 // Isa 36–37 between two once-separate reports of the Assyrian embassy that were only secondarily combined.[30] Some elements of the shorter 2 Chr 32 correspond to material in one of these sources and some to material in the other. It follows that it must have been after their combination that the Chronicler had written his abbreviated account. However, just one of the benefits of a *Fortschreibung* or "successive rewriting" approach to the longer version in Kings/Isaiah as advocated by Reinhard Kratz is this: it enables the relation-

---

30. Bernhard Stade, "Anmerkungen zu 2 Kö. 15–21," *ZAW* 6 (1886): 156–92. His analysis was minimally modified by Brevard S. Childs, *Isaiah and the Assyrian Crisis*, SBT 2/3 (London: SCM, 1967), 74–75.

ship with Chronicles to be reconsidered.³¹ What if Chronicles was based not on the completed report in Kings and Isaiah but on an earlier stage in its complex development? If that longer report had been drafted in several stages, not every element of the so-called B¹ need have been in its present position before B² began to be drafted: the several stages in the successive rewriting of B could in principle have included some reordering of the material. And, if B had its origins in a narrative much shorter than Stade's B¹, then comparison with the relevant portion of 2 Chr 32 that is also shorter could be relevant and should be explored.

10.4. Focus on Chronicles / Kings + Isaiah

10.4.1. General Overview

The two most distinct forms of the Hezekiah story are most readily compared and contrasted in 2 Kgs 18:17–20:19 (along with Isa 36–39) and 2 Chr 32:9–31. As for comparisons:

- Both use a cognate infinitive absolute at the same stage in the argument (2 Kgs 18:30 // 2 Chr 32:13).
- They use the same temporal transition: בימים ההם חלה [י]חזקיהו [עד] למות ("In these days Hezekiah was sick to the point of dying," 2 Kgs 20:1a // 2 Chr 32:24a).
- Negatively, and in contrast with the intermediation vocabulary already reviewed (ch. 4 above), neither שאל ("ask") nor דרש ("inquire") is used within either report.³²

The narratives are most similar in their opening sections: 2 Kgs 18:17–37 may be roughly twice as detailed as 2 Chr 32:9–19; but the essentials of the story are shared, including a major emphasis on the verb הציל ("deliver").³³ The single most telling difference over wording in this first

---

31. Reinhard G. Kratz, "Isaiah and the Siege of Jerusalem," in Thelle, Stordalen, and Richardson, *New Perspectives on Prophecy,* 143–60.

32. דרש is differently used in 2 Chr 32:31 from its synoptic use in 1 Kgs 22:5, 7, 8 // 2 Chr 18:4, 6, 7 and 2 Kgs 22:13, 18 // 2 Chr 34:21, 26—there of consulting Yahweh or a prophet, but here of interpreting a sign.

33. The details are charted in my "Prophetic Narrative," 56–60. A table published there is reproduced below (12.3.18).

section is that בטח ("trust") and האמין ("be confident") are mentioned just twice in the shorter version (2 Chr 32:10, 15), while בטח is much more prominent in the longer. We find it twice in the wider immediate context (2 Kgs 18:5; 19:10) and seven times in the fuller parallel (18:19, 20, 21 [2x], 22, 24, 30).

Some of the contrasts are quite striking.

1. "Life" and "living" are totally absent from 2 Chr 32. By contrast, they are not just present in the Kings (and Isaiah) version but actually constitute *a prominent element* of the longer narrative they offer. As already noted (2.3–5), it is the "living God" that Sennacherib mocks (2 Kgs 19:4, 16), and it is the continuing life of Jerusalem's human king that is brought into question (20:1, 7).

2. דבר יהוה ("Yahweh's word") has been used synoptically in 2 Chr 11:2 // 1 Kgs 12:22 and 18:4, 18 // 1 Kgs 22:5, 19, and appears often elsewhere in Chronicles. However, this most common expression is also absent from 2 Chr 32, although it is used in 2 Kgs 20:4, 16, 19 (// Isa 38:4; 39:5, 8) where the latter part of the same story is reported. Similarly the cognate verb דבר ("speak") has Yahweh as its subject in 2 Kgs 19:21 and 20:9, but never in 2 Chr 32. It is hard to see why no mention of Yahweh speaking and no mention of Yahweh's word—not to mention the other features of synoptic prophetic stories faithfully preserved elsewhere by the Chronicler—should have survived in 2 Chr 32 *if they were part* of the Chronicler's source.

3. The verb שמע ("hear") is never used in 2 Chr 32, but is a major feature of the longer version (used no less than 17x in the parallel text shared by Kings and Isaiah[34]). This common verb is used throughout the narrative books. Indeed, when it comes to "hearing," we find only minimal variation between Samuel-Kings and Chronicles across almost all synoptic contexts. Given the frequency of its use in 2 Kgs 18–20, its total absence from 2 Chr 32 is quite surprising. If we adopted the normal critical perspective of the priority of Kings, we would expect at least some of the seventeen instances of the verb in the "original" shared by Kings and Isaiah[35] to have survived in the Chronicler's abridgment. The Chronicler was manifestly not averse to this verb: he used it nearby in his own mate-

---

34. 2 Kgs 18:26, 28, 31; 19:1, 4 (2x), 6, 7, 8, 9, 11, 16 (2x), 25; 20:5, 12, 16 // Isa 36:11, 13, 16; 37:1, 4 (2x), 6, 7, 8, 9, 11, 17 (2x), 26; 38:5; 39:1, 5—also 2 Kgs 18:32; 19:20; 20:13; and Isa 37:9.

35. 2 Kgs 18:26, 28, 31; 19:1, 4 (2x), 6, 7, 8, 9, 11, 16 (2x), 25; 20:5, 12, 16 // Isa

10. ISAIAH AND HEZEKIAH

rial, both before chapter 32 in 29:5 and 30:20, and after it in 33:13. From our synoptic viewpoint, we should suppose instead that שמע was added as part of the more ample retelling (*Fortschreibung*) within Kings of both Solomon's vision and the Hezekiah story.

This striking divergence is not unique: and the other instance belongs precisely within the synoptic God-king communication passages (see ch. 4 above). שמע is used in 1 Kgs 3:9 and 11 but is absent from the parallel report in Chronicles, despite appearing nineteen times in the remainder of the Solomon story in 2 Chr 1–9. "A hearing heart" (לב שמע) is a combination unique to 1 Kgs 3:9; and "to hear a case" (לשמע משפט) in 3:11) may also represent the sole combination of these terms in a judicial sense—in Deut 5:1 and 7:12 Israel is required to listen to divine "judgments" (משפטים). The neighboring mention (1 Kgs 3:8) by Solomon of Yahweh's people as chosen is not only a Kings plus, but is the only instance of this Deuteronomic phrase in all of Samuel–Kings (see 11.3).

4. As for dates and times, the shorter Hezekiah story in 2 Chr 32 opens its account of the threat from Assyria with a simple "After this" (אחר זה), and it says nothing about how long the king survived after his serious illness. The longer report in Kings/Isaiah sets the invasion in Hezekiah's fourteenth year, and the king is promised that he will survive fifteen years after his illness. By adding precise years to the shorter account in Chronicles, the account in Kings/Isaiah was achieving several aims very economically.

a. It was insisting that the transitional "in those days" (בימים ההם), as the narrative moved from the death of Sennacherib to the illness of Hezekiah (2 Kgs 20:1 // 2 Chr 32:24), was no vague phrase. Given that Hezekiah reigned for twenty-nine years, his survival for fifteen years placed his illness in exactly the same fourteenth year of his reign when Sennacherib invaded.

b. Survival—living on—for fifteen years after the crisis in Jerusalem added another link to the several synoptic ties between Hezekiah and Amaziah. We already noted (6.3) that they were both twenty-five at accession to the throne, both reigned for twenty-nine years, and Lachish featured in both their stories; and we could add that Jerusalem was endangered under both. Despite the fact that the king of Israel whom Amaziah had foolishly challenged died soon after his victory, the defeated Amaziah lived on for fifteen years. Kings/Isaiah observes the surprise in this synoptic detail, and adds it to the inherited Hezekiah story. I shall note below

---

36:11, 13, 16; 37:1, 4 (2x), 6, 7, 8, 9, 11, 17 (2x), 26; 38:5; 39:1, 5. The instances in 2 Kgs 18:32; 19:20; 20:13; and Isa 37:9b are not shared.

two more features of the expanded Hezekiah story that had their origins in synoptic Amaziah (10.5.1).

c. Second Kings 18:13 employs the same unusually worded date formula as we find twice in relation to synoptic Josiah (see 5.4). This invites comparing the significance of the deliverance experienced by both Jerusalem and Hezekiah in year 14 of his reign with only four other dates in Kings: Solomon building the temple, Josiah repairing the temple, Josiah (in the very same year) reforming the Passover, and the king of Babylon raising the status of exiled king Jehoiachin. Synoptic Josiah both provided the unusual form of words and inspired attention to the coincidence of two major events.

10.4.2. Isaiah

As for the prophet Isaiah, he has hardly even a walk-on part in Chronicles, while in Kings he plays a larger role than any of the intermediaries who feature alongside Jerusalem's other kings. Isaiah is simply mentioned alongside Hezekiah as the king prays in 2 Chr 32:20 (ויתפלל יחזקיהו המלך וישעיהו בן־אמוץ הנביא על־זאת, "and Hezekiah the king prayed—and Isaiah son of Amoz the prophet—about this"). But he is named ten times in text shared by Kings and Isaiah[36] and three more times in Kings pluses.[37] We have noted that the Assyrian envoy questions Jerusalem's grounds for trust in Yahweh much more insistently in Kings than Chronicles. The much larger role for the prophet in Kings than Chronicles in Jerusalem's response to the Assyrian threat is intimately related, for בטח ("trust") is a key Isaianic term.[38]

In expanding Isaiah's role, the authors of Kings/Isaiah drew again on synoptic prophetic materials, but also on materials in the book of Isaiah. Prominent among the former was the Josiah/Huldah narrative:

- Hezekiah weeps and tears his clothes like synoptic Josiah.[39]

---

36. 2 Kgs 19:2, 5, 6, 20; 20:1, 4, 7, 14, 16, 19 // Isa 37:2, 5, 6, 21; 38:1, 4, 21; 39:3, 5, 8.

37. 2 Kgs 20:8, 9, 11.

38. Verb and related nouns are used outside chs. 36–39 in Isa 12:2; 14:30; 26:4; 30:12, 15; 31:1; 32:10, 11, 17; 42:17; 47:8, 10; 50:10; 59:4.

39. In his great grief (2 Kgs 20:3), Hezekiah anticipates and also outdoes Josiah (22:19), the only synoptic character who weeps (indicator 6).

10. ISAIAH AND HEZEKIAH

- Isaiah develops the role played in the older text by Huldah.[40]
- Named messengers sent by Hezekiah to Isaiah (2 Kgs 19:2) reflect the naming of emissaries in the synoptic account of Josiah and Huldah; and this feature may also have influenced the addition of named representatives of both Sennacherib and Hezekiah as the earlier part of the narrative (in 2 Kgs 18) was expanded.

In addition to his similarities with Huldah, Isaiah repeats in 2 Kgs 20:5 // Isa 38:5 Yahweh's assurance to Solomon that he has heard his prayer (1 Kgs 9:3 // 2 Chr 7:12), and in 2 Kgs 20:16 // Isa 39:5, שמע דבר־יהוה ("Hear the word of Yahweh"), a phrase that only Micaiah has uttered synoptically (1 Kgs 22:19[41]), also in the context of a divine warning. He uses this synoptic formula with reference to the visit of the embassy from Babylon at the end of a tale (2 Kgs 20:12–19), which itself was drafted with conscious reference to the visit of the queen of Sheba in the Solomon story (1 Kgs 10:1–10 // 2 Chr 9:1–9).

Isaiah's first speech within the Hezekiah narrative (2 Kgs 19:6–7 // Isa 37:6–7) provides a useful window on his use of the (developing) book of Isaiah. גדף ("revile") and חרף ("scorn") seem to be an established word pair: they are found together three times in the Hebrew Bible: Isa 51:7, Ezek 5:15, and Ps 44:17. When the king sends a message (2 Kgs 19:4 // Isa 37:4) that the Assyrian ambassador has been sent "to *scorn* a living God" (לחרף אלהים חי), it is therefore unremarkable that, when Isaiah responds (2 Kgs 19:6 // Isa 37:6) with a countermessage from Yahweh, he varies the verb and speaks about those who "have *reviled* me" (גדפו אתי). However, that his first speech within the Hezekiah narrative (2 Kgs 19:6–7 // Isa 37:6–7) opens with "do not fear" (אל־תירא) suggests that he was doing more than just drawing on the resource of a familiar word pair: the divine response he passes on to the king includes a conscious recollection of Isa 51:7b: אל־תיראו חרפת אנוש ומגדפיהם אל־תחתו ("Do not fear a human's reproach, and at their revilings be not broken").[42] This

---

40. The sole occurrence of נאם יהוה (3.2.2) in this longer version of the Hezekiah story, spoken by Isaiah (19:33) just a few verses before the king's great weeping, is also unique to 22:19 within the synoptic texts. Similarly, two of the instances of הנה (3.2.5), key elements of the synoptic Huldah story (22:16, 20), are used in the same broad context (19:35; 20:5).

41. Admittedly 2 Chr 18:18 has pl., שמעו.

42. Strangely, Hans Wildberger notes the other occasions in the HB where חרף

first and earliest "Isaiah" within the Kings/Isaiah Hezekiah story develops a text drawn from Second Isaiah. However, a range of prophetic texts has fleshed out the response Isaiah has built on Isa 51:7. Half of the instances in the Hebrew Bible of אל־תירא מפני ("be not afraid in face of") and of גדף ("revile") are found in the Latter Prophets; "see I am setting a spirit in him" (הנני נתן בו רוח) draws on Micaiah's words in 1 Kgs 22:23; "and he will hear a rumor" (ושמע שמועה) has parallels, apart from 1 Sam 4:19, only in Jer 49:14, 23; and Obad 1—and in all three cases the rumor leading to destruction is divinely inspired. This provides a further example of significant linkage between the beginning of Samuel, the end of Kings, and the book of Jeremiah—though in this case not Jer 19 (see the end of 9.9).

It is subsequent Isaiah responses within this story that engage with First Isaiah. The second (2 Kgs 19:21–35 // Isa 37:21–35) is to Hezekiah's prayer on receipt of an Assyrian letter (2 Kgs 19:14–20 // Isa 37:14–20). Its first section draws heavily on several portions of the book of Isaiah:

- בת ציון ("daughter [of] Zion," 2 Kgs 19:21); see Isa 1:8; 10:32; 16:1; 52:2; 62:11[43]
- קדוש ישראל ("holy one of Israel," 2 Kgs 19:22); see Isa 1–31 (11x), 41–60 (13x)[44]
- החריב ("dried up," 2 Kgs 19:24); see Isa 42:15; 50:2; 51:10[45]
- מ/כימי קדם ("from/as days of old," 2 Kgs 19:25); see Isa 23:7; 51:9[46]
- יצר ([divine] "forming," 2 Kgs 19:25); see Isa 22:11 (N.B.); 29:16; 43:1, 21; 44:21; 45:7, 18; 46:11
- שאה ("become ruined," 2 Kgs 19:25);[47] see Isa 6:11
- חתו ובשו ("be shattered and ashamed," 2 Kgs 19:26);[48] see Isa 20:5
- ירק דשא חציר ("greenery/grass/foliage," 2 Kgs 19:26); see Isa 15:6 (only there, all three together)
- רגז ("rage," 2 Kgs 19:28); see Isa 5:25; 14:9; 28:21; 32:10, 11; 64:1

---

and גדף appear together, but not this one instance in Isaiah (*Jesaja 28–39: Das Buch, der Prophet und seine Botschaft*, part 3 of *Jesaja*, BKAT 10.3 [Neukirchen-Vluyn: Neukirchener Verlag, 1982], 1410).

43. Also 19x elsewhere.
44. And only 5x elsewhere: Jer 50:29; 51:5; Pss 71:2; 78:41; 89:19.
45. Also Jer 51:36; Nah 1:4.
46. Also Jer 46:26; Mic 7:20; Ps 44:2; Lam 1:7; 2:17.
47. Reading להשאות with Isa 37:26 rather than להשות as in 2 Kgs 19:25.
48. Reading חתו ובשו with Isa 37:27 rather than חתו ויבשו as in 2 Kgs 19:26.

10. ISAIAH AND HEZEKIAH

- שַׁאֲנָן ("ease," 2 Kgs 19:28); see Isa 32:9, 11, 18; 33:20[49]

The second section (2 Kgs 19:29–31) is also indebted to portions of the book of Isaiah:

- ונטעו כרמים ואכלו פרים ("and they shall plant orchards and eat their fruit," 2 Kgs 19:29); see Isa 65:21
- ויספה פליטת בית־יהודה ("and the remnant of the house of Judah shall again …," 2 Kgs 19:30); see Isa 10:20 (לא יוסיף פליטת בית־יעקב)
- קנאת יהוה תעשה זאת ("the zeal of Yahweh shall perform this," 2 Kgs 19:31); see Isa 9:6

Then the third section (19:32–34) recalls in verse 34 the use of גנן ("shield") in Isa 31:5.

The underlying Hezekiah narrative had been integral to the synoptic Jerusalem royal story; and that is no less true of the rewritten version in Chronicles. But was the expanded Kings/Isaiah narrative more at home in Kings or Isaiah?

1. In addition to the use made of other portions of the *synoptic* narrative (especially about Josiah and Huldah, Micaiah, and Solomon), close *nonsynoptic* links with Samuel–Kings were also inserted by this rewriter. These include (a) the request made by Hezekiah to Isaiah for healing (lit. "life") from illness, like those made by king Amaziah to Elijah in 2 Kgs 1 and the king of Damascus to Elisha in 2 Kgs 8; and (b) elements shared with the critique of Eli by an unnamed "man of God" in 1 Sam 2:27–36.[50] One of these shared elements, הנה ימים באים ("see, days are coming," 1 Sam 2:31; 2 Kgs 20:17 // Isa 39:6), is also found some dozen times in Jeremiah. And the return of Hezekiah's envoys (2 Kgs 18:37) with rent clothes (קרעי בגדים) recalls 1 Sam 4:12; 2 Sam 1:2; 13:31; 15:32; and, outside Samuel, only Jer 41:5.

2. On the other hand, the location by the Fuller's Field (2 Kgs 18:17b) is known elsewhere only in Isaiah (7:3); משענת הקנה הרצוץ הזה ("the

---

49. Further examples are cited in Wildberger, *Jesaja 28–39*, 1429.

50. These include (1) כה אמר יהוה (1 Sam 2:27) used in 2 Kgs 19:6, 32; 20:1, 5; (2) נאם יהוה (1 Sam 2:30) in 2 Kgs 19:33; (3) התהלך (1 Sam 2:30, 35) in 2 Kgs 20:3; (4) הנה ימים באים (1 Sam 2:31) in 2 Kgs 20:17; and (5) וזה־לך האות (1 Sam 2:34) in 2 Kgs 19:29; 20:9.

staff of this broken reed," 2 Kgs 18:21) resonates with נשען ("leaning") in Isa 3:1; 10:20; 30:12; 31:1; the explicit critique of Egypt (2 Kgs 18:20–21, 23–24) echoes Isa 30:1–5; 31:1–3;[51] and קנאת יהוה צבאות תעשה זאת ("the zeal of Yahweh of hosts shall perform this," 2 Kgs 19:31) is known elsewhere only in Isa 9:6. In Kings/Isaiah, both principal spokesmen draw important elements of their arguments from the book of Isaiah: not only Isaiah, but Sennacherib's envoy as well. Together they treat Hezekiah to a debate about the significance of Isaiah's teaching to his situation.

The only mention of Isaiah in the main body of 2 Chr 32 is at the end of the siege (v. 20); and this point in the story is exactly where we meet him for the first time within the longer narrative (2 Kgs 19:1–7 // Isa 37:1–7). On his first appearance in the fuller version, Isaiah is reactive—like a synoptic Micaiah or Huldah. But on later occasions in Kings/Isaiah (of which Chronicles preserves no trace), he is different—proactive, like nonsynoptic Elijah and Elisha. Second Chronicles 32 preserves the earliest stage of this growing narrative about the prophet Isaiah alongside Hezekiah: he simply accompanies the king as he prays. Next, as his role develops in 2 Kgs 19:1–7 // Isa 37:1–7, he responds to the king's staff as Huldah did to Josiah's emissaries. In his third and longest contribution (2 Kgs 19:20–34 // Isa 37:21–35), Isaiah learns directly from Yahweh about a subsequent prayer of Hezekiah (2 Kgs 19:14–19 // Isa 37:14–20) and is sent to the king with the divine response. Each marks a discrete stage in the development of this prophetic legend.[52]

10.5. Focus on Kings/Isaiah

The narratives in Kings and Isaiah have most in common, but there are again two principal areas of difference.

---

51. Chronicles would have had no motive to remove mention of Egypt. The shared tradition mentions Egypt in connection with Solomon (1 Kgs 8:9, 16; 9:9; 10:28, 29 // 2 Chr 5:10; 6:5; 7:22; 9:26, 28), Jeroboam (1 Kgs 12:2 // 2 Chr 10:2), Rehoboam (1 Kgs 14:25 // 2 Chr 12:2), Josiah (2 Kgs 23:29 // 2 Chr 35:20), and Jehoahaz (2 Kgs 23:34 // 2 Chr 36:4). Pharaoh, king of Egypt, is also criticized in very similar terms in Ezek 29:6.

52. It is over her lack of attention to the almost complete "disappearance" of Isaiah from 2 Chr 32 that the argument of Park's *Hezekiah and Dialogue* unravels.

10.5.1. 2 Kgs 18:14–16

Their accounts of the threat from Assyria start the same way (2 Kgs 18:13 // Isa 36:1) and are almost identical (2 Kgs 18:17-37 // Isa 36:2–22). But the short report immediately following the shared opening verse, about Hezekiah paying off Sennacherib (2 Kgs 18:14–16), is not represented at all in Isa 36. In Kings, but not in Isaiah or Chronicles, we have a tension between Hezekiah paying a large tribute to Sennacherib of Assyria in 2 Kgs 18:14–16 and (still) having a treasury to display to his Babylonian visitors in 20:12–19. Isaiah and Chronicles share with Kings only the display at the end; and Chronicles has reported that Hezekiah's wealth had been enhanced through gifts brought to the king after Sennacherib's withdrawal (2 Chr 32:23). Have Chronicles and Isaiah resolved the tension by omission, or has Kings created it by the late addition of 18:14–16?[53]

Given modern assumptions about historical causation, it is very hard not to prefer the brief account in 2 Kgs 18:14–16 (Hezekiah bought off Sennacherib) as more credible than the reports of divine deception of the Assyrian king (19:7–9) or divine plague visited on his forces (19:35–36).[54] Yet what 18:14–16 reports is neither repeated within the extended parallel to 2 Kgs 18–20 in Isa 36–39 nor reflected at all in 2 Chr 32. On the other hand, both Isaiah and Chronicles share with Kings the report of divine plague (and Isa 37:7–9 shares with Kings the divine deception). Analyses of the sources and growth of 2 Kgs 18–19 regularly follow Stade in identifying 18:13–16 as source A, with the longer following narrative as B or B^1 + B^2. Yet, however realistic, however accurate its information could possibly

---

53. For Joseph Blenkinsopp, "The biblical account simply ignores the problem that Hezekiah had only recently handed over all his gold and silver to the Assyrians" (*Opening the Sealed Book: Interpretations of the Book of Isaiah in Late Antiquity* [Grand Rapids: Eerdmans, 2006], 42).

54. Bob Becking's "basic assumption ... that the numbers for the reigns of the kings of Israel and Judah in the Book of Kings are not to be assessed as a deliberate and meaningful 'invention' by the redactors of the Book" appears unexceptionable ("Chronology: A Skeleton without Flesh? Sennacherib's Campaign as a Case-Study," in *"Like a Bird in a Cage": The Invasion of Sennacherib in 701 BCE*, ed. Lester L. Grabbe, JSOTSup 363 [London: Sheffield Academic Press, 2003], 5). In the light of our discussion, however, we should immediately limit the scope of that claim to the older narrative underlying Kings and Chronicles.

be, we should not allow the natural priority of A over B to mislead us about the course of the literary history.[55]

Hezekiah's extra fifteen years of life could be described as an invention by the authors of Kings. But they themselves had considered that they were simply comparing Hezekiah's surprising survival with the similarly noteworthy survival of Amaziah that was already part of the inherited tradition—indeed, that they were simply giving more precision to the transitional בימים ההם ("in those days") in 2 Kgs 20:1 // 2 Chr 32:24, as the older synoptic report moved from the troubles of Jerusalem to the illness of its king. Ray Person has proposed that 2 Kgs 18:14–16 was added for the purpose of "downplaying Hezekiah as a model king."[56]

In a paper whose primary concern is to differentiate 2 Kgs 19:9b–35 (the so-called source B²) from its context in 18:13–19:9a, 19:36–37 (B¹) and to date the later material, Nadav Na'aman has dismissed Person's case as "arbitrary."[57] He holds to the view that 18:14–16 were omitted when the Hezekiah story was copied into the book of Isaiah, and cites the opposite reason: toward "the idealization of the figure of Hezekiah in exilic and postexilic periods." His comparison and contrast of the lists of captured cities and peoples in 18:33–34 and 19:12–13 and the implications of the differences for (up)dating are all persuasive. Less persuasive is Na'aman's retention of the model of an earlier and a later "source" at all: the very evidence that he cites might have been better directed toward alternative models such as a "rolling corpus" or *Fortschreibung*—expansive rewriting. In these more organic models, the newer material has to be understood within the context of the older rather than as over against it.

Indeed, Person's proposal can be strengthened by observing another short word trail that begins in a synoptic text. Although the details of Ahaz's cultic innovations are reported very differently in Kings and Chronicles, they share in 2 Kgs 16:17 // 2 Chr 28:24 the unique instance in synoptic texts of the verb קצץ ("cut off"). The context there is Ahaz's destruction of (or removal of elements from) temple furnishings in favor of or under pressure from Aram and Assyria. The author of 2 Kgs 18:16 ("Hezekiah cut off [the gilt from] the doors of Yahweh's palace") reused a term that his synoptic source had employed only once, in its report of Ahaz; and he

---

55. Here I must part company with Kratz's "Siege of Jerusalem."
56. *Recensions*, 79.
57. "Updating the Messages: Hezekiah's Second Prophetic Story (2 Kings 19:9b–35) and the Community of Babylonian Deportees," in Grabbe, *Like a Bird*, 203.

thereby aligned Hezekiah's action with the behavior of his wicked father. And the fact that the author of Kings combines קצץ with היכל יהוה[58] first in 18:16 and then again only in his report of the Babylonian sack of the temple (24:13) encourages readers of the enhanced Hezekiah story to see his action in 18:14–16 as an anticipation of his foolish dealings with the envoys from Babylon in 20:12–19. However apparently credible the information, we are dealing in 18:14–16 not with a historian's use of archive or of reliable memory, but with exegesis. Hezekiah's extra fifteen years were not well used.

Jeremy Schipper has made the useful proposal that, if we were to "remove 2 Kgs 21:10–15, 23:26–27, and 24:3–4" (all nonsynoptic texts) "from the rest of the text," we would blame Hezekiah and not Manasseh for the exile.[59] However, his argument can be stood on its head: the case against Hezekiah would fail if we were to remove 2 Kgs 18:14–16 and 20:12–19; by contrast, Manasseh is already sufficiently condemned in (synoptic) 2 Kgs 21:1–9 // 2 Chr 33:1–9. Within the so-called source A, it is necessary to distinguish between 2 Kgs 18:13 // Isa 36:1 and 2 Kgs 18:14–16. The synoptic narrative had not provided a specific date for Sennacherib's move on Judah's cities. The specification of the fourteenth year by an author of Kings came first: it anticipated the report of the healing of the king and the deliverance of his city, and was likely added at the same time. Despite positive billing at the outset (2 Kgs 18:3 // 2 Chr 29:2), Hezekiah ends up "true" to his ancestor David, finishing his career by making a bad mistake (2 Kgs 20:12–19 // Isa 39:1–8). Paying the king of Assyria to withdraw (2 Kgs 18:14–16, without parallel in Isaiah or Chronicles) is probably a fresh and secondary anticipation of this final and discreditable episode in the Hezekiah story. It also builds yet again on synoptic Amaziah. Deliverance of Jerusalem had cost him: כל־הזהב־והכסף ואת־כל הכלים הנמצאים בית־יהוה ובאצרות בית המלך ("All the gold and the silver and all the vessels found in the house of Yahweh and in the treasuries of the house of the king"; 2 Kgs 14:14 // 2 Chr 25:24). And now it would cost Hezekiah: כל־הכסף הנמצא בית־יהוה ובאצרות בית המלך ("All the silver found in the house of Yahweh and in the treasuries of the house of the king"; 2 Kgs 18:15).

---

58. We have noted (5.1) that היכל יהוה is also very rare synoptically.
59. "Hezekiah, Manasseh," 81–82.

10.5.2. Hezekiah Healed

The end of the second topic, about the illness of Hezekiah, is written very differently in 2 Kgs 20:1–11 and Isa 38:1–22. The two versions of the healing start in almost identical terms (2 Kgs 20:1–3 // Isa 38:1–3[60]); then 2 Kgs 20:4–6[61] is a little fuller than Isa 38:4–6[62] (and the traditional verse division is different). However, the reports in 2 Kgs 20:7–11 and Isa 38:7–8, 21–22 about signs and treatment by a compress of figs diverge still further:

- Only 2 Kgs 20:5 and 8 talk of "healing" (רפא). The verb occurs in other portions of Isaiah[63] but not in Isa 36–39.
- Only Kings specifies "the third day" for the king's return to the temple in 20:5 and 8. "The third day" does measure time elsewhere in Samuel–Kings;[64] however, it is never found in Isaiah, and appears in Chronicles only in the synoptic 2 Chr 10:12 // 1 Kgs 12:12.
- Then the extra detail in 2 Kgs 20:10 (this verse as a whole is without parallel in Isa 38) about the direction in which the shadow should move includes נקל ("is easy"). This verb too is never found in Isaiah, but is used in several late portions of Samuel–Kings.[65]

On the other hand, Hezekiah's extended response to his recovery (the so-called psalm in Isa 38:9–20) has no parallel at all in Kings.

Yair Zakovitch, when exploring assimilation in biblical narratives, took his start from the version of the story in 2 Kgs 20:1–11 and found that "verse 7 is not only contradictory to verse 8 but is also opposed to the general character of the story … the verse was added to enhance Isa-

---

60. LXX attests ויהי at the opening of Isa 38:1 but simply לאמר at the start of 38:3, where MT has ויאמר אנה יהוה.

61. In place of the puzzling לא יצא העיר (2 Kgs 20:4), "in the hall" (LXX) may attest בחצ[י]ר.

62. In Isa 38:5 "the sound of [your prayer]" is an LXX plus, while in 38:6 ואת העיר הזאת is an MT plus.

63. Isa 6:10; 19:22; 30:26; 53:5; 57:18–19.

64. 1 Sam 30:1; 2 Sam 1:2; 1 Kgs 3:18; 12:12; 2 Kgs 20:5, 8.

65. In a significant plus in 2 Sam 6:22 related to 1 Sam 18:23; in 1 Kgs 16:31; and in 2 Kgs 3:18 (significantly, here part of a divine promise through Elisha—late Isaiah was compared above with Elisha).

iah's similarity to Elisha."[66] This narrative judgment found support in text-critical details of the version in Isa 38. For Zakovitch, the first stage of the story was "*1 [sic] Kings 20:1-6, 8-11,* reflected in abridged form[67] in 1QIsa[a] 38:1-8, minus the later addition of verses 21-22."[68]

Person's starting point was text-critical rather than literary; and he concluded that only a short text such as Isa 38:7-8 originally stood between 38:6 (= 2 Kgs 20:6) and 39:1 (= 2 Kgs 20:12). Five observations combine to suggest to Person the secondary nature of all the other verses: (1) they were added in 1QIsa[a] by a different, later hand at the end of a short line continuing into the margin; (2) we find them in different positions in Kings (both MT and LXX) over against Isaiah (MT, LXX, and 1QIsa[a]); (3) Hezekiah's question in these verses does not receive an answer; (4) these verses are closely related to the addition in 2 Kgs 20:5; and (5) they are lacking in the parallel account in 2 Chr 32:24-26. He suggests that "a probable source for this addition is 19:29 which has references to a sign and three years."[69]

10.5.3. Striking a Balance

That the relevant texts of Kings and Isaiah are otherwise so similar to each other might already suggest that these two larger (sets of) differences arose at the latest stages in the development of each text. The different ordering of the shared verses toward the end (2 Kgs 20:7-11 and Isa 38:7-8, 21-22) reinforces the effect of the pluses in each text. The book of Isaiah stresses the piety of King Hezekiah, but the book of Kings emphasizes the efficacy of the prophet Isaiah. Then the presence in Kings at the beginning, and absence there from Isaiah, of the short report about Hezekiah paying tribute to Sennacherib is also relevant to the estimate of King Hezekiah in each book. The absence from Chronicles of material similar to any one of

---

66. Yair Zakovitch, "Assimilation in Biblical Narratives," in *Empirical Models of Biblical Criticism*, ed. Jeffrey H. Tigay (Philadelphia: University of Pennsylvania Press, 1985), 183.

67. "Abridged" does appear to be a deliberate choice of words, although it is less than clear in ibid., 184 n. 21 just what is "original": "Note that the version of the story in Isaiah was originally shorter than that in Kings and lacked verse 8—part of the original story—as well as verse 7. When 2 Kings 20:7 was interpolated in Isaiah, part of verse 8 was brought along as well."

68. "Assimilation in Biblical Narratives," 185.

69. *Recensions*, 72.

these significant shorter and longer pluses in Kings and Isaiah supports the suggestion that they were all added quite late to Kings and Isaiah. They give further encouragement to comparing the shorter account in Chronicles with that portion of the longer versions that is actually common to Kings and Isaiah.[70] Just as the text of Chronicles often preserves an earlier version of what we read now in Kings, so too Isa 36–39 is our prime witness to a late stage in the development of 2 Kgs 18–20.

10.6. אות AND מופת

Our "trigonometry" has suggested that expansive rewriting can explain many of the divergences among the three accounts of Hezekiah. But at least one important element of the drafting and redrafting of the several versions of Hezekiah was not linear: the shift from אות ("sign") to מופת ("portent"), or the other way round. The shorter version in Chronicles is rather enigmatic: the king prays when close to death and Yahweh grants him a מופת (2 Chr 32:24); and later the Babylonian envoys are sent "to examine the portent there has been in the land" (לדרוש המופת אשר היה בארץ, 32:31). It is unclear what constitutes the מופת in the land; but we may presume it is one and the same as the earlier divine response to the king's prayer. The book of Chronicles nowhere uses the term אות, and it uses מופת only once more (when quoting Ps 105:5 at 1 Chr 16:12[71]). By contrast, only אות is used in Samuel–Kings.[72] It seems more likely that Samuel–Kings has altered מופת to אות—a term that it does use elsewhere—rather than that Chronicles has altered אות to מופת.

Twice in Isaiah (8:18; 20:3) and quite frequently in several other books we find אות and מופת paired. Where this is not the case, אות is much more common than מופת (as in Isa 7:11, 14; 19:20; 44:25; 55:13; 66:19). William Johnstone has shown that in Exodus, מופת on its own refers to bad things done to Egypt, while אות on its own refers to good things done to Israel.[73]

---

70. The relationship of 2 Kgs 20:12–19 // Isa 39 to 2 Chr 32:31 may be a more open question: Chronicles here may depend on the longer story. Yet the theme of Hezekiah having wealth to display is handled in some detail in 2 Chr 32:27–29.

71. Ps 105:27 has אתות and מפתים in parallel, but the citation in 1 Chr 16 finishes at Ps 105:15. The unique combination לדרוש המופת could allude to Ps 105:4–5 (// 1 Chr 16:11–12) as a whole, since Ps 105:4 opens with דרשו.

72. 1 Sam 2:34; 10:7, 9; 14:10; 2 Kgs 19:29; 20:8, 9.

73. William Johnstone, "The Deuteronomistic Cycles of 'Signs' and 'Wonders'

10. ISAIAH AND HEZEKIAH

If there is an element of puzzling menace in the more original מופת, then the expansive authors of Kings/Isaiah may have joined the Babylonian envoys in seeking to decode it.

In Kings and Isaiah, two of the three instances of אות also concern the king's recovery, but are not reported in the same order. Isaiah is shorter than Kings in the relevant verses. Immediately after the double declaration that his God will lengthen the king's life and save both him and his city from the king of Assyria (38:6), the prophet first promises a "sign from Yahweh" that he will do what he has spoken (38:7). This sign is turning back the sun's shadow by ten steps on the steps of Ahaz (38:8). Then, at the end of the episode, the king asks for a sign that he will go up to Yahweh's house; but no response is offered (38:22). In Kings as in Isaiah, we read first the double promise (2 Kgs 20:6 // Isa 38:6). But here Hezekiah goes on to request a sign that Yahweh will heal him and that he will go up to Yahweh's house on the third day (2 Kgs 20:8, similar to but fuller than Isa 38:22[74]), and the prophet announces a more complex version of the sign of the shadow on the steps immediately afterward (2 Kgs 20:9). In the relevant verses, both books use the word אות twice within very similar sentences. In Isaiah, the prophet promises one sign and the king later asks for another. In Kings, despite using many more words, only one sign is narrated: the king asks for it and the prophet announces it.

Kings/Isaiah has already reported a further sign in which Isaiah speaks of gradual relief and recovery of the land. This, his second response to Hezekiah's prayer (2 Kgs 19:15–19 // Isa 37:16–20), is set toward the end of the siege narrative (2 Kgs 19:29–31 // Isa 37:30–32). There is no immediate parallel in Chronicles' account of the siege, but the images in this sign of improvement to agriculture do resonate with "the portent there has been *in the land.*"

---

in Exodus1–13," in *Understanding Poets and Prophets: Essays in Honour of George Wishart Anderson*, ed. A. Graeme Auld, JSOTSup 152 (Sheffield: Sheffield Academic Press, 1993), 166–85.

74. No one else in the Hebrew Bible puts the question מה אות ("What sign?").

11
READING THE WRITTEN KINGS

11.1. FOLLOWING THE WORDS

The origin and development of the book of Kings—even more than the book of Samuel[1]—can best be understood by comparing it with parallel texts. Our study has explored this proposition from many different angles. Our opening probes of sample parallels in Kings/Isaiah and in Samuel/Chronicles (ch. 1) anticipated several later discussions. The longer parallels in Kings and Samuel had each included the theme of "life" and expressed emphasis by cognate infinitives absolute. "Life" and "living" turned out to be a hugely more important theme in Kings than in Chronicles (see ch. 2). Further recurrent differences over word use between Kings and Chronicles and the content they share were then reviewed; adding emphasis to a verb by prefacing cognate infinitives absolute proved to be simply one element in later, more extensive rewriting of several Samuel–Kings passages (see ch. 3). The most interesting indicator of the distinctiveness of the shared material is יש ("there is"): wholly absent from synoptic texts, but used in both (Samuel–)Kings and Chronicles. Minimal interest in "life," lesser use of the infinitive absolute, and nonuse of יש combine to constitute a prima facie case for significant difference between the material shared by Kings and Chronicles and the rest of the book of Kings.

Reference was made in chapter 3 to a study (separately published) of expressions for date and time in synoptic portions.[2] These exhibit only minimal difference between Kings and Chronicles. This also turned out to be true of the notes and narratives about divine/human communica-

---

1. The first parallel text (1 Sam 31 // 1 Chr 10) comes more than halfway through Samuel.
2. See my "Shaping of Israelite History."

tion, whether consultation of the Deity or prophetic utterances or prayer. The summative role of the Huldah oracle supported treating the divine-human communication portions as a group (see ch. 4). The exception that proved this rule was the large-scale variation between Kings and Chronicles as they report on Hezekiah—not surprisingly, the radically divergent accounts of this king provided the context for one of their very few differences over dating. Attention to the shared narrative sheds light on how the במה theme developed divergently in Kings and Chronicles (see ch. 5).

The shared material is significantly different in wording and outlook from Kings as a whole. This is no less true of its relationship with Chronicles as a whole. Several synoptic constituents reviewed are not developed at all in Chronicles: the Chronicler did not simply adopt from his source such material as he found congenial to his purposes. It is hardly plausible that he started by making such an untypical selection from his main source, especially since several elements were not sufficiently useful for reuse by him. Both Kings and Chronicles were constrained by the shape and wording of the material they jointly inherited. The intention and coherence of the source material is sketched (see ch. 6) by listing a series of words and phrases that occur just twice, so suggesting deliberate comparisons and contrasts. Significantly, some of these pairs also come in pairs, such as משח ("anoint") and ברית ("covenant"), or חרף ("scorn") and הציל ("deliver").

A small detour to the book of Samuel (ch. 7) developed the discussion of four passages already treated in my Old Testament Library commentary. All had drawn on distinctive language from 2 Sam 7 // 1 Chr 17, and three of them from 2 Sam 24 // 1 Chr 21. Three samples follow of how much of the familiar book of Kings was generated from these synoptic resources. Important elements of the "northern" prophetic narrative in 1 Kgs 17–2 Kgs 10 drew successively on synoptic 1 Kgs 22 and 2 Kgs 11. As for the northern kings, half of them already feature (or are at least mentioned) in shared text about Jerusalem's monarchs; and many of the rest serve only to make up a total equaling the succession to David in the south. Synoptic texts had blamed the house of Ahab for its pernicious influence. However, Kings overlays the whole story of the north by repeated indictment of Jeroboam I, who is largely depicted like a second David (see ch. 8).

Organic development from the synoptic narrative was next explored in the story of Jerusalem's kings (ch. 9). The book of Kings makes substantial additions to the synoptic portraits of Solomon and Josiah. However, the Hezekiah stories are in a class of their own (see ch. 10 above). The very substantial expansion in Kings of the older narrative about Hezekiah and the Assyrian envoy, Hezekiah's illness, and the visit to Jerusalem of envoys from Babylon was also indebted to other synoptic portions; and the availability of a third parallel text (in the book of Isaiah) permitted triangulation of the development of the prophetic legend of Isaiah and Hezekiah. Though Kings (and Isaiah) had augmented these parts of the older Hezekiah narrative much more than Chronicles, the reverse was true of his religious reforms. In the sparser version still more readily visible in Kings, the narrator had mockingly "set up" the Assyrian envoy to give a misleading account of Judah's king: centralization of sacrifice at a single altar in Jerusalem was not a synoptic issue. A reconstruction of much of the synoptic text follows (see ch. 12).

De Wette and Wellhausen were right to dismiss the notion that the author of Chronicles had access to ancient independent sources about David, Solomon, and the others behind the main connected narrative he inherited. But they were wrong to argue that the inherited narrative was substantially what we know as Samuel–Kings. Instead, both Chronicles and Samuel–Kings were organic developments from a shared integrated and prophetically interpreted narrative. The final shape of the book of Kings, no less than of the book of Samuel, has confused researchers about the course of its development. Many key elements of the portrayal of Saul as well as David had been drawn from and adapted from the powerful story of David insisting on a count of Israel (see ch. 7). The freshly structured *abccba* conclusion in 2 Sam 21–24 may have been intended to add further weight to the culminating census and its awful aftermath. However, these chapters are often misread as a somewhat detached tailpiece. A key element of the fresh perspective informing this study has involved bringing 1 Kgs 22, like 2 Sam 24, into center stage. The equally powerful story of Micaiah with the kings of north and south and his prophetic rivals is integral to the whole narrative in 1 Kgs 17–2 Kgs 10 because much of the rest was generated from it. From Elijah's self-presentation (1 Kgs 17:1) to Jehu's riding to overthrow the two kings (2 Kgs 9:17–27), the language draws on a narrative that was originally part of the (synoptic) prophetic account of Jerusalem's kings (see chs. 5 and 8 above). The final authors of Samuel did recognize the importance of the census, but in a way that misled (modern) readers. A whole series of prophetic stories (set in the north) was generated by and around 1 Kgs 22. It is hardly a surprise that it came to be thought one of them, and that all of them were supposed to reflect northern traditions.

In the older synoptic narrative, both 2 Sam 24 // 1 Chr 21 and 1 Kgs 22 // 2 Chr 18 were integral to a "prophetic" interpretation of Jerusalem and David's line. The destructive role of the divine envoy in the census story was predictive of a series of diminishments of Jerusalem and its Davidic kings. After Solomon, Israel split between north and south. The invitation by a king of Israel to Jehoshaphat to cooperate militarily was a failure. Rivalry between north and south led to damage to Jerusalem under Amaziah. When Sennacherib occupied much of Judah, Jerusalem itself was only just saved. And, by the time of Josiah, the end was already decreed.

11.2. Serial Anticipations

The authors of Samuel–Kings were "serial anticipators." As they rewrote the older synoptic record, they retrojected many of its themes back into earlier times.

1. My discussion of "asking Yahweh" or "asking the Deity" (4.3) noted that every single nonsynoptic occurrence of that phrase preceded the sole synoptic occurrences (2 Sam 5 // 1 Chr 14).³

2. The synoptic record blamed Jehoram and Ahaziah for following in the ways of the house of Ahab in Israel. But Yahweh did not destroy Judah at the time of Jehoram because he had granted a ניר to David (see 3.2.3). Kings moves the first mention of this grant several generations forward, to Solomon and Abijam. They would already have lost everything by their behavior, and not just northern Israel in Solomon's case, had it not been for Yahweh's promise to David.

3. Similarly Rehoboam is blamed in Kings using terms that the synoptic story had reserved for wicked Ahaz and Manasseh: while 2 Kgs 16:4 // 2 Chr 28:4 is the only synoptic verse to use either גבעה ("height") or עץ רענן ("green tree"), Rehoboam is blamed in 1 Kgs 14:23 for resorting to them (see 9.3). Synoptic Rehoboam had been foolish; but Kings heaps blame on David's first three successors in Jerusalem (Solomon, Rehoboam, and Abijam) as well as on Jeroboam I and the following kings of the north.

4. The coronation acclamation יחי המלך ("[Long] live the king"), used first in 2 Kgs 11:12 // 2 Chr 23:11, is found also in 1 Sam 10:24; 2 Sam 16:16; 1 Kgs 1:25, 29, 34, 39 (see 2.4).

---

3. שאל ב־, first used in 2 Sam 5:19, 23 // 1 Chr 14:10, 14, is anticipated in Judg 1:1; 18:5; 20:18, 23, 27; 1 Sam 10:22; 14:37; 22:10, 13, 15; 23:2, 4; 28:6; 30:8; 2 Sam 2:1.

5. Swearing "by living Yahweh" (חי יהוה) provided a further example, but also an interesting exception (2.3). Most use of "Yahweh's life" does anticipate the sole synoptic instance. However, it is the few further instances that follow quite closely on 1 Kgs 22 // 2 Chr 18 that most resemble it in function.

6. Just when Judah became separate from Israel provides another instance. Without lessening Rehoboam's responsibility, the authors set what he did in a wider context. The kingdom of Judah to which his rule was reduced had a past: it was the kingdom over which his grandfather David had already ruled before becoming king of Israel as well. After all, even the older synoptic history had taught that Yahweh had promised David exactly that "landed estate" (ניר) for all time.

7. Important moments in the re-presentation within the book of Samuel of David, Saul, and even Samuel drew on synoptic David (see ch. 7).

8. The retrospective critique of northern Israel (2 Kgs 17) drew on synoptic Hezekiah and Manasseh (2 Kgs 18, 21).

9. The reattribution of developments at Bethel and Dan from eighth-century Jeroboam II to tenth-century Jeroboam I is another plausible case of retrojection (see 8.8.3).

It must remain for a future study to consider how far projection backward to earlier times may already have been a feature of the older synoptic narrative. Whose repertoire of cultic misdemeanors may have been retrojected onto the shoulders of Ahaz or Manasseh?[4] And in what period(s) were the traditions developed that we find ascribed to David and Solomon?

11.3. Deuteronomy and the Narrative Tradition

Beyond such developments in nonsynoptic Samuel and Kings, the book of Deuteronomy is the big anticipation. And we return here to where we began: to the seminal contributions of de Wette, advanced by Wellhausen, on the link between Deuteronomy and Josiah's reform. As noted at the start (1.1), ancient readers had already proposed that Deuteronomy

---

4. Susan Ackerman notes conservatively that "the phrase found in Isa 57:5, 'under every green tree', ... belongs almost exclusively to the language of Jeremiah ... Ezekiel ... and the Deuteronomistic historians ... that is, to the language of the late seventh and sixth centuries" (*Under Every Green Tree: Popular Religion in Sixth-Century Judah*, HSM 46 [Atlanta: Scholars Press, 1992], 113).

or something like it was the book found in the temple during restoration work under King Josiah. Rannfrid Thelle has explored this territory quite usefully in her *Approaches to the "Chosen Place."* In these concluding remarks, I am seeking to support her larger case; and yet, by supplying some of the diachronic argument that she chooses not to deploy, I also advance some modifications. I am exploring just one aspect of a complex relationship, but one that is crucial to exploring the long-perceived link between Deuteronomy and Kings.

Deuteronomy 12 is undoubtedly one of the programmatic chapters in that book. Its opening words ("These are the ordinances and judgments") have themselves been frequently anticipated in Deut 1–11.[5] Now finally they are introducing the big statement toward which expectation has been building—and this chapter states and restates what will be a recurrent theme of the book, the divinely chosen place.[6] All that is clear; but whether Deut 12 is advocating or mandating cultic centralization is another matter. It is also debatable whether Josiah as described in 2 Kgs 22–23 is giving effect to cultic centralization. From her careful reading of the Josiah report in Kings, Thelle notes that it does not even mention Jerusalem or its "house of Yahweh" as chosen: for her, Josiah's wide-ranging cultic reform was prophylactic rather than centralizing. Equally, there was no mention of "the book" in 2 Kgs 23:4–20.[7]

The language of Deut 12 has its closest links with the royal narrative not in 2 Kgs 22–23 but in 1 Kgs 8. We reviewed מקום ("place") in synoptic texts and contexts earlier (5.3.3), and noted that "the place" is an important topic in Solomon's prayer.[8] Yahweh's "choice" of the city of Jerusalem (as also of David as king) is also claimed in Solomon's prayer,[9] and is recalled in three synoptic locations (in Solomon's second vision, in a note about Rehoboam's reign, and in the critique of Manasseh[10]). But the city of Jerusalem is distinct from "the place."

---

5. Deut 4:1, 45; 5:1: 6:1.

6. Deut 12:5, 11, 14, 18, 21, 26; 14:23, 24, 25; 15:20; 16:2, 6, 7, 11, 15, 16; 17:8, 10; 18:6; 23:17 (Yahweh as grammatical subject is assumed here, but not stated); 26:2; 31:11.

7. *Approaches to the "Chosen Place,"* 152–53. And her remarks (200–203) on articles by Gary Knoppers (different Deuteronomists?) and Bernard Levinson relating to Deuteronomy and Kings (see 1.2 above) are also helpful.

8. 1 Kgs 8:29 (2x), 30 (2x), 35 // 2 Chr 6:20 (2x), 21 (2x), 26.

9. 1 Kgs 8:16, 20 // 2 Chr 6:5, 10.

10. 1 Kgs 9:3; 14:21; 2 Kgs 21:7 // 2 Chr 7:16; 12:13; 33:7.

What Yahweh "has chosen" (בחר) in synoptic texts are "the city" or "Jerusalem"[11] and also "David."[12] Nonsynoptic Kings adds choice of "your people" (1 Kgs 3:8[13]); and in 2 Chronicles we find divine choosing of "this place" (7:12), "this house" (7:16), and "you" (Levites, 29:11). As for Deuteronomy: in addition to the many mentions (22x) of "the place that Yahweh will/may choose," Yahweh chose his people (4x),[14] Levi(tes) (2x),[15] and will/may choose a king.[16] The divine choice of Levites and of "this place" are topics shared between Deuteronomy and Chronicles, but not Samuel-Kings. Throughout Deuteronomy, choosing is almost always Yahweh's prerogative. In the single exception (30:19), the people are invited to choose life (and not death).

The crucial issue is this. If divine "choosing" belonged to (proto-)Deuteronomy before it featured in (proto-)Kings, then elements of Deuteronomy's המקום אשר יבחר יהוה ("the [unspecified] place that Yahweh will/may choose") have become specified in different directions in the later royal narrative: the object of "choose" has become "the city" or "Jerusalem," while "the place" has become "the temple within Jerusalem" (or, even more precisely, its inner sanctum). But if choosing Jerusalem and choosing the city were expressions crafted first in the synoptic narrative underlying Kings,[17] then Deuteronomy has conflated these objects of choice with the "place" of which Solomon had also spoken in his synoptic prayer. In the wider context of the manifold serial anticipations just noted (11.2), I find the second option more likely: talk of a divinely chosen place has been pushed forward beyond the Solomon story to the Moses story—Deuteronomy has reformulated Kings.

There are three supporting arguments. On each synoptic occasion, the divine choice of Jerusalem is spelled out as follows: לשום שמי/ו שם ("to set my/his name there") or להיות שמי שם ("for my name to be there"). And the same formula is used in nonsynoptic 1 Kgs 11:36. In three of the related passages in Deuteronomy, לשום שמו שם ("to set his name there")

---

11. 1 Kgs 11:13, 32, 36; 2 Kgs 23:27.
12. 1 Kgs 11:34.
13. A plus, to which nothing in the broadly parallel 2 Chr 1:8–9 corresponds.
14. Deut 4:37; 7:6, 7; 10:15; 14:2.
15. Deut 18:5; 21:5.
16. Deut 17:15.
17. 1 Kgs 8:16, 44, 48 // 2 Chr 6:6, 34, 38; 1 Kgs 14:21 // 2 Chr 12:13; 2 Kgs 21:7 // 2 Chr 33:7.

is used.[18] But in six others we find לשכן שמו שם ("to cause his name to dwell there"),[19] a combination found elsewhere only twice in the Hebrew Bible.[20] Like "the place Yahweh will/may choose" in Deuteronomy, this alternative formulation merges two features of Solomon's great speech: the pervasive לשום שמי/ו שם ("to set my/his name there"), and an element of the possibly ancient fragment in 1 Kgs 8:12–13 // 2 Chr 6:1–2 already discussed (3.3.1): Yahweh had spoken of dwelling (שכן) in darkness, and a house was built for him to live in forever. The verb שכן is used only once more in Kings: in a nonsynoptic addition, Yahweh promises to "dwell" within Israel if they are obedient to him (1 Kgs 6:13). Yahweh "dwelling" in the house built for him and Yahweh choosing Jerusalem "to place his name there" have become merged in Deuteronomy as Yahweh "choosing a place to make his name dwell there." Kings has supplied the components and Deuteronomy reformulated them.

The shift in the sense of שבט, from "staff/scepter" to "tribe," points in the same direction. According to Nathan, Yahweh asks (2 Sam 7:7), "Did I ever speak with one of the staffs/scepters of Israel [את־אחד שבטי ישראל], whom I commanded to shepherd my people Israel?" Context requires that שבט be understood here as an individual "staff-holder." David would be the first such with whom he spoke (7:8). Solomon, also citing Yahweh, voices the theme of divine initiative in respect of David and Jerusalem in similar terms (1 Kgs 8:16), though the ancient texts vary. We read in MT, "I did not choose a[ny] city from all the staffs/tribes of Israel" (לא־בחרתי בעיר מכל שבטי ישראל); LXX attests, "I did not choose a[ny] city, [not] one scepter of Israel." LXX, probably rightly, understands שבט here as it must be understood in 2 Sam 7; Jerusalem and David were the first city and scepter to be chosen. The wording of Moses (Deut 12:14) is similar to both of these but identical to neither: "in the place that Yahweh may/will choose in one of your tribes" (במקום אשר־יבחר יהוה באחד שבטיך).[21] It combines Solomon's use of "choose" with Nathan's "one of the שבטי ישראל," but Moses here most probably understands the latter to be Israel's tribes rather than its staff-holders.

---

18. Deut 12:5, 21; 14:24.

19. Deut 12:11; 14:23; 16:2, 6, 11; 26:2.

20. Jer 7:12; Neh 1:9.

21. The combination "one of Israel's tribes/staff-holders" is found only twice more in the Hebrew Bible: Gen 49:16 and 2 Sam 15:2.

11. READING THE WRITTEN KINGS

The final supporting argument is this. To understand the historical relationship between Kings and Deuteronomy, it is also vital to be attentive to an eloquent silence, to note that one component available from Kings has been significantly omitted in Deuteronomy's reformulating. There is no longer any "forever" (עד־עולם or לעולם) in what Moses envisages for the chosen place. Or, in case that is too strong a statement, "forever" has been displaced. No longer does every mention of Yahweh's choice of a place for his name include "forever"; instead that has simply become part of a concluding exhortation (Deut 12:28): שמר ושמעת את כל־הדברים האלה אשר אנכי מצוך למען ייטב לך ולבניך אחריך עד־עולם ("Watch and listen to all these words that I am commanding you in order that it may be well for you and your sons after you forever"). If Israel is obedient to what has been commanded in this whole chapter, well-being may follow forever. But what has been stated—or has not been stated—in Deut 12:2–27?

By rebuilding Solomon's words, Moses has despecified Jerusalem, has tamed the dangerous notion that Yahweh himself might dwell in his house, and has either removed the component of eternity (עולם) from the statement of divine intention altogether or at least displaced it safely to being an aspiration for the community. By anonymizing and relativizing the city of Jerusalem, they were presumably making their teachings available to a new situation or to different communities.

Deuteronomy can of course be read *as part of* Deuteronomy–Kings (the so-called Deuteronomistic History), or even of Genesis–Kings (the so-called Primary History). When it is read within these larger contexts, the "chosen place" (of which it repeatedly speaks) anonymously but apparently deliberately anticipates Jerusalem, the chosen city of the book of Kings (both synoptic and postsynoptic). But if Deuteronomy is read *apart from* the narratives that follow, whether on its own or as part of a completed and separated Mosaic Torah, then the very anonymity of its chosen place may be quite as deliberately nonspecific; "the place that Yahweh will/may choose" may have been drafted to enable varied answers and to legitimate sanctuaries in other cities.

This recurrent theme through Deuteronomy of "the place that Yahweh will choose" goes unmentioned in Samuel–Kings and appears only once in Chronicles. By contrast, במות are an important theme in Kings and Chronicles; but they pass completely without mention in Deuteronomy, and receive a mention only twice in the Pentateuch altogether. Leviticus 26:30 includes "high places" among features of Israel's illicit cult that Yahweh will destroy; and Num 33:52 looks forward to Israel's entry to its new land as it crosses the Jordan: all the existing במות of the previous inhabitants are to be destroyed (אבד). It is this verb, reinforced by a cognate infinitive absolute, that makes the same point in the programmatic introduction to Deut 12, *but without using the word* במות: אבד תאבדון את־כל־המקמות אשר עבדו־שם הגוים אשר אתם ירשים אתם את־אלהיהם על־ההרים הרמים ועל־הגבעות ותחת כל־עץ רענן ונתצתם את־מזבחתם: "you shall *wholly destroy* all the places where the nations whom you are dispossessing served their gods on the high hills and on the heights and under every green tree; and you shall tear down their altars" (12:2–3). Each element—"high hills," "heights," and "every green tree"—appears only here in Deuteronomy, but "heights" and "every green tree" are together part of the במות theme in synoptic tradition. Like Jerusalem and its temple, the במות have also been anonymized in Deut 12: "places ... on the high hills" (unidentified but looking exactly like במות) are to be eliminated (12:2–3), before we read the very first mention of the "place Yahweh will choose" (12:4–7).[22]

The mismatch in language over this issue between Deuteronomy and the narrative books is almost complete. In each of (nonsynoptic) Kings and (nonsynoptic) Chronicles, there is no more than one comparable pejorative instance of "place(s)." In 2 Chr 33:19, within the summary of Manasseh's career, the term is plural: וכל־חטאתו ומעלו והמקמות אשר בנה בהם במות והעמיד האשרים והפסלים ("and all his sin and his treachery and the places in which he built במות and erected Asherahs and images"). In 2 Kgs 23:14 it is singular: וישבר את־המצבות ויכרת את־האשרים וימלא את־מקומם עצמות אדם ("and he shattered the pillars, and he cut down the Asherahs, and he filled their place with human bones"). Second Kings 23:14 and 2 Chr 33:19 may be among the latest additions to these books.

Deuteronomy 12 has almost certainly been drafted in several stages. Thomas Römer persuasively identifies three (with each addition anticipating the earlier draft): (1) verses 13–18, (2) verses 8–12, and (3) verses 2–7 and 20–27.[23] "The place that Yahweh will/may choose" is pervasive

---

22. While I fully agree with Thelle (*Approaches to the "Chosen Place,"* 143) that "the problem of the *bamot* is ... not to be sought in Deuteronomy, but within the context of Kings itself," she goes too far in denying that they are "not a concern whatsoever, of the book of Deuteronomy, not even of Deut 12." That judgment results from following the one word במות too far, and the several words "on the heights and under every green tree" not far enough.

23. So Römer, *So-Called Deuteronomistic History*, 63–64.

throughout this chapter (vv. 5, 11, 14, 18, 21, 26), and indeed throughout Deuteronomy as a whole: this anonymous coinage is fundamental to the heart of the book. Plotting the relationship of Deut 12:2–3 to the book of Kings nicely illustrates a further radical shift in rhetoric. The book called Kings repeatedly contrasts good kings belonging to the family of David "chosen" (בחר) by Yahweh, who had maintained the cult in Jerusalem, with "the people" (העם) who were sacrificing at the במות. In Deuteronomy, it is "the people" (העם) who are chosen (7:6), and the במות-like "places" they must destroy are now reattributed to "the nations" (הגוים) they would dispossess. The parties have been redefined: chosen-king-over-against-the-people has become chosen-people-over-against-the-nations. How far the religious issue may also have changed must be the business of another study.

Read in such a way from the perspective of the royal story in Kings, Deut 12 is not about centralization, and it must belong in any case to a period after the end of the royal story that had Jerusalem as its center. In short, it cannot have been the program of any Jerusalem-based reform, centralizing or otherwise, carried out by the late-seventh-century king Josiah. Developing the implications of this conclusion should provide more satisfactory solutions to the issues raised in 2001 by Gary Knoppers and Bernard Levinson.[24] The increasing critique of more and more kings as the narrative of Kings was expansively rewritten was not inspired by Deuteronomy, but instead provided part of the inspiration for Deuteronomy. Yet, while Deuteronomy appropriated much of the language of Kings and of its predecessor in the Book of Two Houses, together with many of their concerns, it also reminted these from its fresh perspective on the other side of the collapse. It is less a matter of rival Deuteronomists (Knoppers) and more a matter of rival inheritors of the Book of Two Houses.

The above analysis also strengthens my reluctance to join Ray Person in terming the whole continuum "Deuteronomic": Deuteronomy did not simply depend on important features of the synoptic Book of Two Houses; it also radically altered them. A link between Deuteronomy and a reform undertaken by Josiah is better sought in Passover than centralization; but even there the exclusivity of the chosen place in Deut 16 goes beyond what is reported in 2 Kgs 23:21–23 of that king's celebration in Jerusalem. As

---

24. Knoppers, "Rethinking the Relationship"; Levinson, "Reconceptualization of Kingship." See 1.2 above.

often noted, the much longer account of Josiah's Passover in 2 Chr 35 is much more "Deuteronom(ist)ic" than the short note in Kings.

I noted earlier the following words of Wellhausen:

> In the Chronicles, the pattern according to which the history of ancient Israel is represented is the Pentateuch, *i.e.* the Priestly Code. In the source of Chronicles, in the older historical books, the revision does not proceed upon the basis of the Priestly Code, which indeed is completely unknown to them, but on the basis of Deuteronomy.[25]

In the light of subsequent study, it is a pity that the first sentence did not end with "Pentateuch." While many elements of Chronicles are closely related to the "Priestly Code"—not least the role of Levites alongside priests—other parts are more Deuteronomic than Samuel–Kings. As for his second sentence, Deuteronomy and "the older historical books" do share many of the same key terms. But they are often differently used; and the direction of influence is working the other way round. Following the keywords from Samuel and Kings closely allows several quite radical shifts to be detected in Deuteronomy.

11.4. Afterthought

If Jerusalem's last four kings were original to the Book of Two Houses, then that book cannot have been completed before the fall of Jerusalem to Babylon. If they were not original, then the Book of Two Houses could have been completed any time after Josiah. The move in Deuteronomy to maintain but anonymize the traditions of the Jerusalem temple developed in the Book of Two Houses would in time allow the Samaritan community to worship on Mount Gerizim in fidelity to the same book. However, Deuteronomy may have served first to validate worship at Bethel by the remnant of Judah that Gedaliah ruled over at Mizpah for the Babylonians.[26] Gedaliah's father had been an important Judahite insider: Ahikam son of Shaphan was one of the emissaries from Josiah to Huldah (2 Kgs 22:12 //

---

25. Wellhausen, *Prolegomena*, 294; see 1.1.2.

26. His months in charge before he was assassinated are sketched in 2 Kgs 25:22–26 (the portion of that chapter not included in Jer 52), and presented at greater length within Jer 39–43.

2 Chr 34:20). It had been in his son's interest both to maintain key traditions and to see them reshaped for the new imperial situation.

De Wette was right to date Deuteronomy much later than longstanding tradition had allowed. We must continue to sympathize with the rejection by de Wette and Wellhausen of the Chronicler as historian of David and Solomon or Manasseh and Josiah. But the book of Chronicles has often—not just occasionally but very often—preserved vital evidence for the modern historian of biblical literature, by leaving unchanged the wording of the older text on which it was based where Samuel-Kings has changed it. Only when we follow the words of both Samuel-Kings and Chronicles can we better detect the contours of the narrative that both inherited—that "prophetically" interpreted narrative that supplied Deuteronomy with so many of its themes. Oddly, as it might seem to de Wette, it is by carefully rereading Chronicles alongside Samuel-Kings that we can propose a somewhat later dating of Deuteronomy than even he himself advocated.

12
Shared Text Sampled

12.1. Preliminary Remarks

As we seek to recover elements of the shared text underlying Kings and Chronicles, we need first to recognize several recurrent features as simply "noise" within the scribal system rather than markers that help us to reconstruct significant editorial activity.

We shall ignore instances of common variation such as the following:

- a collective subject (one that is grammatically singular but logically plural) may be associated with a singular verb in one version but a plural in the other
- spelling often varies (plene or not)
- proper names with the divine name as an element vary between יו־/יהו (Jo-/Jeho-) at the start and between יה־/יהו (-iah/-iahu) at the end
- use/nonuse of directional suffix ־ה
- use/nonuse of את as object marker

Some patterns are detected, and some of these discrepancies may reflect the preferences of major contributors to Kings or Chronicles. But they may equally reflect variation in the texts available to these authors or variation during the later scribal process. In any case, although some might be informative about date of composition, none of them informs us about content or purpose.

The divergences over object marking in the texts reproduced later in this chapter can be variously evaluated.

| 1 | 1 Kgs 12:6 | את־פני | 2 Chr 10:6 | לפני |
| 2 | 1 Kgs 12:6 | את־העם | 2 Chr 10:6 | לעם |

3	1 Kgs 15:13	את־מעכה אמו	2 Chr 15:16	מעכה אם אסא המלך
4	1 Kgs 15:19	הפרה את־בריתך	2 Chr 16:3	הפרה בריתך
5	1 Kgs 15:23	חלה את־רגליו	2 Chr 16:12	ויחלא אסא ברגליו
6	2 Kgs 11:7	ושמרו את־משמרת בית־יהוה	2 Chr 23:6	ישמרו משמרת יהוה
7	2 Kgs 11:15	הוציאו אתה	2 Chr 23:14	הוציאוה
8	2 Kgs 11:17	ויכרת יהוידע את־הברית	2 Chr 23:16	ויכרת יהוידע ברית
9	2 Kgs 21:4	אשים את־שמי	2 Chr 33:4	יהיה שמי
10	2 Kgs 21:8	להניד רגל ישראל	2 Chr 33:8	להסיר את־רגל ישראל
11	2 Kgs 22:9	ויבא שפן הספר	2 Chr 34:16	ויבא שפן את־הספר
12	2 Kgs 23:1	ויאספו אליו כל־זקני	2 Chr 34:29	ויאסף את כל־זקני

In cases 1, 2, and 5, the objects are differently marked; in 12, the verb is active in Chronicles but passive in Kings. In 11, Chronicles disambiguates Kings: the presence of את indicates that ויבא must be read as *hiphil*, not *qal*, and that הספר means "the book," not "the scribe." In 4 and 6–8, Chronicles appears to me more original, but Peter Bekins suspects the "removal" of the object marker indicated influence from Late Biblical Hebrew.[1]

There is also the issue of greater or lesser specification in a text. We often find a pronominal suffix or a verb with an unspecified subject in one version and a specified name or noun in the other. Here my preference is to assume that the shorter, less specific option is more original.[2] Greater emphasis may also be secondary, such as adding כל ("all") or a cognate relative clause—and we have already discussed (ch. 3) the greater preference in Samuel–Kings for the cognate infinitive absolute.

While some issues are resolved when viewed more openly and synoptically, others are rendered more problematic. Altered order of pairings (such as "from great to small" or "from Dan to Beer-sheba") is regularly attributed to the Chronicler, but perhaps should not be. Varied order within a list is even harder to assess. And then we find variation between broadly synony-

---

1. Peter Bekins, *Transitivity and Object Marking in Biblical Hebrew: An Investigation of the Object Preposition 'et*, HSS 64 (Winona Lake, IN: Eisenbrauns, 2014), 135–39.

2. This takes the relationship between the shorter LXX and much longer MT of Jeremiah as a relevant analogy. As a whole, MT is some 15 percent longer than LXX; and much of the difference is concentrated in the second half of the book. Many of the pluses in MT appear to be additions to aid disambiguation, naming the subject or object of a verb, specifying a title, and so on.

mous verbs such as נתן/שים ("grant"/"set") or עזב/לא שמר ("abandon"/"not keep"), though all these verbs are also well attested synoptically. Then Samuel–Kings tends to prefer the title המלך ("the king"), whereas Chronicles tends to use the particular king's name. Moving in the opposite direction, Samuel–Kings nearly always uses "Yahweh," while Chronicles varies almost evenly between this divine name and האלהים ("the Deity").

12.2. Synoptic Presentation Explained

The elements of the Masoretic Text shared by Kings and Chronicles are presented in the central column below (C), with text peculiar to Kings in the column to the left (L) and text peculiar to Chronicles to the right (R). The siglum * identifies the joins between material in C and L or R on the same line. Where there is a second, or even third, such join on the same line, the sigla • and ▪ are used. The C siglum indicates the place of the join; the word or phase following the same siglum in the L or R columns is to be placed at the point of the C siglum. Most often, to left and right, we are dealing with whole words or phrases—but sometimes differences of just one or two letters (say, a pronominal suffix or the object marker). Where Kings or Chronicles has a larger body of text not included in the other, this is often noted simply by specifying the relevant range of verses. Any element to the left or right that seems more original is underlined. The whole supposedly more original text—the central column plus any underlined material from left or right—is then translated into rather literal English. In the translation, material from the central Hebrew column is set in normal type, with material drawn from Kings (left) in **bold** and from Chronicles (right) in *italics*. [Square brackets] identify words that are required for good English sense, though not themselves translation equivalents. Each section concludes with a short explanation of the choices made.

Starting with Solomon's second vision is not wholly arbitrary. I have already published two discussions of the text underlying the variant accounts in 1 Kgs 3:4–15 and 2 Chr 1:7–13 of his first vision, and while I am not wedded to every detail proposed in these, I still hold them to be on the right track. The different accounts of Solomon's major building works in Jerusalem (1 Kgs 6–7 and 2 Chr 3–4) are hardly typical of the twin narratives of David's line as a whole. And the reports of the dedication of the temple, including the king's lengthy prayer, are very similar; the few differences over "place" (מקום) have already been noted (5.3). Then, the material in 1 Kgs 3:16–5:32—between the first vision and the start of building—is so different from Chronicles that it too has been separately discussed, within the treatment of how synoptic Solomon was reshaped in 1 Kgs 1–11 (see 9.2).

In Kings as in Samuel, the Greek texts are often closer than the Masoretic Text to the detail of the parallel or synoptic passage in Chronicles.[3] Several sections of the Solomon narrative exemplify more complex relationships. The more extensive material in Kings is arranged very differently in the Masoretic Text and the Septuagint. Julio Trebolle Barrera's largely persuasive discussion of this material is in terms of a triple rather than a double textual tradition.[4] The textual comparisons of variation within the synoptic tradition in 12.3 below are illustrative only; and in several instances it is clear that this approach does not lead to the earliest stage of the tradition. First Kings 8:1–5 // 2 Chr 5:2–6 offers a particularly noteworthy example.

Kings MT +	Kings MT/Kingdoms LXX shared text	Kingdoms +
	אז יקהל * שלמה	* המלך
את־כל־ראשי המטות נשיאי האבות לבני ישראל אל־המלך שלמה ירושלם	את־ * זקני ישראל	* כל
		ציון
	להעלות את־ארון ברית־יהוה מעיר דוד היא ציון	
ויקהלו אל־המלך שלמה כל־איש ישראל		
* בחג הוא החדש השביעי	בירח האתנים *	
* ויבאו כל זקני ישראל	* וישאו הכהנים את־הארון	
* ויעלו את־ארון יהוה	* ואת־אהל מועד ואת־כל־כלי הקדש אשר באהל *	* מועד
ויעלו אתם הכהנים והלוים שלמה * *עדת הנועדים עליו אתו	והמלך * וכל־* ישראל	
	לפני הארון מזבחים צאן ובקר אשר לא־יספרו ולא ימנו מרב	

---

3. Traditionalist enthusiasts for MT have claimed that the Greek translators of Samuel–Kings were influenced by variant readings in Chronicles MT. Since the discovery of the Dead Sea Scrolls, it has been more common to argue that the Chronicler's text of Samuel–Kings had many differences from MT Samuel–Kings.

4. "Kings (MT/LXX) and Chronicles," 483–501.

12. SHARED TEXT SAMPLED

	Then * Solomon assembled	* King
all the heads of the tribes, patriarchal leaders of the sons of Israel, to King Solomon in Jerusalem	* the elders of Israel	* all
		in Zion
	to bring up the ark of Yahweh's covenant from the city of David (that is, Zion).	
And they were assembled to King Solomon, every man of Israel,		
* at the feast (that is, the seventh month).	in the month Ethanin *	
* And all the elders of Israel came	* and the priests carried the ark	
* and they brought up the ark of Yahweh	* and the tent of witness	
	and all the holy vessels that were in the tent *	* of witness.
And the priests and Levites brought them up. * Solomon * the congregation of who had congregated to him with him	And the king * and all * Israel	
	were in front of the ark sacrificing unnumbered sheep and cattle.	

At the start of 1 Kgs/3 Kgdms 8, the Septuagint is the much shorter text: it lacks all of verse 2 except the date, all of verse 3a about the elders, the end of verse 4 that associates Levites with the priests, and the definition of Israel as a "congregation" (קהל) in verse 5. The Septuagint will be our best witness to the older text; unusually, several of the pluses in the Masoretic Text of Kings represent interests typical of Chronicles. It is likely that this version has adopted expansions that were being developed within Chronicles. The final text of the parallel in 2 Chr 5:2–6 exhibits two further developments, and both are alterations rather than additions to the older shared text: it does not include בירח האתנים ("in the month Ethanin"); and it was Levites rather than priests who "carried the ark."[5]

---

5. For discussion of several examples of expansions in Samuel based on Chronicles, see Becker and Betzel, *Rereading the relecture?*

12.3. The Shared Text

12.3.1. Solomon's Second Vision: 1 Kgs 9:1–9 // 2 Chr 7:11–22

1 Kgs 9		2 Chr 7	
	1 ויהי ככלות לבנות *		11 <u>ויכל</u> שלמה
	את־בית־יהוה ואת־בית המלך		
*חשק * אשר חפץ	ואת כל־* שלמה * לעשות		<u>הבא על־לב</u> בבית־יהוה ובביתו הצליח
* שנית כאשר נראה אליו בגבעון	2 * וירא יהוה אל־שלמה		12 * בלילה
* יהוה אליו	3 ויאמר *		* <u>לו</u>
* ואת־תחנתך אשר התחננתה לפני	שמעתי את־תפלתך *		* ובחרתי במקום הזה לי לבית זבח 13–15
* אשר בנתה	*הקדשתי את־הבית הזה *		16 ועתה בחרתי ו *<u>היות</u>
<u>שום</u>*	ל־*שמי שם עד־עולם והיו עיני ולבי שם כל־ הימים		
* בתם־לבב ובישר	4 ואתה אם־תלך לפני כאשר הלך דוד אביך * לעשות ככל אשר צויתיך חקי ומשפטי תשמר		17
* <u>ממלכתך</u> על־ישראל לעולם	5 והקמתי את־כסא *		* מלכותך 18
* <u>דברתי על־</u>	כאשר * דוד אביך * לאמר		* כרתי ל
* מעל כסא ישראל	לא־יכרת לך איש *		<u>משל בישראל</u>
6 *<u>שוב</u>	ואם־* תשובון אתם *		19
* ובניכם מאחרי ולא תשמרו מצותי חקתי			<u>ועזבתם חקותי ומצותי</u>
	אשר נתתי לפניכם והלכתם ועבדתם אלהים אחרים והשתחויתם להם		
7 והכרתי את־ישראל * מעל פני האדמה	* אשר נתתי להם ואת־הבית * אשר הקדשתי לשמי		20 <u>ונתשתים</u> * <u>מעל אדמתי</u> * הזה
* אשלח	מעל פני		* אשליך

12. SHARED TEXT SAMPLED

* והיה ישראל	* למשל ולשנינה בכל־העמים		* ואתננו
8 * יהיה	והבית הזה * עליון כל־עבר עליו ישם *		* 21 * <u>אשר היה</u>
* ושרק * ואמרו על־מה	* עשה יהוה ככה לארץ הזאת ולבית הזה		* <u>ואמר במה</u>
	ואמרו על אשר עזבו את־	9	22
* אלהיהם	יהוה *		* <u>אלהי אבתיהם</u>
	אשר הוציא*		*ם
* את־אבתם	* מארץ מצרים ויחזקו באלהים אחרים וישתחוו להם ויעבדם		
* יהוה	על־כן הביא * עליהם את כל־הרעה הזאת		

1/11 And Solomon *completed* Yahweh's house and the king's house and all *that came upon the heart* of Solomon to do. 2/12 And Yahweh appeared to Solomon. 3 And he said *to* him: "I have heard your prayer. 16 I have sanctified this house, **setting** my name there forever; and my eyes and my heart shall be there all the time. 4/17 And you—if you will walk before me as David your father walked, acting according to all I have commanded you, my decrees and my judgments you shall keep. 5/18 And I shall establish the throne of your **kingly rule as I spoke** to David your father, saying, 'You shall not lack a man *ruling in Israel*.' 6/19 And if [all of] you turn *and abandon my decrees and my commands*, which I set before you, and you go and serve other gods and prostrate to them, 7/20 *I shall root them out from my land* that I gave them; and the house that I have sanctified to my name *I shall throw* from over against my face, *and I shall give it* as a proverb and a taunt among all the peoples; 8/21 and this house *that was* high—everyone passing by it shall be devastated and shall say, 'For what [cause] has Yahweh acted thus to this land and to this house?' 9/22 And they shall say, 'Because they rejected Yahweh *God of their fathers*, who brought *them* out of the land of Egypt, and they took hold of other gods and prostrated to them and served them. Therefore he brought upon them all this evil.'"

Notes

1/11   Synoptic texts use ויהי כ־ with the infinitive five times (1 Kgs 12:2; 15:21; 22:32, 33; 2 Kgs 22:11 // 2 Chr 10:2; 16:5; 18:21, 22; 34:19);

but the combination ויהי ככלות is never synoptic,[6] though ככלות is found separately in both books. ויכל has already been used twice synoptically (2 Sam 6:18 // 1 Chr 16:2; 1 Kgs 7:40 // 2 Chr 4:11); and, because it is also the shorter text, it has been preferred here.

The verb and noun חפץ ("[take] pleasure") are synoptic in 1 Kgs 10:9, 13 // 2 Chr 9:8, 12; but are Kings plus in 1 Kgs 5:22–24 and 9:11 as well as being different from Chronicles here in 1 Kgs 9:1. The verb and noun חשק ("desire") are synoptic in 1 Kgs 9:19 // 2 Chr 8:6. Kings' unique combination of the two terms will anticipate synoptic 1 Kgs 9:19; 10:9, 13. Chronicles' הבא על־לב ("coming upon the heart") resumes יען אשר היתה זאת עם־לבבך ("because this was with your heart"), in Chronicles' account of Solomon's first vision (2 Chr 1:11).[7] חפץ is combined with עשה referring to divine freedom to act in Isa 55:11; Jonah 1:14; Pss 115:3; 135:6; and to royal freedom in Ps 40:9; Qoh 8:3; Esth 6:6.

2/12 The precise combination ובחרתי במקום ("and I chose the place") is found nowhere else; but "place" and "choose" are construed together many times in Deuteronomy and also in Josh 9:27. בית זבח ("a house of sacrifice") appears unique in the Hebrew Bible (as is בית תפלה, "a house of prayer," in Isa 56:7).

4/17 Kings plus בתם־לבב ("in completeness of heart") has parallels only in Gen 20:5, 6; Pss 78:72; 101:2. The Kings plus בישרת לבב ("in straightness of heart") in the report of the earlier vision is a similar combination, and has parallels in Deut 9:5; 1 Kgs 3:6; 1 Chr 29:17; Ps 119:7.

5/18 כסא ישראל is synoptic in 1 Kgs 8:20, 25 // 2 Chr 6:10, 16, and a Kings plus in 1 Kgs 2:4; 9:5 (but LXX = Chronicles); 10:9 (2 Kgs 10:30; 15:12). "Israel" is a plus three times in the Kings report of this vision: twice (9:7) making a pronominal suffix (7:20) more precise, here part of a simple plus.

6/19 עזב—עזב/לא שמר is shared just below, as also in 1 Sam 31:7; 2 Sam 5:21; 1 Kgs 12:8, 13; 2 Kgs 22:17.

7/20 נתש + אדמה: נתש/הכרית, Deut 29:27; Jer 12:14; 2 Chr 7:20; and cf. Amos 9:15; הכרית occurs regularly with other nations, but here uniquely with Israel as object.

---

6. The closest pairing is וַיְהִי ככלות שלמה להתפלל (1 Kgs 8:54), but וַכְּכַלּוֹת שלמה להתפלל (2 Chr 7:1).

7. 1 Kgs 3:11 offers instead יען אשר שאלת את־הדבר הזה (the texts are presented in parallel in Auld, "Solomon at Gibeon: History Glimpsed," in *Samuel at the Threshold*, 99).

אשלח/אשליך: both verbs are used in both Kings and Chronicles, but never synoptically; note דבר as the object of שלח in Lev 26:25; Jer 24:10; 29:17; Ezek 14:19; 28:23; Amos 4:10; 2 Chr 7:13.

8/21 ושרק (Kings +) is paired with synoptic שמם in Jer 19:8, and they are used in parallel in Zeph 2:15 (the nouns are paired in Jer 25:9; 51:37; 2 Chr 29:8).

9/22 על־כן ("accordingly") is used three times in the synoptic David story (2 Sam 5:8, 20; 7:27 // 1 Chr 11:7; 14:11; 17:25). However, the reference is different in the first instance: to the blind and lame in 2 Sam 5:8, but to naming the city of David in 1 Chr 11:7. It is found again near the third instance also at the start of 2 Sam 7:22, where the end of 1 Chr 17:19 is very different: להודיע את־עבדך על־כן גדלת אדני יהוה כי־אין כמוך ואין להודיע את־כל־הגדלות יהוה אין כמוך ואין אלהים זולתך (2 Sam 7:21–22); בעבור אלהים זולתך (1 Chr 17:19–20) (and LXX ἕνεκεν normally renders בעבור in Samuel).[8]

12.3.2. Solomon's Works: 1 Kgs 9:10–28 // 2 Chr 8:1–18

	ויהי מקץ/צה עשרים שנה 10		1
את־שני הבתים *	* אשר בנה שלמה		
* המלך	*את־הבית יהוה ואת־הבית		*ן
11–14	cities exchanged		2
15 וזה דבר המס ...			
16–17a פרעה מלך־מצרים עלה ...			
		3–5 וילך שלמה	
		ויבן את־בית חורון העליון	
	* ואת־בית חרן תחתון	* ערי מצור חומות דלתים וברִיח	
18 * ואת־תמר במדבר בארץ	* ואת־בעלת		6
19	ואת כל־ערי המסכנות אשר היו		
	לשלמה ואת * ערי הרכב		כל *
	* ואת ערי הפרשים ואת חשק		כל *

---

8. Here the links with 2 Sam 5:20 // 1 Chr 14:11 (על־כן קראו) may be instructive: 1 Chr 11:7; 2 Chr 20:26; Genesis, 11x; Exod 15:23; Josh 7:26; Judg 15:19; 18:12; 1 Sam 23:28.

			שלמה אשר חשק לבנות
			בירושלם
			ובלבנון ובכל ארץ
			ממשלתו
7 * <u>החתי האמרי</u>	* כל־העם הנותר מן־ *	20 * האמרי החתי	
	הפרזי החוי והיבוסי		
	אשר לא מ* ישראל המה	*בני	
8 * מן־	* בניהם אשר נתרו	21	
	אחריהם בארץ		
* <u>כלם</u>	אשר לא־ * בני ישראל *	יכלו * להחרימם	
	ויעלם שלמה למס* עד	*־עבד	
	היום הזה		
9	ומבני ישראל לא־נתן	22	
* <u>לעבדים למלאכתו</u>	שלמה *	עבד *	
	כי־הם אנשי המלחמה *	ועבדיו *	
	ושריו ושלשיו ושרי רכבו		
	ופרשיו		
10 * <u>למלך שלמה</u>	ואלה שרי הנצבים אשר *	23 * על־המלאכה לשלמה	
<u>ומאתים</u> *	חמשים *	וחמש מאות *	
	הרדים בעם *	העשים במלאכה *	
11 * <u>ואת</u>	* בת־פרעה	24 * אך	
* <u>העלה שלמה</u> * <u>לבית</u>	* מעיר דוד *	עלתה * אל־ביתה *	
	אשר בנה־לה		
12 כי אמר לא־תשב אשה לי			
בבית דויד מלך־ישראל			
כי־קדש			
המה אשר־באה אליהם			
ארון יהוה			
	* אז *	* בנה את־המלוא	
	העלה שלמה	25 * <u>שלש פעמים בשנה</u>	
	* עלות	ושלמים *	
* <u>על מזבח יהוה</u>	* אשר בנה *	על־המזבח * ליהוה	
לפני האולם		והקטיר אתו אשר לפני	
		יהוה	
13–16a, incl.			
שלש פעמים בשנה			
* בית יהוה	* ושלם		
17 * <u>אז הלך</u> *־ל	* שלמה * עציון גבר	26 * ואני עשה המלך *ב	
* <u>ואל־</u> * <u>הים</u>	* אילות על־שפת * בארץ	* אשר את־ * ים־סוף	
		אדום	
18 * <u>לו</u> * <u>יד</u>	וישלח * חי/ורם ב* עבדיו *	27 *יאני את־	
* ועבדים	* אניות * ידעי הים	* אנשי	

12. SHARED TEXT SAMPLED 215

28	ויבאו * אופירה	* עם־עבדי שלמה
	ויקחו משם זהב	
	ארבע־מאות ועשרים	
	ככר	
	ויבאו אל־המלך שלמה	

10/1 And it came to be at the end of twenty years, in which Solomon built Yahweh's house and his house, ... and Lower Beth-horon, 18/6 and Baalath, 19 and all the store cities that belonged to Solomon and the chariot cities and the cities of the horsemen and the desire of Solomon that he desired to build in Jerusalem and in Lebanon and in all the land of his rule. 20/7 All the people left from the *Hittite, the Amorite*, the Perizzite, the Hivvite, and the Jebusite, who were not from Israel—21/8 their sons who were left after them in the land, whom the sons of Israel *had not finished [off]*—Solomon raised them as corvée until this day. 22/9 But from the sons of Israel Solomon did not set [any] *as servants for his project*; for they were the men of war, his officers, his captains, and the officers of his chariotry and his horsemen. 23/10 And these were the officers of the appointees who belonged to King Solomon: *two hundred* and fifty who had charge of the people. 24/11 *And* the daughter of Pharaoh *Solomon brought up* from the city of David *to the house* that he built for her. 25/12 Then Solomon raised holocausts on Yahweh's altar that he had built—three times a year. And he completed the house. 26/17 *Then* Solomon *went to* Ezion-geber and *to* Eilat by the side of the sea in the land of Edom. 27/18 And Hi/uram sent *him* by *hand of* his servants ships and *servants* knowing the sea, 28 and they came to Ophir and took from there gold (420 talents) and came to King Solomon.

Notes

10/1 After this synoptic verse, the texts diverge until 17b/5b.

- Details of trade with Hiram are provided in 9:11–14; the same trees figure in 1 Kgs 5:22, 24 (part of 5:15–26, where the trade is more fully described) as in 9:11, but also in 2 Sam 5:11 // 1 Chr 14:1 (this, perhaps the ultimate source, is recalled in 5:15).

- Only part of the contents of 1 Kgs 9:15–25 (MT) are represented in synoptic 2 Chr 8:5–12; others appear piecemeal elsewhere in 3 Kingdoms.

17/5 The Chronicles plus that follows "Lower Beth-horon" includes two nonsynoptic phrases: ערי מצור (Pss 31:22; 60:11; 2 Chr 8:6; cf. 11:5,

10, 11, 23; 12:4; 14:5; 21:3), and דלתים ובריח (Deut 3:5; 1 Sam 23:7; Jer 49:31; Ezek 38:11; Job 38:10; 2 Chr 8:5; 14:6).

20/7 The names as listed in the Masoretic Text of Chronicles reappear in the Septuagint. The Masoretic Text of Kings has the first two names in reverse order; the Septuagint starts with "Hittite" like Chronicles, but also includes two further names: the familiar "Canaanite" in fourth place and the rare "Girgashite" in seventh.

21/8 Either כלם (2 Chr 8:8) became doubly represented in יכלו להחרימם (1 Kgs 9:21): the consonants כלו- were retained in יכלו, while the content ("finished them off") was reexpressed in the metaphor of the ban; or the longer phrase in Kings was neatly encapsulated in Chronicles' כלום. Each has a synoptic pairing: כלה ("finish") reappears in a military sense in 1 Kgs 22:11 // 2 Chr 18:10; and החרים ("put to the ban") is attributed to earlier Assyrian kings in 2 Kgs 19:11 // 2 Chr 32:14.

22–23/9–10 עבד ("servant") is apparently emphasized in 1 Kgs 9:21–22 (3x), over against the single negation in 2 Chr 8:9. It is odd to find "his servants" within the list of his Israelite staff, when we have just been told that he did not treat Israel as servants. The two occurrences of מלאכה ("project") in 1 Kgs 9:23 do not correspond to the single instance in 2 Chr 8:9. In synoptic contexts, the noun is only used in connection with Solomon,[9] Joash,[10] and Josiah.[11] העשים במלאכה at the end of 1 Kgs 9:23 is anticipated in 1 Kgs 5:30, which is also a plus. Elsewhere this combination is found only in 2 Chr 34:12 (also +) and Neh 4:10, 11, 15. It seems likely that the text of Kings has been adjusted toward the large plus in 1 Kgs 5.

24–25/11–12 The notes on Pharaoh's daughter and sacrifice at the altar both link עלה and בנה, and Millo (1 Kgs 9:15) is another case of construction (בנה).

12.3.3. Queen of Sheba: 1 Kgs 10:1–13 // 2 Chr 9:1–12

1 * שמעה	ומלכת־שבא * את־שמע * 1	שמעת
* את־שלמה	* שלמה	* לשם יהוה
* בירושלם	ותבא לנסת* בחידות *	*־ו 2
	* בחיל כבד מאד	* ותבא ירושלמה

---

9. 1 Kgs 7:40, 51 // 2 Chr 4:11; 5:1 are synoptic; but 1 Kgs 5:30 (2x), 7:14 (2x), and 2 Chr 8:16 are also pluses.

10. 2 Kgs 12:12, 15, 16 broadly correspond to 2 Chr 24:12, 13 (2x).

11. 2 Kgs 22:5 (2x), 9 // 2 Chr 34:10 (2x), 17 are synoptic; 2 Chr 34:12, 13 are pluses.

12. SHARED TEXT SAMPLED

* <u>לרב</u>	גמלים נשאים בשמים	* רב־מאד	
	ואבן יקרה		
* <u>עמו</u>	ותבא אל־שלמה ותדבר *	אליו	
	את כל־אשר היה עם־		
	לבבה		
2	ויגד־לה שלמה את־כל־	3	
	דבריה		
<u>ולא־נעלם דבר משלמה</u>		לא־היה דבר נעלם מן־	
	אשר לא הגיד לה	המלך	
3	ותרא מלכת־שבא	4	
	את * חכמת שלמה	* כל־	
	והבית אשר בנה		
4	ומאכל שלחנו ומושב	5	
	עבדיו		
	ומעמד משרתיו		
	ומלבושיהם		
* ומלבושיהם ועליתו	ומשקיו *	<u>ועלתו</u>	
	אשר יעלה בית יהוה		
5	ולא־היה עוד בה רוח		
	ותאמר אל־המלך	6	
	אמת * הדבר	* היה	
	אשר שמעתי בארצי על־		
	דבריך ועל־חכמתך		
6	ולא־האמנתי לדברי[ה]ם	7	
	עד אשר־		
	באתי ותראינה עיני והנה		
* חצי מרבית חכמתך	לא־הגד־לי *	<u>החצי</u>	
* <u>יספת על־</u>	* השמועה אשר שמעתי	* הוספת חכמה וטוב אל־
7	אשרי אנשיך ואשרי	8	
	עבדיך אלה		
	העמדים לפניך תמיד		
	ו/השמעים את־חכמתך		
8	יהי יהוה אלהיך ברוך	9	
	אשר חפץ בך		
*יָ למלך ליהוה אלהיך	לתתך על־כסא* *	• ישראל	
	באהבת יהוה את־		
* להעמידו	ישראל * לעלם		
* ויתנך	למלך לעשות משפט	<u>וישימד</u>	
	וצדקה		
9	ותתן למלך מאה ועשרים	10	
	ככר זהב		

* הרבה	* ובשמים * מאד ואבן יקרה	* לרב
* לא־בא * עוד לרב	* כבשם ההוא • אשר־נתנה מלכת־שבא למלך שלמה	* ולא היה
* אני 11 *נשא	* וגם * חירם • אשר־* זהב מאופיר הביא[ו] * עצי אלמגים ואבן יקרה	10 * עבדי *ועבדי שלמה *הביאו
* מאפיר * הרבה מאד	ויעש המלך את־עצי האלמגים	11
* מסעד * לא בא־כן עצי אלמגים * עד היום הזה	* לבית־יהוה ולבית המלך • וכנרות ונבלים לשרים * * ולא נראה/ו	* מסלות
12 13		* כהם לפנים בארץ יהודה 12
	והמלך שלמה נתן למלכת־שבא את־כל־חפצה אשר שאלה	
* נתן־לה כיד המלך שלמה	* מלבד אשר *	* הביאה אל־המלך
* ותפן	* ותלך לארצה היא ועבדיך	* ותהפך

1/1 And the queen of Sheba *had heard* the fame of Solomon and she came to test him by riddles, 2 with a very massive array: camels bearing spices *in quantity* and precious stone; she came to Solomon and spoke *with him* all that was on her mind. 3/2 And Solomon declared to her all her words, *and no word was hidden from Solomon* that he did not declare to her. 4/3 And the queen of Sheba saw the wisdom of Solomon and the house that he had built 5/4 and the food of his table and the seating of his servants and the stance of his attendants and their clothing and his butlers and **his holocausts** that he raised at Yahweh's house, and there was no more spirit in her. 6/5 And she said to the king, "True is the word that I heard in my land about your words and your wisdom. 7/6 But I did not believe the words till I came and my eyes saw—and look, **the half** was not told me: *you have added to* the fame that I heard. 8/7 Happy are your men, and happy these your servants who stand before you continually and hear your wisdom. 9/8 May Yahweh your God be blessed, who has taken pleasure in you, setting you on *his* throne, in Yahweh's love of Israel for ever, and has **placed** you as king practicing laws and right." 10/9 And she gave the king 120 talents of gold and very **much** spices and precious stone—*there has not been* like that spice that the queen of Sheba gave to King Solomon. 11/10

Also the **fleet**/*servants* of Hiram who brought gold from Ophir brought almug wood and precious stone. 12/11 And the king made [of] the almug wood ... for Yahweh's house and for the king's house, and harps and pipes for the singers.... 13/12 And King Solomon gave the queen of Sheba all her desire that she asked for apart from what *she had brought to the king*; and she turned and went to her land, she and her servants.

Notes

1/1 לשם יהוה is synoptic (following "building a house") in 1 Kgs 5:17, 19; 8:17, 20 // 2 Chr 2:3; 6:7, 10.

7/6 מרבית—חכמתך מרבית means "greater part" in 1 Chr 12:30; 2 Chr 9:6; 30:18; and "increase" in Lev 25:37; 1 Sam 2:33.

9/8 Kings has supplied "Israel" from the following phrase.

• עמד *hiphil* is never synoptic: 1 Kgs 12:32, 15:4, and 2 Kgs 8:11 are all Kings pluses; it is found 26 times in Chronicles, and also in Daniel and Ezra-Nehemiah.

12/11 מסעד/מסלות: Mandelkern reports both as "unexplained" (*unerklärt*)!

• Elsewhere ארץ יהודה is never synoptic but is used in both Chronicles (1 Chr 6:40; 2 Chr 9:11; 15:8; 17:2) and the end of Kings (2 Kgs 23:24; 25:22). נראו is combined once more with בארץ יהודה: in 2 Kgs 23:24, of bad things that Josiah removed.

13/12 כיד המלך (Kings) is found elsewhere only in Esther and Ezra-Nehemiah.

12.3.4. Solomon Epilogue: 1 Kgs 10:14–29 + 11:41–43 // 2 Chr 9:13–31

	14	ויהי משקל הזהב אשר בא לשלמה בשנת אחת שש מאות וששים ושש ככר זהב	13
ומחסר הרכלים	15 *	לבד מאנשי התרים * וכל־מלכי *ערב ופחות	* 14 והסחרים מביאים
*ה			* מביאים זהב וכסף לשלמה הארץ *
	16	ויעש המלך שלמה מאתים צנה זהב שחוט שש מאות זהב *	15
			* שחוט *

16	יעלה על־הצנה האחת	
	ושלש־מאות מגנים זהב	17
	שחוט	
*מאות	שלשת * זהב יעלה על־	*מנים
	המגן האחת	
*ב	ויתנם המלך *בית יער	
	הלבנון	
17	ויעש המלך כסא־שן גדול	18
*טהור	ויצפהו זהב *	*מופז
18 *ן * וכבש בזהב	*שש מעלות לכסא •	• וראש עגל
לכסא מאחזים		לכסא מאחריו
	וידות מזה ומזה ע/אל־	
	מקום השבת	
	ושנים אריות עמדים אצל	
	הידות	
19	ושנים עשר אריות עמדים	20
	שם	
	על־שש המעלות מזה	
	ומזה	
*ממלכה	לא־נעשה כן לכל־*	*ממלכות
20	וכל כלי משקה המלך	21
	שלמה זהב	
	וכל כלי בית־יער הלבנון	
	זהב סגור	
	אין כסף * נחשב בימי	* לא
	שלמה למאומה	
21	כי אני תרשיש למלך בים	22
	עם אני חירם	
	אחת לשלש שנים	
	תבוא[נה]	
	אני[ות] תרשיש נשא[ו]ת	
	זהב וכסף שנהבים וקפים	
	ותכיים	
22	ויגדל המלך שלמה מכל	23
	מלכי הארץ	
	לעשר ולחכמה	
* 23 * מלכי	וכל * הארץ מבקשים	24
	את־פני שלמה	
	לשמע את־חכמתו אשר־	
* ה	נתן *אלהים בלבו	
24	והמה מבאים איש מנחתו	25
	כלי כסף	

12. SHARED TEXT SAMPLED

		וכלי זהב ושלמות [ו]נשק ובשמים
		סוסים ופרדים דבר־שנה בשנה
26 ויאסף שלמה רכב ופרשים	25 *ויהי־*	25 *לשלמה ארבעת אלפים אריות*
לו אלף וארבע־מאות רכב		* סוסים ומרכבות
	ושנים־עשר אלף פרשים	
	וינ[י]חם בערי הרכב ועם־המלך בירושלם	
		26 ויהי מושל בכל־המלכים
		מן־הנהר ועד־ארץ פלשתים
		ועד־גבול מצרים
	27 ויתן המלך את־הכסף בירושלם	27
	כאבנים ואת־הארזים נתן כשקמים	
	אשר־בשפלה לרב	
28 * ומוצא הסוסים	אשר לשלמה ממצרים •	28 * ומוציאים סוסים
ומקוה סחרי המלך יקחו מקוה		ומכל־הארצות
במחיר 29 ותעלה ותצא מרכבה		
ממצרים בשש מאות כסף וסוס		
בחמשים ומאה וכן לכל־מלכי		
החתים ולמלכי ארם בידם יצאו		
11:1–40		
41 * ויתר	* דברי שלמה	29 * ושאר הראשנים והאחרונים
וכל־אשר עשה וחכמתו	הלא־הם כתובים על־*	* דברי נתן הנביא ועל־נבואת אחיה
* ספר דברי שלמה		השילוני ובחזות יעדו החזה
		על־ירבעם בן־נבט

30 * <u>וימלך</u>	* שלמה בירושלם על־כל־ישראל ארבעים שנה	42 * והימים אשר מלך
31 *הו	וישכב שלמה עם־אבתיו ויקבר* בעיר דוד אביו וימלך רחבעם בנו תחתיו	43

14/13 And the weight of the gold that came to Solomon in one year came to be 666 talents of gold, 15/14 apart from the men of the merchants **and the business of the traders**, and all the kings of Arabia and the governors of the earth. 16/15 And king Solomon made two hundred [large] shields of beaten gold: six hundred of gold went up into one shield; 17/16 and three hundred shields of beaten gold: three **minas** of gold went up into one shield; and the king put them in the House of the Forest of Lebanon. 18/17 And the king made a large ivory throne and overlaid it with fine gold; 19/18 and the throne had six steps. The throne had a round head at its back and armrests at this side and that of the place of the seat, and two lions standing beside the armrests. 20/19 And twelve lions were standing on the six steps this side and that. Such was not made for any kingdom. 21/20 And all King Solomon's drinking vessels were of gold, and all the vessels of the House of the Forest of Lebanon were of pure gold: silver was not reckoned in the days of Solomon at all. 22/21 For the king had a Tarshish fleet on the sea with Hi/uram's fleet: once in three years would come the Tarshish fleet bearing gold and silver, ivory, apes, and peacocks. 23/22 And King Solomon was greater than all the kings of the earth in wealth and wisdom. 24/23 And all the earth sought Solomon's face, to hear his wisdom that a God had set in his heart. 25/24 And these were bringing each his gift: vessels of silver and vessels of gold, and clothing, weaponry, and spices; horses and mules—so much year by year. 26/25 **And Solomon gathered chariots and horses: and he had fourteen hundred chariots** and twelve thousand horses; and he settled them in the chariot cities and with the king in Jerusalem. 26 And he was ruling over all the kings from the river and as far as the land of Philistines and as far as the border of Egypt. 27 And the king made silver in Jerusalem like stones, and cedars he made like sycamores in the Shephelah for multitude. 28 **And the export of the horses** belonging to Solomon was from Egypt. And the king's traders from Que would take from Que for a price. 29 And a chariot went up and out from Egypt for six hundred silver and a horse for one hundred fifty, and thus they go out to all the kings of the Hittites and the kings of Aram by their hands. 41/29 And the rest of the acts of Solomon **and all that he did and his wisdom**—are these not written **in the book of the acts of Solomon**? 42/30 *And Solomon reigned* in Jerusalem over all Israel forty years. 43/31 And Solomon lay with his fathers and was buried in the city of David his father; and Rehoboam his son reigned in his place.

Notes

15 הרכלים (and cognate רכלה) predominate in Ezekiel, and are never used in Chronicles; elsewhere only Nah 3:16; Nehemiah (3x); Song 3:6.

18/17 מופז is a unique verbal form related to פז (a very high quality gold). זהב טהור ("pure gold") is used in 1 Chr 28:17 and 2 Chr 3:4 relating to the temple, in 2 Chr 9:17 relating to the palace, and many times in Exod 25–40 relating to the tabernacle.

Second Chronicles 9:26 is placed much earlier in Kings, at 1 Kgs 5:1.

12.3.5. Rehoboam at Shechem: 1 Kgs 12:1–19 // 2 Chr 10:1–19

1	וילך רחבעם שכם*		1 ה*
	כי שכם בא* כל־ישראל להמליך אתו		ו*
2	ויהי כשמע ירבעם בן־נבט		2
* עודנו	והוא * במצרים		* שלמה המלך
* המלך שלמה	אשר ברח מפני *		* ממצרים
* במצרים	וישב ירבעם *		
3	וישלחו ויקראו לו		3
*קהל	ויבאו ירבעם וכל־* ישראל וידברו אל־רחבעם לאמר		
4	אביך הקשה את־עלנו		4
*אתה	ו* עתה הקל מעבדת אביך הקשה ומעלו הכבד אשר נתן עלינו ונעבדך		
5 * לכו עד שלשה	ויאמר אליהם * ימים		5 * עוד שלשת
* וילכו	ושובו אלי * העם		* וילך
6	ויועץ המלך רחבעם את־הזקנים		6
	אשר־היו עמדים * שלמה * את־פני אביו		* לפני

	בהיתו חי לאמר איך אתם נועצים	
*לְ	להשיב *עם־הזה דבר	*את־ה
7	וידברו אליו לאמר	7
• לטוב	אם־* תהיה • להעם	*היום • עבד
* ורציתם	הזה *	* ועבדתם וענתים
	ודברת אלהם דברים טובים	
	והיו לך עבדים כל־הימים	
8	ויעזב את־עצת הזקנים	8
	אשר יעצהו	
	ויועץ את־הילדים אשר	
	גדלו אתו	
	* העמדים לפניו	* אשר
9	ויאמר אלהם מה אתם	9
	נועצים ונשיב דבר את־	
	העם הזה	
	אשר דברו אלי לאמר	
	הקל מן־העל אשר־נתן	
	אביך עלינו	
* אתו	וידברו * הילדים אשר	10 * אליו
10	גדלו אתו	
	לאמר כה־תאמר לעם *	* הזה
	אשר דברו אליך לאמר	
	אביך הכביד את־עלנו	
	ואתה הקל מעלינו	
	כה תדבר אליהם קטני	
	עבה ממתני אבי	
11	ועתה אבי העמיס עליכם	11
	על כבד	
	ואני אוסיף על־עלכם	
	אבי יסר אתכם בשוטים	
	ואני * בעקרבים	* איסר אתכם
12	ויבו ירבעם וכל־העם	12
	אל־רחבעם ביום השלישי	
	כאשר דבר המלך לאמר	
	שובו אלי ביום השלישי	
13 *ם	ויען* המלך • קשה	13 • את־העם
* המלך רחבעם	ויעזב * את־עצת הזקנים •	* אשר יעצהו
14	וידבר אליהם כעצת	14
	הילדים לאמר	
* אכביד	* את־עלכם	* אבי הכביד
* עליו	ואני אסיף *	* על־עלכם

12. SHARED TEXT SAMPLED

	אבי יסר אתכם סשוטים	
* איסר אתכם	ואני * בעקרבים	
15	ולא־שמע המלך אל־העם	15
* סבה מעם יהוה	כי־היתה *	* נסבה מעם האלהים
	למען הקים * את־דברו	יהוה
* אחיה השילני	אשר דבר יהוה ביד *	* אחיהו השלוני
	אל־ירבעם בן־נבט	
* ירא 16	ו * כל־ישראל כי לא־שמע	16
* אליהם	המלך *	* להם
* דבר	וישבו העם את־המלך *	
	לאמר	
	מה־לנו חלק בדוד ולא־	
	נחלה בבן־ישי	
	* לאהליך ישראל עתה	* איש
	ראה ביתך דוד	
	וילך * ישראל לאהליו	* כל
	ובני ישראל הישבים בערי 17	17
	יהודה	
	וימלך עליהם רחבעם	
18	וישלח המלך רחבעם	18
*אדרם	את־*	*הדרם
	אשר על־המס	
* כל־ישראל בו	וירגמו * אבן וימת	* בן בני ישראל
	והמלך רחבעם התאמץ	
	לעלות במרכבה לנוס	
	ירושלם	
	ויפשעו ישראל בבית דוד 19	19
	עד היום הזה	

1 And Rehoboam went to Shechem, for to Shechem came all Israel to make him king. 2 And it came to be as Jeroboam son of Nebat heard (and he was in Egypt to which he had fled from the face of **King Solomon**) and Jeroboam returned *from Egypt*. 3 And they sent and called for him, and Jeroboam and all Israel came and spoke to Rehoboam, saying, 4 "Your father made our yoke heavy. And now make reduction from the hard service of your father and his heavy yoke that he put on us, and we shall serve you." 5 And he said to them, "*Three days more*, and come back to me." And the people went. 6 And King Rehoboam took counsel with the elders who were standing before his father Solomon when he was alive, saying, "How are you counseling to return this people a word?" 7 And they spoke to him, saying, "If you *will be for good* for this people and *will*

please them, speak good words to them and they will be servants to you all the time." 8 And he abandoned the counsel of the elders that they counseled him, and he took counsel with the children who had grown up with him and who were standing before him; 9 and he said to them, "What are you advising that we return this people a word who have spoken to me, saying, 'Make reduction from the yoke that your father put on us.'" 10 And the children who had grown up with him spoke *with* him, saying, "Thus shall you say to the people who have spoken to you saying, 'Your father made our yoke heavy. Now you make lighter what is on us.' Thus shall you speak to them: 'My little thingie is thicker than my father's loins. 11 And now, my father loaded on you a heavy yoke, but I shall add to your yoke. My father taught you with whips, but I with scorpions.'" 12 And Jeroboam and all the people came to Rehoboam on the third day, just as the king had spoken, saying, "Return to me on the third day." 13 And the king answered *them* hardly and abandoned the counsel of the elders, 14 and spoke to them according to the counsel of the children, saying, "My father made heavy your yoke, but I shall add to it. My father taught you with whips, but I with scorpions." 15 And the king did not listen to the people, because it was **a change from Yahweh**, in order to establish his word that Yahweh had spoken by the hand of Ahijah the Shilonite to Jeroboam son of Nebat. 16 And all Israel **saw** that the king had not listened, and the people returned the king [a word], saying, "What portion have we in David and what inheritance in the son of Jesse? To your tents, Israel. Now see your [own] house, David." And Israel went to its tents. 17 And as for the sons of Israel who were living in the cities of Judah, Rehoboam became king over them. 18 And King Rehoboam sent *Hadoram* who was over the corvée, and *the sons of Israel* pelted him with stones and he died. As for King Rehoboam, he made efforts to mount on his chariot to flee to Jerusalem. 19 And Israel rebelled against the house of David to this day.

Notes

Most differences in 12:1–19 // 10:1–19 are insignificant, but the following should be noted.

2b במצרים/ממצרים ("in/from Egypt") imply different readings of וישב ("and he lived" [from ישב] or "and he returned" [from שוב]).

7 As already discussed (3.1.2), היום ("today") is never attested synoptically, and so at least some rewriting has taken place in Kings. Chronicles' לטוב may be compared with Deut 30:9. רצה ("please") is also a plus in all of 2 Sam 24:23; 1 Chr 28:4; 29:3, 17; 2 Chr 10:7.

16–18 Interesting shifts at the end between כל־/בני ישראל/ישראל ישראל.

17 ובני ישראל הישבים בערי יהודה—closest parallels may be Amos 3:12 בני ישראל ויהודה) and 2 Chr 31:6 (בני ישראל הישבים בשמרון הישבים בערי יהודה).

12.3.6. Rehoboam as King: 1 Kgs 12:21–24; 14:21–31 // 2 Chr 11:1–4; 12:2–16

	1 Kgs	2 Chr
	21 ויבא רחבעם ירושלם ויקהל	1
*כל־ • את־שבט	את־* בית יהודה ו בנימין	
	מאה ושמנים אלף בחור עשה מלחמה להלחם עם־* ישראל	*ממלכה
*בית • המלוכה • בן־שלמה	להשיב את־* לרחבעם	2 * יהוה
22 * האלהים	ויהי דבר * אל־שמעיה איש האלהים לאמר	
23	אמר אל־רחבעם בן־שלמה מלך יהודה	3
*בית • יתר העם	ואל־כל־* יהודה ובנימין * לאמר	*ישראל ב
24	כה אמר יהוה לא־תעלו ולא־תלחמון	4
* בני־ישראל	עם־אחיכם * שובו איש לביתו כי מאתי נהיה הדבר הזה וישמעו את־דבר* יהוה	
* ללכת כדבר יהוה	וישבו *	*י מלכת אל־ירבעם
21 * ורחבעם בן־שלמה מלך ביהודה	* בן־ארבעים ואחת שנה במלכו	13 * ויתחזק המלך רחבעם בירושלם וימלך כי
	ושבע עשרה שנה מלך בירושלם העיר אשר־בחר יהוה לשום את־שמו שם מכל־שבטי ישראל ושם־אמו נעמה העמנית	

14 • כי לא הכין לבו לדרש את־יהוה	ויעש • הרע •	22 • יהודה • בעיני יהוה
2	ויהי בשנה החמישית למלך רחבעם עלה שישק מלך־מצרים על־ירושלם	25
9	ויקח את־אצרות בית יהוה ואת־אצרות בית־המלך את־הכל לקח	26
	ויקח את־* מגני הזהב אשר עשה שלמה	*כל־
10	ויעש המלך רחבעם תחתם מגני נחשת והפקיד על־יד שרי הרצים השמרים פתח בית המלך	27
11 • באו הרצים ונשאום	ויהי מדי בא המלך בית יהוה * והשיבום אל־תא הרצים	28 * ישאום הרצים
12–14		
15 • הראשנים והאחרונים * בדברי שמעיה הנביא ועדו החזה להתיחש * ומלחמות *	ו* דברי רחבעם • הלא־הם כתובים * רחבעם * וי־רבעם כל־הימים	29 *יתר • וכל־אשר עשה * על־ספר דברי הימים למלכי יהודה * 30 * ומלחמה היתה בין *בין
16	וישכב רחבעם עם־אבתיו ויקבר * בעיר דוד	31 * עם־אבתיו

21/1 And Rehoboam came to Jerusalem and assembled the house of Judah and Benjamin, one hundred eighty thousand elite warriors, to make war with Israel, to return the kingdom to Rehoboam. 22/2 And the word of *Yahweh* came to Shemaiah the man of God, saying, 23/3 "Say to Rehoboam, son of Solomon king of Judah, and to all Judah and Benjamin, saying: 'Thus says Yahweh, 24/4 "You shall not go up, and you shall not fight with your brothers. Return each to his house; for from me has come this word."'" And they heard the word of Yahweh and turned *from going to Jeroboam*.

21/13 **And Rehoboam son of Solomon became king over Judah.** He was forty-one years old when he became king, and seventeen years he was king in Jerusalem, the city that Yahweh chose to put his name there. 22/14 And he did evil.... 25/2 And in the fifth year of King Rehoboam, Shishak king of Egypt went up against Jerusalem. 26/9 And he took the treasures of Yahweh's house and the treasures of the king's house—everything he took—and he took the golden shields that Solomon had made. 27/10 And King Rehoboam made in their place shields of bronze; and he consigned them to the hand of the officers of the runners who were guarding the entrance of the king's house; 28/11 and it came to be, as often as the king came to Yahweh's house, **the runners would pick them up** and bring them back to the chamber of the runners.... 29/15 And the deeds of Rehoboam, are they not written.... 30/15 And there was war between Rehoboam and Jeroboam all the time. 31 And Rehoboam lay with his fathers and was buried in the city of David.

Notes

30/15   Chronicles is briefer, without the prepositions בין ("between").

12.3.7. Abijam/h: 1 Kgs 14: 31b –15:8 // 2 Chr 12:16b–13:23

ם* 31b	וימלך אבי* בנו תחתיו		ה* 16b
ו* 1	*בשנת שמנה עשרה		1
* בן־נבט	למלך ירבעם *		
ם*	מלך אבי* על־יהודה		*ה
2	שלש שנים מלך בירושלם		2
* מעכה *אבישלום	ושם־אמו * בת־*		* מיכיהו *אוריאל מן־
			גבעה
3–5			
ם* 6	ומלחמה היתה בין אבי*		ה
* כל־ימי חייו	ובין ירבעם *		
			3–21
ם* 7 *וכל־אשר עשה	ויתר דברי אבי*		*ה ודרכיו ודבריו 22
* הלוא־הם * על־ספר	* כתובים *		• במדרש הנביא עדו
דברי הימים למלכי יהודה			
ם* 8	וישכב אבי* עם־אבתיו		ה* 23
	ויקברו אתו בעיר דוד		

31b/16b And Abija**m** his son became king after him. 1 In the eighteenth year of King Jeroboam, Abija**m** became king over Judah. 2 Three years he was king in Jerusalem, and the name of his mother was **Maacah** daughter of **Abishalom**. 6/2 And there was war between Abijam and Jeroboam. 7 And the rest of the acts of Abijam **and all that he did** are written.... 8 And Abijam lay with his fathers and they buried him in the city of David.

Notes

1 Kings adds the patronymic "son of Nebat."

2 Substantial variation over the mother's name: Chronicles adds "from Gibeah."

8/23 There was no shared evaluation in the heading of this report; but (unusually) the king's burial is reported in identical terms by Kings and Chronicles in their conclusion: ויקברו אתו ("and they buried him"). This precise form is repeated synoptically only once (2 Kgs 15:7 // 2 Chr 26:23), and in a synoptic context in 1 Kgs 12:22; 2 Chr 25:28; 27:9. The alternative form ויקברהו (with pronominal suffix) is never synoptic, but is found in synoptic contexts in 2 Kgs 23:30 and nine times in 2 Chronicles.[12] ויקבר *niphal* ("and he was buried") is synoptic twice (in 1 Kgs 14:31 // 2 Chr 12:16; 1 Kgs 22:51 // 2 Chr 21:1), and is used in a synoptic context six times in Kings[13] and in 2 Chr 35:24.

12.3.8. Asa: 1 Kgs 15:8b–24a // 2 Chr 13:23aβ–16:14

8b	וימלך אסא בנו תחתיו		23aβ
10 ארבעים ואחת שנה מלך בירושלם ושם־אמו מעכה בת־אבישלום			בימיו שקטה הארץ עשר שנים
11 * כדוד אביו	ויעש אסא * הישר בעיני * יהוה		14:1 * הטוב ו * אלהיו 14:2–15:15
12 * הקדשים מן־הארץ ויסר את־כל־הגללים אשר עשו אבתיו	* ויעבר		15:8 * השקוצים מכל־ ארץ יהודה
13 * את־ • אמו * ויסרה	וגם * מעכה * מגבירה		16 • אם אסא המלך * הסירה

---

12. 2 Chr 9:31; 16:14; 21:20; 22:9; 24:16, 25; 28:27; 32:33; 33:20. It is also used in later portions of Samuel (1 Sam 25:1; 28:3; 2 Sam 2:32) and of Kings (2 Kgs 13:9, 20; 23:30).

13. 1 Kgs 15:24; 2 Kgs 8:24; 14:20; 15:38; 16:20; 21:18.

12. SHARED TEXT SAMPLED

	אשר־עשתה מפלצת		
	לאשרה		
	ויכרת אסא את־מפלצתה		
ויִדק *	וישרף בנחל קדרון		
17 * מישראל	והבמות לא־סרו *	14	
	רק לבב־אסא היה שלם * עם־יהוה		
	כל־ימיו		
18	ויבא את־קדשי אביו	15	
* האלהים	וקדשיו בית *	יהוה *	
	כסף וזהב וכלים		
19 * לא * עד שנת	ומלחמה * היתה *	16 * בין אסא ובין בעשא	
שלשים וחמש למלכות		מלך־ישראל כל־ימיהם	
אסא			
16:1 * בשנת שלשים		17 * ויעל	
וחמש למלכות אסא עלה	* בעשא מלך־ישראל		
	על־יהודה ויבן את־הרמה		
	לבלתי תת יצא ובא		
	לאסא מלך יהודה		
2 * ויצא	* אסא * כסף וזהב	18 * ויקח * את־כל־ה יה	
*מ	*אצרות בית־יהוה	*הנותרים ב	
	ו * בית המלך *	את־אוצרות * ויתנם	
		ביד־עבדיו	
	וישלח* אל־בן־הדד *	*ס המלך אסא * בן־	
		טברמן בן־חזיון	
ר*	מלך ארם היושב בד־*משק		
	לאמר		
3	ברית ביני ובינך בין אבי	19	
	ובין אביך		
	הנה שלחתי לך * כסף וזהב * שחד		
	לך הפרה *בריתך את־	*את־	
	בעשא		
	מלך־ישראל ויעלה מעלי		
4	וישמע בן־הדד אל־המלך	20	
	אסא		
	וישלח את־שרי החילים		
	אשר־לו		
* ויכו	על־ערי ישראל * את־	* ויַד	
	עיון ואת־דן		
* מים	ואת אבל *	* בית־מעכה	
*מסכנות ערי	ואת כל־* נפתלי	*כנרות על כל־ארץ	
5	ויהי כשמע בעשא ויחדל	21	
* וישבת את־מלאכתו	מבנות את־הרמה *	וישב בתרצה	

22 * השמיע * אין נקי	והמלך אסא * את־כל־יהודה * וישאו את־אבני הרמה ואת־עציה אשר בנה בעשא	6 * לקח
		ה*
* המלך אסא * בנימן	ויבן ב*ם * את־הגבע * ואת־המצפה	
		7–10
23 ויתר כל־* וכל־גבורתו וכל־אשר עשה הלא־הם * דברי הימים למלכי יהודה רק לעת זקנתו חלה את־רגליו	*דברי אסא * כתובים על־ספר	11 והנה * הראשנים והאחרונים הנם * המלכים ליהודה ולישראל
		12 ויחלא אסא ברגליו
24a	וישכב אסא עם־אבתיו	13
* עם־אבתיו * אביו	ויקבר* * בעיר דוד *	14 *הו בקברתו אשר כרה־לו

8b/23aβ And Asa his son became king in his place. 11/14:1 And Asa did what was right in Yahweh's eyes. 12 **And he put away the cult prostitutes from the land, and removed all the idols that his fathers had made.** 13/15:16 And Maacah **his mother** too he turned away from being queen mother, who had made an image for Asherah, and Asa cut her image and burned it at the Kidron Brook. 14/17 And the high places were not removed; however, Asa's heart was complete all his days. 15/18 And he brought his father's votive gifts and his [own] votive gifts into **Yahweh's** house, silver and gold and vessels. 16/19 And there was war **between Asa and Baasha king of Israel all their days.** 17/16:1 And Baasha king of Israel went up against Judah and built Ramah not allowing going or coming to Asa king of Judah. 18/2 And Asa *brought out* silver and gold *from* the treasuries of Yahweh's house and of the king's house, and sent [them] to Ben-Hadad king of Aram who was enthroned in Damascus, saying, 19/3 "There is a pact between me and you and between my father and your father. See, I hereby send you silver and gold. Go, break your pact with Baasha king of Israel, that he goes up from against me." 20/4 And Ben-Hadad listened to King Asa, and he sent the leaders of the troops he had against the cities of Israel; and **he** struck Iyyon and Dan and Abel-beth-**maacah** and all *the storage facilities of the cities* of Naphtali. 21/5 And it came to be as Baasha heard, and he stopped building Ramah **and resided at Tirzah.** 22/6 And King Asa *took* all Judah and they lifted the stones of

Ramah and its timbers, with which Baasha had built, and he built with them Geba and Mizpah.... 24a/13–14 And Asa lay with his fathers; and he was buried in the city of David.

Notes

10/23 Kings has the same mother's notice as for Abijam (none in Chronicles)—Maacah is called his mother in the body of report (13/16).

11/14:1 Kings adds "like David his father"; Chronicles adds "good and" and "his God."

13/16 Apart from removal of the queen mother, Chronicles' Asa account only uses סור *hiphil* in 2 Chr 14:2, 4—is גללים a plus in Kings? Certainly אשר עשו אבתיו ("that his fathers had done") only appears again with two of the last four kings (2 Kgs 23:32, 37), and את־כל may suggest supplementation.

- The unusually more specific אם אסא המלך (2 Chr 15:16) is occasioned by the large Chronicles plus.
- סור *hiphil* is synoptic in 2 Sam 6:10; 7:15; 1 Kgs 15:13; 2 Kgs 18:22. It is used also in 2 Chr 36:2, where synoptic 2 Kgs 23:23 uses אסר.

14/17 שלם עם־יהוה occurs only in 1 Kgs 8:61; 11:4; 15:3, 14; cf. באמת ובלבב שלם והטוב בעיניך in 2 Kgs 20:3 // Isa 38:3. Chronicles uses only בלבב שלם (1 Chr 12:39; 28:9; 29:9; 2 Chr 15:17; 16:9 [closest to Kings with שלם אליו]; 19:9; 25:2).

- כל־ימיו is synoptic only here (15:14—2 Kgs 12:3; 15:18; 2 Chr 18:7; 34:33 are all pluses).
- כל־ימיהם: unique to 1 Kgs 15:16, 32—verse 16 may be original, and altered in Chronicles; but verse 32 is a plus.

17/16:1 לבלתי is synoptic only here (once more in 1 Chr 4, but often in Deuteronomy, Joshua, Judges, Samuel, Kings).

18/2 Kings adds "all the [gold]," and so on, and many other pluses in the embassy.

19/3 Kings שחד ("present") is an interesting plus: it anticipates Ahaz (2 Kgs 16:8), who also takes silver and gold from both "houses." Has Chronicles removed it for the sake of Asa's reputation (cf. 2 Chr 19:7—אין עם־יהוה מקח שחד), or is it a case of added precision?

20–21/4–5 Note different place names.

22/6 אין נקי ("none in the clear") in Kings is unique; and Chronicles never uses either noun or verb.

12.3.9. Jehoshaphat: 1 Kgs 15:24b; 22:4-35, 41-51 // 2 Chr 17-20

17:1a	וימלך יהושפט בנו תחתיו	15:24b	
18:3 * אחאב מלך־ישראל * מלך יהודה	ויאמר * אל־יהושפט * התלך אתי למלחמה רמת גלעד	4	
4	ויאמר יהושפט אל־מלך ישראל	5	
* ועמך במלחמה	כמוני כמוך כעמי כעמך * כסוסי כסוסיך ויאמר יהושפט אל־מלך ישראל דרש־נא כיום את־דבר יהוה		
5	ויקבץ מלך־ישראל את־הנביאים	6	
* הַנֵלֵךְ	*ארבע מאות איש ויאמר אלהם * אל־רמת גלעד למלחמה אם־אחדל	* האלך	*כ
* האלהים	ויאמרו עלה ויתן * ביד־המלך	* אדני	
6	ויאמר יהושפט האין פה נביא ליהוה עוד ונדרשה מאתו	7	
7	ויאמר מלך־ישראל אל־יהושפט עוד איש־אחד לדרוש את־יהוה מאתו	8	
*איננו מתנבא * לטובה * כל־ימיו לרעה הוא	ואני שנאתיהו כי־* עלי * כי * מיכיהו בן־ימלה/א ויאמר יהושפט אל־יאמר המלך כן	* לא יתנבא * טוב * אם־רע	
8	ויקרא מלך ישראל אל־סריס אחד ויאמר מהר[ה] מיכהו בן־ימלה/א	9	
9	ומלך ישראל ויהושפט מלך יהודה ישבים איש על־כסאו מלבשים בגדים	10	

12. SHARED TEXT SAMPLED

	* וישבים		* בגרן פתח שער שמרון וכל־הנביאים מתנבאים לפניהם
10		11	ויעש לו צדקיה בן־כנענה קרני ברזל ויאמר כה אמר יהוה באלה תנגח את־ארם עד־כלתם
11		12	וכל־הנביאים נבאים כן לאמר עלה רמת גלעד והצלח ונתן יהוה ביד המלך
12 *ל		13	והמלאך־אשר־הלך לקרא *מיכיהו
	*־נא		דבר אליו לאמר הנה* דברי הנבאים פה־אחד טוב אל־המלך
	*דבר		ויהי־נא דברך כ* אחד מהם ודברת טוב
13		14	ויאמר מיכיהו חי־יהוה כי את־אשר־יאמר אלהי אתו אדבר
14		15	ויבא אל־המלך ויאמר המלך אליו מיכה הנלך אל־רמת גלעד למלחמה אם־* ויאמר •
*<u>אחדל</u> <u>עלו והצליחו ויְנַתְנוּ בְיֶדְכֶם</u>		*נחדל • אליו <u>עלה והצלח</u> ונתן יהוה ביד המלך	
15		16	ויאמר אליו המלך עד־כמה פעמים אני משביעך אשר לא־תדבר אלי רק־אמת בשם יהוה
16		17	ויאמר ראיתי את־כל־ ישראל נפצים אל־ההרים כצאן אשר אין־להם רעה ויאמר יהוה לא־אדנים לאלה ישובו איש־לביתו בשלום

17		18	ויאמר מלך־ישראל אל־יהושפט
			הלוא אמרתי אליך
*ל			לוא־יתנבא עלי טוב כי־אם *רע
18 *ו		19	ויאמר לכן שמע* דבר־יהוה
			ראיתי את־יהוה ישב על־כסאו
* עמדים			וכל־צבא השמים * עמד
על־ימינו ושמאלו			עליו מימינו ומשמאלו
19		20	ויאמר יהוה מי יפתה את־אחאב *
* מלך־ישראל			ויעל ויפל ברמת גלעד
* אמר ככה * ככה			ויאמר זה * וזה אמר * בכה * בכה
20		21	ויצא הרוח ויעמד לפני יהוה ויאמר
			אני אפתה/נו ויאמר יהוה אליו במה
21 *ל		22	ויאמר אצא והייתי *רוח שקר
			בפי כל־נביאיו ויאמר תפתה
			וגם־תוכל צא ועשה־כן
22		23	ועתה הנה נתן יהוה רוח שקר בפי
			*נביאיך אלה ויהוה דבר * כל־עליך רעה
23		24	ויגש צדקיהו בן־כנענה
			ויך את־מיכיהו על־הלחי
* הדרך			ויאמר אי זה * עבר רוח־יהוה
			מאתי לדבר אתך
24		25	ויאמר מיכיהו הנך ראה ביום ההוא
			אשר תבוא חדר בחדר להחבא/ה
25		26	ויאמר מלך ישראל קחו את־מיכיהו
			והשיבהו אל־אמן שר־העיר
			ואל־יואש בן־המלך

12. SHARED TEXT SAMPLED

	27	ואמרתם כה אמר המלך	26
		שימו זה בית הכלא	
		והאכלהו לחם לחץ ומים	
		לחץ	
* באי	*	עד * בשלום	*שובי
	28	ויאמר מיכיהו אם־שוב	27
		תשוב בשלום	
		לא־דבר יהוה בי	
		ויאמר שמעו עמים כלם	
	29	ויעל מלך־ישראל	28
		ויהושפט	
		מלך־יהודה *רמת גלעד	* אל־
	30	ויאמר מלך־ישראל אל־	29
		יהושפט	
		התחפש ובא במלחמה	
		ואתה לבש בגדיך	
		ויתחפש מלך ישראל	
		ויבוא במלחמה	
	31	ומלך ארם צוה את־שרי	30
* שלשים ושנים		הרכב אשר־לו *	
		לאמר	
		לא תלחמו את־הקטן ואת־	
		גדול	
		כי אם־את־מלך ישראל	
		לבדו	
	32	ויהי כראות שרי הרכב	31
		את־יהושפט	
* אך		והמה אמרו * מלך־	
		ישראל הוא	
* ויסרו		* עליו להלחם ויזעק	* ויסבו
		יהושפט	
		ויהוה עזרו ויסיתם אלהים	
		ממנו	
	33	ויהי כראות שרי הרכב	32
* הוא		כי־לא־* מלך ישראל *	*היה
		וישובו מאחריו	
	34	ואיש משך בקשת לתמו	33
		ויכה את־מלך ישראל	
		בין הדבקים ובין השרין	
* והוציאני		ויאמר לרכבו הפך ידך *	* והוצאתני
		מן־המחנה כי החליתי	
	35	ותעל המלחמה ביום ההוא	34

המלך • מעמד • בערב	ו* היה • במרכבה • נכח ארם * וימת *	*מלך ישראל • מעמיד * עד־הערב • לעת בוא השמש 20:31
42	בן־שלשים וחמש שנה במלכו ועשרים וחמש שנה מלך בירושלם ושם אמו עזובה בת־שלחי	
43 *כל־	וילך ב* דרך אסא אביו לא סר ממנו לעשות הישר בעיני יהוה	32
44 * מזבחים ומקטרים בבמות 45 וישלם יהושפט עם־מלך ישראל 46 * וגבורתו אשר עשה * הלא־הם Cult prostitute remnant 47 King in Edom 48 49–50	אך הבמות לא סרו עוד העם * ויתר דברי יהושפט * כתובים ... Ships to Tarshish	33 * לא־הכינו לבבם לאלהי אבתיהם 34 * הראשנים והאחרונים הנם * 20:35–36 Prophecy against ships 20:37
51	וישכב יהושפט עם־אבתיו ויקבר עם־אבתיו בעיר דוד	21:1

The story of the joint military operation by the kings of Israel and Judah in Gilead and the key role of Micaiah ben Imlah is so similarly told in Kings and Chronicles that it is unnecessary to offer a translation until the final verses. The majority of the very few earlier differences are quite trivial.

42/31 He was thirty-five years old when he became king, and twenty-five years he was king in Jerusalem. 43/32 And he walked in the way of Asa his father; he did not turn from it—doing the right in Yahweh's eyes. 44/33 However, the high places were not removed; still the people.... 46/34 And the rest of the deeds of Jehoshaphat are written.... 51/21:1 And Jehoshaphat lay with his fathers, and he was buried with his fathers in the city of David.

Notes

6/5 אדני may anticipate the unique shared אדנים (17/16)—do both אדני (6) and האלהים (5) derive from a common יהוה?

19/18 לכן here is unique in Chronicles: it is a plus in 2 Kgs 22:20, and not found elsewhere in a synoptic context (except 2 Kgs 19:32 // Isa 37:33). It is common throughout the Latter Prophets.

In Kings (MT) and Chronicles, the main story appears before most of the formula (but not in Kings LXX); different versions also set the invasion of Shishak at different points in the Rehoboam story (12.3.6).

12.3.10. Jehoram: 2 Kgs 8:16b–24 // 2 Chr 21:1b–20

16b	וימלך יהורם בנו תחתיו		1b
			2–4
17	בן־שלשים ושתים שנה היה במלכו ושמנה שנים מלך בירושלם		5
18	וילך בדרך מלכי ישראל כאשר עשו בית אחאב כי בת־אחאב היתה לו לאשה ויעש הרע בעיני יהוה		6
19	ולא־אבה יהוה להשחית את־* *יהודה		7 *בית דויד * הברית אשר כרת לדויד ו
*דוד עבדו	למען * כאשר אמר		*ו
	לתת לו ניר *לבניו כל־הימים		
20	בימיו פשע אדום מתחת יד־יהודה וימלכו עליהם מלך		8
21 * *יורם צעירה	ויעבר * וכל־הרכב עמו		9 * יהורם עם־שריו
* הוא * ויכה	ויהי * קם לילה * את־אדום הסובב אליו ואת שרי הרכב *		• *ויך*
* וינס העם לאהליו			
22	ויפשע אדום מתחת יד־יהודה עד־היום הזה		10

	אז תפשע לבנה בעת	* מתחת ידו
	ההיא *	כי עזב את־יהוה אלהי
		אבתיו
		11a גם־הוא עשה במות
		בהרי יהודה
23 ויתר דברי יורם וכל־		11b–20a
אשר עשה		
הלא־הם כתובים על־ספר		20b וילך בלא חמדה
דברי הימים למלכי יהודה		
24 וישכב יורם עם־אבתיו		
ויקבר עם־אבתיו *	* בעיר דוד	* ויקברהו
		ולא בקברות המלכים

16b/1b And Jehoram his son became king in his place. 17/5 He was twenty-two years old when he became king; and eight years he was king in Jerusalem. 18/6 And he walked in the way of the kings of Israel, just as the house of Ahab did; for the daughter of Ahab was his wife. And he did evil in Yahweh's eyes. 19/7 But Yahweh was not willing to destroy **Judah** for the sake of **David his servant**, as he had spoken of giving him land to till for his sons for all time. 20/8 In his days Edom rebelled from under the hand of Judah, and they kinged a king over themselves. 21/9 And **Joram** passed over **to Zair** and the chariotry with him; and he rose by night and struck Edom that was surrounding him and the officers of the chariotry. 22/10 And Edom rebelled from under the hand of Judah to this day. Then Libnah rebelled at that time....

Notes

19/7 Whether "Judah" or "house of David" is more original here, the counterpart in 2 Kgs 13:23 is "Israel." שחת hiphil is used synoptically twice more, in 2 Sam 11:1; 24:16 // 1 Chr 20:1; 21:15, where the objects are Ammon and "Israel." The Assyrian envoy will claim Yahweh's complicity in the orders to destroy "this place" and "this land" (2 Kgs 18:25).

20/8 בימיו ("in his days") is unique here in synoptic texts.

21/9 Though this king is introduced in both texts (16b/1b) as יהורם (Jehoram), Kings prefers the shorter יורם (Joram) here and in 8:24.

12.3.11. Ahaziah: 2 Kgs 8:24b–29 // 2 Chr 22:1b–6

	24b	וימלך אחזיהו בנו תחתיו	1b
	26	בן־עשרים ושתים שנה	2
		אחזיהו במלכו	
		ושנה אחת מלך בירושלם	
		ושם־אמו עתליהו בת־	
מלך ישראל *		עמרי *	
וילך בדרך *	27	בית אחאב *	3 * גם־הוא הלך בדרכי
			כי אמו היתה יועצתו
			להרשיע
		ויעש הרע בעיני יהוה	
כי חתן בית־אחאב הוא *		כבית אחאב *	
			4b + 5aα
	28	וילך את־יורם בן־אחאב	5aβ–b
		למלחמה	
		עם־חזהאל מלך־ארם	
		ברמת גלעד	
		ויכו ארמים את־יורם	
יורם המלך *	29 *	וישב * להתרפא	6
		ביזרעאל מן־המכים	
		אשר יכהו ארמים ברמה	
		בהלחמו את־חזהאל מלך	
		ארם	
ואחזיהו *		בן־יהורם מלך יהודה *	* ועזריהו
		ירד	
		לראות את־יורם בן־	
		אחאב ביזרעאל	
		כי־חלה הוא	

24b/1b And Ahaziah his son became king in his place. 26/2 Ahaziah was twenty-two years old when he became king, and one year he was king in Jerusalem. And his mother's name was Athaliah, daughter of Omri. 27/3 **And he walked in the way** of the house of Ahab; and he did evil in Yahweh's eyes like the house of Ahab, **for he was an in-law of the house of Ahab**. 28/5 And he went with Joram son of Ahab to war with Hazael king of Aram in Ramoth-gilead; and Aramaeans struck Joram. 29/6 And he returned to be healed in Jezreel from the wounds when Aramaeans struck him in Ramah in his warring with Hazael king of Aram. And **Ahaziah** son of Joram king of Judah went down to see Joram son of Ahab in Jezreel because he was sick.

Notes

27/3 Chronicles often pluralizes original singulars (like בדרכי here). Both texts vary the spelling of י[ה]ורם (J[eh]oram), yet context indicates which king is intended.

12.3.12. Athaliah: 2 Kgs 11 // 2 Chr 22:10–23:21

1	ועתליהו אם אחזיהו ראתה כי מת בנה		22:10
* ותאבד	ותקם * את־כל־זרע הממלכה		* ו‎תדבר
2 * יהושבע	ותקח * בת־המלך		11 * יהושבעת
*־יורם אחות אחזיהו	את־יואש בן־אחזיהו		
	ותגנב אתו מתוך בני־ המלך המומתים		
	* אתו ואת־מינקתו בחדר המטות		* ותתן
	ויסתרו אתו מפני עתליהו ולא הומת		
3 * אתה בית יהוה	ויהי * מתחבא שש שנים ועתליהו מלכת על־הארץ		12 * אתם בבית האלהים
4 * שלח	ובשנה השביעית * יהוידע		23:1 * התחזק
* לכרי ולרצים	ויקח את־שרי המאות *		* לעזריהו ... לישראל
ויבא אתם אליו בית יהוה			ויבאו אל־ירושלם
* להם • וישבע אתם	ויכרת * ברית •		3 * כל־הקהל
יהוה	בבית *		* האלהים
* וירא אתם את־	*בן־המלך		* ויאמר להם הנה
5 ויצום לאמר			ימלך כאשר דבר יהוה על־בני דויד
	זה הדבר אשר תעשו השלשית מכם באי השבת		4
ושמרי משמרת בית יהוה			לכהנים וללוים לשערי הספים
6 * בשער סור	* והשלשית		5 * בבית המלך
* בשער אחר הרצים	* והשלשית		* בשער היסוד
ושמרתם את־משמרת הבית מסח			וכל־העם בחצרות בית יהוה
7 ושתי הידות בכם כל יצאי השבת			6 ואל־יבוא בית־יהוה
			כי אם־הכהנים והמשרתים ללוים

12. SHARED TEXT SAMPLED

ושמרו את־משמרת בית־יהוה אל־המלך	* על־המלך סביב איש וכליו בידו	8 * והקפתם *השדרות	המה יבאו כי־קדש המה וכל־העם ישמרו משמרת יהוה 7 * <u>והקיפוּ</u> הלוים <u>הבית</u>
	והבא אל־* יומת ויהיו את־המלך בצאתו ובבאו		
<u>שרי המאיות</u> 9 *	ויעשו * ככל אשר־צוה יהוידע הכהן ויקחו איש את־אנשיו באי השבת עם יצאי השבת		8 * הלוים וכל־יהודה
			כי לא פטר יהוידע הכהן את־המחלקות 9 * <u>ואת־המגנות</u> * בית האלהים
	ויתן הכהן לשרי המאיות את־החניתים * ואת־השלטים אשר למלך	10	
<u>בבית יהוה</u> *	דוד אשר *		10 * את־כל־העם ו* שלחו
<u>ן הרצים</u> <u>וכליו</u> *	ויעמד * איש * בידו מכתף הבית הימנית עד־כתף הבית השמאלית למזבח ולבית על־המלך סביב	11	
	ויוצא* את־בן־המלך ויתן עליו את־הנזר ואת־העדות	12	יו 11 *
ויכו־כף *	וימלכו אתו וימשחהו * ויאמרו יחי המלך		* יהוידע ובניו
<u>הרצין העם</u> *	ותשמע עתליהו את־קול * ותבוא אל־העם בית־יהוה	13 *	12 * העם הרצים והמהללים את־המלך
<u>העמוד כמשפט</u>*	ותרא והנה המלך עומד על־* והשרים והחצצרות על־המלך וכל־עם הארץ שמח ותקע בחצצאות *	14	13 *עמודו במבוא
			* והמשוררים בכלי השיר ומודעים להלל
ותקרא *	ותקרע עתליה את־בגדיה * קשר קשר		* ותאמר

14 * ויוצא	* יהוידע הכהן	15 * ויצו
	את־שרי המאות פקדי החיל	
*ה	ויאמר אליהם הוציאו* אל־מבית לשדרות והבא אחריה	* אתה
* יומת	* בחרב כי אמר הכהן	* המת
* לא תמיתוה	* בית יהוה	* אל־תומת
15	וישמו לה הידים	16
* אל־ * שער	ותבוא *מבוא * הסוסים	* דרך־
* ומיתוה	בית המלך * שם	* ותומת
16	ויכרת יהוידע *ברית	17 * את־ה
בינו ובין כל־העם ובין המלך	להיות לעם ליהוה *	בין יהוה ובין המלך ובין העם
	* ובין המלך ובין העם	
17 *העם	ויבאו כל־* בית הבעל	18 *עם הארץ
*ו	ויתצהו *את־מזבחתיו ואת־צלמיו שברו * ואת־מתן כהן הבעל הרגו לפני המזבחות	* היטב
18 * יהוידע	וישם * פקדות על־בית יהוה	* הכהן
20 * ואת־האדירים	ויקח את־שרי המאות *	19 * ואת־הכרי
* ואת־המושלים בעם	* ואת כל־עם הארץ ויורד את־המלך מבית יהוה	* ואת־הרצים
* בתוך־שער העליון	ויבאו * בית המלך	* דרך שער הרצים
* את־המלך * הממלכה	וישב * על־כסא *	* המלכים
21 *ו	וישמח* כל־עם־הארץ והעיר שקטה ואת־עתליהו המיתו בחרב *	20
		* בית מלך

1/22:10 And Athaliah mother of Ahaziah had seen that her son had died. And she rose and **destroyed** [drove out?] the whole royal seed. 2/11 And Jehosheba[th] daughter of the king took Joash son of Ahaziah and stole him from among the sons of the king put to death, him and his nurse in the room of the staffs, and hid him from Athaliah and he was not put to death. 3/12 And he was **with her,** hidden in **Yahweh's** house, six years; and Athaliah was ruling as king over the land. 4/13 And in the seventh year Jehoiada **sent** and took the officers of hundreds of the **Carites** and of the runners;

and they came to Jerusalem and he made covenant in **Yahweh's** house, **and he showed them** the king's son; 5/23:3 **and he commanded them, saying,** "This is the action you will take, the third of you coming on the Sabbath **and attending to the guarding of Yahweh's house,** 6/5 **and the third at the gate Sur,** and the third **at the gate after the runners; and you will attend to the guarding of the house in turn. 7/6 And the two divisions among you, all that come out on the Sabbath—they shall attend to the guarding of Yahweh's house.** 8/7 And *they shall surround* the king round about each with his weapons in his hand, and whoever comes *to the house* shall be put to death. And they shall be with the king at his going out and coming in. 9/8 And **the officers of the hundreds** did according to all that Jehoiada the priest had ordered; and they took each his men, those coming in on the Sabbath and those going out on the Sabbath. 10/9 And the priest gave the leaders of the hundreds the spears and shields belonging to King David that were **in Yahweh's house;** 11/10 and **the runners** stood, each with **his weapons** in his hand, from the right wing of the house to the left wing of the house around the altar and the house close to the king. 12/11 And he brought out the king's son and put on him the crown and the protocol, and they made him king and anointed him, and said, "[Long] live the king." 13/12 And Athaliah heard the voice **of the runners/the people**, and she came to the people in Yahweh's house; 14/13 and she saw—and there was the king standing **by the pillar according to the rule**, and the officers and the trumpeters close to the king and all the people of the land rejoicing and sounding on trumpets, and she rent her clothes, and she **cried,** "A plot! A plot!" 15/14 And Jehoiada the priest **commanded** the officers of the hundreds set over the army and said to them, "Bring her out ... to the ranks, and put whoever comes after her to death by the sword." For the priest said, "Let her not be put to death in Yahweh's house." 16/15 And they put hands on her, and she came **by way of** the horses' entrance to the king's house and was put to death there. 17/16 And Jehoiada made a covenant **between Yahweh and the king and the people**, that the people should belong to Yahweh. 18/17 And all *the people* came to Baal's house and tore it down: its altars and its images they shattered, and Mattan the priest of Baal they slaughtered in front of the altars; and **the priest** set appointees over Yahweh's house. 19/20 And he took the officers of the hundreds **and the Carites and the runners** and all the people of the land and brought down the king from Yahweh's house; and they came **by way of the Runners' Gate** to the king's house, and he sat on the seat of the **kings**. 20/21 And all the people of the land rejoiced and the city was at rest—and Athaliah they had put to death by the sword.

Notes

1/10 ותאבד/ותדבר: Kings uses אבד *piel* four times: 2 Kgs 11:1 (דבר); 13:7 (+); 19:18 (+); 21:3 (נתץ), but Chronicles never. Many instances of אבד occur in the late book of Esther (10x). דבר II could bear the same sense.

3/12 In more than thirty synoptic instances, Kings/Chronicles agree in reading בית יהוה.[14] Here and in 10/9 below, Chronicles reads בית האלהים and in 22:4 // 34:5 בית אלהים.

4/1 התחזק, while not unique to Chronicles, is one of its commonplaces (15x out of 27x in the HB). Only one instance is synoptic (2 Sam 10:12 // 1 Chr 19:13), and it is found four more times in Samuel–Kings.

4/3 Chronicles nowhere uses ראה *hiphil*, while we find it also in 2 Kgs 6:6; 8:10, 13—and notably in 20:13, 13, 15 (// Isa 39:2, 2, 4). Cf. ראה in 2 Sam 7:2 (MT) but הנה in the Septuagint and 1 Chr 17:1.

5-7/4-6 The version in Kings may not be original, but it commands more confidence than Chronicles. סור and יסוד (6/5) are probably unintentional variants.

11/10 שלח ("missile") is never found in the Former Prophets, but is used again in 2 Chr 32:5—it is more specific than כליו.

12/11 A synoptic instance of העדות in this sense is unusually never repeated in either Kings or Chronicles.

13/12 רצים ("runners") is synoptic in 1 Kgs 14:27–28 // 2 Chr 12:10–11 (תא); and here the unusual הרצין העם in Kings corresponds to הרצים העם in Chronicles. It is a Kings plus in 2 Kgs 11:4, 6, 11, 19 (2x), and 10:25 (2x) (just before a synoptic context); and it is a Chronicles plus in 2 Chr 30:6, 10.

14/13 עם הארץ ("people of the land") is synoptic three times in this passage (14/13, 19/20, 20/21) and occurs once in Kings (18) where Chronicles (17) has simply העם. It is synoptic in three different passages elsewhere (2 Kgs 15:5 // 2 Chr 26:21; 2 Kgs 21:24 // 2 Chr 33:25; 2 Kgs 23:30 // 2 Chr

---

14. 1 Kgs 6:37 // 2 Chr 3:1; 1 Kgs 7:45 // 2 Chr 4:16; 1 Kgs 7:51 // 2 Chr 5:1; 1 Kgs 8:11 // 2 Chr 5:11–14(!);1 Kgs 8:64 // 2 Chr 7:7; 1 Kgs 9:1 // 2 Chr 7:11; 1 Kgs 9:10 // 2 Chr 8:1; 1 Kgs 10:5, 12 // 2 Chr 9:4, 11; 1 Kgs 14:26, 28 // 2 Chr 12:9, 11; 1 Kgs 15:18 // 2 Chr 16:2; 2 Kgs 11:13, 15, 18, 19 // 2 Chr 23:12, 14, 17, 18; 2 Kgs 12:10 // 2 Chr 24:8; 2 Kgs 12:8–14 // 2 Chr 24:9–16; 2 Kgs 14:14 // 2 Chr 25:24; 2 Kgs 15:35 // 2 Chr 27:3; 2 Kgs 16:8 (, 18) // 2 Chr 28:21 (, 24); 2 Kgs 21:4, 5 // 2 Chr 33:4, 5; 22:3, 5 (2x), 8, 9; 2 Kgs 23:2 (2x) // 2 Chr 34:8, 10 (2x), 15, 17, 30 (2x).

36:1), and a Kings plus in 2 Kgs 16:15; 23:35; 24:14; 25:19 (all in material without correspondents in Chronicles)—it is never a Chronicles plus.

15/14 אל־מבית is unique in the Hebrew Bible and is left untranslated above. This verse concludes in Kings with the command stated in the active המת and reinforced by a negated passive אל תומת. In Chronicles, the jussive יומת refers to the fate of whoever is following Athaliah, and only the negated active תמיתוה to the erstwhile ruler. Such interchange between actives and passives is most frequent—and almost regular—in regnal closing formulae.

18/17 בית הבעל ("Baal's house") is the object of נתץ ("tear down") only once more, in 2 Kgs 10:27. However, "tear down" has "house" as its object five more times in the Hebrew Bible: Lev 14:45; 2 Kgs 23:7; Isa 22:10; Jer 31:28; Ezek 26:12.

- This is the sole synoptic use of צלם ("image"), and צלם and מזבח ("altar") are nowhere else paired in the Hebrew Bible. שבר *piel* ("shatter") is found synoptically once more (2 Kgs 18:4 // 2 Chr 31:1), where its object is מצבת ("standing stones").

- David Clines compares שברו היטב in 2 Kgs 11:18 (where the verb is strengthened by a noncognate infinitive absolute) with שבר תשבר מצבתיהם (cognate infinitive absolute) in Exod 23:24.[15]

19/20 המושלים בעם ("those ruling in the people," Chronicles) corresponds to the penultimate instance in 2 Kgs 11 of רצים. משל ("rule") is used synoptically of Solomon (1 Kgs 5:1 // 2 Chr 9:26) and, in the phrase ארץ ממשלתו ("land of his rule") in 1 Kgs 9:19 // 2 Chr 8:6—and it may be original in 2 Chr 7:18. Then ממשלה has a broadly Hezekian connection in 2 Kgs 20:13; 2 Chr 32:9; Isa 22:21; 39:2.

- "Gate of the Runners" (Kings) corresponds here to "Upper Gate" (Chronicles), which is found synoptically in 2 Kgs 15:35 // 2 Chr 27:3.

12.3.13. Jehoash: 2 Kgs 12 // 2 Chr 24

1 * יהואש בן־שבע שנים * במלכו		1 * יואש
2 וארבעים שנה מלך בירושלם		
ושם אמו צביה מבאר שבע		
3 ויעש י[ה]ואש הישר בעיני יהוה		2

---

15. *DCH* 8:251.

כל־ימי* יהוידע הכהן *ו אשר הורהו
3 וישא־לו יהוידע נשים   4 רק הבמות לא־סרו
שתים ויולד בנים ובנות ...   עוד העם מזבחים
                                        ומקטרים בבמות ...

1/1 J[eh]oash was seven years old when he became king, 2/1 and forty years he was king in Jerusalem. And his mother's name was Zibiah from Beer-sheba. 3/2 And And J[eh]oash did what was right in Yahweh's eyes all the days of Jehoiada the priest....

Notes

4/3 These are quite different continuations from the introduction; and the material in 2 Chr 24:15–22 is a typical set of Chronicles pluses.

• עלה על־לב also occurs in Isa 65:17 and Jer 3:16 (cf. Jer 12:11; Mal 2:2; 2 Chr 7:11).

6-9, 13 בדק is mostly the object of חזק *piel*, but not in 2 Kgs 12:8; in Chronicles only 2 Chr 34:8 // 2 Kgs 22:5—here typical multiplication within a Kings plus.

9 אות: "consent"; cf. only Gen 34 (3x).

• Second Chronicles 24:4-7 includes several related expressions as well as מדוע: לחזק את־ (2 Kgs 12:5 // 2 Chr 24:4), עלה על־לב/היה עם־לב בית (2 Kgs 12:15 // 2 Chr 24:5, 12), קדשי בית יהוה (2 Kgs 12:19 // 2 Chr 24:7). Typically Levites are included, and blamed (2 Chr 24:5, 6, 11); and the tax is משאת משה (2 Chr 24:6, 9).

• אז opens both 2 Kgs 12:18 and 2 Chr 24:17b—is there an earlier correspondence there? If so, Chronicles is saying that the Aramaean invasion (at the solstice) was a response to Joash listening *then* to the bad advice of his ministers.

Further Remarks

The accounts of Joash in Kings and Chronicles diverge immediately after the formulaic opening; and it appears that both have substantially rewritten the shared tradition they inherited. Kings develops differently from Chronicles the king's efforts to strengthen the house of Yahweh, drawing on language from the synoptic presentation of Josiah. Chronicles emphasizes still further the positive role of Jehoiada the priest and of his prophetic son. Jehoiada's first-noted contribution to Joash as king (2 Chr 24:3) was arranging his two marriages. The first of the series of four Kings pluses about continuing "high places" (2 Kgs 12:4) emphasizes that not all cultic problems had been solved by the overthrow of Athaliah.

The main themes of the Joash reports are as follows:

1.	Joash speaks to the priests about repairing the house of the Lord	5–6	4–5a
2.	Nothing happens [fast]	7	5b
3.	Joash *questions* (מדוע) Jehoiada the priest	8–9	6–7
4.	Chest for contributions as one entered house of Yahweh	10–11	8–11
5.	Paying those who did the work	12–13	12–13
6.	Sacred implements were [not] made	14–17	14a
7.	Beneficial role of Jehoiada and his death	—	14b–17a
Then (אז)			
8.	King listened to the officials	—	17b
9.	Abandoned house of Yahweh	—	18
10.	Yahweh sent prophets, including the son of Jehoiada	—	19–20
11.	Zechariah stoned in the house of Yahweh	—	21–22
12.	Hazael of Aram invaded and was bought off/plundered	18–19	23–24
13.	Conspiracy against Joash, and his end	20–22	25–27

The underlying structure can be detected in shared words and phrases rarely or uniquely found in the synoptic record:

- מדוע ("why") (2 Kgs 12:8 // 2 Chr 24:6) and אז ("then") (2 Kgs 12:18 // 2 Chr 24:17b)
- the pattern of repetitions of בית יהוה and variants of it
- the use of חזק ("strengthen") with [יהוה] בית ("[Yahweh's] house"), which is synoptic only in 2 Kgs 12:6 // 2 Chr 24:5 and 2 Kgs 12:12 // 2 Chr 24:12[16] (// 5, 12), and חדש (// 2 Chr 24:4, 12)
- שמרי הסף in 2 Kgs 12:10 become the Levites in 2 Chr 24:11, as in the Chronicles plus in 2 Kgs 22:4 // 2 Chr 34:9

---

16. The linkage is Kings plus in 2 Kgs 12:7, 8, 9, 13, 15, with בדק (imported from Josiah [2 Kgs 22:5 // 2 Chr 34:10] normally interposed (2 Kgs 12:6 [2x], 7, 8, 9, 13).

- עשי המלאכה, "doing the work" (2 Kgs 12:12, 15, 16 // 2 Chr 24:12, 13)

The questioning of Jehoiada by the king (2 Kgs 12:8 // 2 Chr 24:6) is the only point at which the priest appears in the shared text. He had been instrumental in bringing Joash to power (2 Kgs 11 // 2 Chr 23), and is given general credit for the king's conduct in a plus in 2 Kgs 12:3; and in 2 Kgs 12:9 it was he who made arrangements for the collection chest; but he and his son play a much larger role in Chronicles (themes 7–11 above).

Chronicles interprets the shared "then" (2 Kgs 12:18 // 2 Chr 24:17b) not as temporal but as logical: only when the advice of the priest was exchanged for that of fawning officials did Hazael invade.

1   The only shared elements of the king's original instruction are כסף ("money") in 2 Kgs 12:5 and 2 Chr 24:5 and חזק ("strengthen") in the context of repairs to the divine בית ("house") in 2 Kgs 12:6 and 2 Chr 24:5.

2   כסף הקדשים and כסף נפשית ערכו (in 2 Kgs 12:5) are unique in the Hebrew Bible, and כסף עובר is found only in Gen 23:16.

3   מכר(ים) ("assessor" or "acquaintance") is unique in the Hebrew Bible to 2 Kgs 12:6, 8.

4   בדק is synoptic only in 2 Kgs 22:5 // 2 Chr 34:8, and has been introduced from there to 2 Kgs 12.

5   However, 2 Chr 24:7 will report that Athaliah had used for the Baals "all the sacred donations of the house of Yahweh" (כל־קדשי בית־יהוה).

6   The specific date (the twenty-third year of Joash) in 2 Kgs 12:7 where there is none in 2 Chr 24:5b already makes it unlikely that that date had been part of the shared tradition. Additionally, this dating formula (ויהי בשנת עשרים ושלש שנה למלך יהואש) using a second שנה is never found in Chronicles, and so is never synoptic; but it is a frequent element (14x) of synchronic introductions throughout Kings.[17] It will be part of a rewriting within the book of Kings of the synoptic Joash story; and, since the very same date marks the accession in Samaria of Jehoahaz (2 Kgs 13:1), some relationship may have been intended.

7   Second Kings 12:8 and 2 Chr 24:6 open with several words in common: ויקרא המלך ליהוידע ויאמר מדוע ("And the king called to Jehoiada and said, 'Why'"), though they are differently expanded in Kings

---

17. 1 Kgs 16:8, 15, 23; 2 Kgs 8:25; 13:1, 10; 14:23; 15:1, 8, 13, 17, 23, 27; 16:1.

and Chronicles. The concluding מדוע ("why") is the unique synoptic instance of this interrogative.[18] However, while מדוע לא (as in 2 Chr 24:6) is common, מדוע אין in 2 Kgs 12:8 is unique.

8 Second Kings 12:10 and 2 Chr 24:8 share the information that "one chest" (ארון אחד) was "placed" (נתן) "as one entered the house of Yahweh" (Kings) or "outside the gate of the house of Yahweh" (Chronicles). Similarly 2 Kgs 12:11 and 2 Chr 24:11 share that, "when they saw that the money had grown great" (ויהי כראותם כי־רב הכסף), "the king's scribe" (ספר המלך) dealt with it, along with either the chief priest (Kings) or his representative (Chronicles).

9 They gave the money (2 Kgs 12:12 and 2 Chr 24:12) to those doing the work in Yahweh's house (Kings and Chronicles specifying different trades). The end of the work is reported quite differently in 2 Kgs 12:13 and 2 Chr 24:13.

10 Second Chronicles 24:14a reports quite briefly that a number of utensils (or vessels) were made for temple and sacrificial service from the balance of the money collected. Two of the items are utensils (or vessels) of gold and silver. Only this detail is shared with the list in 2 Kgs 12:14, which makes the categorical denial of any such manufactures: it was given to those who did the work, and they strengthened Yahweh's house. Both כסף אשם and כסף חטאות in 2 Kgs 12:17 seem to be unique expressions, and apparently return us to the topic mentioned in 2 Kgs 12:5 of specific sacral monies.[19] All in all, the brief statement in 2 Chr 24:14a, or an earlier form of it, will have been prior to the more extended denial in 2 Kgs 12:14(–17).

11 It was *then* (אז) that Hazael invaded, and again the reports in Kings and Chronicles are very differently stated. Second Chronicles 24:23 tells only of an attack on Jerusalem in which its officials were destroyed and booty sent to Damascus. Second Kings 12:18 reports a first assault by Aram on Gath, while 2 Kgs 12:19 has Jehoash collecting dedications made by several of his predecessors and all the gold in the house of Yahweh and the house of the king and sending them to Hazael in Damascus.

Instances of בית יהוה in both Kings and Chronicles:

2 Kgs 12:5 (2x), 10 (2x), 11, 12 (2x), 13, 14 (2x), 15, 17, 19
2 Chr 24:4, 7, 8, 12 (3x), 14 (2x), 18, 21

---

18. It is found only once (more) in a synoptic context (2 Sam 24:21a has no parallel in 1 Chr 21).

19. For guilt money going to Yahweh being for the priests, see Num 5:8.

12.3.14. Amaziah: 2 Kgs 12:22b; 14:2-22 // 2 Chr 24:27b-25:28

	2 Kings		2 Chronicles	
12:22b	וימלך אמציה בנו תחתיו		ויהי	24:27b
14:2	בן־עשרים וחמש שנה היה במלכו ועשרים ותשע שנה מלך בירושלם ושם אמו יהועדן מירושלם			25:1
3	ויעש הישר בעיני יהוה			2
	* רק לא *		* <u>בלבב שלם</u>	
	* כדוד אביו ככל אשר־עשה יואש אביו עשה			
4 רק הבמות לא־סרו עוד העם מזבחים ומקטרים בבמות				
5	ויהי כאשר חזקה הממלכה בידו			3
	את־עבדיו המכים את־ המלך אביו	* <u>ויך</u>	* ויהרג	
6 * המכים	ואת־בני* לא המית		* <u>הם</u>	4
* בספר תורת משה	* ככתוב * אשר צוה יהוה לאמר לא־* אבות על־ בנים		* כי * <u>בתורה בספר משה</u> *ימותו	
*יומתו	ובנים לא־* על־אבות		*ימותו	
* אם־ * יומת	כי *איש בחטאו *		ימותו	
7 הוא־הכה את־אדום <u>בגיא־המלח</u> <u>עשרת אלפים</u> <u>ותפש את־הסלע</u> <u>במלחמה</u> <u>ויקרא את־שמה יקתאל</u> <u>עד היום הזה</u>				
8 * <u>אז שלח אמציה</u> מלאכים	* אל־יהואש בן־יהואחז		17 * ויועץ אמציה מלך יהודה וישלח	
	בן־יהוא מלך ישראל לאמר			
* לכה	* נתראה פנים		* לך	18
	וישלח יהואש מלך־ישראל 9 אל־אמציה מלך־יהודה לאמר			

12. SHARED TEXT SAMPLED

	החוח אשר בלבנון שלח אל-הארז		
	אשר בלבנון לאמר		
	תנה-את-בתך לבני לאשה		
	ותעבר חית-השדה אשר בלבנון		
	ותרמס את-החוח		
הכה 10	* הכית את-אדום ונשאך לבד	* אמרת הנה	19
הכבד ושב	* בביתך למה תתגרה ברעה	* להכביד עתה שבה	
	ונפלת אתה ויהודה עמך		
11	* ולא-שמע אמציה	* כי מאלהים היא למען תתם ביד כי דרשו את אלהי אדום	20
			21
	ויעל יהואש מלך-ישראל		
	ויתראו פנים הוא ואמציה מלך-יהודה		
	בבית שמש אשר ליהודה		
12	וינגף יהודה לפני ישראל וינסו איש לאהלו		22
13	ואת-אמציה מלך-יהודה בן-יהואש		23
אחזיהו	בן-* תפש יהואש מלך-ישראל בבית שמש	*יהואחז	
ויבאו	* ירושלם ויפרץ בחומת ירושלם	* ויביאהו	
ב	*שער אפרים עד-שער הפנה ארבע מאות אמה	*מ	
14 *לקח את-	ו* כל-הזהב-והכסף ואת כל-הכלים הנמצאים		24
*יהוה	בית-*	*האלהים	
וב	*אצרות בית המלך ואת-בני התערבות וישב שמרונ[ה]	*עם-עבד אדום ואת-	
17	ויחי אמציהו בן-יואש מלך יהודה		25
	אחרי מות יהואש * מלך ישראל חמש עשרה שנה	* בן-יהואחז	
18	* ויתר דברי אמציהו הלא-* כתובים	26 * הראשניםוהאחרונים	
*הם		*הנם	

וְיִשְׂרָאֵל •
27 וּמֵעֵת אֲשֶׁר־סָר אֲמַצְיָה
מֵאַחֲרֵי יְהוָה

עַל־סֵפֶר •מַלְכֵי יְהוּדָה •   • דִּבְרֵי הַיָּמִים לְ

19   וַיִּקְשְׁרוּ עָלָיו קֶשֶׁר
בִּירוּשָׁלַ͏ִם
וַיָּנָס לָכִישָׁה וַיִּשְׁלְחוּ
אַחֲרָיו לָכִישָׁה
וַיְמִתֻהוּ שָׁם

28 • וַיִּקְבְּרוּ אֹתוֹ   וַיִּשָּׂאֻהוּ עַל־הַסּוּסִים •   20 • וַיִּקָּבֵר בִּירוּשָׁלַ͏ִם
• יְהוּדָה   עִם־אֲבֹתָיו בָּעִיר •   • דָּוִד

12:21b/24:27b And Amaziah his son became king in his place. 14:2/25:1 He was twenty-five years old at his becoming king; and twenty-nine years he was king in Jerusalem. And his mother's name was Jehoaddin from Jerusalem. 3/2 And he did right in Yahweh's eyes, only not *with a complete heart.* 5/3 And it came to be, as the kingdom became firm in his hand, he **struck down** his servants who struck down his father. 6/4 But *their* sons he did not put to death, as written *in the Torah, in the book of Moses that Yahweh commanded,* saying, "Fathers *shall not die* for sons, and sons *shall not die* for fathers, for *they shall die* each for his [own] sin." 7 **He it was struck Edom in the Valley of Salt—ten thousands—and seized Selah in battle. And he called its name Yoqteel till this day.** 8/17 Then Amaziah sent to Jehoash son of Jehoahaz son of Jehu king of Israel, saying, "Come, let us see each other's face." 9/18 And Jehoash king of Israel sent to Amaziah king of Judah, saying, "The thornbush on Lebanon sent to the cedar on Lebanon, saying, 'Give your daughter to my son as wife.' But a wild beast of Lebanon passed by and trampled the thornbush. 10/19 You have **indeed** struck down Edom, and your heart has lifted you. **Be honored and dwell** in your house. Why should you … and fall—you and Judah with you?" 11/20 And Amaziah did not listen. 11/21 And Jehoash king of Israel went up, and they saw each other's face—he and Amaziah king of Judah—in Beth-shemesh, which belongs to Judah. 12/22 And Judah was struck down before Israel, and each man fled to his tent. 13/23 And Amaziah king of Judah son of Jehoash son of Ahaziah was seized by Jehoash king of Israel in Beth-shemesh. And **they came** to Jerusalem, and he broke through in the wall of Jerusalem *from* the Ephraim Gate to the Corner Gate, four hundred cubits. 14/24 And **he took** all the gold and the silver, and all the vessels found in **Yahweh's** house **and in** the treasuries of the king's house and the pledged sons and returned to Samaria. 17/25 And

Amaziah son of Joash king of Judah lived [on] after the death of Jehoash king of Israel fifteen years. 18/26 And the rest of the deeds of Amaziah, are these not written in the book of the kings of Judah? 19/27 And they plotted against him a plot in Jerusalem; and he fled to Lachish, and they sent after him to Lachish and put him to death there. 20/28 And they lifted him on horses; and he was buried with his fathers in the city of **David**.

Notes

7/5–16   2 Chr 25:11 is built from 2 Kgs 14:7a, while elements of 14:7b feature in 25:12.

10/19   Kings' הכבד ושב ("Be honored and dwell") has become in Chronicles להכביד עתה שב ... (" ... making [you] honored. Now dwell").

• The addition of אמרת in 19 poses the question of preferring הנה over הכה.

13/23   תפש ("seize") is unique here in Chronicles, but it occurs eleven times more in Kings (1 Kgs 11:30; 13:4; 18:40; 20:18 [2x]; 2 Kgs 7:12; 10:14; 14:7; 16:9; 18:13; 25:6). (Note that these include 2 Kgs 18:13, one of many links beween Amaziah and Hezekiah.) If תפש was an original element of 2 Kgs 14:7, it was not adopted into 2 Chr 25:11–12 along with "Valley of Salt," "ten thousand," and "Sela."

14/24   שמרונה in Kings, but שמרון in Chronicles (contrast שכם in 1 Kgs 12:1, but שכמה in 2 Chr 10:1).

18/26   הלא הנם (Chronicles) may be a simple mistake for הלא הם (Kings)—הנם is used eleven times in Chronicles' tailpieces (Asa, Jehoshaphat, Amaziah, Jotham, Ahaz, Hezekiah, Manasseh [2x], Josiah, Jehoiakim).

12.3.15. Azariah/Uzziah: 2 Kgs 14:21; 15:2–7 // 2 Chr 26

1 *עזיהו	ויקחו כל־עם יהודה את־* 21 *<u>עזריה</u>
והוא בן־שש עשרה שנה	
	וימלכו אתו תחת אביו
	אמציהו
2 הוא בנה את־אילת	
וישבה ליהודה	
אחרי שכב־המלך עם־	
אבתיו	
3 * עזיהו	בן־שש עשרה * במלכו * 2 * <u>היה</u>

		וחמשים ושתים שנה מלך	4
		בירושלם	
		ושם אמו יכליהו מירושלם	
	3	ויעש הישר בעיני יהוה	
		ככל אשר־עשה אמציהו	
		אביו	
4 רק הבמות לא־סרו עוד			
העם מזבחים ומקטרים			
בבמות			
5 <u>וינגע יהוה את־המלך</u>			5–20
	ויהי * מצרע עד־יום מתו	עזיהו המלך *	21
	וישב בית החפשית *	מצרע כי נגזר מבית	
		יהוה	
* בן־המלך על־הבית	ויותם *	<u>בנו על־בית המלך</u> *	
	שפט את־עם הארץ		
6 * <u>עזריהו</u>	ויתר דברי *	עזיהו *	22
וכל־אשר עשה הלא־הם		הראשנים והאחרנים	
כתובים			
על־ספר דברי הימים		כתב ישעיהו בן־אמוץ	
למלכי יהודה		הנביא	
7 * <u>עזריה</u> *	וישכב * עם־אבתיו	עזיהו *	23
* בעיר דוד	ויקברו אתו עם־אבתיו *	בשדה הקבורה אשר *	
		למלכים	
		כי אמרו מצורע הוא	

1/1 And all the people of Judah took Azariah/Uzziah and made him king instead of his father Amaziah. 2/3 He was sixteen years old at his becoming king; and fifty-two years he was king in Jerusalem. And the name of his mother was Jecoliah of Jerusalem. 3/4 And he did what was right in Yahweh's eyes, according to all that his father Amaziah had done. 5/20 **And Yahweh struck the king**, 5/21 and he became leprous till the day of his death; and he lived in a ... house, and Jotham *his son was over the king's house* ruling the people of the land. 6/22 And the rest of the deeds of **Azariah**.... 7/23 And **Azariah** lay with his fathers, and they buried him with his fathers....

Notes

5/20 נגע *piel* opens 2 Kgs 15:5 and closes the long insert in Chronicles (26:5–20)—elsewhere only Gen 12:17.

5b/21 It is impossible to choose between "son of the king was over the house" (Kings) and "his son was over the house of the king" (Chronicles).

12.3.16. Jotham: 2 Kgs 15:32b–38 // 2 Chr 26:23b–27:9

		32b	וימלך יותם בנו תחתיו	26:23b
		33	בן־עשרים וחמש יותם במלכו	27:1
			ושש עשרה שנה מלך בירושלם	
			ושם אמו ירושא בת־צדוק	
		34	ויעש הישר בעיני יהוה	2
			ככל אשר־עשה עזיהו	
	* עשה		* אביו	
* הבמות לא־סרו	35		* רק	* לא־בא אל־היכל יהוה
* מזבחים ומקטרים בבמות			*עוד העם •	*ו * משחיתים
			הוא בנה את־שער בית־	
			* יהוה העליון *	* ובחומת העפל בנה לרב 3
		36	ויתר דברי יותם	7
* הלא־הם			* כתובים	* וכל־מלחמתיו ודרכיו הנם
* דברי הימים ל			* על־ספר * מלכי *יהודה	* ישראל ו
			בן־עשרים וחמש יותם במלכו	8
			ושש עשרה שנה מלך בירושלם	
		38	וישכב יותם עם־אבתיו	9
* ויקבר * אביו			* עם־אבתיו בעיר דוד *	* ויקברו אתו

15:32b/26:23b And Jotham his son became king instead of him. 33/27:1 Jotham was twenty-five years old when he became king, and sixteen years he was king in Jerusalem; and the name of his mother was Jerushah daughter of Zadok. 34/2 And he did what was right in Yahweh's eyes according to all that Uzziah his father had done; 35/2 only … the people were still…. 35/3 He it was built the Upper Gate of Yahweh's house. 36/7 And the rest of the deeds of Jotham … written on the book of the kings of Judah. 38/9 And Jotham lay with his fathers and **was buried** with his fathers in the city of David.

Notes

34/2 Jotham's father is given as עזיהו in Kings as well as Chronicles—in Kings perhaps under the influence of nonsynoptic 15:32.

35/3 לרב is used synoptically in 1 Kgs 10:10 and 27 but is a favorite of Chronicles (more than 30x).

12.3.17. Ahaz: 2 Kgs 15:38b–16:20 // 2 Chr 27:9b–28:27

	15:38b	וימלך אחז בנו תחתיו	27:9b
	16:2	בן־עשרים שנה אחז במלכו	28:1
		ושש עשרה שנה מלך בירושלם	
		ולא עשה הישר בעיני	
* אלהיו		יהוה * כדוד אביו	
3 * בדרך		וילך * מלכי ישראל	2 * בדרכי
		וגם *	* מסכות עשה לבעלים
			3 והוא הקטיר בגיא בן־הנם
* את־בנו העביר		* באש כתעבות הגוים אשר הוריש יהוה מפני בני ישראל	* ויעבר את־בניו
	4	ויזבח ויקטר בבמות ועל־הגבעות ותחת כל־עץ רענן	4
	5–18		5–25
19 *אחז אשר עשה		ויתר דברי*	26 *ו וכל־דרכיו הראשנים והאחרונים
* הלא־הם		* כתובים על־ספר	* הנם
* דברי הימים ל		*מלכי יהודה •	• וישראל
	20	וישכב אחז עם־אבתיו	27
* עם־אבתיו • דוד		ויקבר* בעיר •	*הו • בירושלם
			כי לא הביאהו לקברי מלכי ישראל

15:38b/27:29b And Ahaz his son became king in his place. 16:2/28:1 Ahaz was twenty years old when he became king; and sixteen years he was king in Jerusalem; and he did not do what was right in Yahweh's eyes like David his father. 3/2 And he walked in the **way** of the kings of Israel. 3/3 **And even his son he made pass** in the fire like the abominations of the nations that Yahweh had dispossessed before the sons of Israel. 4/4 And he sacrificed and offered incense [enthusiastically] at the high places and on the hills and under every green tree.... 20/27 And he lay with his fathers, and he was buried....

Notes

2/1 ולא עשה הישר ("and he did not do what was right") in place of ויעש הרע ("and he did what was bad") is unique—it comes after the longest series (4x) of kings who had "done right" (Joash, Amaziah, Azariah, Jotham).

- Also unique is the addition of אלהיו in Kings after the divine name: in three introductions and one conclusion it is part of a Chronicles plus. אלהיו (on its own) is synoptic only in 2 Kgs 19:37 // 2 Chr 32:21—where it follows יהוה in a synoptic context it is always a plus. It may depend here on Isa 7:11, where Isaiah challenges Ahaz: "Ask yourself a sign from Yahweh your God" (שאל־לך אות מעם יהוה אלהיך).

- Chronicles plus in verses 2–3 takes off from גם in the older text and anticipates ויקטר ("offered incense") in verse 4.

- After this substantial shared introduction, common content in the reports of Ahaz in Kings and Chronicles is even more elusive than in the case of Jehoash (12.3.13). The main themes of the Ahaz reports are:

1.	War with Aram and Israel	5	5–15
2.	Role of Edom	6	17
	N.B. בעת ההיא in 6 and 16!		
3.	Appeal to Assyria	7	16
4.	Philistine raids		18
5.	Judah brought low by Ahaz's faithlessness		19
6.	Treasures sent and Assyria does [not] listen	8–9	20–21
7.	Ahaz, Uriah (Isa 8:2), and the altar seen in Damascus (7:8; 8:4)	10–16	22–23
8.	Further cultic actions	17–18	24–25

Second Kings 16:10–16 features the altar copied from a model in Damascus. Second Chronicles 28:5–15 offers much more detail on Judah's war with Israel and Aram[20] before Ahaz's appeal to Assyria for help against

---

20. The note about booty and plunder (2 Chr 28:8) will be related to Maher-shalal-hash-baz in Isa 8:1, 3.

them. And the brief mention of Edom is placed differently in each. It is no surprise that בית יהוה features in themes 6 and 8 (in fact, בית האלהים in 2 Chr 28:24), and also in the report of the Damascus altar (2 Kgs 16:14).

בעת ההיא ("at that time") is also similarly, but not identically, placed (themes 2 and 3): in 2 Kgs 16:6 it introduces the note about Edom; but in 2 Chr 28:16, the appeal to Assyria. The same is true, at least at first sight, of אז ("then") in 2 Kgs 12:18 and 2 Chr 24:17. However, like that temporal connective, בעת ההיא can be seen here as pointing to an earlier shared text.

Prior to the Ahaz story, Damascus had featured only twice in the synoptic record: David's victory over Aram-Damascus (2 Sam 8:5-6 // 1 Chr 18:5-6) and Asa sending tribute there (1 Kgs 15:18 // 2 Chr 16:2). In the Ahaz story, both Kings and Chronicles assign an important role to Damascus—but differently. In Kings, Damascus features repeatedly, but only in the central account of the new altar commissioned by Ahaz on the model of one he had seen in that city (2 Kgs 16:9, 10 [2x], 11 [2x], 12[21]). In Chronicles, the city appears twice, immediately after the shared introduction (2 Chr 28:5) and shortly before the shared conclusion (28:23).

2 The notes about the Edomites (2 Kgs 16:6; 2 Chr 28:17) share two features: (1) the plural gentilic אדמים is synoptic only here;[22] both verses end with a clause including וישבו. However, Kings understands this as "they lived [there]" (from ישב), while Chronicles reads it as "they took away captives" (from שבה, which has been used 3x already in this expanded narrative: 2 Chr 28:5, 8, 11).

Second Chronicles 28:17 notes more briefly that Edom had regained the upper hand over Judah. Second Kings 16:6 contributes more precision: Edom's ascendancy over Judah was achieved by the king of Aram who restored Elat to them—they drove out the Judahites and settled it themselves. The port of Elat is synoptic twice: in the Solomon story (1 Kgs 9:26 // 2 Chr 8:17), and as rebuilt and restored to Judah by Azariah/Uzziah (2 Kgs 14:22 // 2 Chr 26:2). The victory over Edom by Amaziah (2 Kgs 14:7; cf. 2 Chr 25:11-12) that led to this recovery of Elat by Azariah his son had brought to an end the revolt by Edom reported in 2 Kgs 8:20-22 // 2 Chr 21:8-10. That synoptic report included the immediately previous synoptic instance of בעת ההיא ("at that time"); and two further elements of the report may be the origin of two pluses in 2 Kgs 16—אז ("then") at the start

---

21. The final two instances do not appear in LXX.

22. In 2 Chr 25:14 it is part of an expansion corresponding to 2 Kgs 14:7, which uses the normal singular אדום.

of 16:5, from 2 Kgs 8:21 // 2 Chr 21:9; and עד היום הזה ("until this day") at the end of 2 Kgs 16:6, from 2 Kgs 8:22 // 2 Chr 21:10.

If as in 2 Chr 28:16 בעת ההיא ("at that time") originally introduced the appeal to Assyria, we must suppose that Kings promoted the note about Judah and Edom as well as expanding it. Two linguistic features of 2 Kgs 16:6 are unusual and possibly late: (1) היהודים ("the Judahites") is never found in Chronicles, and appears elsewhere in the Former Prophets only in 2 Kgs 25:25 (part of the Kings plus vv. 22–26 not in Jeremiah).[23] The verb נשל is rare, and the *piel* unique to this verse; in Deut 7:1 and 22 the *qal* is used apparently in the same sense "drive out."

7   When Ahaz met his Assyrian benefactor in Damascus, he saw an altar and had it copied in Jerusalem. Against an older interpretation that Ahaz was thereby demonstrating allegiance to Tiglath-pileser, it has been observed that the Assyrians did not practice animal sacrifice. Whether or not more original, 2 Chr 28:23 reports that Ahaz sacrificed to the gods of Damascus who had shown their superiority by defeating him.

Much of the terminology in 2 Kgs 16:10–16 is quite unusual. דמות (v. 10) is unique in the Former Prophets, and appears only in 2 Chr 4:3 within the Hebrew Bible narrative books. תבנית appears in the Former Prophets only in (the probably related) Josh 22:28; and also 1 Chr 28:11, 12, 18, 19. קטר *hiphil* (2 Kgs 16:13, 15) is never synoptic. דם השלמים appears only in 2 Kgs 16:13 and Lev 7:14, 33; and דם עלה (2 Kgs 16:15) is unique. זרק ("sprinkle," 2 Kgs 16:13, 15) appears only here in the Former Prophets.

הסך נסכים ("to pour libations," also 2 Kgs 16:13 and 15) is a common theme in Jeremiah: to other gods (7:18; 19:13;[24] 32:29), and to the queen of heaven (5x in Jer 44). When 2 Chr 28:23 portrays Ahaz praying to the gods of Damascus because they had helped Aram defeat him, it may be reflecting this.

12.3.18. Hezekiah: 2 Kgs 18–20 // 2 Chr 28:27b–32:32

28:27b		וימלך חזקיהו בנו תחתיו	
29:1	היה במלכו *	בן־עשרים וחמש שנה *	18:1
		ועשרים ותשע שנה מלך	
		בירושלם	

---

23. It is more common in Jeremiah (6x), Nehemiah (7x), and often in Esther.
24. Note yet another link between themes in Kings and Jer 19 (see the end of 9.9 above).

2	ושם אמו אבי[ה] בת־זכריה		
	ויעש הישר בעיני יהוה	3	
	ככל אשר עשה דוד אבי		
			4 **הוא הסיר את־הבמות**
32:32 • וחסדיו	• ויתר דברי חזקיה	20:20 • וכל־גבורתו	
		ואשר עשה את־הברכה	
		ואת־התעלה ויבא את־	
		המים העירה	
• הנם • בחזון ישעיהו	• כתובים •	הלא־הם •	
בן־אמוץ הנביא			
• וישראל	על־ספר •		
	*מלכי יהודה •	ל •	
		דברי הימים •	
33	וישכב חזקיה עם־אבתיו	21	
*הו במעלה קברי בני דוד	ויקבר *	עם־אבתיו בעיר דוד *	
וכבוד עשו־לו במותו כל־			
יהודה וישבי ירושלם			

18:1/28:27b And Hezekiah his son became king in his place, 2/29:1 twenty-five years old; and twenty-nine years he was king in Jerusalem; and his mother's name was Abi(jah) daughter of Zechariah. 3/2 And he did what was right in Yahweh's eyes according to all that David his father did. 4 **He it was removed the high places.**...

I argued in chapter 10 that the very different accounts of the reign of Hezekiah had resulted from expansive rewriting of shared material, just as in other portions of Kings and Chronicles, although much more substantially expansive than elsewhere. The previously published table below illustrates the content common to the most similar portions: 2 Kgs 18:17–37 and 2 Chr 32:9–19.[25] However, as in the cases of Jehoash and Ahaz, any reconstruction would be very tentative.

2 Chr 32:9–19	2 Kgs 18:17–37	Elsewhere in 2 Kgs 18–20	Notes
9 שלח, "send"	18:17		
9 מלך אשור, "the king of Assyria"	18:17		
9 לכיש, "Lachish"	18:17		

---

25. Slightly modified from Auld, "Prophetic Narrative," 56–57.

12. SHARED TEXT SAMPLED 263

9 ירושלם, "Jerusalem"	18:17		
10 כה אמר מלך אשור, "so says the king of Assyria"	18:19		
10 בטח, "trust" (verb)	18:19–24 (6x) + בטחון (noun) in 18:19	18:5; 19:10	nowhere else in Kings
11–17 ... יציל (8x), "deliver"	18:29–35 (7x)	19:12; 20:6; and cf. 19:11 20:6	only 2 Kgs 17:39
11 מכף מלך אשור, "from the hand of the king of Assyria"			
11, 15 מסית, "entice"	18:32	cf. 19:10	
12 הסיר את־במתיו ואת־מזבחתיו, "he removed his high places and his altars"	18:22	18:4 הוא הסיר את־הבמות	unique in the Hebrew Bible (occasionally one of these two objects is construed with הסיר; but both, nowhere else)
12 ויאמר ליהודה ולירושלם, "and he said to Judah and Jerusalem"	18:22		unique in the Hebrew Bible
12 לפני מזבח אחד תשתחוו, "before one altar you shall prostrate yourselves"	18:22 לפני המזבח הזה תשתחוו, "before this altar ..."		
13–15 יכול, "is able" 13 infinitive absolute	18:23, 29 18:30, 33 (Kings +)		
13, 17 אלהי גוי הארצות, "gods of the nations of the lands"	אלהי הארצות in 18:35		
13–17 מידי, "from the hands of"	18:34–35		

14 אלהי הגוים, "gods of the nations"	18:33	19:12	Deut 29:17
14 הגוים אשר החרימו, "the nations that they put to the ban"		cf. 19:11, but there with הארצות	
15 ישיא, "deceive"	18:29	19:10	
15 ואל-תאמינו לו, "and do not rely on him"	18:30 ואל-יבטח אתכם		האמין in 2 Kgs 17:14
17 ספרים, "letters"		19:14; 20:12	different purpose
17 לחרף, "to scorn"		19:4, 16, 22, 23	
17 "any god save people from the hand of the king of Assyria"	18:33		
18 ויקרא בקול גדול, "and he called in a loud voice"	18:28		
18 יהודית, "Judean"	18:26, 28		only Neh 13:24
18 אשר על-החומה, "who are on the wall"	18:26, 27		
19 מעשה ידי ה[ה]אדם, "work of human hands"		19:18	cf. 2 Kgs 22:17 // 2 Chr 34:25

- Synoptic אלהי only in 2 Kgs 19:37 // 2 Chr 32:21.
- Synoptic יהוה אלהינו only in 2 Kgs 18:22; 19:19 // 2 Chr 32:8, 11; and singular יהוה אלהי in 1 Kgs 5:19; 8:28 // 2 Chr 2:3; 6:19.
- Only in 1 Kgs 10:9 // 2 Chr 9:8 is יהוה אלהיך synoptic—that is, not in 2 Kgs 19:4, 10; and, as for יהוה אלהיכם, 2 Chr 35:3 may be influenced by 2 Kgs 23:21.
- וחסדיו (2 Chr 32:32) is shared only with Josiah (35:26)—both recall חסדי דויד in 6:42.
- וכל-גבורתו (2 Kgs 20:20) is shared with 1 Kgs 15:23 (Asa) and 2 Kgs 10:34 (Jehu). וגבורתו is commoner: 1 Kgs 16:5 (Baasha), 27 (Omri); 22:46 (Jehoshaphat); 2 Kgs 13:8 (Jehoahaz), 12 (northern Joash); 14:15 (northern Jehoash), 28 (Jeroboam); 1 Chr 29:30 (David).
- Elsewhere כבוד is the object of עשה only in Gen 31:1.

12. SHARED TEXT SAMPLED

12.3.19. Manasseh: 2 Kgs 20:21b–21:18 // 2 Chr 32:33b–33:20

	20:21b	וימלך מנשה בנו תחתיו	32:33b
	21:1	בן־שתים עשרה שנה מנשה במלכו וחמשים וחמש שנה מלך בירושלם *	33:1
* ושם אמו חפצי־בה			
	2	ויעש הרע בעיני יהוה כתעבות הגוים אשר הוריש יהוה מפני בני ישראל	2
	3	וישב ויבן את־הבמות אשר * חזקיהו אביו ויקם מזבחת * ויעש *	3
* אבד			<u>נתץ</u> *
<u>לבעל</u> • <u>אשרה</u> כאשר עשה אחאב מלך ישראל			* לבעלים • אשרות
		וישתחו לכל־צבא השמים ויעבד אתם	
	4	ובנה מזבחת בבית יהוה אשר אמר יהוה בירושלם * שמי • *	4
<u>אשים את־</u> *			* יהיה • לעולם
	5	ויבן מזבחת לכל־צבא השמים בשתי חצרות בית־יהוה	5
	6	ו* העביר את־* באש •	6 *הוא יבניו • בגי בן־הנם
<u>יבנו</u> *			* וכשף
		וענן ונחש * ועשה אוב וידענים הרבה לעשות הרע בעיני יהוה להכעיסו	
<u>האשרה</u> *	7	וישם את־פסל * אשר עשה	7 * הסמל
<u>יהוה</u> *		בבית * אשר אמר • אל־דוד ואל־שלמה בנו בבית הזה ובירושלם אשר בחרתי מכל שבטי ישראל אשים את־שמי לעולם	* האלהים • אלהים
<u>להניד</u> *	8	ולא אסיף * רגל ישראל מן־האדמה אשר * רק אם־ישמרו לעשות ככל אשר צויתים	8 * להסיר את־ * העמדתי לאבתיכם
<u>נתתי לאבותם</u> *			

* אשר צוה אתם עבדי 9 ולא שמעו *ם	* משה * ולכל־התורה ביד	* והחקים והמשפטים
	ויתע* מנשה * לעשות את־הרע מן־הגוים אשר השמיד יהוה מפני בני ישראל	9 * את־יהודה וישבי ירושלם
10 * ביד־עבדיו הנביאים לאמר	* וידבר יהוה	10 * אל־מנשה ואל־עמו ולא הקשיבו
11-16 17	* ויתר דברי מנשה	11-17 18 * ותפלתו אל־אלהיו ודברי החזים המדברים אליו בשם יהוה אלהי ישראל הנם על־ דברי מלכי ישראל
*אשר עשה ו * אשר חטא * הלא־הם על־ספר דברי הימים למלכי יהודה 18 * בגן־ * בגן־עזא	* וכל־ * חטאתו * כתובים וישכב מנשה עם־אבתיו ויקבר* *ביתו *	19 * ותפלתו והעתר־לו * ומעלו ... הכנעו * הנם * על־דברי חוזי 20 *הו

20:21b/32:33b And Manasseh his son became king in his place. 21:1/33:1 Twelve years old was Manasseh at his becoming king, and fifty-five years he was king in Jerusalem. 2/2 And he did what was evil in Yahweh's eyes like the abominations of the nations that Yahweh had dispossessed before the sons of Israel. 3/3 And he rebuilt the high places that Hezekiah his father had *torn down*, and raised altars to **Baal** and made **an Asherah** and prostrated to the whole host of heaven and served them. 4/4 And he built altars in Yahweh's house, where Yahweh had stated, "In Jerusalem I shall set my name." 5/5 And he built altars to the whole host of heaven in the two courts of Yahweh's house. 6/6 And he made his **son** pass in the fire,... and multiplied doing evil in Yahweh's eyes, vexing *him*. 7/7 And he set the image of the Asherah he had made in Yahweh's house, who had stated to David and to Solomon his son, "In this house and in Jerusalem which I have chosen from all Israel's staffs I shall set my name forever. 8/8 And I shall not again make Israel's foot **wander** from the land which **I gave to their fathers**—only if they keep to doing according to all I have commanded them and all the Torah ... Moses...." 9/9 ... and Manasseh misled

them, doing more evil than the nations that Yahweh had blotted out before the sons of Israel. 10/10 And Yahweh spoke.... 17/18 And the rest of the deeds of Manasseh ... and his sin ... written.... 18/20 And Manasseh lay with his fathers, and they buried him in his house.

Notes

3/3 נתץ (Chronicles) may have the support of LXX in Kings. אבד (Kings) is never used in Chronicles (whether *qal*, *piel*, or *hiphil*); yet its usage in Samuel–Kings does not appear early (see 12.3.12 above on 2 Kgs 11:1).

5/5 בשתי חצרות בית־יהוה ("in the two courts of Yahweh's house") is unique synoptically, but repeated in 2 Kgs 23:12.

6/6 The details of the various divinatory procedures need not concern us here, and they have been left untranslated. Four are specified in both Kings and Chronicles, and a fifth (in third place) in Chronicles. ענן never reappears in Samuel–Kings or Chronicles; נחש never reappears in Chronicles but is used in 1 Kgs 20:33 and 2 Kgs 17:17; and [ם]אוב וידעני reappears in 2 Kgs 23:24 as well as featuring largely in 1 Sam 28.

• The absence in Kings of the suffix at the end appears accidental.

8/8 The combination רגל ישראל ("Israel's foot") is unique, as is Kings' הניד. Chronicles' הסיר is attested both synoptically and separately in both Kings and Chronicles. Chronicles' use both of a common verb and of the object marker את־ may suggest it is derivative.

• Chronicles' והחקים והמשפטים may be compared with Deut 4:45; 5:28; 6:20 (cf. Deut 4:5, 8, 14; Mal 3:22)—yet the closest parallel may be synoptic וחקי ומשפטי תשמור in 1 Kgs 9:4 // 2 Chr 7:17.

12.3.20. Amon: 2 Kgs 21:18b–26 // 2 Chr 33:20b–24

	18b	וימלך אמון בנו תחתיו	20b
	19	בן־עשרים ושתים שנה	21
		אמון במלכו	
		ושתים שנים מלך	
ושם אמו משלמת בת־ *		בירושלם *	
חרוץ מן־יטבה			
	20	ויעש הרע בעיני יהוה	22
וילך בכל־הדרך *	21 *	כאשר עשה מנשה אביו	
אשר הלך אביו			ולכל־הפסילים אשר *
			עשה מנשה אביו

ויעבד את־הגללים		זבח אמון ויעבדם
אשר עבד אביו וישתחו		
להם		
22 ויעזב את־יהוה אלהי		23 ולא נכנע מלפני יהוה
אבתיו		כהכנע מנשה אביו
ולא הלך בדרך יהוה		כי הוא אמון הרבה
		אשמה
	ויקשרו עבדי* עליו	24 *וַ
23 * אמון	וימיתו* בביתו	*הו
* את־המלך	ויכו עם־הארץ את כל־	25
24	הקשרים על־המלך אמון	
	וימליכו עם־הארץ את־	
	יאשיהו בנו תחתיו	
25 ויתר דברי אמון אשר		
עשה הלא־הם כתובים		
על־ספר דברי הימים		
למלכי יהודה		
26 ויקברו אתו בקברתו		
בגן־עזה		
וימלך יאשיהו בנו תחתיו		

18b/20b And Amon his son became king in his place. 19/21 Amon was twenty-two years old on becoming king, and two years he was king in Jerusalem. 20/22 And he did what was evil in Yahweh's eyes as Manasseh his father had done. 21/22 **And he served the "idols" that his father had served and prostrated himself to them.** 23/24 And *his* servants plotted against him and put *him* to death in his house. 24/25 And the people of the land struck down all the plotters against King Amon; and the people of the land made Josiah his son king in his place.

Notes

21/22 הגללים (Kings) corresponds to הפסילים in Chronicles (shared use of עבד suggests a link). It never appears in Chronicles, is commonest in Ezekiel (some 40x), combined with תועבותיך (16:36), טמא (20:7, 18; 22:4; 23:7, 30; 36:18; 37:23), טהר (36:25), חטא (23:49), and תעה (44:10).[26] In 2 Kgs 23:24 הגללים end a list summed up by כל־השקוצים.

---

26. See also Lev 26:30; Deut 29:16; 1 Kgs 15:12 (see 5.4.1 above); 21:26; 2 Kgs 17:12; 21:11, 21; 23:24; Jer 50:2.

12. SHARED TEXT SAMPLED

26 וימלך יאשיהו בנו תחתיו (Kings only) looks like a recap after an insertion.

12.3.21. Josiah: 2 Kgs 22:1–23:30 // 2 Chr 34:1–36:1

*שמנה שנה 22:1	בן־* יאשיהו במלכו ושלשים ואחת שנה מלך בירושלם *	34:1 *<u>שמנה שנים</u>
	ושם אמו ידידה בת־עדיה מבצקת	
	2 ויעש הישר בעיני יהוה	2
<u>בכל־דרך</u> *	וילך * דוד אביו ולא־סר ימין ושמאול	* בדרכי
3 <u>ויהי בשמנה עשרה</u> <u>שנה</u> למלך יאשיהו		8 ובשנת שמונה עשרה <u>למלכו</u> לטהר הארץ והבית
המלך *	שלח * את־שפן בן־אצליהו * בן־משלם הספר בית יהוה	ואת־מעשיהו שר־העיר ואת יואח בן־יואחז המזכיר לחזק את־בית יהוה
4 לאמר עלה *	אל־חלקיהו הכהן הגדול	9 * ויבאו
* יהוה ויתם * את־הכסף המובא בית * אשר אספו * שמרי הסף <u>מאת העם</u>		* אלהים * ויתנו הלוים מיד מנשה ואפרים ומכל שארית ישראל ומכל־יהודה ובנימין וישבי ירושלם
5	ויתנה על־יד עשי המלאכה המפקדים בבית יהוה	10
* <u>לעשי</u>	ויתנו אתו * המלאכה אשר * בבית יהוה	* עושי * עשים
* <u>לחזק בדק</u>	* הבית	* לבדוק ולחזק
6 * <u>ולגדרים</u> <u>ולקנות עצים ואבני מחצב</u>	* לחרשים ולבנים *	11 * ויתנו לקנות אבני מחצב ועצים למחברות ולקרות את־הבתים אשר השחיתו מלכי יהודה
לחזק את־הבית 7 אך לא־יחשב אתם הכסף הנתן על־ידם כי		

12 והאנשים עשים באמונה 12aβ–14		<u>באמונה הם עשים</u>
15 ויען חלקיהו ויאמר * על־שפן הספר * ספר התורה מצאתי בבית יהוה ויתן חלקיה את־הספר אל־שפן * ויקראהו *		8 * <u>ויאמר חלקיהו הכהן הגדול</u> 9
16 את־ * לאמר כל אשר־נתן ביד־עבדיך הם עשים	ויבא שפן *הספר אל־המלך וישב את־המלך דבר *	<u>ויאמר</u> *
17 ויתיכו * יהוה	את־הכסף הנמצא בבית *	<u>התיכו עבדיך</u> *
* המפקדים ועל־יד עשי המלאכה	ויתנהו על־יד *	* <u>עשי המלאכה המפקדים בית יהוה</u> 10
18	ויגד שפן הספר למלך לאמר ספר נתן לי חלקיה הכהן	
*־בו	ויקרא* שפן לפני המלך	*הו 11
19	ויהי כשמע המלך את־ דברי * התורה ויקרע את־בגדיו	* ספר 12
20	ויצו המלך את־ חלקיה * ואת־אחיקם בן־שפן ואת־* בן־מיכיה ואת־שפן הספר ואת עשיה עבד־המלך לאמר לכו דרשו את־יהוה בעדי	* הכהן *עכבור
עבדון 21 הנשאר בישראל וביהודה ובעד־ אשר נמצא	ועד־* העם * על־דברי הספר * כי־גדולה חמת יהוה אשר־	13 *<u>העם ובעד־כל יהודה</u> * הנמצא הזה
נתכה *<u>שמרו</u> * <u>את־דבר יהוה</u> על־הספר הזה 22 ואשר המלך	היא * בנו * על אשר לא־* אבתנו * לעשות ככל־הכתוב * וילך חלקיהו אל־חלדה הנביאה אשת שלם בן־* בן־* שמר הבגדים	* נצתה *שמעו * על־דברי הספר הזה * <u>עלינו</u> 14 * <u>הכהן ואחיקם ועכבור ושפן ועשיה</u>
*תוקהת *חסרה		*<u>תקוה</u> *<u>תרחס</u>

12. SHARED TEXT SAMPLED

	והיא ישבת בירושלם במשנה		
	וידברו אליה *	* כזאת	
* אליהם 15	ותאמר * כה־אמר יהוה אלהי ישראל אמרו לאיש אשר־שלח אתכם אלי	להם *	23
16	כה אמר יהוה הנני מביא רעה על־המקום הזה ועל־ישביו את		24
*דברי *	כל־* הספר אשר קרא* מלך יהודה	* האלות הכתובות על־ו לפני	
17	תחת אשר עזבוני ויקטרו לאלהים אחרים למען הכעיסני בכל מעשה ידיהם		25
* ונצתה	* חמתי במקום הזה ולא תכבה	* ותתך	
18	ואל־מלך יהודה השלח אתכם		26
* את־יהוה	לדרש * כה תאמרו אליו * כה אמר יהוה אלהי ישראל הדברים אשר שמעת	* ביהוה	
* מפני יהוה 19 * אשר דברתי	יען רך־לבבך ותכנע * בשמעך * על־המקום הזה ועל־ישביו * להיות לשמה ולקללה	מלפני האלהים * את־דבריו * ותכנע לפניו	27 *
	ותקרע את־בגדיך ותבך לפני		
	וגם אנכי שמעתי נאם־יהוה		
* לכן 20	* הנני אספך על־אבתיך ונאספת אל־קברתיך בשלום ולא־תראינה עיניך בכל־הרעה אשר־אני מביא על־המקום הזה *		28
	וישיבו את־המלך דבר	ועל־ישביו *	
23:1 * ויאספו אליו	וישלח המלך * כל־זקני יהודה וירושלם	* ויאסף את	29

30 ויעל המלך בית יהוה	2 ויעל המלך בית יהוה	
והלוים וכל־איש יהודה וי ישבי	*כל־	
מגדול ועד־קטן ירושלם *	*אתו	
	והכהנים * וכל־העם *	*והנביאים
		למקטן ועד־גדול
	ויקרא באזניהם	
	את־כל־דברי ספר הברית	
	הנמצא *בית יהוה	*ב
31 *עמדו	ויעמד המלך על־	3 *העמוד
	ויכרת את־הברית לפני	
	יהוה	
*י	ללכת אחר* יהוה ולשמר	
*את־	מצותיו ו* עדותיו ו חקיו	*את־ *את
*בו יו	בכל־לב* ובכל־נפש•	
*לעשות	* את־דברי הברית •	להקים * הזאת
	הכתבים על־הספר הזה	
	ויעמד *	*כל־העם
32 * את כל־הנמצא		
בירושלם ובנימין		ברבית
ויעשו ישבי ירושלם		
כברית		
אלהים אלהי אבותיהם		
33 ויסר יאשיהו את כל־		
התועבות		
מכל־הארצות אשר לבני		
ישראל		
ויעבד את כל־הנמצא		
בישראל		
לעבוד את־יהוה אלהיהם		
כל־ימיו לא סרו		
מאחרי יהוה אלהי		
אבותיהם		
		21 ויצו המלך את־כל־
		העם לאמר
		עשו פסח ליהוה אלהיכם
		ככתוב על ספר הברית
		הזה
35:18 *ן • פסח כמהו	*לא נעשה •	22 * כי • בפסח הזה
בישראל		
*שמואל הנביא	מימי *	* השפטים אשר שפטו
		את־ישראל
	וכל * מלכי ישראל •	* ימי • ומלכי יהודה

12. SHARED TEXT SAMPLED

		לא־עשו כפסח אשר־עשה יאשיהו
		והכהנים והלוים וכל־יהודה
		וישראל הנמצא ויושבי ירושלם
23 * כי אם־	*בשמנה עשרה שנה	19
* <u>למלך</u>	* יאשיהו	* למלכות
* ליהוה בירושלם	נעשה הפסח הזה *	
28 * וכל־אשר עשה	* ויתר דברי יאשיהו	26 * וחסדיו ככתוב בתורת יהוה
		27 ודבריו הראשנים והאחרנים
* הלא־הם • דברי הימים	* כתובים על־ספר •	* הנם
*ל	*מלכי ־יהודה	• ישראל ו
29 בימיו		20 אחרי כל־זאת אשר הכין יאשיהו את־הבית
* פרעה	עלה * נכו מלך־מצרים	* להלחם בכרכמיש
* על־מלך אשור • נהר־	* על־ ־פרת	ויצא לקראתו יאשיהו
וילך המלך יאשיהו לקראתו		

וימיתהו במגדו כראותו אתו		
30 וירכבהו עבדיו מת ממגדו ויבאהו ירושלם ויקברהו בקברתו		
	ויקח עם־הארץ את־יהואחז בן־יאשיהו	36:1
* וימשחו אתו	* וימלכהו תחת אביו	• בירושלם

22:1/34:1 Josiah was eight years old on becoming king, and thirty-one years he was king in Jerusalem. 2/2 And he did what was right in the eyes of Yahweh, and walked in the way of David his father and did not turn to right or left. 3/8 **And it came to be in the eighteenth year** *of his being king*, he sent Shaphan son of Azaliah 4/9 to Hilkiah the great priest, that he might melt down the silver brought in to Yahweh's house, that the keepers of the threshold had collected from the people, 5/10 and put it in the hands of those doing the work—those appointed in Yahweh's house, that they should give it to those doing the project that is in Yahweh's house,

strengthening the ruptures of the house, 6/11—to the carpenters and the builders—7/12 trustworthily they are dealing. 8/15 **And Hilkiah said** to Shaphan the scribe, "The Torah book have I found in Yahweh's house," and Hilkiah gave the book to Shaphan, 9/16 and Shaphan brought the book to the king and returned the king word and said, 9/17 "Your servants have melted the silver found in the house and put it in the hands of those doing the project, those appointed in Yahweh's house." 10/18 And Shaphan the priest declared to the king: "A book has Hilkiah the priest given to me." And Shaphan read *in it* before the king. 11/19 And it came to be as the king heard the words of the Torah, he rent his clothes, 12/20 and the king commanded Hilkiah and Ahikam son of Shaphan and Achbor son of Micaiah and Shaphan the scribe and Asaiah the king's servant, saying, 13/21 "Go and seek Yahweh for me and for **the people and for all Judah** about the words of this found book, for great is Yahweh's wrath that has been kindled on us, because our fathers *have not observed the word of Yahweh*, acting according to all that is written **about us**." 14/22 And Hilkiah the priest **and Ahikam and Achbor and Shaphan and Asaiah** went to Huldah, wife of Shallum son of **Tikvah** son of **Harhas**, keeper of the clothes, and she was living in Jerusalem in the Second [City], and they spoke to her. 15/23 And she said to them: "Thus says Yahweh God of Israel—say to the man who sent you to me—16/24 thus says Yahweh, 'See I am bringing evil on this place and on its inhabitants—all **the words** of the book that the king of Judah read—17/25 for that they have abandoned me and burned incense to other gods in order to vex me with all the work of their hands, and my anger will be **kindled** in this place and will not be quenched.' 18/26 And to the king of Judah who is sending you to seek **Yahweh** thus shall you say to him, 'Thus says Yahweh God of Israel, "As for the words that you have heard—19/27 because your heart was soft and you were humble before **Yahweh**, on your hearing **what I had spoken** against this place and against its inhabitants, and you rent your clothing and wept before me, I too have heard—utterance of Yahweh. 20/28 I shall clearly gather you to your fathers and you shall be gathered to your graves in peace, and your eyes shall not look on all the evil that I am bringing against this place."'" And they brought the king back word. 23:1/29 And the king sent and *he gathered* all the elders of Judah and Jerusalem, 2/30 and the king went up to Yahweh's house and every man of Judah and the inhabitants of Jerusalem and the priests and the **prophets** and all the people, and he read in their ears all the words of the covenant book found in Yahweh's house. 3/31 And the king stood by **the pillar** and instituted the covenant before

Yahweh, to follow Yahweh and to keep his commandments and his decrees and his statutes with all heart and with all soul, practicing the words of the covenant written on this book. **And all the people stood in the covenant.** 23:21 **And the king commanded all the people, saying, "Make Passover to Yahweh your God as written on this covenant book."** 22/35:18 And there was not made **like this Passover** from the days *of Samuel the prophet* and all the kings of Israel. 23/19 In the eighteenth year of **King** Josiah this Passover was made. 29/20 Neco king of Egypt went up.... 30/36:1 And the people of the land took Jehoahaz son of Josiah and made him king in place of his father.

Notes

1/1 Unless we prefer the irregular שמנה שנה as being more original.

2/2 בדרכי (Chronicles) is found six times in Chronicles and three times elsewhere.

4/9 לאמר עלה (Kings): לאמר is most often synoptic, but more often in Kings pluses (where there is more direct speech) than in Chronicles pluses.

• The detailed listing of tribal elements in Chronicles is clearly secondary to מאת העם ("from the people").

7/12 עשים [הם] באמונה: only here and in 2 Kgs 12:16 (+) do we find באמונה ("reliably") and עשה ("act") combined.

• והאנשים here (2 Chr 34:12) and in related 2 Kgs 12:16 may be a plus. The plural "men," in any of its forms, is remarkably rare synoptically (only 6x: 2 Sam 10:5; 23:17 // 1 Chr 19:5; 11:19; 1 Kgs 9:22; 10:8, 15 // 2 Chr 8:9; 9:7, 14; 2 Kgs 11:9 // 2 Chr 23:8). It is a plus in the following synoptic contexts (11x in Samuel–Kings, and just once—here—in Chronicles): 1 Sam 31:3, 6; 2 Sam 5:6, 21; 7:14; 2 Kgs 9:27; 12:16; 18:27; 20:14; 23:17; 24:16; 2 Chr 34:12. In 1 Sam 31:1 and 7, it corresponds to singular איש.

19/27 לשמה ולקללה (Kings +) resembles very many expressions in Jeremiah (some 20x). Neither the verb קלל nor the noun קללה ("slight/curse") is ever used in Chronicles; but the noun (especially) is frequent in Deuteronomy and Jeremiah, though elsewhere in Kings only in 1 Kgs 2:8 and 2 Kgs 2:24. לשמה ("as a desolation") is used twice in Chronicles' Hezekiah narrative: in 2 Chr 30:7 alone and in 29:8, where it is part of the longer לזועה לשמה ולשרקה ("as a horror, a desolation, and a hissing").

29/20 "Neco king of Egypt" is introduced in 2 Chr 35:20 in the same style as synoptic "Shishak king of Egypt" in 1 Kgs 14:25 // 2 Chr 12:2; but 2 Kgs 23:29 adds "Pharoah." Twice immediately below, Kings reads only "Pharoah" and Chronicles only "king of Egypt." Pharaoh is synoptic only once, in "the daughter of Pharoah" (1 Kgs 9:24 // 2 Chr 8:11).

• The substantial body of shared text—temple renovation, national covenant, Passover—hardly constitutes an explicit response to Manasseh's cultic malpractice. The measures on religious reform that do correspond are very differently reported in 2 Kgs 23:4–20 and 2 Chr 34:3–7, and were discussed above (9.10).

12.3.22. Last Four Kings: 2 Kgs 23:31–24:20a // 2 Chr 36:2–13

		Chronicles
23:31 *עשרים ושלש	בן־* שנה יהואחז במלכו ושלשה חדשים מלך בירושלם	2 *שלוש ועשרים
ושם אמו חמוטל בת־ ירמיהו מלבנה		
32 ויעש הרע בעיני יהוה ככל אשר־עשו אבתיו		
33 ויאסרהו פרעה נכו ברבלה	בירושלם	3 ויסירהו מלך־מצרים
* בארץ חמת במלך ויתן־ענש על־	*הארץ מאה ככר־כסף וככר זהב	* ויענש את־
34 פרעה נכו בן־יאשיהו תחת יאשיהו אביו	וימלך * את־אליקים	4 * מלך־מצרים אחיו על־יהודה וירושלם
ויבא מצרים וימת שם 36	ויסב את־שמו יהויקים ואת־יהואחז * לקח	* אחיו * נכו ויביאהו מצרימה
	בן־עשרים וחמש שנה יהויקים במלכו ואחת עשרה שנה מלך בירושלם	5
ושם אמו זבידה בת־פדיה מן־רומה		
37 * ככל אשר־עשו אבתיו	ויעש הרע בעיני יהוה *	* אלהיו
24:1 * בימיו	* עלה נבכדנאצר מלך בבל	6 * עליו

12. SHARED TEXT SAMPLED

1b–4			6b–7
5 * וכל	* ויתר דברי יהויקים * אשר־עשה *		8 * ותעבתיו * והנמצא עליו * הנם * מלכי ישראל ויהודה
* הלא־הם • דברי הימים למלכי יהודה 6 וישכב יהויקים עם־אבתיו	* כתבים על־ספר •		
7	וימלך יהויכין בנו תחתיו		9
8 * <u>עשרה</u>	בן־שמנה * שנה יהויכין במלכו		
	ושלשה חדשים * מלך בירושלם		* ועשרת ימים
ושם אמו נחשתא בת־אלנתן מירושלם			
9 * ככל אשר־עשה אביו	ויעש הרע בעיני יהוה *		10 ולתשובת השנה * שלח המלך ויבאהו בבלה עם־כלי חמדת בית־יהוה
10 <u>בעת ההיא</u> * עלה עבדי	* נבכדנאצר		
17 * מלך בבל את־מתניה דדו תחתיו * ויסב את־שמו 18	וימלך *		
	* צדקיהו •		* אחיו על־יהודה וירושלם
	בן־עשרים ואחת שנה צדקיהו במלכו ואחת עשרה שנה מלך בירושלם		11
ושם אמו חמיטל בת־ירמיהו מלבנה			
19 * ככל אשר־עשה יהויקים	ויעש הרע בעיני יהוה *		12 * אלהיו
20a			12b
וימרד צדקיהו במלך בבל			13 וגם במלך נבכדנאצר מרד

23:31/36:2 And Jehoahaz was twenty-three years old on his becoming king, and three months he was king in Jerusalem. 33/3 And *the king of Egypt removed* him in Jerusalem, and *fined* the land one hundred talents of silver and a talent of gold. 34/4 And *the king of Egypt* made Eliakim *his brother* king over Judah and he changed his name to Jehoiakim. And Jehoahaz he took, **and he came** to Egypt. 36/5 Twenty-five years old was

Jehoiakim on his becoming king, and eleven years he was king in Jerusalem, 37/5 and he did what was evil in Yahweh's eyes. 24:1/6 **In his days** Nebuchadnezzar king of Babylon went up.... 5/8 And the rest of the deeds of Jehoiakin that he did are written in the book ... 6/8 and Jehoiachin his son became king in his place. 8/9 Eight**een** years old was Jehoiachin on his becoming king, and three months he was king in Jerusalem. 9/9 And he did what was evil in Yahweh's eyes. 10/10 At that time ... Nebuchadnezzar ... 17/10 and made Zedekiah king. 18/11 Zedekiah was twenty-one years old on his becoming king and eleven years he was king in Jerusalem. 19/12 And he did what was evil in Yahweh's eyes ...

Notes

31/2 Chronicles uses the normal numerical order, "three and twenty."

33/3 As already noted, Kings and Chronicles differ here and in the following verse between "Pharaoh" and "king of Egypt."

- The verbs used look very similar: Kings ויאסרהו ("and he confined him") and Chronicles ויסירהו ("and he removed him").

- Chronicles' simpler "he fined" has been adopted rather than Kings' "and he set a fine on."

34/4 This repeats the situation in 2 Kgs 14:13 // 2 Chr 25:23. In unpointed Hebrew, ויבא is ambiguous: read as *qal*, it means "and he came"; read as *hiphil*, "and he brought." Kings has opted for the simpler "came"; once Chronicles opted for "brought," it was natural to add the suffixed object "him."

Bibliography

Ackerman, Susan. *Under Every Green Tree: Popular Religion in Sixth-Century Judah*. HSM 46. Atlanta: Scholars Press, 1992.
Arrian. *Anabasis Alexandri*. Translated by E. Iliff Robson. LCL. London: Heinemann, 1929.
Auld, A. Graeme. *I and II Samuel: A Commentary*. OTL. Louisville: Westminster John Knox, 2011.
———. "Chronicles—Isaiah—Kings." In *Imperial Visions: The Prophet and the Book of Isaiah in an Age of Empires*. Edited by Joachim Schaper. Göttingen: Vandenhoeck &Ruprecht, forthcoming.
———. "David's Census: Some Textual and Literary Links." Pages 19–34 in *Textual Criticism and Dead Sea Scrolls Studies in Honour of Julio Trebolle Barrera: Florilegium Complutense*. Edited by Andrés Piquer Otero and Pablo A. Torijano Morales. JSJSup 158. Leiden: Brill, 2012.
———. "Did the Assyrian Envoy Know the *Venite*? What Did He Know? What Did He Say? And Should He Be Believed?" Pages 42–53 in *Torah and Tradition*. Edited by Klaas Spronk. OTS 70. Leiden: Brill, 2017.
———. "Elijah and the Prophets of Baal and of Asherah: Towards a Discussion of 'No Prophets?'" Pages 7–16 in *New Perspectives on Prophecy and History: Essays in Honour of Hans M. Barstad*. Edited by Rannfrid I. Thelle, Terje Stordalen, and Mervyn E. J. Richardson. VTSup 168. Leiden: Brill, 2015.
———. "Isaiah and the Oldest 'Biblical' Prophetic Narrative." Pages 45–63 in *Prophets and Prophecy in Stories: Papers Read at the Fifth Meeting of the Edinburgh Prophecy Network, Utrecht, October 2013*. Edited by Bob Becking and Hans Barstad. OTS 65. Leiden: Brill, 2015.
———. "Jeremiah—Manasseh—Samuel: Significant Triangle? Or Vicious Circle?" Pages 1–9 in *Prophecy in the Book of Jeremiah*. Edited by Hans M. Barstad and Reinhard G. Kratz. BZAW 388. Berlin: de Gruyter, 2009.
———. *Kings without Privilege*. Edinburgh: T&T Clark, 1994.

———. "Prophets Shared—but Recycled." Pages 19-28 in *The Future of the Deuteronomistic History*. Edited by Thomas Römer. BETL 147. Leuven: Peeters, 2000. Repr. as pages 127-34 in *Samuel at the Threshold: Selected Works of Graeme Auld*. SOTSMS. Aldershot: Ashgate, 2004.

———. "Prophets through the Looking Glass: Between Writings and Moses." *JSOT* 27 (1983): 3-23.

———. "Reading Genesis after Samuel." Pages 459-69 in *The Pentateuch*. Edited by Thomas B. Dozeman, Konrad Schmid, and Baruch J. Schwartz. FAT 78. Tübingen: Mohr Siebeck, 2011.

———. "Reading Kings on the Divided Monarchy: What Sort of Narrative?" Pages 337-43 in *Understanding the History of Ancient Israel*. Edited by Hugh G. M. Williamson. Proceedings of the British Academy 143. Oxford: Oxford University Press, 2007.

———. "Re-telling the Disputed 'Altar' in Joshua 22." Pages 281-93 in *The Book of Joshua*. Edited by Ed Noort. BETL 250. Leuven: Peeters, 2012.

———. "Righting Israel's Kings: Israel's Kings in Synoptic Perspective." Pages 147-58 in *A King Like All the Nations? Kingdoms of Israel and Judah in the Bible and History*. Edited by Manfred Oeming and Petr Sláma. Beiträge zum Verstehen der Bibel 28. Berlin: LIT, 2015.

———. *Samuel at the Threshold: Selected Works of Graeme Auld*. SOTSMS. Aldershot: Ashgate, 2004.

———. "The Shaping of Israelite History in Samuel and Kings." *RB* 121 (2014): 195-216.

———. "Solomon at Gibeon: History Glimpsed." Pages 97-107 in *Samuel at the Threshold: Selected Works of Graeme Auld*. SOTSMS. Aldershot: Ashgate, 2004.

———. "The Text of Chronicles and the Beginnings of Samuel." Pages 31-40 in *Rereading the relecture? The Question of (Post)chronistic Influence in the Latest Redactions of the Books of Samuel*. Edited by Uwe Becker and Hannes Bezzel. FAT 2/66. Tübingen: Mohr Siebeck, 2014.

———. "Vision of a New Future?" *TZ* 48 (1992): 343-55.

———. "What If the Chronicler Did Use the Deuteronomistic History?" Pages 137-50 in *Virtual History and the Bible*. Edited by J. Cheryl Exum. BibInt 8. Leiden: Brill, 2000.

———. "What Was the Main Source of the Books of Chronicles?" Pages 91-99 in *The Chronicler as Author: Studies in Text and Texture*. Edited by M. Patrick Graham and Steven L. McKenzie. JSOTSup 263. Sheffield: Sheffield Academic, 1999.

———. "Writing Time and Eternity in Samuel and Kings." Pages 1–10 in *Far from Minimal: Celebrating the Work and Influence of Philip R. Davies*. Edited by Duncan Burns and John W. Rogerson. LHBOTS 484. London: T&T Clark, 2012.
Ausloos, Hans. *The Deuteronomist's History: The Role of the Deuteronomist in Historical-Critical Research into Genesis–Numbers*. OTS 67. Leiden: Brill, 2015.
Barrick, W. Boyd. *The King and the Cemeteries: Toward a New Understanding of Josiah's Reform*. VTSup 88. Leiden: Brill, 2002.
Becker, Uwe. "Wie 'deuteronomistisch' ist die Samuel-Rede in I Sam 12?" Pages 131–45 in *Rereading the relecture? The Question of (Post)chronistic Influence in the Latest Redactions of the Books of Samuel*. Edited by Uwe Becker and Hannes Bezzel. FAT 2/66. Tübingen: Mohr Siebeck, 2014.
Becker, Uwe, and Hannes Bezzel, eds. *Rereading the relecture? The Question of (Post)chronistic Influence in the Latest Redactions of the Books of Samuel*. FAT 2/66. Tübingen: Mohr Siebeck, 2014.
Becking, Bob. "Chronology: A Skeleton without Flesh? Sennacherib's Campaign as a Case-Study." Pages 46–72 in *"Like a Bird in a Cage": The Invasion of Sennacherib in 701 BCE*. Edited by Lester L. Grabbe. JSOTSup 363. London: Sheffield Academic, 2003.
Bekins, Peter. *Transitivity and Object Marking in Biblical Hebrew: An Investigation of the Object Preposition 'et*. HSS 64. Winona Lake, IN: Eisenbrauns, 2014.
Ben Zvi, Ehud. "The Account of the Reign of Manasseh in II Reg 21,1–18 and the Redactional History of the Book of Kings." *ZAW* 103 (1991): 362–63.
———. "The House of Omri/Ahab in Chronicles." Pages 41–53 in *Ahab Agonistes: The Rise and Fall of the Omri Dynasty*. Edited by Lester L. Grabbe. LHBOTS 421. London: T&T Clark, 2007.
Blenkinsopp, Joseph. *Opening the Sealed Book: Interpretations of the Book of Isaiah in Late Antiquity*. Grand Rapids: Eerdmans, 2006.
Carr, David. *The Formation of the Hebrew Bible: A New Reconstruction*. New York: Oxford University Press, 2011.
Childs, Brevard S. *Isaiah and the Assyrian Crisis*. SBT 2/3. London: SCM, 1967.
Cogan, Mordechai, and Hayim Tadmor. *II Kings: A New Translation with Introduction and Commentary*. AB 11. Garden City, NY: Doubleday, 1988.

Cross, Frank Moore. *Canaanite Myth and Hebrew Epic: Essays in the History of the Religion of Israel*. Cambridge: Harvard University Press, 1973.
Cross, Frank Moore, Donald W. Parry, Richard J. Saley, and Eugene Ulrich. *Qumran Cave 4.XII: 1–2 Samuel*. DJD XVII. Oxford: Clarendon, 2005.
Dietrich, Walter. "Die Vorderen Propheten." Pages 167–282 in *Die Entstehung des Alten Testaments*, by Walter Dietrich, Hans-Peter Mathys, Thomas Römer, and Rudolf Smend. ThW 1. Stuttgart: Kohlhammer, 2014.
———. "Josia und das Gesetzbuch (2 Reg. XXII)." *VT* 27 (1977): 13–35.
———. *Prophetie und Geschichte: Eine redaktionsgeschichtliche Untersuchung zum deuteronomistischen Geschichtswerk*. FRLANT 108. Göttingen: Vandenhoeck & Ruprecht, 1972.
Edenburg, Cynthia, and Juha Pakkala, eds. *Is Samuel among the Deuteronomists? Current Views on the Place of Samuel within a Deuteronomistic History*. AIL 16. Atlanta: Society of Biblical Literature, 2013.
Eichhorn, Johann Gottfried. *Einleitung in das Alte Testament*. 3rd ed. Leipzig: Weidmann, 1803.
Fernández Marcos, Natalio, and José Ramón Busto Saiz. *1–2 Reyes*. Vol. 2 of *El Texto Antioqueno de la Biblia Griega*. TECC. Madrid: Instituto de Filología del CSIC, 1992.
Finkelstein, Israel. *The Forgotten Kingdom: The Archaeology and History of Northern Israel*. ANEM 5. Atlanta: Society of Biblical Literature, 2013.
Gilmour, Rachelle. *Juxtaposition and the Elisha Cycle*. LHBOTS 594. London: Bloomsbury T&T Clark, 2014.
Goldstein, Ronnie. "On Treaties, Military Assistance and Divine Support in Isaiah 1–39." In *Imperial Visions: The Prophet and the Book of Isaiah in an Age of Empires*. Edited by Joachim Schaper. Göttingen: Vandenhoeck & Ruprecht, forthcoming.
Goswell, Greg. "The Literary Logic and Meaning of Isaiah 38." *JSOT* 39 (2014): 165–86.
Graham, M. Patrick, Kenneth G. Hoglund, and Steven L. McKenzie, eds. *The Chronicler as Historian*. JSOTSup 238. Sheffield: Sheffield Academic, 1997.
Gray, John. *I and II Kings*. 3rd ed. OTL. London: SCM, 1977.
Halpern, Baruch, and André Lemaire. "The Composition of Kings." Pages 123–53 in *The Books of Kings: Sources, Composition, Historiography and Reception*. Edited by Baruch Halpern and André Lemaire. VTSup 129. Leiden: Brill, 2010.

Ho, Craig (Yuet-Shun). "Conjectures and Refutations: Is 1 Samuel XXXI 1–13 Really the Source of 1 Chronicles X 1–12?" *VT* 45 (1995): 82–106.

———. "The Troubles of David and His House: Textual and Literary Studies of the Synoptic Stories of Saul and David in Samuel–Kings and Chronicles." PhD thesis, Edinburgh University, 1994.

Hoffmann, Hans-Detlef. *Reform und Reformen: Untersuchungen zu einem Grundthema der deuteronomistischen Geschichtsschreibung*. ATANT 66. Zurich: Theologischer Verlag, 1980.

Hornkohl, Aaron D. *Ancient Hebrew Periodization and the Language of the Book of Jeremiah: The Case for a Sixth-Century Date of Composition*. SSLL. Leiden: Brill, 2014.

Japhet, Sara. *I and II Chronicles: A Commentary*. OTL. Louisville: Westminster John Knox, 1993.

Johnstone, William. "The Deuteronomistic Cycles of 'Signs' and 'Wonders' in Exodus1–13." Pages 166–85 in *Understanding Poets and Prophets: Essays in Honour of George Wishart Anderson*. Edited by A. Graeme Auld. JSOTSup 152. Sheffield: Sheffield Academic Press, 1993.

Kalimi, Isaac. "Kings *with* Privilege: The Core Sources of the Parallel Texts between the Deuteronomistic and Chronistic Histories." *RB* 119 (2012): 498–517.

———. "Die Quelle(n) der Textparallelen zwischen Samuel–Könige und Chronik." Pages 11–30 in *Rereading the* relecture? *The Question of (Post)chronistic Influence in the Latest Redactions of the Books of Samuel*. Edited by Uwe Becker and Hannes Bezzel. FAT 2/66. Tübingen: Mohr Siebeck, 2014.

———. "Was the Chronicler a Historian?" Pages 73–89 in *The Chronicler as Historian*. Edited by M. Patrick Graham, Kenneth G. Hoglund, and Steven L. McKenzie. JSOTSup 238. Sheffield: Sheffield Academic, 1997.

———. *Zur Geschichtsschreibung des Chronisten*. BZAW 226. Berlin: de Gruyter, 1995.

Keulen, Percy S. F. van. *Manasseh through the Eyes of the Deuteronomists*. OTS 38. Leiden: Brill, 1996.

Klein, Ralph W. *1 Chronicles*. Hermeneia. Minneapolis: Fortress, 2006.

———. *2 Chronicles*. Hermeneia. Minneapolis: Fortress, 2012.

Knoppers, Gary N. "Rethinking the Relationship between Deuteronomy and the Deuteronomistic History: The Case of Kings." *CBQ* 63 (2001): 393–415.

Kratz, Reinhard G. "Isaiah and the Siege of Jerusalem." Pages 143–60 in *New Perspectives on Prophecy and History: Essays in Honour of Hans M. Barstad*. Edited by Rannfrid I. Thelle, Terje Stordalen, and Mervyn E. J. Richardson. VTSup 168. Leiden: Brill, 2015.

Kropat, Arno. *Die Syntax des Autors der Chronik verglichen mit der seiner Quellen: Ein Beitrag zur historischen Syntax des Hebräischen*. BZAW 16. Giessen: Töpelmann, 1909.

Kucová, Lydie. "Common Source Theory and Composition of the Story of the Divided Monarchy in Kings with Special Emphasis on the Account of Josiah's Reform." PhD thesis, Edinburgh University, 2005.

———. "Obeisance in the Biblical Stories of David." Pages 241–60 in *Reflection and Refraction: Studies in Biblical Historiography in Honour of A. Graeme Auld*. Edited by Robert Rezetko, Timothy H. Lim, and W. Brian Aucker. VTSup 113. Leiden: Brill, 2007.

Levin, Christoph. "Joschija im deuteronomistischen Geschichtswerk." *ZAW* 96 (1984): 351–71.

Levinson, Bernard M. "The Reconceptualization of Kingship in Deuteronomy and the Deuteronomistic History's Transformation of Torah." *VT* 51 (2001): 511–34.

Linville, James R. *Israel in the Book of Kings: The Past as a Project of Social Identity*. JSOTSup 272. Sheffield: Sheffield Academic, 1998.

Mandelkern, Solomon. *Veteris Testamenti Concordantiae*. 2nd ed. Tel Aviv: Schocken, 1971.

McKenzie, Steven L. "The Chronicler as Redactor." Pages 70–90 in *The Chronicler as Author: Studies in Text and Texture*. Edited by M. Patrick Graham and Steven L. McKenzie. JSOTSup 263. Sheffield: Sheffield Academic, 1999.

———. *The Chronicler's Use of the Deuteronomistic History*. HSM 33. Atlanta: Scholars Press, 1985.

———. *The Trouble with Kings: The Composition of the Book of Kings in the Deuteronomistic History*. VTSup 42. Leiden: Brill, 1991.

Monroe, Lauren A. S. *Josiah's Reform and the Dynamics of Defilement: Israelite Rites of Violence and the Making of a Biblical Text*. Oxford: Oxford University Press, 2011.

Montgomery, James A. *A Critical and Exegetical Commentary on the Books of Kings*. Edited by Henry Snyder Gehman. ICC. Edinburgh: T&T Clark, 1951.

Na'aman, Nadav. "Updating the Messages: Hezekiah's Second Prophetic Story (2 Kings 19.9b–35) and the Community of Babylonian Deportees." Pages 201–20 in *"Like a Bird in a Cage": The Invasion of Sennacherib in 701 BCE*. Edited by Lester L. Grabbe. JSOTSup 363. London: Sheffield Academic, 2003.

Nelson, Richard. *The Double Redaction of the Deuteronomistic History*. JSOTSup 18. Sheffield: JSOT Press, 1981.

Nihan, Christophe. "Samuel, Chronicles, and 'Postchronistic' Revisions: Some Remarks of Method." Pages 57–78 in *Rereading the relecture? The Question of (Post)chronistic Influence in the Latest Redactions of the Books of Samuel*. Edited by Uwe Becker and Hannes Bezzel. FAT 2/66. Tübingen: Mohr Siebeck, 2014.

Noll, Kurt L. "Deuteronomistic History or Deuteronomic Debate? (A Thought Experiment)." *JSOT* 31 (2007): 311–45.

Noth, Martin. *The Chronicler's History*. Translated by H. G. M. Williamson. JSOTSup 50. Sheffield: Sheffield Academic, 1987.

———. *The Deuteronomistic History*. JSOTSup 15. Sheffield: JSOT Press, 1981.

———. *Könige: 1 Könige 1–16*. BKAT 9.1. Neukirchen-Vluyn: Neukirchener Verlag, 1968.

———. *Überlieferungsgeschichtliche Studien: Die sammelnden und bearbeitenden Geschichtswerke im Alten Testament*. Halle: Niemeyer, 1943.

Park, Song-Mi Suzie. *Hezekiah and the Dialogue of Memory*. Emerging Scholars. Minneapolis: Fortress, 2015.

Parry, Donald W., and Elisha Qimron, eds. *The Great Isaiah Scroll (1QIsa^a): A New Edition*. STDJ 32. Leiden: Brill, 1999.

Peltonen, Kai. "Function, Explanation and Literary Phenomena: Aspects of Source Criticism as Theory and Method in the History of Chronicles Research." Pages 18–69 in *The Chronicler as Author: Studies in Text and Texture*. Edited by M. Patrick Graham and Steven L. McKenzie. JSOTSup 263. Sheffield: Sheffield Academic, 1999.

Person, Raymond F., Jr. "The Deuteronomic History and the Books of Chronicles: Contemporary Competing Historiographies." Pages 315–36 in *Reflection and Refraction: Studies in Biblical Historiography in Honour of A. Graeme Auld*. Edited by Robert Rezetko, Timothy H. Lim, and W. Brian Aucker. VTSup 113. Leiden: Brill, 2007.

———. *The Deuteronomic History and the Book of Chronicles: Scribal Works in an Oral World*. AIL 6. Atlanta: Society of Biblical Literature, 2010.

———. *The Deuteronomic School: History, Social Setting, and Literature*. SBLStBL 2. Atlanta: Soceity of Biblical Literature, 2002.

———. *The Kings–Isaiah and Kings–Jeremiah Recensions*. BZAW 252. Berlin: de Gruyter, 1997.

———. "The Problem of 'Literary Unity' from the Perspective of the Study of Oral Traditions." Pages 217–37 in *Empirical Models Challenging Biblical Criticism*. Edited by Raymond F. Person Jr. and Robert Rezetko. AIL 25. Atlanta: SBL Press, 2016.

Polzin, Robert. *David and the Deuteronomist. Literary Study of the Deuteronomic History 2*. San Francisco: Harper & Row, 1989.

———. *Moses and the Deuteronomist. Literary Study of the Deuteronomic History 1*. New York: Seabury, 1980.

———. *Samuel and the Deuteronomist. Literary Study of the Deuteronomic History 3*. Bloomington: Indiana University Press, 1993.

Press, Michael D. "'Where Are the Gods of Hamath?' (2 Kings 18.34 // Isaiah 36.19): The Use of Foreign Deities in the Rabshakeh's Speech." *JSOT* 40 (2015): 201–23.

Provan, Iain W. *Hezekiah and the Books of Kings: A Contribution to the Debate about the Composition of the Deuteronomistic History*. BZAW 172. Berlin: de Gruyter, 1988.

Rezetko, Robert. *Source and Revision in the Narratives of David's Transfer of the Ark: Text, Language and Story in 2 Samuel 6 and 1 Chronicles 13, 15–16*. LHBOTS 470. London: T&T Clark, 2007.

Rhyder, Julia. "Holiness Language in II Kings 23? A Note on a Recent Proposal." *ZAW* 127 (2015): 497–501.

Rogerson, John W. *W. M. L. de Wette, Founder of Modern Biblical Criticism: An Intellectual Biography*. JSOTSup 126. Sheffield: Sheffield Academic, 1992.

Römer, Thomas C. *The So-called Deuteronomistic History: A Sociological, Historical and Literary Introduction*. London: T&T Clark, 2007.

Schipper, Jeremy. "Hezekiah, Manasseh, and Dynastic or Transgenerational Punishment." Pages 81–105 in *Soundings in Kings: Perspectives and Methods in Contemporary Scholarship*. Edited by Mark Leuchter and Klaus-Peter Adam. Minneapolis: Fortress, 2010.

Sergi, Omer. "Die Schlacht von Ramot-Gilead und der Niedergang der Omriden-Dynastie: Versuch einer historischen Rekonstruktion." Pages 33–49 in *A King Like All the Nations? Kingdoms of Israel and Judah in the Bible and History*. Edited by Manfred Oeming and Petr Sláma. Beiträge zum Verstehen der Bibel 28. Berlin: LIT, 2015.

Smend, Rudolf. "Das Gesetz und die Völker." Pages 494–509 in *Probleme biblischer Theologie: Gerhard von Rad zum 70. Geburtstag*. Edited by Hans Walter Wolff. Munich: Kaiser, 1971.

———. *Wilhelm Martin Leberecht de Wettes Arbeit am Alten und am Neuen Testament*. Basel: Helbing & Lichtenhahn, 1958.

Stade, Bernhard. "Anmerkungen zu 2 Kö. 15–21." *ZAW* 6 (1886): 156–92.

Sweeney, Marvin A. *I and II Kings: A Commentary*. OTL. Louisville: Westminster John Knox, 2007.

———. "Prophets and Priests in the Deuteronomistic History: Elijah and Elisha." Pages 35–49 in *Israelite Prophecy and the Deuteronomistic History: Portrait, Reality, and the Formation of a History*. Edited by Mignon R. Jacobs and Raymond F. Person Jr. AIL 14. Atlanta: Society of Biblical Literature, 2013.

Thelle, Rannfrid Irene. *Approaches to the "Chosen Place": Accessing a Biblical Concept*. LHBOTS 564. London: T&T Clark, 2012.

———. "Reflections of Ancient Israelite Divination in the Former Prophets." Pages 7–33 in *Israelite Prophecy and the Deuteronomistic History: Portrait, Reality, and the Formation of a History*. Edited by Mignon R. Jacobs and Raymond F. Person Jr. AIL 14. Atlanta: Society of Biblical Literature, 2013.

Trebolle Barrera, Julio. "Kings (MT/LXX) and Chronicles: The Double and Triple Textual Tradition." Pages 483–501 in *Reflection and Refraction: Studies in Biblical Historiography in Honour of A. Graeme Auld*. Edited by Robert Rezetko, Timothy H. Lim, and W. Brian Aucker. VTSup 113. Leiden: Brill, 2007.

Van Seters, John. *In Search of History: Historiography in the Ancient World and the Origins of Biblical History*. New Haven: Yale University Press, 1983.

Veijola, Timo. *Das Königtum in der Beurteilung des deuteronomistischen Historiographie*. AASF 198. Helsinki: Academia Scientiarum Fennica, 1977.

Wellhausen, Julius. *Briefe*. Edited by Rudolf Smend. Tübingen: Mohr Siebeck, 2013.

———. "Die Composition des Hexateuchs." *JDT* 21 (1876): 392–450, 531–602; *JDT* 22 (1877): 407–79.

———. *Die Composition des Hexateuchs und der historischen Bücher des Alten Testaments*. Berlin: Reimer, 1889.

———. *Geschichte Israels*. 2 vols. Berlin: Reimer, 1878.

———. *Prolegomena to the History of Israel.* Reprints and Translations. Atlanta: Scholars Press, 1994.

———. *Der Text der Bücher Samuelis.* Göttingen: Vandenhoeck & Ruprecht, 1871.

Wette, W. M. L. de. *Beiträge zur Einleitung in das Alte Testament.* 2 vols. Halle: Schimmelpfennig, 1806–1807.

Wiggins, Steve A. *A Reassessment of Asherah: With Further Considerations of the Goddess.* Gorgias Ugaritic Studies 2. Piscataway, NJ: Gorgias, 2007.

Wildberger, Hans. *Jesaja 28–39: Das Buch, der Prophet und seine Botschaft.* Part 3 of *Jesaja.* BKAT 10.3. Neukirchen-Vluyn: Neukirchener Verlag, 1982.

Wright, Jacob L. *David, King of Israel, and Caleb in Biblical Memory.* Cambridge: Cambridge University Press, 2014.

Würthwein, Ernst. *1. Kön. 17–2. Kön. 25.* Vol. 2 of *Die Bücher der Könige.* ATD 11.2. Göttingen: Vandenhoeck & Ruprecht, 1984.

———. "Erwägungen zum sog. deuteronomistischen Geschichtswerk: Eine Skizze." Pages 1–11 in *Studien zum deuteronomistischen Geschichtswerk.* BZAW 227. Berlin: de Gruyter, 1994.

———. "Die Josianische Reform und das Deuteronomium." Pages 188–216 in *Studien zum deuteronomistischen Geschichtswerk.* BZAW 227. Berlin: de Gruyter, 1994.

Zakovitch, Yair. "Assimilation in Biblical Narratives." Pages 175–96 in *Empirical Models of Biblical Criticism.* Edited by Jeffrey H. Tigay. Philadelphia: University of Pennsylvania Press, 1985.

Hebrew Bible Index

Genesis		48:15	160
1–11	36	49:16	198
3:14	35		
3:17	35	Exodus	
12:17	256	3:12	161
17:1	160	14:31	110
18:24	43	15:23	213
20:5	212	15:26	100
20:6	212	17:17	43
23:8	43	23:20–33	7, 18
23:16	250	23:24	247
24:23	43	23:33	152
24:40	160	34:1	148
24:42	43	34:4	148
24:49	43		
28:16	43	Leviticus	
31:1	264	7:14	261
31:29	43	7:33	261
33:9	43	14:45	247
33:11	43	18:27	152
34	248	20:13	152
39–50	36	25:37	219
39:4	43	26:25	213
39:5	43	26:30	81, 199, 268
39:8	43		
42:1	43, 95	Numbers	
42:2	43	5:8	251
42:15	36	9:20	43
42:16	36	9:21	43
43:4	43	13:20	43
43:7	43	14:21	34
44:19	43	14:28	34
44:20	43	22:29	43
44:26	43	33:52	199
47:6	43		

Deuteronomy		12	196, 200–201
1–11	38, 196	12–15	38
4:1	38, 196	12:1	30, 38
4:1–8:3	38	12:2	150
4:4	38, 144, 267	12:2–3	200–201
4:5	267	12:2–7	200
4:8	267	12:2–27	199
4:9	35, 38, 144	12:4–7	200
4:10	38, 144	12:5	196, 198, 201
4:14	267	12:8	100
4:19	136	12:8–12	200
4:33	38	12:11	196, 198, 201
4:37	197	12:13–18	200
4:43	38	12:14	196, 198, 201
4:45	196, 267	12:18	196, 201
5:1	177, 196	12:20–27	200
5:3	38, 144	12:21	196, 198, 201
5:9	136	12:25	100
5:23	34	12:26	196, 201
5:24	38	12:28	100, 199
5:26	38	12:31	152
5:28	267	13:4	43
5:33	38	13:15	152
6:1	196	13:18	100
6:2	35, 38, 144	14:2	197
6:18	100	14:23	196, 198
6:20	267	14:24	196, 198
6:24	38	14:25	196
7–8	22	15:20	196
7:1	261	16	201
7:6	197, 201	16–18	115
7:7	197	16–20	38
7:12	177	16:2	196, 198
7:12–14	22	16:3	35, 38, 144
7:22	261	16:6	196, 198
8:1	38	16:7	196
8:3	38	16:11	196, 198
8:7–9	22	16:15	196
8:10	22	16:16	196
8:19	136	16:18–18:22	14
9:5	212	16:20	38
10:1	148	17:3	136
10:3	148	17:4	152
10:15	197	17:8	196
11:16	136	17:10	196

HEBREW BIBLE INDEX

17:14–18	115	33:6	38
17:14–20	14		
17:15	197	Joshua	
17:19	35, 38, 144	1:5	35, 37, 144
18:5	197	2:13	37
18:6	196	3:10	34, 37
18:15–22	115	4:14	35, 37, 110, 144
19:4	38	5:8	37
19:5	38	6:17	37
19:10	153	6:25	37
19:13	153	7:26	213
20:16	38	8:23	37
21–27	38	9:15	37
21:5	197	9:20	37
21:8	153	9:21	37
21:9	100, 153	9:27	212
21:23	156	13:1	110
23:7	196	14:10	37
24:4	152	22	151
25:19	152	22:28	261
26:2	196, 198	23	110
26:10	136	23:1	110
27:25	153	24	110
28–33	38	24:14	110
28:26	37	24:16	110
28:66	38	24:22	110
29:14	43	24:27	110
29:16	81, 268		
29:17	43, 264	Judges	
29:19	152	1:1	63, 194
29:25	136	4:20	43
29:27	212	6:13	43
30:6	38	6:36	43
30:9	227	8:18	37
30:16	38	8:19	37
30:17	136	8:22–32	37
30:19	38	15:19	37, 213
30:20	38, 144	16:30	37
31:11	196	17–18	5
31:13	38, 144	17–21	5
31:27	38, 144	17:6	100
32:21	148	18:5	63, 194
32:39	38	18:12	213
32:40	34, 38	18:14	43
32:47	30, 38	19–21	5

Judges (cont.)

19:19	43	7:13	47
20:18	63, 194	7:15	32, 35, 144
20:23	63, 194	7:16	80
20:27	194	8:1	110
20:27–28	63	8:7	115
21:14	37	8:9	44, 50
21:25	100	9:9	61, 62
		9:11	42, 61
		9:12	42
1 Samuel		9:18	61
1–2	173	9:19	61
1–8	42, 160	9:22	80
1–30	80	10:7	188
1:7	68	10:9	188
1:8	68	10:16	50
1:9	69	10:22	63, 194
1:10	68	10:24	32, 34, 194
1:11	32, 35, 144	11:4	68
1:22	32	11:5	68
1:23	44	12	8, 109–15
1:26	32, 36	12:1–5	111
2	50, 161	12:2	110, 160
2:6	32	12:5	110
2:15	32	12:8	80, 111
2:20	80	12:9–15	111
2:27	160, 181	12:14–15	111, 114
2:27–36	160, 181	12:16–18	111, 114
2:30	126, 160, 181	12:18b	110
2:31	160, 181	12:20	44
2:33	219	12:22	111
2:34	160, 181, 188	12:23	110–11, 113–14
2:35	132, 160, 181	12:24	44, 110
3	161	12:25	50, 111–12, 114
3:1	61	13	110
3:2	80	13:1	8
3:3	69	13:13–14	109
3:9	80	13:20	47
3:11	161	14:10	161, 188
3:12	50	14:27–28	122
4:12	68, 181	14:28	50, 56
4:17	47	14:30	56
5:3	80	14:37	63, 194
5:11	80	14:39	31–32, 42
6:2	80	14:43–44	55
6:3	50	14:43–45	56

14:45	31–32	22:15	63, 194
14:46	80	22:15–16	56
15	110	22:22	50
15:8	32	23:2	63, 194
15:22	66	23:4	63, 194
15:23	50	23:22	80
15:27	68	23:23	42
16	106, 110	23:28	80, 213
16:6	44	24	56
17:16	50	24:9	35
17:26	32, 34, 91, 158	24:11	56
17:35	91	24:17	68
17:36	32, 34, 91, 158	24:20	56
17:37	91	24:21	56
17:44	37	25–30	42, 57, 105
17:46	32, 37	25:1	110, 230
17:48	42	25:21	44
17:51	47	25:26	31–33, 36, 50
17:52	47	25:28	132
17:55	32, 36	25:29	32
18:8	44	25:33	50
18:17	44	25:34	31, 33
18:23	186	26	56, 103
19	106	26:5	80
19:6	31–32	26:8	56
19:15	153	26:10	31, 33, 112
20:3	31–32, 36	26:13	80
20:8	42	26:16	31, 33
20:14	32	26:17	35
20:17	122	26:19	35
20:19	80	26:21	56
20:21	31–32	26:23	56
20:25	80	26:24	56
20:27	80	26:25	56, 80
20:27–28	56	27	103, 104
20:31	32	27:1	112, 132
20:37	80	27:1–28:2	105
20:39	44	27:5	80
20:41	68	27:9	32
21:3	80	27:11	32, 103–5, 113
21:4	42	27:12	50, 103, 104
21:5	42, 44	28	103, 267
21:9	42	28:1	103–4
22:10	63, 194	28:2	103–4
22:13	63, 194	28:3	110, 230

1 Samuel (cont.)

28:6	63, 194	5:1–2	105
28:7	62	5:2	108, 132
28:10	31, 33	5:3	91, 92
28:15	65	5:6	275
29:4	80	5:6–9	29, 108
29:6	31, 33	5:9	5, 30
29:9	44	5:10	47, 53, 57
30	146	5:11	215
30:1	186	5:13	108
30:4	68	5:16	83
30:8	50, 63, 194	5:19	47, 54, 59, 63, 92, 194
30:16	147	5:20	63, 76, 83, 213
30:31	80	5:21	212, 275
31	16, 92, 108–10, 191	5:23	59, 63, 92, 194
31:1	275	6	92
31:3	275	6:8	63, 76
31:6	275	6:10	233
31:7	212, 275	6:12	92, 147
		6:17	50, 79, 80
		6:18	50, 212
2 Samuel		6:20	56
1–4	42	6:22	186
1:2	68, 181, 186	7	59, 105–6, 109, 111, 115, 192, 198
1:10	32	7:2	45, 61, 62, 246
1:11	68	7:5	61, 161
1:12	68	7:7	65, 96, 198
1:23	32	7:8	61, 161, 198
1:24	68	7:10	76–77
2–4	146	7:13	106–7
2:1	63, 194	7:14	275
2:10	44	7:15	233
2:16	80	7:16	106, 132
2:23	80	7:17	61
2:27	31, 33	7:18	61
2:32	230	7:19	61, 65
3:2–5	108	7:20	61
3:13	44	7:21	61, 213
3:16	68	7:22	213
3:21	35	7:24	106
3:31	68	7:25	61, 65, 106
3:32	68	7:26	61, 106, 158
3:34	68	7:27	61, 158, 213
4:9	31, 33	7:28	61, 65
5	19, 63, 92, 98, 106, 194	7:29	61, 106, 111
5:1	45	8	24, 27, 92, 98

HEBREW BIBLE INDEX

8:2	24–27, 32, 46, 47, 51, 53, 105	15:23	68
8:5–6	260	15:30	68
8:15–18	146, 147	15:32	68, 181
9–20	11, 147	16:4	35
9:1	42	16:9	35
9:11	35	16:10	120
10	105, 107, 115	16:16	32, 34, 194
10:1–11:1	107	17:9	80
10:5	275	17:12	80
10:12	246	18:9	113
11	107	18:14	32
11–12	17, 108, 132	18:18	32
11:1	107, 240	18:31	35
11:2–12:25	105	18:32	35, 127
11:3	62	19:1	68
11:11	32	19:2	68
11:16	80	19:7	32
11:25	108	19:20	35
12:3	32	19:21	35
12:5	31, 33	19:23	120
12:10	107	19:27	35
12:14	55	19:28	35
12:18	32	19:29	42
12:20–23	133	19:31	35
12:21	32, 68	19:36	35
12:22	32, 68	19:38	35
12:25	65	19:40	80
12:26–31	107	20:24	147
13:19	68	21	92
13:31	68, 181	21–24	5, 9, 19, 106, 193
13:33	35	21:10	32, 37
13:36	68	21:12	47
14:9	35	21:18–22	19
14:11	31, 33	21:21	92, 158
14:12	35	22:47	31, 33–34
14:15	35	23	19, 29, 98
14:17	35	23:10	44, 54
14:18	35	23:12	92
14:19	32, 35, 42	23:34	106
14:22	35	23:39	106
14:32	42	24	19, 56, 59, 90, 92, 106, 109, 112–13, 115, 192–94
15:2	198	24:1–9	146
15:15	35	24:2	96
15:19	80	24:3	35
15:21	31–33, 35–36, 80		

2 Samuel (cont.)

24:9	157
24:10	106
24:11	61, 66–67
24:11–12	48
24:12	47, 53–54, 161
24:12–13	106
24:14	169
24:16	107, 113, 240
24:17	47, 52, 53, 106, 132
24:18	69
24:20	169
24:21	35, 69, 78, 251
24:23	227
24:24	47, 137
24:25	50, 69, 78

1 Kings

1	36, 106
1–2	11
1–11	208
1:2	120
1:13	35
1:16	136
1:18	35
1:20	35
1:21	35
1:23	136
1:25	32, 34, 147, 194
1:27	35
1:29	31, 33, 35, 194
1:31	32, 35, 136
1:34	32, 34, 194
1:36	35
1:37	35
1:39	32, 34, 194
1:47	136
2:4	212
2:8	275
2:12	142
2:13	127
2:19	136
2:24	31, 33
2:38	35
2:42	122
2:46b	142
3–11	111
3:1	99, 142
3:2	143
3:3	50, 75, 143
3:4	92
3:4–15	59, 92, 207
3:5	61
3:5–15	142, 144
3:6	212
3:8	177, 196
3:9	92, 177
3:11	177, 212
3:15	50
3:16–28	144
3:16–5:32	207
3:18	186
3:25	32
3:26	32, 51
3:27	32, 51
4:1–19	144–45
4:6	147
4:20	145–47
4:20–5:5	145
4:20–5:8	145
4:20–5:32	145, 147
5	148, 216
5:1	32, 35, 91, 145, 147, 247
5:2–3	145
5:4	145
5:5	145–46
5:6	145
5:8	80
5:9	145
5:9–14	145–46
5:10	146
5:11	146
5:12–13	146
5:14	146
5:15–26	145, 215
5:17	219
5:19	219
5:22	215
5:23	79
5:24	215

5:27	146–47	8:33–34	111
5:28	147	8:34	114
5:30	147, 216	8:35	77, 196
5:31	147	8:35–36	111, 113–14
5:32	148	8:36	30, 111, 113–14
6–7	69, 144, 207	8:39	114
6:1	86	8:40	29–30
6:13	198	8:44	197
6:37	246	8:48	197
7:14	145, 216	8:50	114
7:40	212, 216	8:50b–61	168
7:45	246	8:53	65
7:51	216, 246	8:54	168–69, 212
8	92, 111, 115, 196, 209	8:56	65
8:1	92	8:61	71, 233
8:1–5	208–9	8:63	50
8:3–4	96	8:64	50, 69, 246
8:5	72, 92	8:66	92, 147
8:6	76	9	18
8:7	76	9:1	211–12, 246
8:9	74, 182	9:1–9	60, 69, 209–13
8:11	246	9:2	61, 212
8:12–13	198	9:3	78, 179, 196
8:12b–13	51	9:4	212, 267
8:13	47, 54	9:5	65, 212
8:14	101	9:6	47–49, 54, 67, 84, 92, 169, 212
8:15	65	9:7	30, 212–13
8:16	96, 182, 196–98	9:8	213
8:17	219	9:9	67, 84, 92, 169, 182, 213
8:19	74	9:10	215, 246
8:20	65, 78–79, 196, 219	9:10–28	213–16
8:21	79	9:11	212, 215
8:22	61, 101, 168–69	9:11–14	215
8:22–50a	60	9:15	142
8:23	30	9:15–25a	49, 215
8:24	30, 65	9:17	215–16
8:25	30, 74	9:19	212, 247
8:26	30, 65	9:20	216
8:27	45	9:21	95, 216
8:28	41, 61	9:21–22	216
8:29	61, 76, 78, 196	9:22	275
8:30	30, 61, 76, 114, 196	9:22–23	216
8:31	168	9:23	146–47, 216
8:31–32	111	9:24	18, 44–45, 142, 276
8:31–50	114	9:24–25	216

1 Kings (cont.)

9:25	47, 50–51, 53, 69	11:32	197
9:25b	49, 50	11:33	135
9:26	92, 260	11:34	32, 35, 144, 197
10	142	11:34–36	131
10:1	219	11:36	43, 144, 149, 197
10:1–10	179	11:38	132
10:1–13	216–19	11:39	44, 144
10:5	246	11:41–43	219–23
10:7	45, 219	12–13	153
10:8	275	12:1	255
10:9	132, 212, 219	12:1–19	128, 223–27
10:10	258	12:2	211, 226
10:12	219, 246	12:6	29–30, 93, 205
10:13	212, 219	12:7	41, 226–27
10:14–29	219–23	12:8	93, 212
10:15	223, 275	12:12	186
10:18	223	12:13	93, 212
10:19	77	12:15	10, 13, 60, 64–65, 67
10:23	146	12:16–18	227
10:24	146	12:17	227
10:26–29	145	12:18	146
10:27	258	12:21	97–98
10:28	182	12:21–24	227–29
10:29	98, 182	12:22	230
11	64, 143–44, 148	12:22–24	60
11–14	10	12:23	97
11:1	143	12:24	65, 161
11:1–8	143	12:25–33	155
11:2	164	12:26–29	132
11:4	71, 233	12:29	139
11:5	143, 155	12:30	132
11:7	75, 143, 148, 155	12:31–33	132
11:8	50, 143	12:32	219
11:9	143	12:33	50
11:9–13	131	13	140, 155, 161
11:12	44, 144	13:1	50
11:13	144, 197	13:1–32	132
11:14–22	144	13:2	50
11:23–25	144	13:4	255
11:26–40	142, 144	13:8	80
11:27–28	131	13:16	80
11:28	147	13:22	80
11:29–39	64–65	13:32	132
11:30	68, 255	13:33	155
		13:33–34	132

HEBREW BIBLE INDEX

Reference	Pages	Reference	Pages
14:1–18	132	15:20–21	233
14:2	65	15:21	211
14:5	62	15:22	233
14:15	118	15:23	206, 264
14:18	65, 133	15:24	230, 234–39
14:20	133	15:25–32	137
14:21	96, 196–97	15:27	137
14:21–31	227–29	15:29	65
14:22	148	15:30	133
14:22–24	75, 148	15:31	133
14:23	75, 118, 148, 150, 165, 194	15:32	233
14:24	148	15:33–16:7	136
14:25	182, 276	16–2 Kings 10	129
14:26	246	16:2	133
14:27–28	123, 246	16:5	264
14:28	246	16:7	64–65, 133
14:30	229	16:8	133, 250
14:31–15:8	229–30	16:8–14	137
15	75	16:9–12	133
15–16	136	16:11	139
15:1	128, 230	16:12	64, 65
15:1–2	93, 99	16:13	133, 159
15:1–8	149	16:15	137, 250
15:2	230	16:15–20	137
15:2b	99	16:21–22	137
15:3	71, 100, 233	16:23	250
15:3–5	100	16:23–28	136
15:4	43, 100, 144, 219	16:24	137
15:5	32, 35, 100, 144, 149	16:26	133, 159
15:6	32, 35, 144	16:27	264
15:8	230	16:29–22:40	137
15:9–24	80, 149, 230–33	16:31	135, 186
15:10	233	16:31–33	137
15:10b	99	16:32	148
15:11	233	16:32–33a	117
15:12	81, 268	16:33	118, 133
15:13	44, 81, 93, 117, 156, 206, 233	16:34	65
15:14	70–71, 74, 100, 233	17	32
15:15	81	17–19	9, 137
15:16	95, 233	17–2 Kings 10	11, 192, 193
15:17	93, 233	17:1	31, 33, 120–21, 193
15:17–22	94, 128	17:12	31, 33, 42
15:18	98, 233, 246, 260	17:13	44
15:19	45, 206, 233	17:16	65
15:20	96	17:18	120

1 Kings (cont.)

17:21	26
17:22	32, 37
17:23	32
18	121, 124–25, 137, 140
18:5	32
18:10	31, 33, 42, 122, 124
18:15	31, 33, 120, 124
18:19	118
18:22	118, 124
18:25	118
18:40	118, 255
20	9, 124
20:4	35
20:18	32, 255
20:24	80
20:31	32
20:32	32
20:33	267
20:37	51
21	9, 126, 137
21:15	32
21:19	80
21:22	133
21:26	81, 152, 268
21:27	68
21:29	68
22	9, 33, 60, 62, 93, 98–99, 119, 120–25, 128, 192–95
22:1–3	95
22:1–35	129, 137
22:4	119, 124
22:4–35	95, 234–39
22:5	67, 93, 175
22:6	239
22:7	62, 93, 118–19, 124, 175
22:8	62, 93, 119, 124, 175
22:11	95, 161, 216
22:13	45
22:14	29–30, 120, 124
22:16	30, 74, 121–22, 124
22:17	61, 121, 239
22:18	121
22:19	61, 67, 83, 93, 239
22:19–22	121
22:20	169, 239
22:21	120, 124
22:22	123–24
22:23	45, 65, 123–24
22:25	45, 61, 123, 125
22:28	47, 65
22:30	47, 57, 95
22:32	44–45, 211
22:33	211
22:34	123, 125
22:35	132
22:41–51	234–39
22:43	74, 133
22:44	44, 70, 72–73, 93
22:46	264
22:47	149
22:50	45
22:51	230
22:54	133, 135

3 Kingdoms (LXX)

2:35g	49
8	96, 209
8:53	51
9:9	45
12:21	97–98
12:23	97
12:24x	97
12:24y	97
14:22a	148

2 Kings

1	32, 62, 181
1:2	32, 35
1:17	35
2:2	31, 33, 36
2:4	31, 33, 36
2:6	31, 33, 36
2:12	68
2:15	136
2:16	42
2:24	275
3	9, 33, 119–20, 124, 129
3:2	165
3:4–5	120

HEBREW BIBLE INDEX 301

3:4–27	120	8:14	32, 35
3:6–25	120	8:15	158
3:7	119–20, 124	8:16–24	239–40
3:9b–17	120	8:16–29	129
3:10–19	120	8:17	158
3:11	62, 118–19, 124	8:18	73, 128
3:12	42, 119, 122	8:19	43, 61, 100, 144, 149, 240
3:13	120	8:20	158, 240
3:14	31, 33, 119–20	8:20–22	260
3:18	186	8:21	240, 261
3:26–27	120	8:22	261
4:2	42	8:23	158
4:7	32	8:24	230, 240
4:13	42	8:24–29	241–42
4:16	32	8:25	158, 250
4:17	32	8:26	121, 128, 158
4:30	31, 33, 36	8:27	73, 93, 128, 242
4:37	136	8:28	93, 98, 128
4:43	51	8:29	95, 98, 128
5:7	32, 35, 44, 68	9	124, 127
5:8	42, 68, 135	9–10	9–10, 122–25
5:11	80	9:2	123–24
5:16	31, 33, 120	9:12	123–24
5:20	31, 33	9:15	42, 123
6:1	80	9:17	123, 125
6:2	80	9:17–27	193
6:6	80, 246	9:18	120
6:8	80	9:19	120
6:9	80	9:21	128
6:10	80	9:23	123, 125
6:12	35	9:24	123, 125
6:24–7:20	9, 124	9:26	126
6:26	35	9:27	128, 275
6:30	68	9:36	65
7:4	32	10:10	65
7:12	32, 255	10:14	32, 255
8	98, 181	10:15	42, 123
8:1	32	10:18–27	118
8:5	32, 35	10:19	32, 118
8:8	32, 35, 62	10:21	118
8:9	32, 35	10:22	118
8:10	32, 35, 246	10:23	42, 118, 123
8:11	68, 219	10:25	123, 125, 246
8:12	68	10:26	165
8:13	246	10:27	123, 127, 165, 247

2 Kings (cont.)

10:30	212
10:34	264
11	83, 121–25, 140, 149, 192, 242–47, 250
11:1	246, 267
11:1–3	81
11:3	246
11:4	91, 122, 246
11:4–12	121
11:5–7	246
11:6	246
11:7	206
11:9	275
11:10	246
11:11	69, 246
11:12	29–30, 92, 138, 194, 246
11:13	123, 125, 246
11:14	45, 67, 92, 147, 246
11:15	51, 206, 246–47
11:17	91, 206
11:18	47, 51, 81, 121–23, 125, 168, 246–47
11:19	246–47
11:20	92, 147, 247
12	149, 247–51
12:3	233, 250
12:4	44, 73, 75, 149, 248–49
12:5	248, 250–51
12:5–6	249
12:6	249–50
12:6–9	248
12:7	249–50
12:8	249–51
12:8–9	249
12:8–14	246
12:9	248–50
12:9–16	44
12:10	246, 249, 251
12:10–11	249
12:11	251
12:12	216, 249–51
12:12–13	249
12:13	248–49, 251
12:14	44, 251
12:14–16	44
12:14–17	249, 251
12:15	248–51
12:15–16	149, 216
12:16	250, 275
12:17	251
12:18	248–51
12:18–19	249
12:19	248, 251
12:20–22	249
12:22b	252–55
13	32
13:1	250
13:6	44, 118, 126
13:7	246
13:8	264
13:9	230
13:10	250
13:10–11	138
13:12	264
13:12–13	138
13:13	139
13:14	68, 126
13:20	230
13:21	32, 37
13:23	240
13:24–25	138
14	30, 98, 139
14:1–14	138
14:2–22	252–55
14:3	74
14:4	44, 73–75, 149
14:7	255, 260
14:8	95, 128
14:8–14	128, 138
14:9	29, 31–32, 37
14:10	46–47, 51, 169, 255
14:11	95
14:13	96, 255, 278
14:14	171, 185, 246, 255
14:15	264
14:15–16	138–39
14:17	29–30, 32, 35, 128, 138
14:17–20	138
14:18	255

14:19	93	16:8	233, 246
14:20	230	16:8–9	259
14:22	92, 260	16:9	255, 260
14:23	250	16:10	260–61
14:23–29	139	16:10–16	150, 172, 259, 261
14:25	64–65, 139	16:11	260
14:28	139, 264	16:12	260
15	75	16:13	50, 261
15:1	250	16:14	260
15:1–7	140, 255–57	16:15	50, 151, 247, 261
15:3	133	16:17	184
15:4	44, 73–75, 149	16:17–18	150, 259
15:5	92, 246, 256–57	16:18	246
15:7	230	16:19–20	150
15:8	250	16:20	230
15:8–12	140	17	117, 125, 134, 143, 160, 173, 195
15:12	212	17:1–6	140
15:13	250	17:7–17	75, 133
15:13–16	140	17:8	134, 143
15:17	250	17:9	134
15:17–22	129, 140	17:10	118, 134, 150, 165
15:18	233	17:12	81, 268
15:23	250	17:13	61, 65
15:23–26	140	17:13–14	66
15:27	250	17:14	135, 264
15:27–31	140	17:15	159
15:30	140	17:16	118, 135
15:32	258	17:16–17	117, 134
15:32–38	140, 257–58	17:17	267
15:34	74, 133, 258	17:19	143
15:35	44, 73–75, 149, 246–47, 258	17:23	65
15:38	230	17:33	147
15:38b–16:20	258–61	17:35	135, 173
16	98	17:36	135–36, 173
16:1	250	17:39	135, 263
16:2	133, 259	17:41	147
16:2b–4	70, 150	18	92, 151, 166, 179, 195
16:3	81, 148	18–19	183
16:3–4	134	18–20	22, 29, 36, 53, 60, 92, 164, 171, 174, 176, 183, 188, 261–64
16:4	67, 70, 72, 75, 92, 194		
16:5	129, 259, 261	18–25	160
16:5–6	150	18:1–8	99
16:6	259–61	18:3	133, 185
16:7	259	18:4	70, 75, 118, 164–68, 172, 247, 263
16:7–9	150		

2 Kings (cont.)

18:4–8	164
18:5	158, 164, 176, 263
18:6	164
18:7	164–65
18:8	165
18:9–12	99
18:13	40, 86, 174, 178, 183, 185, 255
18:13–16	183
18:13–19:9a	184
18:13–19:37	173
18:14–16	183–85
18:15	185
18:16	69, 184–85
18:17	93, 181, 262–63
18:17–37	175, 183, 262–64
18:17–19:37	174
18:17–20:19	175
18:19	176, 263
18:19–24	263
18:19–35	263
18:20	44, 165, 176, 182
18:21	176, 182
18:22	70, 81, 136, 165–66, 168–69, 173, 176, 233, 263
18:23	263
18:23–24	182
18:23a	170
18:24	176
18:25	79, 240
18:26	176, 264
18:27	264, 275
18:28	176, 264
18:29	263–64
18:30	51, 56, 175–76, 263–64
18:31	176
18:31a	23
18:31b–33	22
18:32	263
18:33	263–64
18:33–34	184
18:34–35	263
19:1	68, 176
19:1–7	182
19:2	178–79
19:4	29, 32, 34, 36, 158, 176, 179, 264
19:5	178
19:6	160, 176, 178–79, 181
19:6–7	179
19:7	161, 176
19:7–9	183
19:8	176
19:9	176
19:9b–35	184
19:10	263–64
19:11	96, 176, 216, 263–64
19:12	263–64
19:12–13	184
19:14	264
19:14–19	182
19:15	158
19:15–19	174
19:16	29, 32, 34, 36, 176, 264
19:18	246, 264
19:20	158, 176, 178
19:20–34	174, 182
19:21	176, 180
19:22	180, 264
19:23	264
19:24	180
19:25	176, 180
19:26	180
19:28	180–81
19:29	160–61, 181, 187–88
19:29–31	181
19:30	181
19:31	181–82
19:32	160, 181, 239
19:32–34	181
19:33	126, 160, 179, 181
19:34	174, 181
19:35	179
19:35–36	183
19:36–37	184
19:37	135
20:1	29, 32, 36, 160, 175–78, 181, 184
20:1–3	186
20:1–6	187
20:1–11	173, 186
20:2–3	174

20:3	68, 71, 160, 178, 181, 233	21:12	152–53
20:4	176, 178, 186	21:12–14	159
20:4–6	186	21:12–15	151–52
20:5	160, 176, 179, 181, 186–87	21:13	152
20:5–6	174	21:14	152
20:6	36, 174, 187, 189	21:15	152
20:7	22, 29, 32, 35–36, 176, 178, 186	21:16	151–52
20:7–11	22, 186–87	21:17	152
20:8	178, 186, 188–89	21:17–18	82
20:8–11	187	21:18	230
20:9	160–61, 176, 178, 181, 188–89	21:18b–26	267–69
20:10	186	21:20	74
20:11	178	21:21	81, 101, 133, 135, 268
20:12	174, 176, 187	21:23	93
20:12–19	173, 179, 183, 185, 188	21:24	246
20:13	176, 246–47	21:26	269
20:14	178, 275	22	1, 62
20:15	246	22–23	196
20:16	176, 178–79	22:1	275
20:17	160, 181	22:1–2	84, 153
20:19	176, 178	22:1–23:3	153
20:21b–21:18	265–67	22:1–23:30	269–76
21	195	22:2	133, 275
21:1–2	82	22:3	86, 246
21:1–9	117, 125, 151, 185	22:3–7	84
21:2	93, 134, 151	22:4	246, 249, 275
21:2–7	134	22:5	216, 246, 248–50
21:3	67, 70, 82–83, 92, 93, 117–18, 134, 152, 169, 246, 267	22:7	44, 275
		22:8	246
21:3–5	82	22:8–10	84
21:3–7	154	22:9	206, 216, 246
21:3–9	82, 151	22:11	67, 211
21:3b–7a	117	22:11–23:3a	84
21:4	70, 83, 206, 246	22:12	202
21:5	70, 83, 246, 267	22:13	93, 135
21:6	67, 133–34, 152, 267	22:14–22	60
21:7	67, 83, 93, 96, 117, 196–97	22:15	62, 158, 161
21:8	30, 74, 132, 206, 267	22:16	45, 77, 111, 161, 179
21:9	135	22:17	67, 72, 77, 92–93, 133, 152, 212, 264
21:9–10	60, 66		
21:10	65, 159	22:18	93, 158, 161
21:10–15	161, 185	22:19	43, 77, 93, 111, 178, 275
21:10–16	82	22:20	45, 77, 179
21:11	81, 151–52, 268	23:1	93, 206
21:11–16	151	23:2	246

2 Kings (cont.)

23:3	84–85, 87
23:4	69, 118, 153–55
23:4–20	84, 86, 153–56, 196, 276
23:5	118, 155
23:6	118, 153–54, 156–57
23:7	118, 148, 154–55, 247
23:8	75, 155–57
23:8a	153
23:9	44, 154–55
23:10	156
23:11	154–55
23:12	154, 157, 267
23:12–14	153
23:13	85, 148, 156
23:13–14	155
23:14	118, 155, 157, 165, 200
23:15	118, 154–56
23:16	153–54, 156–57
23:16–18	155
23:17	154, 275
23:19	85, 157
23:20	153–55, 157
23:21–23	86, 201
23:21a	85
23:22–23	85
23:23	86–87, 233
23:24	81, 157, 219, 267, 268
23:24–27	85
23:25	153
23:26	44
23:26–27	185
23:27	197
23:28–30	153
23:29	182, 276
23:30	91, 230, 246
23:31	278
23:31–24:20a	276–78
23:32	233
23:33	278
23:34	182, 278
23:35	44, 247
23:37	233
24:2	65
24:3	44
24:3–4	185
24:3b–4a	153
24:10	40
24:12	87
24:13	69, 185
24:14	247
24:16	275
25:1	87
25:6	255
25:19	247
25:22	219
25:22–26	202, 261
25:25	261
25:27	86
25:29–30	32, 35, 87, 144

Isaiah

1–31	180
1:8	180
3:1	182
5:25	180
6:10	186
6:11	180
7:1	140
7:3	181
7:9	135
7:11	188
7:14	188
8:1	259
8:3	259
8:18	188
9:6	181–82
10:20	181–82
10:32	180
12:2	178
14:9	180
14:30	178
15:6	180
16:1	180
18:6	37
19:20	188
19:22	186
20:3	188
20:5	180
22:10	247

HEBREW BIBLE INDEX

22:11	180	37:2	178
22:21	247	37:4	29, 32, 36, 176, 179
23:7	180	37:5	178
26:4	178	37:6	176, 178–79
28:7	61	37:6–7	179
28:16	135	37:7	161, 176
28:17	152	37:7–9	183
28:21	180	37:8	176
29:16	180	37:9	176
30–31	61	37:11	176
30:1–5	182	37:14–20	180
30:2	61	37:15–20	174, 182
30:10	61	37:16–20	189
30:12	178, 182	37:17	29, 32, 36, 176
30:15	178	37:21	178
30:26	186	37:21–35	174, 180, 182
31:1	61, 178, 182	37:26	176, 180
31:1–3	182	37:27	180
31:5	181	37:30	161
32:9	180	37:30–32	189
32:10	178, 180	37:35	174
32:11	178, 180	37:38	171
32:17	178	38	32, 186–87
32:18	181	38:1	29, 32, 36, 178, 186
33:20	181	38:1–3	186
36	183	38:1–8	187
36–37	173–74	38:1–22	173, 186
36–39	22, 29, 36, 53, 174–75, 183	38:2–3	174
36:1	183, 185	38:3	186, 233
36:2–22	183	38:4	176, 178
36:7	165	38:4–6	186
36:7–8	166	38:5	36, 176, 179, 186
36:7b	166	38:5–6	174
36:8	170	38:6	174, 186–87, 189
36:11	176	38:7–8	22, 187, 189
36:13	176	38:7–11	186
36:16	176	38:8	161, 186
36:16–17	32	38:9	29
36:16a	23	38:9–20	22, 29, 36, 186
36:16b–18	22	38:11	29
36:17	36	38:12	29
36:17–18	26	38:16	29
36:19	134	38:20	29
37:1	176	38:21	29, 32, 36, 178
37:1–7	182	38:21–22	22, 187

Isaiah (cont.)		65:21	181
38:22	189	66:19	188
39	188		
39:1	174, 176, 187	Jeremiah	
39:1–8	173, 185	1:2	86–87
39:2	246–47	2:2	48
39:3	178	2:5	159
39:4	246	2:20	150
39:5	176, 178–79	2:34	153
39:6	181	2:35	44
39:8	176, 178	3:6	150
41–60	180	3:11	159
42:15	180	3:12	48
42:17	178	3:13	150
42:22	152	3:15	51
42:24	152	3:16	248
43:1	180	4:2	34, 160
43:8	43	4:3	44
43:21	180	4:10	51
44:8	43	5:1	43
44:21	180	5:2	34, 160
44:25	188	7:5	51
45:7	180	7:6	153
45:18	180	7:9	51
46:11	180	7:12	198
47:8	178	7:13	51
47:10	178	7:18	51, 261
49:18	34	7:25	51
50:2	180	7:32	161
50:10	178	7:33	37
51:7	179–80	9:24	51, 161
51:9	180	10:5	51
51:10	180	11:7	51
52:2	180	11:12	51
53:5	186	12:11	248
55:11	212	12:14	212
55:13	188	12:16	34, 160
56:7	79, 212	13:1	48
57:5	195	14:22	43
57:18–19	186	15:3	37
59:4	178	16:4	37, 161
59:7	153	16:14	34, 160
62:11	180	16:15	34, 160
64:1	180	17:19	48
65:17	248	19	180, 261

19:1	48, 153	35:14	51
19:3	152–53, 161	35:15	51
19:4	153	36:16	51
19:6	153, 161	36:23	51
19:7	37, 153, 161	37:17	43
19:8	153	37:20	35
19:13	51, 153, 261	38:9	35
22:3	153	38:15	51
22:17	153	39–43	202
22:19	51	39:2	86
22:24	34	39:16	48
23:5	161	41:5	181
23:7	34, 160–61	44	261
23:8	34, 160	44:4	51
23:26	43	44:17	51
23:32	51	44:18	51
23:36	34	44:19	51
24:10	213	44:25	51
25:4	51	44:29	161
25:9	213	46:18	34
26:5	51	46:26	180
26:15	153	48:12	161
26:19	51	49:2	161
27:18	43	49:14	180
28:13	48	49:23	51, 180
29:17	213	49:31	216
29:19	51	50:2	81, 268
30:3	161	50:29	180
30:16	152	50:37	171
31:6	43	51:5	180
31:16	43	51:25	152
31:17	43	51:36	180
31:27	161	51:37	213
31:28	247	51:47	161
31:31	161	51:52	161
31:38	161	51:59	87
32:29	261	52	202
32:33	51	52:4	87
32:44	51	52:31	86
33:14	161	52:33–34	32, 144
34	14		
34:2	48	Ezekiel	
34:15	100	1:1	86
34:20	37	5:11	34
35:13	48	5:14	34

Ezekiel (cont.)

5:15	179	36:25	268
5:16	34	37:23	268
5:18	34	38:11	216
5:20	34	40:1	86
6:13	150	44:10	268
6:14	152		
8:16	101	Hosea	
14:9	152	1:1	139
14:13	152	2:1	34
14:19	213	4:15	34, 160
16:36	268	10:5	155
16:48	34	10:12	44
17:16	34		
17:19	34	Joel	
18:3	34	4:19	153
18:14	100		
20:3	34	Amos	
20:7	268	3:12	227
20:18	268	3:14	140
20:31	34	4:2	161
20:33	34	4:4	140
22:4	268	4:10	213
23:7	268	5	160
23:30	268	5:5–6	140
23:49	268	7:10–17	132, 140, 161
25:13	152	8:11	161
26–33	86	8:14	34, 140
26:1	86	9:13	161
26:12	247	9:15	212
28:23	213		
29:6	182	Obadiah	
29:17	86	1	
30:20	86		
31:1	86	Jonah	
32:1	86	1:14	153, 212
32:17	86	4:11	43
33:11	34		
33:21	86	Micah	
33:27	34	1:1	139
34:8	34	2:1	43
35:3	152	4:2	113
35:6	34	6:10	43
35:11	34	7:20	180
36:18	268		

HEBREW BIBLE INDEX

Nahum
  1:4
  3:16 — 223

Habakkuk
  2:7 — 152
  2:18 — 148

Zephaniah
  1:4 — 152, 155
  1:13 — 152
  2:9 — 34
  2:15 — 213

Zechariah
  14:20

Malachi
  1:14 — 43
  2:12 — 147
  3:3 — 147
  3:22 — 267

Psalms
  7:4 — 43
  14:2 — 43
  18:47 — 34
  23:6 — 35
  25 — 114
  25:8 — 114
  25:11 — 114
  27:4 — 35
  31:22 — 215
  40:9 — 212
  42:3 — 34
  44:2 — 180
  44:17 — 179
  50:16 — 120
  53:3 — 43
  56:14 — 160
  58:12 — 43
  60:8 — 26
  60:11 — 215
  61:7 — 36
  62:10–11 — 159
  71:2 — 180
  73:11 — 43
  78:41 — 180
  84:3 — 34
  88 — 146
  89 — 146
  89:19 — 180
  94:21 — 153
  95:6 — 169
  103:3 — 114
  105:4–5 — 188
  105:5 — 188
  105:15 — 188
  105:27 — 188
  106:35 — 170
  106:38 — 153
  108:8 — 26
  115:3 — 212
  116:9 — 160
  119:7 — 212
  128:5 — 35, 144
  135:6 — 212
  135:17 — 43

Job
  1:13 — 147
  1:18 — 147
  27:2 — 34
  27:12 — 159
  38:10 — 216
  40:28 — 105
  42:16 — 37

Proverbs
  6:17 — 153
  10:16 — 132
  10:27 — 36
  14:10 — 170
  20:19 — 170
  24:21 — 170–71
  31:12 — 35, 144

Ruth
  1:12 — 43
  3:12 — 43

Ruth (cont.)
3:13	34

Song of Songs
3:6	223

Qoheleth
2:3	35, 144
2:17	35
3:12	35
4:2	35
4:15	35
5:5	152
5:17	35, 144
5:19	35, 144
6:3	35
6:6	35
6:8	35
6:12	35
7:2	35
7:12	35
8:3	212
8:15	35, 144
9:3	35
9:4	35
9:5	35
9:9	35
10:9	147
10:19	35
11:8	35

Lamentations
1:7	180
1:12	43
2:17	180
3:3	123
3:29	43

Esther
1:3	87
3:8	43
6:6	212

Daniel
1:10	35
2:4	35
5:10	35
6:7	35
6:19	169
6:21	34
6:22	35
6:27	34
9:2	87

Ezra
9:2	170
10:2	43
10:44	43

Nehemiah
1:9	198
4:10	216
4:11	216
4:15	216
5:2	43
5:3	43
5:4	43
5:5	43
13:24	264
13:26	152

1 Chronicles
2:6	146
4	233
5:17	139
6:40	219
9:22	61
10	16, 108, 191
10:13–14	62
11	19, 30
11:1	45
11:2	108, 132
11:3	65, 91
11:4–8	29, 108
11:7	213
11:8	6, 29–30, 53, 113
11:9	47, 53
11:14	44, 54
12:30	219
12:39	71, 233

13	63	21:3	35
13:11	63, 76	21:5	157
14	63, 194	21:9	61, 66–67
14:1	215	21:9–10	48
14:3	108	21:12	111–112
14:7	83	21:13	169
14:10	47, 59, 63, 194	21:15	240
14:11	63, 76, 213	21:16	113
14:14	59, 63, 194	21:17	47, 51–52, 111–112
15	80	21:18	69
15:1	80	21:21	169
15:3	80	21:22	69, 78, 113
15:12	80	21:23	35
15:25	147	21:24	47, 137
16:1	50, 79–80	21:25	78, 137
16:2	50, 212	21:26	50, 69
16:11–12	188	22:12	44
16:12	188	26:28	61
16:27	78	28:4	227
16:29	136	28:9	71, 233
17	59, 105–6, 115	28:11	261
17:1	45, 61–62, 246	28:12	261
17:6	96	28:18	261
17:9	76–77	28:19	261
17:14	132	29:3	42, 227
17:19–20	213	29:5	40
17:24	158	29:9	71, 233
17:25	213	29:17	212, 227
17:27	111	29:19	71
18	24, 27	29:20	136
18:2	24, 26–27, 47	29:29	61
18:5–6	260	29:30	264
18:14–17	146		
19	105, 107, 115	2 Chronicles	
19:1–20:1	107	1	50
19:13	246	1–9	177
20:1	240	1:3–13	59, 69
20:1–3	108	1:7–13	142, 144, 207
20:2–3	107	1:8–9	197
20:4–8	9, 19	1:11	212
20:7	158	2:1–17	145
21	9, 19, 59, 90, 106, 112–13, 115, 194, 251	2:3	219, 264
		2:9	51
21:1–5	146	2:11	40
21:2	96	2:12	145

2 Chronicles (cont.)

Reference	Pages
2:15	79
3–4	69, 144, 207
3:1	78, 246
4:11	212, 216
4:16	246
5:1	216, 246
5:2–6	208–9
5:6	72
5:7	76
5:8	76
5:10	182
5:11–14	246
6	115
6:1b–2	51
6:3	101
6:4	158
6:4–5	96
6:5	182, 196
6:6	96, 197
6:7	158, 219
6:10	78, 158, 196, 212, 219
6:12	101, 168, 170
6:12–39	59
6:13–14	169
6:14	30, 158
6:15	30
6:16	30, 158, 212
6:17	30, 158
6:18	45
6:19	30, 41, 264
6:20	76, 78, 196
6:21	30, 76, 196
6:22	168
6:22–23	111
6:24–25	111
6:26	77, 196
6:26–27	111, 113
6:27	30, 111
6:31	29
6:34	197
6:38	197
6:40	78
6:42	264
7:3	136
7:7	50, 69, 246
7:10	147
7:11	211–12, 246, 248
7:11–22	69, 201–13
7:12	179, 197, 212
7:12–16	79
7:12–22	59, 136
7:12b	78–79
7:12b–15	78
7:13	213
7:14	68
7:15	78
7:16	78, 196–97
7:17	212, 267
7:18	212, 247
7:19	48–49, 169, 212
7:20	212–213
7:21	213
7:22	169, 182, 213
8:1	215, 246
8:1–18	213–216
8:5	215–16
8:5–12	215
8:6	212, 215, 247
8:7	216
8:8	95, 216
8:9	146–47
8:9–10	216
8:11	16, 18, 45, 276
8:11–12	216
8:12	49, 69
8:13	50
8:13–16a	49
8:16	216
8:16b	49
8:17	45, 260
9	142
9:1	219
9:1–9	179
9:1–12	216–19
9:4	246
9:6	45, 219
9:8	132, 212, 219, 264
9:11	219, 246
9:12	212

9:13–31	219–23	13:1	128, 230
9:15	223	13:1–2	99
9:17	223	13:2	230
9:18	77	13:3–21	100, 229
9:22	146	13:23	230
9:23	146	14–16	80, 149
9:25	145	14:2	73, 81, 165, 233
9:25–28	145	14:2–15:15	81
9:26	91, 145, 182, 223, 247	14:4	73, 81, 233
9:28	182	14:5	216
9:31	230	14:6	216
10	64	15:7	42
10:1	255	15:8	81, 219
10:1–19	128, 223–27	15:15–16	34
10:2	182, 211, 227	15:16	81, 117, 156, 206
10:6	29–30, 206	15:17	44, 70–71, 73–74, 100, 233
10:7	41, 227	15:18	81
10:15	10, 13, 59, 64–65, 67	16:1–6	94, 128
10:16–18	227	16:2	246, 260
10:17	227	16:3	45, 87, 206
10:18	146	16:4	96
11:1	97	16:5	211
11:1–4	227–29	16:7	61
11:2	176	16:9	42, 71, 233
11:2–4	59	16:10	61
11:3	97	16:12	206
11:5	215	16:14	230
11:10	216	17–20	234–39
11:11	216	17:2	219
11:23	216	17:6	73
12:2	182, 276	17:7	87
12:2–16	227–29	18	33, 59, 119, 121, 123–24, 137, 194–95
12:4	216	18:1	95, 99
12:6	68	18:1–2	95
12:7	68	18:2–34	9
12:9	246	18:3	119
12:10–11	123, 246	18:3–34	95
12:11	246	18:4	67, 175–76
12:12	68	18:5	239
12:13	96, 196–97	18:6	118, 175
12:14	148	18:7	175, 233
12:15	229	18:10	95, 216
12:16	230	18:12	45
12:16–13:23	229–30	18:13	29
13	149		

2 Chronicles (cont.)

18:15	122	23:9	246
18:16	239	23:10	69, 246
18:18	67, 176, 179, 239	23:11	29–30, 138, 194, 246
18:19	169	23:12	123, 246
18:21	211	23:13	45, 147, 246
18:22	45, 211	23:14	206, 246, 247
18:24	45	23:16	91, 206
18:27	47	23:17	51, 122–23, 168, 246–47
18:29	47, 95	23:18	246
18:31	45	23:20	247
18:34	132	23:21	147
19:7	233	24	139, 149, 247–51
19:9	71, 233	24:3	248–49
20:15	66	24:4	248–49, 251
20:18	136	24:4–5a	249
20:20	110	24:4–7	248
20:26	80, 213	24:5	248–50
20:32	74	24:5b	249–50
20:33	44, 70, 72–73	24:6	248–51
21:1	230	24:6–7	249
21:1–20	239–40	24:7	248, 250–51
21:3	216	24:8	246, 251
21:6	73, 128	24:8–11	249
21:7	43, 61, 100, 240	24:8–14	44
21:8	240	24:9	248
21:8–10	260	24:9–16	246
21:9	240, 261	24:11	80, 248–49, 251
21:10	261	24:12	216, 248–51
21:11	73, 75	24:12–13	249
21:20	230	24:13	216, 250–51
22:1–6	241–42	24:14a	249, 251
22:2	128	24:14b–17a	249
22:3	73, 128, 242	24:15–22	248
22:6	95	24:16	230
22:7–9	9–10, 128	24:17	248, 260
22:9	230	24:17b	249–50
22:10	246	24:18	249, 251
22:10–23:21	242–247	24:19–20	249
22:12	246	24:21	251
23	121–23, 149, 250	24:21–22	249
23:1	91, 246	24:23	251
23:1–3	122	24:23–24	249
23:3	206, 246	24:25	230
23:4–6	246	24:25–27	249
		24:27b–25:28	252–55

HEBREW BIBLE INDEX

25	30	28:8	259–60
25–26	139	28:9	118
25:2	71, 74, 233	28:9–15	150
25:5–16	255	28:11	260
25:8	42	28:16	259–61
25:10	80	28:16–23	150
25:11	255	28:17	259–60
25:11–12	260	28:18	259
25:12	29–31, 255	28:19	259
25:14	260	28:20–21	259
25:17	95, 128	28:21	246
25:17–24	128	28:22	99
25:18	29, 37	28:22–23	259
25:19	46, 51, 169, 255	28:23	260–61
25:21	95	28:24	150, 172, 184, 246, 260
25:23	96, 255, 278	28:24–25	150
25:24	171, 185, 246, 255	28:25	73
25:25	29–30, 35, 128, 138	28:26–27	150
25:26	255	28:27	230
25:27	93	28:27b–32:32	261–64
25:28	230	29–30	167
26	255–57	29–31	165–67, 172
26:2	260	29–32	29
26:4	74	29:2	185
26:5–20	256	29:3	87, 172
26:16	69, 74	29:5	177
26:21	246, 257	29:7	167
26:23	230	29:8	213, 275
26:23b–27:9	257–58	29:11	197
27	139	29:15	155
27:2	69, 74, 149, 258	29:16	69, 155–56
27:3	246–47, 258	29:18	155
27:9	230	29:19	172
27:9b–28:27	258–61	29:28	136
28:1	259	29:29	136
28:1–2a	150	29:30	136
28:1b–4	70	29:35	50
28:2–3	259	30:5–6	99
28:2b–3a	150	30:6	246
28:3b–4	150	30:7	275
28:4	70, 72–73, 172, 194, 259	30:10	246
28:5	260	30:11	44, 68
28:5–8	150	30:14	156
28:5–15	259	30:18	219
28:6	129, 140	30:20	177

2 Chronicles (cont.)

30:22	50
31:1	70, 164–65, 167, 247
31:2	50
31:6	227
31:10	51
31:15	51
32	36, 59, 175–77, 182–83
32:5	246
32:8	264
32:9	40, 93, 247, 262–63
32:9–19	175, 262
32:9–23	173
32:9–31	175
32:10	263
32:11	263–64
32:11–17	263
32:12	70, 81, 165, 167, 169, 263
32:13	47, 56, 175, 263
32:13–15	263
32:13–17	263
32:14	96, 216, 264
32:15	135, 263–64
32:17	158, 263–64
32:18	264
32:19	264
32:20	174, 178, 182
32:21	259, 264
32:23	183
32:24	36, 174–75, 177, 184, 188
32:24–26	173, 187
32:26	36, 68
32:27–31	173
32:31	174, 188
32:32	61, 264
32:33	230
32:33b–33:20	265–67
33:1–2	82
33:1–9	117, 185
33:3	67, 70, 73, 82, 117–18, 169, 267
33:3–5	82
33:3–9	82, 151
33:4	70, 83, 206, 246
33:5	70, 83, 246, 267
33:6	267
33:7	67, 96, 117, 156, 196–97
33:8	65, 132, 206, 267
33:9–10	59, 66
33:10	66, 135
33:10–17	82, 151
33:12	68
33:13	177
33:15	156
33:16	50
33:18–20	82
33:19	68, 73, 151–52, 155, 165, 200
33:20	230
33:20b–24	267–69
33:22	74, 81, 268
33:23	68
33:25	246
34	155
34–35	155
34:1	275
34:1–2	84
34:1–36:1	269–76
34:2	275
34:3	87, 155, 157
34:3–7	84, 87, 153, 156, 276
34:3b–5	155
34:4	156–57
34:4–5	153
34:5	155, 157, 246
34:6–7	155, 157
34:7	156
34:8	87, 155, 246, 248, 250
34:8–12a	84
34:9	249, 275
34:9–13	155
34:10	216, 246, 249
34:12	216, 275
34:12–13	84–85
34:13	216
34:14	65, 84
34:14–18	155
34:15	246
34:15–18	84
34:16	206
34:17	216, 246
34:19	211

34:19–31	84
34:20	203
34:20–28	59
34:21	135, 175
34:23	158
34:24	45, 77, 111
34:25	67, 72, 77, 264
34:26	158, 175
34:27	43, 77, 111, 275
34:28	45, 77
34:29	206
34:30	246
34:31	85
34:32	84–85
34:32–33	156
34:33	84–85, 157, 233
35	202
35:1–17	85, 165
35:1–19	86
35:3	264
35:6	65
35:18–19	85
35:19	86
35:20	85, 182
35:21	40, 120
35:21–23	85
35:24	85, 230
35:25	85
35:26	264
35:26–27	85
36:1	91, 247
36:2	233, 278
36:2–13	276–78
36:3	278
36:4	182, 278
36:10	40
36:13	34, 122
36:15	65

Author Index

Ackerman, Susan — 195, 279
Auld, A. Graeme — 9, 11–21, 30, 39, 42, 54, 56, 89, 105, 107, 127, 142, 151, 161, 163, 168, 175, 191, 212, 262, 279–81
Ausloos, Hans — 18, 281
Barrick, W. Boyd — 154, 281
Becker, Uwe — 55, 113, 209, 281
Becking, Bob — 183, 281
Bekins, Peter — 206, 281
Ben Zvi, Ehud — 117, 125, 281
Bezzel, Hannes — 55, 209, 281
Blenkinsopp, Joseph — 183, 281
Busto Saiz, José Ramón — 49, 281
Carr, David — 15, 281
Childs, Brevard S. — 174, 281
Clines, David — 170, 281
Cogan, Mordechai — 120, 123–24, 281
Cross, Frank Moore — 10, 130–31, 282
Dietrich, Walter — 10, 153, 282
Edenburg, Cynthia — 109, 282
Eichhorn, Johann G. — 2–3, 5, 282
Fernández Marcos, Natalio — 49, 282
Finkelstein, Israel — 129–30, 139, 282
Gehman, Henry S. — 170, 284
Gilmour, Rachelle — 120, 282
Goldstein, Ronnie — 171, 282
Graham, M. Patrick — 3, 282
Gray, John — 119, 123, 282
Halpern, Baruch — 89, 98, 282
Ho, Craig (Yuet-Shun) — 15, 283
Hoffmann, Hans-Detlef — 10, 283
Hoglund, Kenneth G. — 3, 283
Hornkohl, Aaron D. — 46, 283
Japhet, Sara — 167, 283
Johnstone, William — 188, 283
Kalimi, Isaac — 13, 55, 79, 283
Keulen, Percy S.F. van — 117, 283
Klein, Ralph W. — 26, 73, 91, 108, 283
Knoppers, Gary N. — 14, 196, 201, 283
Kratz, Reinhard G. — 174–75, 184, 284
Kropat, Arno — 55, 284
Kucová, Lydie — 14–15, 44, 156–57, 169, 284
Lemaire, André — 89, 98, 284
Levin, Christoph — 153–54, 284
Levinson, Bernard M. — 14, 196, 201, 284
Linville, James R. — 14, 284
McKenzie, Steven L. — 3, 11–13, 64, 284
Monroe, Lauren A.S. — 154, 284
Montgomery, James A. — 170, 284
Na'aman, Nadav — 184, 284–85
Nelson, Richard — 10, 285
Nicholson, Ernest W. — 7, 285
Nihan, Christophe — 107–8, 285
Noll, Kurt L. — 15, 285
Noth, Martin — 6–12, 52, 109–10, 285
Pakkala, Juha — 109, 285
Park, Song-Mi Suzie — 163, 182, 285
Parry, Donald W. — 166, 285
Peltonen, Kai — 5, 285
Person, Raymond F., Jr. — 15–18, 40, 64, 108, 184, 187, 201, 285–86
Polzin, Robert — 10, 286
Press, Michael D. — 134, 171, 286
Provan, Iain W. — 75, 286
Qimron, Elisha — 166, 286
Rezetko, Robert — 15–16, 79, 286
Rhyder, Julia — 154, 286
Rogerson, John W. — 1, 151, 286
Römer, Thomas C. — 13, 109, 200, 286

Schipper, Jeremy   127, 185, 286
Sergi, Omer   123, 286
Smend, Rudolf   1–2, 4, 10, 287
Stade, Bernhard   174, 183, 287
Sweeney, Marvin A.   52, 120, 122–23, 147, 170, 287
Tadmor, Hayim   120, 123–24, 281
Thelle, Rannfrid Irene   62, 168, 196, 200, 287
Trebolle Barrera, Julio   18, 208, 287
Van Seters, John   11, 287
Veijola, Timo   10, 287
Wellhausen, Julius   3–9, 29, 52, 110, 124, 140, 193, 195, 202–3, 287–88
Wette, W. M. L. de.   1–3, 5, 8, 19, 84, 151, 193, 195, 203, 288
Wiggans, Steve. A.   83, 288
Wildberger, Hans   179–80, 288
Williamson, Hugh G.M.   7–8, 27, 288
Wright, Jacob L.   151, 288
Würthwein, Ernst   12–13, 17, 120, 123, 153–54, 166, 288
Young, Ian   16, 288
Zakovitch, Yair   186–87, 288

www.ingramcontent.com/pod-product-compliance
Lightning Source LLC
Chambersburg PA
CBHW030434300426
44112CB00009B/996